The Revelation of Jesus Christ

The Revelation of Jesus Christ

A Disciple's Commentary

JON SCOTT BIRCH

RESOURCE *Publications* · Eugene, Oregon

THE REVELATION OF JESUS CHRIST
A Disciple's Commentary

Copyright © 2022 Jon Scott Birch. All rights reserved. Except for brief quotations in critical publications or reviews, no part of this book may be reproduced in any manner without prior written permission from the publisher. Write: Permissions, Wipf and Stock Publishers, 199 W. 8th Ave., Suite 3, Eugene, OR 97401.

Resource Publications
An Imprint of Wipf and Stock Publishers
199 W. 8th Ave., Suite 3
Eugene, OR 97401

www.wipfandstock.com

PAPERBACK ISBN: 978-1-7252-8114-1
HARDCOVER ISBN: 978-1-7252-8115-8
EBOOK ISBN: 978-1-7252-8116-5

08/01/22

Unless otherwise indicated, all Scripture quotations are taken from the New King James Version (NKJV). Copyright © 1979, 1980, 1982, by Thomas Nelson Inc. Used by permission. All rights reserved.

Scripture quotations marked (ESV) are taken from The Holy Bible, English Standard Version (ESV), copyright © 2001 by Crossway, a publishing ministry of Good News Publishers. Used by permission. All rights reserved.

Scripture quotations marked (NRSV) are taken from The Holy Bible, The New Revised Standard Version (NRSV) © 1989 by the Division of Christian Education of the National Council of the Churches of Christ in the United States of America. Used by permission. All rights reserved.

Scripture quotations marked (KJV) are taken from The Holy Bible, King James Version (public domain).

For Jesus Christ,
who set His revelation in my heart and set my spirit free.

Blessed is he that reads, and they that hear the words of this prophecy, and keep those things which are written therein: for the time is at hand.

—Revelation 1:3

Contents

Preface | ix

Introduction | 1

1 A Key to Understanding Revelation | 15
2 A Vision of Jesus Christ in Full Majesty | 17
3 The Seven Churches | 21
4 The Rapture: No Wrath For His Bride | 57
5 The Throne of God | 70
6 The Time of Jacob's Trouble | 79
7 The Breaking of the Seals | 89
8 Prophets and Martyrs: Parenthetic Revelation I | 98
9 The Blowing of the Trumpets | 106
10 The Little Scroll and the Two Witnesses: Parenthetic Revelation II | 126
11 Dramatis Personae and the Cosmic War: Parenthetic Revelation III | 139
12 The Antichrist and the False Prophet: Parenthetic Revelation III | 150
13 Harvest and Vintage: Parenthetic Revelation III | 173

14   The Overturning of the Bowls of God's Wrath | 185
15   Babylon 101 | 196
16   The Doom of Ecclesiastical and Commercial Babylon: Parenthetic Revelation IV | 212
17   The Marriage of the Lamb and Return of the King | 223
18   The Millennial Kingdom and Final Judgment | 231
19   The New Heaven, New Earth, New Jerusalem, and Eternity | 253

Postscript | 276

Acknowledgments | 283
Appendix A: Ancient Texts | 287
Appendix B: Expanded Commentary | 291
Bibliography | 307

Preface

THE BOOK OF REVELATION is a subject that may evoke mixed emotions, for people often approach this final book of God's Word with a tentative or skeptical outlook. Some may feel intimidated or threatened by its contents, believing that Revelation is an insolvable book of mystery that cannot be—or should not be—figured out. This stands in contrast, however, to the purpose of the book which is to "reveal" that which was previously unrevealed.

Others feel that all the judgments, symbols, events, and peculiar language of Revelation are fanciful tales spun to put fear into those who are less learned. Still others believe that the events of Revelation have already come to pass, or that the book is merely a collection of strictly spiritual metaphors meant to be taken as lessons by the believer while on his/her spiritual journey through life. This is in contrast, however, to the whole of God's plan for humanity, including the truth of prophecy, fulfilled and unfulfilled, contained throughout his Word.

The book of Revelation is in fact one of the most majestic books of the Bible, filled with beauty and hope. It is also a book that reveals exactly who Jesus is, clarifying that the Revelation itself was given by Christ and received by John, as noted in chapter 1, verse 1: "The revelation of Jesus Christ, which God gave unto him [John]." Indeed, this book of prophecy has spoken a bold and living Christ-centric word to every generation of Christians since it was written. It warns the heart, quickens the imagination, hones moral and spiritual judgment, and brings both comfort and inspiration to the attentive reader and contemplative disciple.

The apprehension and various flawed views concerning Jesus' revelatory book are primarily due to a lack of widespread understanding of prophetic literature because of less time spent in personal prayerful study of its magnificent message (or study of the Bible overall). Even with a multitude of sound resources, thorough examination and contemplation of the book of Revelation can be intimidating! The unique literary style that Revelation consists of hearkens back to Old Testament prophetic literature found in books such as Daniel, Ezekiel, Jeremiah, Isaiah, Zechariah, Joel, Psalms, and others. This fact alone challenges the church toward humble immersion in *all* of Scripture while in-step with the Spirit (1 Corinthians 2:13; Galatians 5:25).

Of course, one cannot come to a full comprehension of the book of Revelation at one sitting; in fact, a *lifetime* of study will not result in such (this holds true for the entire Word of God). But the beginning of understanding comes with study and contemplation, which means *time spent in the Word and in prayer with God*.

Second Timothy 2:15 (KJV) states, "Study to show thyself approved unto God, a workman that needeth not to be ashamed, rightly dividing the word of truth." In mining the truth-veins of Scripture our lives become richer, and they become richer still as the prophetic vein leads into the deepest lode—into the very heart of God, for "the testimony of Jesus is the spirit of prophecy" (Revelation 19:10).

Consider that Jesus spoke in parables to veil truth from foolish and evil souls (Matthew 13:10–23). Likewise with the enigmatic style of prophetic visionary literature. Amidst the dark days when Revelation was written and first circulated in the churches, the vibrant symbolism and cryptic messages—all rooted in Scripture—would have been widely understood by the scripturally literate Christian who relied upon the Holy Spirit for interpretive wisdom. Yet any Roman or other party hostile to Christ would remain confused and ignorant concerning such mysteries of God. It is the same today.

Without a working knowledge of prophetic literature (as found in the Old Testament) and how it is used, one cannot hope to comprehend the deeper revelation that can be found in the book of Revelation. Personal discipline toward vigilant prayer, study, and contemplation is well-rewarded with a progressive and systematic revelation of truth as Christ *opens our understanding that we might comprehend the scriptures* (Luke 24:45).

Preface

Second Timothy 2:16 (KJV) goes on to say, "shun profane and vain babblings: for they will increase unto more ungodliness." This passage is a warning to shy away from the act of simply taking someone's word for absolute truth concerning God's Word. Unfortunately, many people (even Christians) are kept in the dark when it comes to subjects and topics involving the book of Revelation (or prophecy in general), all due to presumptions that Bible prophecy is either irrelevant or can be fully understood just by reading a good book about it. To be sure, doctrinally sound resources are great tools that assist in our research and application, yet when one relies *solely* on the information extolled by pastors, teachers, friends, television, radio, commentaries, and authors rather than learning *directly* from the Bible and the Holy Spirit, one can become complacent, unknowingly exposing themselves to (and possibly adopting) a false or compromised doctrine or interpretation.

Sincere and disciplined time with God in prayer and in his Word assists us in discerning his truth from the chatter of human intellect and world influence. Humanity is imperfect; Almighty God is absolute perfection. Who do you believe is the better teacher? *Prophecy is not of any private interpretation, it is revealed and taught by the Holy Spirit* (1 Corinthians 2:7–16; 2 Peter 1:20–21).

In reference to discipleship, too many of Jesus' disciples have left their first love, which is Jesus himself (Revelation 2:4). And too many souls overall miss out on the wonder, inspiration, and comfort that are bestowed upon those who venture into an endeavor toward greater comprehension of the book of Revelation:

> Blessed is he who reads and those who hear the words of this prophecy, and keep those things which are written in it; for the time is near (Revelation 1:3).

Slothfulness, unbelief, intimidation, and the ongoing confusion and distraction generated by competing interpretations and bad theology are the primary obstacles between an individual and the liberation to be had by reading the last book of the Bible. And let us not forget that though the apostle John *wrote* the book of Revelation, its author is Jesus Christ and he is not an author of confusion but of peace (1 Corinthians 14:33).

Despite the apocalyptic imagery and hard (though just) judgment that shall befall those who reject Jesus Christ as the Son of God and humanity's Savior, God has given those who have indeed trusted Jesus as Savior and King the assurance of an awesome, holy, joyful, and peaceful love-filled eternity with him! The end of the age is nothing to be feared, for it heralds the beginning anew of how things ought to be, according to God's eternal design now made possible through Christ.

Compiling this book has been a wonderful and humbling experience. If I were to begin again, the sojourn would surely offer further wonders and an entirely different experience altogether (and such has been the case, this being the third edition[1]). That is the beauty of the Lord God. He is a God of fresh revelation.

My purpose in presenting this commentary is to provide a brief yet detailed guide designed to accompany one on a journey through the book of Jesus' Revelation. I strongly encourage the reader's own personal in-depth research of Scripture under the tutelage of the Holy Spirit, for by no means does this study (or myself) have all the answers or insight concerning Christ's awesome book of revelatory truth.

My prayer is that whosoever partakes of such a journey will be encouraged to search out the scriptures for deeper and grander understanding and experiences that always lead to reclaiming that "first love" or toward finding it for the first time!

—*Jon Scott Birch*

---

1. The first edition was self-printed for a church Bible study in December 2000. The second edition was extensively restructured, expanded, and professionally printed (though not widely published) in May 2011. This third edition carries more expansive additions and new formatting better suited for widespread publication.

Introduction

> Known unto God are all his works from the beginning of the world.
>
> —Acts 15:18 KJV

THE BOOK OF REVELATION is based upon and is a fuller explanation of Jesus' discourse on things to come, as found in Matthew 24, Mark 13, and Luke 21. Also, much Old Testament prophecy finds its parallel and further exhortation in the final book of the biblical canon.

As Genesis is a book of beginnings, Revelation is a book of consummation. Within its pages the divine plan of redemption is brought into completion, and the holiness of God is vindicated before all creation. Numerous prophecies reside in the Gospels and Epistles; however, Revelation is the only New Testament book that focuses primarily on the prophetic, while also containing more unfulfilled prophecy than any other book in the Bible (383 of 404 verses are prophetic, equaling 95 percent of the book!).

The word "revelation" (Greek *apokalupsis*) means "an unveiling, revealing, explaining, or a disclosure." Thus, the book is an unveiling of the character and plan of God. It was written to unfold the future and to chart the destiny of the Jews, Gentiles, and the church. It has been said that prophecy is history written in advance, an aspect well understood by students of the Bible. A more engaging definition of prophecy could describe it as past, current, and future history, i.e., God's blueprint for humanity. And though the word "prophecy" itself causes consternation for some, it is important to recall that God's love is behind that prophecy. He desires that his children know what lies ahead, and to anticipate such; *for the testimony of Jesus is the spirit of prophecy* (Revelation 19:10).

AUTHORSHIP AND CANONICITY

The book of Revelation contains visions and symbols of the resurrected Christ, who alone has authority to judge the earth, to remake it, and to rule it in righteousness. The author of Revelation is, of course, God himself; this is even the book's first statement. God himself dictated it, through Christ and by an angel, to John, who wrote it out and sent the completed message to seven churches, from which it spread.

John the Apostle (Gk. *apostolos*, meaning "one who is sent out"), the Beloved Disciple, most intimate earthly friend of Jesus, and the writer of the Gospel of John and the epistles 1, 2, and 3 John, is almost invariably believed to be the human writer of Revelation. The suggestion by some scholars that it was another John who wrote Revelation, possibly born of a desire to discredit the book, is without solid foundation (as is most Gnostic propaganda, such as the Gospel of Judas, the Gospel of Thomas, the Jesus papers, etc.). At its beginning and at its end the book of Revelation claims to be the prophecy of *John* (Revelation 1:1, 4, 9; 22:8). Although the Revelation contains no explicit identifiers proving its writer to be John the apostle and evangelist, such identification was effectively universal in the early church. Notably, Isbon Beckwith has stated that "so much external testimony to the personality of the author, traceable back to almost contemporaneous sources, is found in the case of almost no other book of the New Testament."[1]

From the dissemination of the Revelation text among the seven original churches in Asia Minor at the end of the first century and onward, its authenticity was readily and faithfully recognized, though primarily by western Christianity in that its circulation seemed to flow more west than east for various reasons. Thus, the book of Revelation is included with those books listed as canonical Scripture by the third Council of Carthage in 397, receiving support and comment by western

---

1. Beckwith, *The Apocalypse of John*, 351; Oden and Weinrich, *Revelation*, xvii.

writers such as "Victorinus of Petovium through those of Tyconius, Primasius, Apringius, Caesarius of Arles, the Venerable Bede, Ambrosius Autpertus, Beatus of Liebana, Alcuin, and Haimo of Auxerre." Some eastern writers include Theophilus of Antioch, Clement and Cyril (both of Alexandria), Origen, Athanasius, Epiphanius, and Basil of Caesarea. And while the Revelation continues to encourage, inspire, fascinate, and frighten western churchgoers even today, it has had minimal impact and scant to no liturgical recitation in the eastern church for the past one thousand years.[2]

THE HISTORICAL CONTEXT—THEN AND NOW

John had been banished to the Aegean island of Patmos during the reign of the Roman emperor Domitian (AD 81–96).[3] He was released in 96, but it is believed that he penned Revelation around AD 95 during his imprisonment, which is when John experienced the visions recorded in the book.[4]

Why was the Revelation given to John at this point in history rather than at another? Let us examine a brief historical tour of the events surrounding John's exile and his receiving Jesus' Revelation.

The visions were given, and the book written, it could be said, in the light of burning martyrs. The church was sixty-six years old and had made tremendous growth. It had suffered, and continued to suffer, great persecutions.[5]

The First Imperial Persecution of Christians occurred under the Roman emperor Nero in AD 64–67, being thirty years after Jesus' ascension into heaven and thirty years prior to Revelation being penned. In this persecution multitudes of Christians were crucified, thrown to wild beasts, or wrapped in combustible garments and burned to death. During this persecution both Paul and Peter suffered martyrdom. The Jewish-Roman War of AD 66–70 also erupted, eventuating the AD 70 destruction of the Jewish temple and the end of Sadducean and Pharisaical overlordship.

---

2. Oden and Weinrich, *Revelation*, xix–xx.
3. Bede, *Explanation of the Apocalypse* 1.9
4. See Appendix B Expanded Commentary #1.
5. For a superb source of historical documentation concerning the woes and victory of the early church, examine Eberhard Arnold's *The Early Christians: In Their Own Words*.

The Second Imperial Persecution was issued by the emperor Domitian in AD 95. While brief, this persecution was severe with over 40,000 Christians being tortured and slain. It was during this persecution that John was sent to Patmos.

The Third Imperial Persecution began in AD 98 under emperor Trajan. Living through the first two and about to enter the third of Rome's imperial efforts to destroy the Christian faith, John would soon witness persecution from *within* the church itself, as corruption and apostasy began to manifest.

God gave these visions recorded in Revelation to help steady the church for the awful days ahead, then and now. Therefore, it should be no surprise that Revelation "was from a very early time one of the most systematically read and used books of the New Testament."[6]

Concerning the book of Revelation as a whole, it is a very practical book. Though it is a book with some *mystery* (something that is hidden until God makes it known by revelation), there is much that we can indeed comprehend. As the time of the end approaches, further mysteries are revealed to those diligent disciples of Christ who spend time searching the scriptures; thus the ignorance of the first centuries of the church kept Christians in anticipation of Christ's return, while the accumulated knowledge and progressive revelation of God over the last few thousand years now has present-day Christians anticipating his return due to the prophetic and historic *evidence* revealing how soon his return truly is! Matthew 16:1–3 and 24:3–8 are great primers.

Buried within Revelation's curious imagery are some of the most sincere warnings and most precious promises of all Scripture. It is very likely that John himself did not immediately understand much of what he saw and recorded, for God had woven hidden meaning into some of the visions that would be progressively revealed only with the unfolding of history.

Alternating simplest truth with strange symbolism, Revelation is a book of ultimate optimism for the children of God, assuring us again and again that we are under his protection and thus preserved toward a life of everlasting peace and love that is to come. And alternating scenes between heaven and earth, Revelation is a book of the wrath of God, juxtaposing the joys of the redeemed with the agonies of the lost. Few souls enjoy the straightforward imagery and references to hell and judgment,

---

6. Oden and Weinrich, *Revelation*, xvii.

but the reality of God and his divine purpose cannot be softened. God is a God of love, but he is also a God of reconciliation and justice, which is precisely what humanity needs in our careless and godless generation!

BLESSED IS HE THAT READS

Revelation is the only book in the Word of God that emphasizes the promise of a blessing to those who read and hear it. "Blessed" is a strong word that is often taken for granted. There are seven blessings, or beatitudes, recorded in Revelation:

1. "Blessed is he who reads and those who hear the words of this prophecy" (1:3).
2. "Blessed are the dead who die in the Lord" (14:3).
3. "Blessed is he who watches" [for the Lord's return] (16:15).
4. "Blessed are those who are called to the marriage supper of the Lamb" (19:9).
5. "Blessed is he who has part in the first resurrection" [the rapture] (20:6).
6. "Blessed is he who keeps the words of the prophecy of this book (22:7).
7. "Blessed are those who do his commandments" [or wash their robes] (22:14).

THE NUMBER SEVEN

In light of the seven beatitudes, the book of Revelation appears to be built around a system of sevens. Seven letters to seven churches (chapters 1–3). Seven aspects of God's throne (chapter 4). Seven seals and seven trumpets (chapters 4–11). Seven bowls/vials (chapters 15–16). Seven lampstands (1:12, 20). Seven stars (1:16, 20). Seven angels (1:20). Seven spirits of God (1:4; 4:5). Seven lamps of fire (4:5). Seven thunders (10:3, 4). Seven mountains (17:9). Seven kings (17:10). A lamb with seven horns and seven eyes (5:6). A red dragon with seven heads and seven crowns (12:1). A leopard-like beast with seven heads (13:1). A scarlet-colored beast with seven heads (17:3, 7).

However, the number seven—effectively God's signature—is found throughout the Bible. The Sabbath is the seventh day and the Levitical system of the Old Testament was founded upon a cycle of sevens. Jericho fell after seven priests with seven trumpets, for seven days, marched around its walls and blew their trumpets seven times on the seventh day.

Naaman dipped in the Jordan seven times to become free of leprosy. Enoch was translated into heaven without seeing death—he was the seventh from Adam. Pharaoh hardened his heart six times consecutively from the miracle of staff-to-serpent through the first five plagues brought upon Egypt, whereas it was God who hardened Pharaoh's heart the *seventh* time (prior to the sixth plague).

In Matthew 18:21 Peter asks Jesus how many times he should forgive those who sin against him. Jesus answers him by saying, "Seventy times seven." Though this equals 490, Jesus' point was that our forgiveness should have no limit. In the book of Daniel we read that God has decreed 490 years to deal directly with Israel, again referencing the 70 x 7 equation with the numbers representing timeframes, specifically the Seventy Weeks of Daniel in which a prophetic "week" is a period of seven years on the Jewish calendar (a Jewish year being 360 days divided into 12 months of 30 days).

Additional interesting incidents of the number seven include the creation week becoming the model for our seven-day calendar week. There are seven notes in music, and seven major chords. There are even seven colors in a rainbow. Not all of these are biblically sanctioned, of course. But it would seem that the number seven signifies wholeness or completion.

GENESIS TO REVELATION

Revelation concludes the awesome story initiated in Genesis. In Genesis the heavens and earth were created; in Revelation we see a new heaven and a new earth. In Genesis there is a garden; in Revelation there is a holy city. In Genesis we witness the fall of mankind to a place lower than the angels; in Revelation we behold mankind reestablished to a place above the angels. In Genesis there is the marriage of the first Adam; in Revelation there is the marriage celebration of the second Adam, Jesus Christ. In Genesis we see the beginning of sin; in Revelation sin is removed. In Genesis we see the appearance of Satan; in Revelation we witness his destruction. In

Genesis we read the first messianic prophecy of a coming Savior; in Revelation we read of his kingdom being established on earth forever.

THE CHRISTOLOGY OF REVELATION

Revelation presents a glorious, reigning Christ. The Gospels present him as a Savior, taking on the curse of sin for humanity. But in the last book of God's Word we see no humiliation. Indeed, the Jesus viewed in the Gospels and Acts is a bit different than the Jesus witnessed in the Revelation. Instead of turning the other cheek, Jesus judges the world with an iron rod!

John's vision of Christ can be read in Revelation 1:12–20. His reaction to the vision can be read in verse 17: "And when I saw him, I fell at his feet as dead." This should be the response of every soul blessed to behold in worship the raw glory of Jesus Christ, for he is at once the prime example and complete explanation of Christian theology in relation to the nature of reality and our place in it (John 1:1–18).[7]

John beheld what words fail to express, yet he successfully documented Jesus holding the seven angels/stars of the churches in his right hand; his hair as white as snow; his eyes like fire; his countenance like the sun; his feet like burnished brass; his voice as the voice of many waters; a sharp two-edged sword proceeding out of his mouth! This is how the meek and humble Jesus now presents himself to his church. And *with* his church, Christ is girded for battle. He is a Warrior and a Conqueror in the truest sense and he bids his church to have confidence in his leadership. He also sternly warns his church, with its increasing signs of corruption and apostasy, that he will not tolerate half-heartedness or disloyalty.

In reference to such disloyalty, recurrent deviant ideologies often separate *what* Jesus said with *who* he was, dismissing the divine nature of Jesus while exalting his ethical teachings.[8] The opposite is also trending, wherein Jesus' divinity and forgiveness of sin is overemphasized to the point of abusing his grace as a license to entertain vice toward being forgiven all the more; the Christian ethic is abandoned outright (Romans 6:1–6; Galatians 5:13). These are false gospels born of attempts at theological understanding in the flesh devoid of direct revelation in the Spirit (Romans 8:1–17; 1 Corinthians 2:11–14). Indeed, the postmodern world needs the Revelation of Jesus Christ more than ever; the Christology of

---

7. McGrath, *Genesis of Doctrine*, 74–75.
8. Shelley, *Church History*, 3rd ed., 46.

Scripture overall and the book of Revelation specifically prove Jesus as the eternal and incarnate Word of God so that we may believe he is the Christ and thus have life in his name (John 20:31).

SUFFERING WITH CHRIST—ISRAEL, THE CHURCH, AND THE WRATH OF GOD

Though the flesh seeks to escape persecution of any kind, every disciple of Jesus Christ (and thus the church universal) must learn obedience through suffering as he did (Isaiah 26:9; Matthew 26:39). Not everyone will experience financial or health challenges, public ridicule, personal intellectual mockery, physical or psychological torture, life or death persecution, or ultimate martyrdom for their faithfulness to Christ. Yet we will all suffer in some way—physically, emotionally, spiritually—unto death.

The seven letters to the seven churches in Revelation 2–3 reveal a paradigm of discipleship wherein we learn that by means of affliction on any level, while bearing our crosses with Christ, we make progress in sanctification. William Hendriksen states that "the church needs these trials in order that it may be cleansed and purified and in order that true believers may be brought closer to God."[9]

Hendriksen's encouragement is welcome and poignantly true concerning discipleship, yet concerning prophecy he mistakenly believed the church would suffer the seal, trumpet, and bowl judgments of the end of the age (Revelation 6–19). This is due to his writing in 1939, several years prior to Israel's rebirth as a modern nation in 1947–48 which miraculously fulfilled the prophecies of Isaiah 66:8; Ezekiel 36; and 37:1–14 and devastated the false teaching of *replacement theology*.[10] As

---

9. Hendriksen, *More Than Conquerors*, 26.

10. Israel's restoration after Christ's return nullifies the false teaching of replacement theology, which insists that the church *forever replaces* Israel as the priesthood/light among nations. Israel will ultimately enjoy a place beside Christ and his church as a distinct but equal entity sharing in the priestly rule of Christ's kingdom (Romans 11). Revelation 21:9–27 reveals the holy city as having twelve *gates* with the names of the twelve tribes of Israel inscribed on them, and also having twelve *foundations* inscribed with the names of the twelve apostles of the Lamb. Gates and foundations are *separate* and *distinct* entities. That Israel's identity is inscribed on the gates possibly represents the idea that it was *through* Judaism that Christianity came into the world, while the church's identity inscribed on the foundations is made explicitly clear in Ephesians 2:19–20, Luke 22:29–30, and Matthew 16:18–19. For more detail see Rhodes, *8 Great Debates of Bible Prophecy*, 37–43; Hampson, *The End Times*, 89–91.

Introduction

we shall learn, the seal, trumpet, and bowl judgments entail the *wrath of God* specifically purposed for an unrepentant Israel and an unbelieving world, not the church.

Indeed, the church now experiences tribulation in the world, but such trials are an aspect of a cursed world, a spiritual enemy, and sinful human nature, not God's wrath. *Jesus Christ himself suffered his Father's wrath in the church's stead when he endured the cross* (2 Peter 2:5–9; Revelation 3:10). This is scriptural proof for a pre-tribulation rapture, a sure and blessed hope (Titus 2:13). We will examine this too in intimate detail in chapter four.

True discipleship is not easy; it is a lifestyle of worship, of persevering joy, and of engaging spiritual warfare. However, in confronting the hard realities of Jesus' revelation to John (and us), we have an awesome future that awaits, for the apostle Paul reminds us in Romans 8:16–18 (ESV):

> The Spirit himself bears witness with our spirit that we are children of God, and if children, then heirs—heirs of God and fellow heirs with Christ, provided we suffer with him in order that we may also be glorified with him. For I consider that the sufferings of this present time are not worth comparing with the glory that is to be revealed in us.

INTERPRETATION

Admittedly, much of Bible prophecy and specifically the book of Revelation is intimidating when first approached and confronted with the oft-times peculiar language, including symbols, metaphors, historical reflections, typology, and double or multiple meanings. It can be difficult to determine what is to be taken as literal, spiritual, metaphorical, or any combination of such.

The late Dr. David L. Cooper offered a profound and useful interpretive tool: "When the plain sense of Scripture makes common sense, seek no other sense; therefore, take every word at its primary, ordinary, usual, literal meaning unless the facts of the immediate text, studied in the light of related passages and axiomatic and fundamental truths, clearly indicate otherwise."

Literal interpretation of Scripture does not exclude symbols, figures of speech, or parables. However, when passages cannot be understood fully in the literal sense by the surface text alone due to unfamiliar symbolism or typology, Scripture interprets itself through previous and/or later passages relative to the passage of study. Particularly concerning prophecy found in the book of Revelation, previous passages in the Bible—whether prophetic, poetic, prose, or historical—are extremely helpful toward attaining comprehension of what is being revealed; therefore, cross-referencing is a vital aspect in studying eschatology (prophecy of the last days). The books of Genesis, Daniel, Ezekiel, Jeremiah, Isaiah, Zechariah, and Joel are heavily referenced.

Scripture also, in some cases, indicates when a specific reference is to be taken spiritually or metaphorically, as in Revelation 11:8 which speaks of Jerusalem as "the great city which *spiritually* is called Sodom and Egypt." The meaning is meant to put forth Jerusalem as being *comparable to* Sodom and Egypt, for Jerusalem in this context has become spiritually corrupt and is in essence (literally) practicing spiritual adultery against Almighty God as had Sodom and Egypt formerly; thus, we see historical reflection *and* spiritual symbolism utilized to convey the specific literal truth of disobedience. Also see Galatians 4:22–26 where the apostle Paul employs allegory to stress literal truth concerning law and grace.

There is likewise a need to note the contemporary background events and immediate circumstance of the book of Revelation, being that the initial purpose of the book was to fortify the failing hearts of believers in the first century AD. Additionally, the multitude of symbols found throughout the book are rooted foremost in the entirety of Scripture but also within the prevailing historical context of the time. Hendriksen reminds us that the apostle John was wholly immersed in all present Scripture and traditions of his day. And though the Revelation was given to bless all believers of all times, we must understand and interpret the prophecy "in the light not only of external events but also of the entire religious heritage held in reverence by believers who lived when these visions were seen and recorded."[11]

It is further helpful to remember that symbols in prophetic literature always convey *literal* truths, and it is these truths that are meant to be revealed whilst not getting lost in the symbolism. To spiritualize or allegorize overtly is to deny the purpose of prophecy, specifically the book of Revelation whereas the divine intent is to *reveal* a former mystery, not further mystify it.

---

11. Hendriksen, *More Than Conquerors*, 46.

Introduction

Symbols are concrete or abstract objects that represent, suggest, or indicate literal, moral, ideological, or spiritual truths (or any combination of these). An example of a *literal symbol* representing a full combination of literal, moral, ideological, and spiritual truth can be seen in the object of the American flag. The literal, tangible flag (its design and colors) recalls America's history, culture, and purpose; and it signifies *liberty*, while simultaneously representing the actual *land* from sea to shining sea. Our flag may evoke fear, hope, power, freedom, or Christian truth. It may even wrongfully represent *tyranny* to our enemies, who are ultimately enemies of freedom. Of course, there will always be some who misinterpret out of ignorance, pride, or outright rebellion.

Finis Dake offers an excellent rule list for practical and proper prophetic interpretation, primarily in regard to the book of Revelation. The following points are condensed from Dake's commentary *Revelation Expounded*:

1. *Give the same meaning to the words of prophecy that are given to words of history*; that is, give the same meaning to the words of the entire Bible that are given to the same words outside the Bible. The common theory that just because a word is found in prophecy, or because it is in the Bible, it automatically has a mystical meaning and cannot be understood in the literal sense is entirely wrong.

2. *Do not change the literal to a spiritual or symbolic meaning*; this does away with the literal meaning of God's own revelation and substitutes man's theories instead.

3. *Do not seek to find hidden meanings to the words of Scripture, or add to Scripture.* Be satisfied with what God has seen fit to reveal and never read between the lines or add to Scripture in order to understand it.

4. *Believe that prophecy can be understood just as it is without any changes or additions and that it is simply a record of things yet to happen sometime after its utterance.* After all, history is simply a record of what has happened and prophecy is a record of what is going to happen.

5. *Forget the idea that prophecy must be fulfilled before it can be understood.* If prophecy must be fulfilled before it can be understood, then it has failed in its purpose of revealing to man beforehand what is to happen.

6. *Do not interpret God's own interpretation of any symbol or prophecy or change God's meaning from that which is plainly and obviously clear.* God always interprets his own symbols as plainly seen in Daniel 2:28–44; 7:17, 23–26; 8:20–23; 9:20–27; 11:2–45; 12:1–13; Revelation 1:20; 12:9; 13:18; 17:8–18. These are only a few examples.[12]

BIBLICAL LITERACY

Concerning scriptural interpretation, it is highly important to maintain an awareness of the "overall plan" or "big picture" that God has woven from Genesis to Revelation. This includes careful consideration of the grammatical, historical, cultural, and contextual methods of interpretation while not allowing our reason, traditions, or experiences to "be seen as a higher authority than Scripture by which Scripture could be trumped *on some issue that Scripture directly addresses* and about which it makes claims on God's people."[13]

Taking choice passages of Scripture out of context to construct a new (or deviant) idea or doctrine is a dangerous practice that has resulted in many divergent schools of thought that have in turn led to ultra-dogmatism within some denominations and institutions. Such dogmatic views have resulted in unintentional doctrinal apostasy, which only leads to confusion, spiritual cynicism, and ultimately spiritual pride and/or false teaching. The majority of these schools of thought (amillennialist, preterist-historical, idealist, et al.) often assail those who hold to a literal interpretation of Scripture—many of those attacks being very unChristlike.

To be sure, elements of truth and uncertainty may exist within each varying view; therefore, it is imperative to be more fluent in Scripture than in any particular human devised tradition. Knowing God through his Word enables us to truly know his Word as instructed by his Spirit and not our own understanding (Proverbs 3:5–7; 1 Corinthians 2:14). We must approach each traditional perspective with the authority of Scripture and never impose upon Scripture our imperfect suppositions. This guards against accidental heresy and promotes humility. And once a biblical worldview is established, a working knowledge of the pros and cons of

---

12. Dake, *Revelation Expounded*, 16–21. See also Hayes/Holladay, *Biblical Exegesis*, 178–90.

13. Witherington, *Is There a Doctor in the House?*, 103. Emphasis in original.

humanity's traditional views—on prophecy in general and Revelation in particular—will enrich one's studies rather than enrage one's sensibilities![14]

One point of contention held by anti-literal views is that which denies Israel its proper doctrinal purpose; but God does have a plan for his chosen people and he will carry out that plan in its entirety as shown in simplistic clarity throughout the pages of Scripture (albeit hidden in plain sight from those in search of nonexistent fiction as they cut and paste the Word of God in blatant violation of Revelation 22:18-19).

To illustrate, the preterist view insists that the majority of the book of Revelation is historical, primarily describing the events of AD 70, with most (if not all) of the prophecies except Jesus' return having been fulfilled long ago. The term "preterism" originates from the Latin word *preter*, which means "past." Thus even the context of Revelation 20-22 is believed by some preterists to be describing events that have generally already taken place, thereby assuming (unintentionally?) that Satan has been removed from world influence (Revelation 20:10), so there is no more death, sorrow, or pain (Revelation 21:4), and believers are now able to see the Father's face (Revelation 22:4). If these chapters in Revelation describe our *present* state, then most of the New Testament can be dismissed also. The admonition to "resist the devil" is useless according to the preterist view. Moreover, if the devil has no influence in the world, why are we instructed to "put on the whole armor of God"?

Parallel prophecies in the Old Testament are likewise dismissed by the preterist reckoning. Zechariah 14:1-3 details Jerusalem's devastation and reveals the Lord himself going forth to fight against the nations as when he fights in a day of battle. History starkly reveals that when Jerusalem was sacked in AD 70 the Roman army was in no way deterred, nor did Christ stand in its way. The plethora of discrepancies that plague the preterist view (among other nonliteral views) are usually dismissed without any serious consideration or legitimate practice of true scholarship.

Sadly, doctrines that dismiss or deny prophecy in its proper divine perspective effectively deny disciples of Christ a richer scriptural experience. A pastor friend within a preterist denomination once asked me about my personal understanding of biblical prophecy. He had been informed by a mutual colleague that I was passionate about the same. During our discussion he expressed his curiosity concerning prophecy and

---

14. For detailed analysis on the main interpretive traditions, see Gregg, *Revelation: Four Views*; Rhodes, *8 Great Debates of Bible Prophecy*; Hitchcock, *The End*; and Hampson, *The End Times*.

Revelation specifically, but said the seminary he had attended rendered Bible prophecy irrelevant since every prediction was said to be fulfilled except Jesus' return to earth. My friend confessed he had no particular bias or enough information about the topic to form an educated or even an opinionated view. I then proceeded to expound prophetic Scripture to him, showing all things concerning Christ from Genesis to Revelation, and particularly highlighting those things that are indeed yet unfulfilled having to do with Israel, the rapture, the end of the age, the Day of God's Wrath, the binding of Satan, the necessity of a literal thousand-year kingdom on earth with Jesus as King in Jerusalem, the great white throne, and hell itself being cast into the lake of fire.

Of course, he asked many clarifying questions and our discussion lasted for hours. I saw the burning in my friend's heart as the Holy Spirit opened up the scriptures (Luke 24:32). Within months he resigned his pastorship at his local charge, left the church denomination he was a part of, and moved away to begin a season of newfound biblical and self-examination. I did not counsel or expect such action, but it was refreshing to see genuine heartfelt conviction at the Spirit's direction result in obedience when so many in the church today rest on pretense and assumption, i.e., comfort and ignorance. I thank Jesus Christ for his testimony and the Holy Spirit's revelation of truth! Amen!

Regarding the literal interpretive view of the Word of God, there is indeed an acceptance of symbolism, allegory, and metaphor where it is utilized and clarified by context and Scripture itself.

However, the arbitrary and overt designation of symbolism, allegorizing, and/or spiritualization is abhorred for reasons aforementioned.

Now, ere we progress and in reference to the previously mentioned systematic revelation of God to diligent disciples and students of his Word, I will quote C. I. Scofield from his own commentary notes on Revelation:

"Doubtless, much which is designedly obscure to us will be clear to those for whom it was written *as the time approaches*."[15]

---

15. See the Introduction to the book of Revelation in *The Scofield Reference Bible* (Oxford University Press, 1999). Emphasis mine.

1

A Key to Understanding Revelation

It is no mystery that the book of Revelation is a book of prophecy requiring an intimate knowledge of the Old Testament for its fullest comprehension. Although the mystery often arises when a simple observation is overlooked or not considered closely.

One observation is this: Prophecy has a *chronological order*, being future-oriented, and Christ's revelation to John is an exemplar of such, with a few parenthetical interludes adding historical and spiritual detail toward fuller comprehension of the text.

The key verse priming the student toward a chronological understanding of Revelation is in chapter 1 verse 19: "Write the things which you have seen, and the things which are, and the things which will take place after this."

The template that John is given clearly consists of three distinct categories:

"*The things which you have seen . . .*"

Reference: Revelation 1. This section contains a prologue (1:1–3), a salutation (1:4–8), and an awesome vision of the "Son of Man," Jesus Christ in full majesty (1:9–20).

"*The things which are . . .*"

Reference: Revelation 2 and 3. The focus of this section is on the seven letters to the seven churches and the geopolitical and spiritual climate surrounding the church's widespread growth in the first century.

John's powerful vision of Christ is detailed, as are the messages to the churches, each containing a command, commendation, condemnation, a correction, and a challenge—perfect counsel from Jesus Christ as the hardship of constant attack descends upon the church at its birth and is prophesied to last until he returns.

The dual historical/prophetic nature of these letters is staggering and carries incalculable importance as the church draws ever nearer to the apostate situation of the last days, characterized in the letter to the church of Laodicea. Evidence of current trends within Catholic, Protestant, Orthodox, and Independent denominations and institutions suggests that the Laodicean church-type is a *clear and present reality*.

"The things which will take place after this . . ."

Reference: Revelation 4–22. In chapter 4 John is translated into heaven, where he is given yet another tremendous vision of God's throne and heavenly worship. The event of John being called up into heaven to witness these things is a shadow of the rapture of the church, further reinforced by the absence of the church from the ensuing judgment (Tribulation) period on earth outlined in chapters 6–19. Chapters 4 and 5 of Revelation are together indicative of events immediately following the rapture of the church prior to the commencement of God's wrath upon the earth, namely the exposing of the church to both God's glory and to Christ himself in worshipful essence.

As said, the events of Revelation chapters 6–19 will take place *after* the rapture of the church. These final events, including those of chapters 20–22, outline the Tribulation (and the events therein), the second advent of Christ (and the events thereof), the binding of Satan, the millennial reign of Christ on earth, the judgment of the unrighteous at the great white throne, and the passing of the old heaven and earth into the new heaven and earth that ushers in eternity future with God Almighty.

The book of Revelation concludes with an awesome epilogue (22:6–21), reassuring humanity that Jesus is indeed coming quickly (22:7, 12, 20).

In order to keep this commentary brief and inviting I have utilized a narrative style of exposition rather than a critically stark exegetical method. My hope is that this book might become an encouraging supplement to the reader's own primary immersion in Scripture, and/or perhaps used as a devotional or small group Bible study guide. Godspeed as you encounter the Revelation of Jesus Christ firsthand!

2

A Vision of Jesus Christ in Full Majesty

> "The things which you have seen..."
> —REVELATION 1

A PROLOGUE OPENS THE book of Revelation and the book's overall structure resembles the Gospel of John. True to form, John closes both his Gospel and the Revelation with a tidy and enticing epilogue.

A blessing is promised to the readers and hearers of the prophetic truths of the book of Revelation (1:3). Note, however, that said blessing only holds for those who "keep those things which are written in it." The context of "keep" here means to treasure the revealed truths in one's heart and to live under obeisance to them. Indeed, one must likewise approach *all* the beatitudes of Revelation (listed in the Introduction to this commentary).

Chapter 1, verse 4 is John's salutation. Though he addresses the "seven churches which are in Asia," the fact that the church universal is also ultimately meant as recipient is proven by Jesus' own words (Revelation 2:23; 22:16). Accompanying John's personal greeting are extended greetings from each Person of the triune Godhead. God the Father is "him who is and who was and who is to come," which shows his omnipresence and sovereignty over time—past, present, future.

The Holy Spirit is referenced as "the seven Spirits who are before his throne," which is simply an Old Testament emphasis on the seven-fold ministry of the Spirit in history (Isaiah 11:2).

And Jesus Christ is honored via many titles that are each worthy of independent examination toward his glory (Revelation 1:5, 8). John also reminds us of who we are in Christ and that he is coming soon (Revelation 1:6–7)!

Chapter 1, verses 9–11 express John's solidarity in suffering with persecuted believers, as well as his commissioning by Jesus to write the Revelation. Upon hearing Jesus' voice, John turns and witnesses a terrifying vision of Christ in full majesty, then writes: "And when I saw him, I fell at his feet as dead. But he laid his right hand on me, saying to me, 'Do not be afraid.'" (1:17).

The context of John's vision shows Jesus walking amidst seven golden lampstands with seven stars in his right hand. Christ himself revealed the lampstands to represent the seven churches, and the stars to represent seven angels assigned to those churches (1:20).

ANGELS WE HAVE HEARD ON HIGH

Consider that via the Holy Spirit and a host of ministering and guarding angels, Jesus' ministry to his church worldwide remains active and relational (Matthew 18:20). Yet how many churches, despite the encompassing spiritual war, fail to abide by this profound truth? How many churches fail to grow by the power of the Spirit as they struggle to be relevant in the flesh?

Concerning the seven "angels," there is much disagreement as to whether they are in fact *heavenly* messengers or *human* elders/shepherds of each respective church. In that Jesus is specifically revealing a "mystery" concerning the lampstands and stars, we must defer to his own clear literal interpretation: the stars are angels, i.e., heavenly messengers, and the lampstands are churches. Jesus specifically says: "The mystery of the seven stars which you saw in my right hand, and the seven golden lampstands: *The seven stars are the angels of the seven churches, and the seven lampstands which you saw are the seven churches*" (Revelation 1:20; emphasis mine).

Extant shoddy scholarship and opinion insists that the angels of the seven churches (and therein any church) are *human* shepherds. However,

A Vision of Jesus Christ in Full Majesty

a survey of the extensive ministry of heavenly angels in both Old and New Testament Scripture will show a literal interpretation of Revelation 1:20 to be altogether consistent with biblical history. Paul even refers to active angelic presence in 1 Timothy 5:21. Also, stars are often identified with angels in Scripture—the symbolism being quite appropriate (e.g., Revelation 9:1–11; 12:3–9), along with an implication of divine command in light of the stars being in Christ's right hand (Job 38:31).

Some contend that both the Hebrew and Greek words for "angel" (*mal'ak* and *aggelos/angelos* respectively, meaning "one sent forth, or messenger") are applied to celestial beings and humans alike. Though true, this does nothing toward changing Jesus' own meaning, for he never referred (even loosely) to humans as angels. Moreover, *every* time he spoke of angels he meant "heavenly angels" in the literal sense as contexts will show (e.g., Matthew 13:39). Jeffrey Weima adds,

> Key considerations in this debate include the fact that elsewhere in the book of Revelation *angelos* always (69x) refers to a supernatural being, early Christian texts rarely use *angelos* to refer to a human being, and Jewish writings from this time period frequently depict heavenly angels as guiding and safeguarding the actions of earthly kings and nations (e.g., Daniel 10:13, 20–21).[1]

Jesus not once interpreted one symbol by the use of another, and for us to reinterpret his own interpretation is simultaneously presumptuous and hazardous.[2] It also lacks imagination by dismissing the ever-present supernatural activity of God's celestial agents, whom are in our midst even today.

Indeed, the circumstance of presiding or protecting angels charged to churches is not commonly taught today, yet is a sobering thought bringing to mind Jesus' reference to personal angelic guardians (Matthew 18:10; Acts 12:15). And recall that angels have a vested interest in the prophetic and transforming aspects of Christ's salvation (1 Peter 1:10–12), as well as the church's progress on a local level (Ephesians 3:8–10; 1 Timothy 3:16; 5:21; Hebrews 1:14; 13:2). Divine truth is never determined by our limited human reason, teaching, insistence, or indifference.

---

1. Weima, *Sermons to the Seven Churches*, 28.

2. Smith, *A Revelation of Jesus Christ*, 57–58; *The New Strong's Exhaustive Concordance*, Hebrew word #4397; Greek word #32.

Lampstands recall Old Testament temple liturgy. The lampstand is a *vessel* that carries the living light/flame of God; it is not itself light. Likewise with the church, for it is only Christ who illuminates.

And finally, the angel who signifies the book of Revelation to John (Revelation 1:1) testifies that he is a *fellow-servant of God* to the apostles, to the prophets, and to those who keep the words of the book of Revelation (Revelation 22:9). Plainly, this angel has an interest in the contents of the book John is charged to write. Perhaps this same angel delivered copies of the completed volume to the angels of the other churches, vouchsafing the message regarding its urgency.

3

The Seven Churches

"The things which are..."

—REVELATION 2–3

IN THE HISTORICALLY IMMEDIATE context, the seven churches are timely messages meant specifically for the targeted communities. Prophetically, the seven epistles speak to all churches of every age, and the seven churches may be seen to foreshadow seven church eras that are to commence within the church age (Pentecost to rapture). Why were only seven churches chosen out of the thousands that existed at the time?

In accord with his undying wisdom, Jesus chose these seven churches of Asia Minor and listed them in specific order pertaining to their positive and negative attributes and the struggles they faced. Inspired by the Spirit, even Paul singled out seven specific churches to receive his epistles—Rome; Corinth; Ephesus; Thessalonica; Galatia; Philippi; Colossae—his additional letters are addressed to individuals. It is clear in the Spirit-inspired message contexts from both Paul and Jesus that *seven* churches indicates a *universal* church intent.

In retrospect, we now can see these church exemplars as ideal for instructing all Christians in discipleship; and the qualities and struggles of each example have turned out to be prophetic revelation revealing applicable aspects of the entire (future/current) history of the church universal—a sentiment likewise expressed by early church father Venerable Bede.[1] Furthermore, the seven churches were personally familiar to John.

Reinforcing the *prophetic* character of the seven churches is the fact that chapters 2 and 3 constitute a part of "the words of this prophecy" (Revelation 1:3; 22:18). The mystery of the seven churches is revealed in the fact that they outline an appropriate approach to the history of the church—institutionally and per discipleship—from Pentecost to the rapture, a period some refer to as the "age of grace." From the humble, sincere, and zealous beginning to the prideful, blind, and heretical end, the seven letters to the seven churches offer spiritual lessons concerning proper conduct and direction for the church that is of as much importance today as when first written.

Although I do not adopt rigid dispensationalism, particularly concerning the church age, I do see prophetic evidences, or trends, that Jesus embedded (not encoded!) within his seven epistles which would gain clarity as history progressed. This is not interpretation as much as it is *application*. Professor Jeffrey Weima nicely summarizes:

> As a basic interpretive principle, these sermons should be viewed as *forthtelling* God's word to seven ancient churches. In other words, they are divine messages addressing first and foremost seven specific churches located in Asia Minor at the end of the first century AD. However, like all Scripture, these texts are also relevant to the twenty-first century church. This interpretive principle differs from an older, once popular approach that saw the sermons as *foretelling* seven future church periods. That approach arose primarily within classic dispensationalism and asserted that the seven sermons were not so much letters to historical churches as they were predictions of seven future periods of church history covering the time between Christ's first coming and his second coming.[2]

Thus the seven churches, their prophetic type, and the *hypothesized* associative historical era are as follows:

1. Ephesus—Apostolic church {AD 30–100}

---

1. Bede, *Explanation of the Apocalypse* 1.1. Also, Andrew of Caesarea, *Commentary on the Apocalypse* 1.4; Apringius of Beja, *Tractate on the Apocalypse* 1.4; and Victorinus of Petovium, *Commentary on the Apocalypse* 1.7.

2. Weima, *Sermons to the Seven Churches*, 19–20. Emphasis in original.

2. Smyrna—Persecuted church {AD 100-313}
3. Pergamum—State church {AD 313-590}
4. Thyatira—Papal church {AD 590-517}
5. Sardis—Reformed church {AD 1517-1750?}
6. Philadelphia—Missionary church {AD 1750-?}
7. Laodicea—Apostate church {AD 1900?-?}[3]

For each church I will briefly outline both historic and prophetic characteristics. To introduce each church I have included a fourfold template listing a commendation, a condemnation, instructive counsel, and a challenge. Though these were each given to the respective churches by Jesus himself, I must give credit to the late pastor, author, and scholar Tim Lahaye for this fourfold template that comprehensively captures the profound simplicity of Jesus' message.[4]

THE CHURCH OF EPHESUS—APOSTOLIC CHURCH: REVELATION 2:1-7

Commendation: Good works, labor, patience, hated Nicolaitans (see church of Pergamos).

Condemnation: You have left your first love.

Counsel: Remember from where you have fallen and repent.

Challenge: "To him who overcomes . . ." will be given to eat of the tree of life.

Founded by Athenian colonists around BC 1000, Ephesus was centered around worship of the goddess Artemis, yet is considered by numerous Bible scholars to have birthed one of the greatest New Testament churches. For information on the founding of this church, read Acts 18-20. The name Ephesus means "desired one," a fitting description of the church for it was highly notable of all the churches in its purpose and practice. However, its one flaw was inexcusable, as we shall see.

Ephesus, a seaport, was only about fifty miles northeast of Patmos. At the time of John's sentence to the infamous island he was one of the

3. Cohen, *Understanding Revelation*, 53-54.
4. Lahaye, *Revelation Unveiled*, 43.

elders of the church in Ephesus. On John's release from imprisonment, Clement of Alexandria commented, "the Apostle John . . . on the tyrant's [Domitian's] death . . . returned to Ephesus from the isle of Patmos, he went away, being invited, to the contiguous territories of the nations, here to appoint bishops, there to set in order whole churches, there to ordain such as were marked out by the Spirit."[5]

Apostolic Foundation

The early church unashamedly preached the Gospel around the entire known world, showing us that bold evangelism was a major requisite for widespread conversion to Christianity. The church in Ephesus truly displayed this trait, undoubtedly kindled by apostolic zeal; for of the seven churches mentioned in Revelation 2 and 3, Ephesus is the only one in which the apostles are referred to, as they assisted in the establishment of this church personally. This fact alone offers sound reason for the awesome strength and endurance of the early church, as well as scriptural support for *not* commissioning apostles in the post-apostolic/modern era in that such work and *doctrinal authority* are laid out in the New Testament canon (in its finality). Anyone commissioned as or assuming the title *apostle* (meaning "one who is sent") today must be understood to simply be an itinerant elder or missionary/church planter, not one who establishes new doctrine.

The apostle Paul, after establishing the Ephesian church (Acts 19:1–8), remained in Ephesus and for two years daily disputed in the school of Tyrannus, after which "upon the eve of a great revival, believers made a great bonfire of books of magical arts valued at 50,000 pieces of silver."[6]

A few years later, Paul's letter to the Ephesian church shows his labor there to have been well rewarded (Ephesians 1:1–3). And in subsequent years Ephesus would celebrate Paul's protege Timothy as its first long-term shepherd-bishop (1 Timothy 1:3). As mentioned above in Clement's statement, John would follow Timothy in this function upon his release from Patmos, living out his days preaching and teaching until dying a natural death (ca. AD 98) around age 100.

---

5. Clement of Alexandria, *Who Is the Rich Man That Shall Be Saved?* (homily) XLII.
6. Smith, *A Revelation of Jesus Christ*, 62; Acts 19:9–20.

No Love, No Light—Know Love, Know Light

Ephesus was a working, pure, autonomous, and uncompromising church. However, Jesus accused it of forsaking its "first love." The people in this church were very bold and zealous for the Lord, but eventually the natural tendency to take something for granted began to pervade the assemblies, resulting in no less than losing the intimate awareness of the spiritual power and privileges and wonder of *knowing* Christ! Perhaps "heresy-hunting had killed love; it may well be that eagerness to root out all mistaken men had ended in a sour and rigid orthodoxy."[7] Or that legalistic orthodoxy and underlying universal suspicion had been achieved at the cost of fellowship with Christ. It is indeed possible to cling tighter to doctrine than to Jesus himself (John 5:39–40).

Too often it is doctrine that determines our relationships when it is our relationships (with God, self, and others) that must determine our doctrine, founded in Scripture. For, as Alister McGrath articulates, doctrine is "a *living tradition* representing the significance of Jesus of Nazareth within the *lived experience of a community of faith*, reflected at all levels of life—in liturgy, prayer, patterns of spirituality, in pastoral practice, and in theological speculation."[8] Therefore, true Christian doctrine can only be appropriately appreciated and applied in the context of genuine loving relationships, not a context of rigid behavioral legalism.

It is for this reason that the Lord Jesus counseled these early believers to repent and remember the things that they had done in the beginning upon first being born into his kingdom. He wanted them (and us today) to always remember, and abide in, the absolute excitement of knowing our first love and realizing our place in the kingdom of heaven, following and serving Jesus. And for those who *live for Christ continuously*, without becoming lukewarm in devotion to him (see the Laodicean church), there is the promise of everlasting life!

A most frightening verse is found in Revelation 2:5, wherein after Christ encourages the church to repentance after forsaking its first love, he then threatens to remove the church's lampstand, meaning that upon a church's departure from sound doctrine and/or upon its removal (even unintentionally) of Christ as the authoritative Head, he will do no less than remove that church's influence as a light in the world—effectively rendering a church as democratically-driven rather than Spirit-driven. This fell

---

7. Barclay, *The Revelation of John*, vol. 1, 77.
8. McGrath, *Genesis of Doctrine*, 197. Emphasis mine.

reality is not uncommon among modern congregations, and the churches of today would do well to practice continual (individual *and* corporate) prayerful spiritual evaluation of the leadership and laity alike so as to keep constant in both devotion to Christ and discernment of his direction.

In Revelation 2:6 Jesus states a commendable trait for the Ephesian congregation, saying, "But this you have, that you hate the deeds of the Nicolaitans, which I also hate."

It may be odd to hear Jesus commending hate when he had earlier commanded and exemplified loving one's enemies (Matthew 5:44; Luke 6:27), but note that it is the *deeds* and *doctrines* of the Nicolaitans that were hated, not the perpetrators themselves. We will more closely examine the Nicolaitans in our look at the Pergamos church.

THE CHURCH OF SMYRNA—PERSECUTED CHURCH: REVELATION 2:8-11

Commendation: Works, tribulation, poverty.

Condemnation: none given

Counsel: Fear not, be faithful.

Challenge: "To him who overcomes . . ." will not be hurt by the *second death*—the lake of fire.

The church in Smyrna was heavily persecuted in a city of wealth that despised Christians. It was here that Polycarp, the famed disciple of the apostle John and once bishop of the Smyrna church, was executed circa AD 155.[9] His martyrdom (among others) was actually triggered by a large sect of apostate (non-Christian) Jews, i.e., "synagogue of Satan" (Revelation 2:9), who were agitating Roman city officials against Christianity.[10] Recall Jesus' former biting words to the Pharisees: "You are of your father the devil, and the desires of your father you want to do" (John 8:44).

That the word *smyrna* (from "myrrh") means bitter seems to prophetically correlate to the severe persecutions endured by Christians in

---

9. See *The Martyrdom of Polycarp* recorded by his disciple, Pionus. After the account of Stephen's death in Acts, this is the oldest extant record of Christian martyrdom. Also D'Ambrosio, *When the Church Was Young*, 29–37.

10. Apostate Jews often were the most volatile instigators of Christian persecution. The book of Acts records some of their heinous machinations against Christian leaders in Antioch (Acts 13:50); Iconium (14:2, 5); Lystra (14:19); and Thessalonica (17:5).

this region. Myrrh was used in embalming the dead and had to be crushed to release its fragrance—likewise the church. Comfort then can be had in the sovereignty and deity of Jesus in that he is the "First and the Last, who was dead, and came to life" (Revelation 2:8; Isaiah 41:4; 44:6; 48:12).

In Revelation 2:10 Jesus encourages believers to be fearless and faithful even unto death as they endure the suffering of trials, imprisonment, and torment *specifically for being a Christ-follower*. This is not a reference to general suffering. Indeed, many New Testament texts reflect the same expectation of affliction for believers, e.g., Matthew 10:22; 2 Timothy 3:12; 1 Peter 4:12; Hebrews 10:32–34. A warning of "ten days" of tribulation is given to the Smyrna assembly. Most commentators agree that the ten days is a symbolic reference alluding to both a short duration and "to the ten general persecutions of the early Christian church which all historians recognize."[11]

Though this understanding is possible, I believe such a specific reference carries an immediately literal fulfillment for those believers who first received the letter to the church at Smyrna. Jesus' words and the supernatural circumstances surrounding their record and timing of deliverance would have offered a threatened church the necessary resolve to personally withstand violent persecution and death with holy boldness (James 1:12).

Not many details are known concerning the history of the church at Smyrna beyond what is offered in the book of Revelation. However, the *city* was founded by Alexander the Great little more than three centuries before the birth of Christ, and despite boasting a temple to Athena, it was eventually known for being conquered by Attila the Hun in the fifth century AD. Also prominently known was the fierce loyalty to Rome that Smyrnaeans possessed, an attribute rewarded by Rome's own laud for Smyrna's populace. Notably, in AD 26 Tiberius selected Smyrna over ten other regional cities for the privilege of constructing a second imperial temple (the first being in Pergamos) in honor of the deceased Caesar Augustus.[12]

What Scripture does tell us is that the *church* at Smyrna was very faithful (to Christ, not Rome) despite relentless persecution. Thus we can predict that Christ will reveal this church to be a most noteworthy local body of believers in all of church history.

---

11. Smith, *A Revelation of Jesus Christ*, 67.
12. Weima, *Sermons to the Seven Churches*, 71.

A History of Spiritual Warfare

The Smyrna era of church history is likely the greatest time of persecution the church has ever known; after all, the greatest mystery of the ages (the passion, crucifixion, and resurrection), "kept secret since the world began but now revealed" (Romans 16:25–26), birthed an unwelcome entity—the church—into Satan's earthly kingdom. When Satan realized that the apostolic church and its faithful preaching of the Gospel was a threat to his godless/pagan empire, he unleashed an unholy offensive against the church in an attempt to annihilate it.

However, he learned an invaluable lesson, for his attack was unsuccessful. The more Satan attacked the church, the more the church overcame the one condemning characteristic of the apostolic age—that of having left its first love. Therefore, *not one condemnation was uttered against Smyrna*. As a result, the supernatural nature of the church was evidenced in the fact that it reached its greatest numbers in proportion to world population during this period of persecution.

The works of the Smyrna church era, in addition to the establishment of churches around the world, included the production of numerous hand-copied manuscripts of Scripture and the translation of Scripture into many languages. The more that Scripture was dispersed and studied, especially amidst persecution, the more the church advanced in number until it reached a level of influence within the Roman Empire that resulted in Christianity being officially legalized by Constantine via the Edict of Milan in AD 313, and soon thereafter established as the state religion in AD 323. A few years later on May 20, 325, Constantine oversaw a great church council in the Asian city of Nicaea—for better and worse.[13] However, from this came the Nicene Creed that can still today be heard in Protestant, Orthodox, and Catholic churches, hinting at a time long prior when Christ's church was wholly unified.[14]

In response to exponential growth in genuine Christian faith, Satan craftily initiated a check on persecution which proved to be a masterfully effective strategy, leading to great tragedy for the church. The devil then buttressed his tactics by infiltrating the church from *within* through the

---

13. The next two centuries witnessed lively debate and painful forging of the core teachings of Christianity by four successive ecumenical councils wherein the biblical canon of New Testament books was finalized. D'Ambrosio, *When the Church Was Young*, 3, 150–61; Scott, *Ancient Worlds*, 283–85. Nicaea is modern Iznik, Turkey.

14. Brownworth, *Lost to the West*, 18–19.

avenues of indulgence and endorsement. This is outlined in Christ's next message to the church in Pergamos which became plagued by paganism and complacency.

Along with physical and spiritual persecution, the Smyrna church also suffered immense poverty, in what amounts to *financial* persecution—compare this with the opposite Laodicean claim in Revelation 3:17. Because of such widespread hatred of Christians, economic security for believers was hard to achieve for the common individual or family. This affected the church in that there was little, if any, donations, tithing, or other inroads of financial support.

These dire circumstances were often the catalyst for spiritual growth, as could be seen in the strength of Smyrna's local church and the associative church era of the second and third centuries. This reveals a marked observation that the churches of the first three centuries were marked by material poverty and spiritual wealth, while the churches of our day are marked by material wealth and spiritual poverty. The lesson being that the more we suffer for Christ, the more blessings (though not always monetary) God will provide as we turn to him in our weakness and humility (Philippians 4:19).

Referencing again the blessing of having no condemnation brought against her, the church at Smyrna would appear to be the ideal church model that Jesus laid the foundation for when he said, "Go and make disciples of all the nations" (Matthew 28:19-20). And it is upon this foundation that the apostle Paul outlined a dual purpose for the church (Ephesians 3 and 4):

1. *Edification* is needed for equipping the saints for the work of ministry (Ephesians 4:12) so that disciples *can be made* of all nations. Without being edified (built up, encouraged, strengthened) disciples would lose their zeal and effectiveness; indeed a must when martyrdom becomes a method of evangelizing at any given time or place.

2. *Glorification of Christ*: To him be glory in the church by Christ Jesus to all generations, forever and ever. Amen (Ephesians 3:21).

THE CHURCH OF PERGAMOS—STATE/POLITICAL CHURCH: REVELATION 2:12–17

Commendation: Works, held fast to my name, have not denied my faith.

Condemnation: You have false teachers of Balaam and the Nicolaitans.

Counsel: Repent.

Challenge: "To him who overcomes . . ." I will give hidden manna and a white stone.

Pergamos (also Pergamum), located in modern Turkey, was the capital city of the Roman province of Asia until the end of the first century. Saturated in the worship of Greek and other idols and unable to cope with the plethora of religious divides, the local Roman rulers demanded the cooperation of all groups, despite their differences. This resulted in heavy emphasis on the city's great altar of Zeus, on the Sanctuary of Asclepius (god of healing/medicine), and Pergamos' subsequent evolution into a center of emperor worship. And with Pergamos also being Rome's administrative center for Asia, politics was another religion of prominence.

Politics as Religion

As the "spirit of Rome" became incarnated in the Emperor, there arose widespread construction of temples in his honor. Notably, this effort was not forced upon Roman citizens, for it was often the people who initiated such projects, giving rise to a civil competition between cities toward out-worshiping each other. The Roman government viewed this as a necessary unifying principle and sought to reinforce it via promotion, especially in Pergamos.

Thus it became law that every Roman citizen must annually visit their local temple of the Emperor and burn incense to the godhead (or image) of Caesar and recite "Caesar is Lord." Fulfillment of this duty was rewarded with a certificate proving the performed ritual. This was much more an act of political loyalty than spiritual worship; and Rome did not expect such to be exclusive in that after confessing Caesar as Lord one remained free to venerate any other god(s).

Nevertheless, for Christians it was unthinkable to utter such words stating anyone other than Jesus Christ was Lord. William Barclay explains that the "Roman government was incapable of understanding this point of view, and Christians were regarded as disloyal and revolutionary citizens, and were, therefore, proscribed and outlawed."[15]

This brought a severe test for Jesus' disciples, serving to weed out the nominal followers from the true. Revelation 2:12 introduces the letter to Pergamos with Jesus identifying himself as "he who has the sharp two-edged sword." Again, Barclay offers keen historical insight:

> Under the Roman government Roman governors were divided into two classes—those who had the *ius gladii*, the right of the sword, and those who had not. Those who had the right of the sword had the power of life and death; on their word a man could be executed on the spot. Humanly speaking, the proconsul, who had his headquarters at Pergamum, had the *ius gladii*, the right of the sword, and at any moment he might use it against any Christian; but the letter bids the Christian not to forget that the last word is still with the risen Christ.[16]

Even the apostle Paul called out the symbolic power of the sword, writing that the ruler "does not bear the sword in vain, for he is the servant of God, an avenger who carries out God's wrath on the wrongdoer" (Romans 13:4 ESV).

It is therefore certain that Jesus' words are purposefully recalling his earlier admonishment of his not coming to bring peace to the earth, but rather a sword of division and judgment (Matthew 10:34; Luke 12:51). First-century disciples would hold fast to this truth rather than compromise, encouraged by the boldness of Antipas in Pergamos. Though there is scant record of this martyr named Antipas, Jesus treasures his example and immortalizes him in both Scripture and name, calling him "my faithful witness" (Revelation 2:13).

Sadly, disciples in later centuries and at present have often allowed political considerations to replace the authority of moral and spiritual judgment, thus heralding the rise of political idolatry.

Darkness Falls

Revelation 2:13 refers to Pergamos as the place "where Satan has his throne" or "where Satan lives."[17] Ancient Babylon has long possessed

---

15. Barclay, *The Revelation of John*, vol. 1, 111.

16. Barclay, *The Revelation of John*, vol. 1, 111.

17. The "place of Satan's throne" in Turkey factors into the future Antichrist's kingdom, as we shall explore later.

the reputation of being the capital city of all things evil. However, when Babylon's glory began to decline and was eventually deserted, Satan sought another physical location. Pergamos suited due to its being a Roman seat of political power coupled with multitudinous idolatry, particularly its cultic emperor worship and eventually its devilishly heavy-handed intolerance for Christianity. Indeed, Babylon will once again find itself as the center of all things pagan as prophecy unfolds toward God's final judgment (Revelation 17–18).

Keeping in mind that the letters to the local churches comprise a broader prophetic message to all historical Christendom, it is easier to comprehend church history in light of local church circumstances. And being that the Pergamos era of church history begins a trend toward darkness, the unveiling of the fact that Satan has his physical throne in Pergamos is an intentional hint toward satanic strongholds being established *within* church communities and should thus be taken as a warning to prepare against such, both in the local immediate sense and universally.

It is under this consideration that we may comprehend the prophetic meaning of the word *pergamos*, which is "to be elevated, or married." J. B. Smith observes: "The church prophetic lost her pilgrim character by her elevation to a state religion; [and] her position as a called-out body, by her union or marriage to the state political system."[18]

When Constantine became emperor of Rome, he became emperor of the western world. Having come to prominence at the battle of Milvian Bridge in AD 312 conquering under a visionary sign of the true cross,[19] and then styling himself as "the protector of the Christian faith," Constantine issued an edict of toleration (AD 313) for Christianity throughout the empire and gave handsomely to the Christian church. Government gifts to the church included the changing of many laws to benefit Christians, massive land grants, the conversion of pagan temples to Christian churches, and near unlimited monetary provision. After an extended period of poverty and severe persecution, such financial assistance appeared to be a true blessing from God.

Although Constantine's conversion has been historically accepted and evidenced as genuine, and though he was a "godsend" to the church, his interpretation of Christianity for the masses was of an ecumenical and cosmopolitan slant.[20] Even as many conservative church leaders took

---

18. Smith, *A Revelation of Jesus Christ*, 71.
19. See Appendix B Expanded Commentary #2.
20. Stark, *Triumph of Christianity*, 170–80, 184–87.

note of his liberal intonations and tolerant support of some paganism, few spoke ill of him as they were desirous to please the new world leader, opting not to risk a reversal of his tolerant edict.

Thus in open expressions of gratitude and at Constantine's request, the local churches began to adopt customs and rituals that were in reality Christianized pagan practices. Inevitably, one compromise leads to another and what at first appeared to be a true blessing became, over time, a great curse. The next three centuries of this church era witnessed the rise of heathen practices within church liturgy and ceremony, eventually stealing from the church its fire and evangelistic zeal. Truly, evil never compromises; only good does at evil's discretion.

Indulging in the power that came with financial wealth, the church succumbed to liberal theology due to the increasing influence of paganism, whereas church leaders that succumbed to (spiritual) pride began to create an aura of *mystery* and ritualism in which to enshroud the church, furthering a patriarchal and elitist agenda that would send the world into a spiritual "dark age." Man-contrived traditions would ultimately trump biblical doctrine. Even today, and by dogmatic design, the biblically illiterate often mistakenly believe that such traditions are in fact biblical!

The rosary, of pagan origin, was introduced during this era. Likewise, the celibacy of priests and nuns has no scriptural basis and is a reworked form of the ritual of virgin sacrifice in order to "appease a god." Further unscriptural changes introduced during this era are listed below. Over time such changes regularly usurped the original teachings of Christianity.

AD 300—Prayers for the dead

300—Making the sign of the Cross

375—Worship of saints and angels

394—Mass introduced

431—Worship of Mary introduced

500—Priests adopt distinguished attire to separate from laity

593—Doctrine of purgatory introduced

600—Worship services conducted in Latin (further distancing clergy from laity)

600—Prayers directed to Mary[21]

---

21. Adapted from Boettner, *Roman Catholicism*, 8. Also see Lutzer, *Rescuing the*

The Great Divorce

From AD 312 the church became less Christian and more Roman in its practices. Prior to AD 312 the church was an independent body of local churches working together whenever possible, with Christ and Scripture as the Head (Acts 2:42–47), as opposed to being dominated by a central human authority. Satan, however, was able to subtly influence the marriage of the church to state authority, and thus her divorce from Jesus Christ.

As a result, the church declined in spiritual power and blessing. The doctrine of the *Nicolaitans* finally found itself accepted within church teaching (Revelation 2:15). The Ephesian church/Apostolic era rejected this heretical idealism while the Pergamos church/State era invited the false doctrine. Of course, at any given point in church history there will be evidence *of* each church era *within* each church era at the local church level.

Nicolaitanism is the doctrine of a strong ecclesiastical (church) hierarchy *ruling over* the laity. The word derives from two Greek words: *nikao* means "to conquer or overthrow"; *laos* means "people, or laity." Hence, "laity-conquerors."

Souls in this category would include Diotrephes "who loves to have preeminence" (3 John 9). Likeminded souls are pride-stained church shepherds who have fallen to serving self.

> The fault of the Nicolaitans was that they were seeking to adjust Christianity to the level of the world rather than lift the world to the level of Christianity . . . they were following a policy of compromise simply and solely to save themselves from trouble they were afraid and unwilling to face.[22]

Note that the *deeds* of the Nicolaitans (Revelation 2:6) have *become doctrine* in the letter to Pergamos. This is likely the beginning of priestcraft, the operating order that developed into Roman church hierarchy. Such a divide has been the root of spiritual pride, spiritual cynicism, and an overall weakened spiritual condition within the church; it is this very circumstance that fueled the rise of the Roman Catholic Church. Protestantism brought much healing of this after the Reformation, but even today there are clergy/laity divisions that do more harm than good. Whenever clergy lose proper contact with the laity, they cease to be effective tools in the hands of God.

Gospel, 63–65.

22. Barclay, *The Revelation of John*, vol. 1, 115.

The mention of Balaam (Revelation 2:14) is meant to parallel the circumstance of the Nicolaitans, in that through the intrigue of Balaam, a (false) prophet hired by Balak, king of Moab, Israel was deceived into illicit relations with the daughters of Moab (Numbers 31:15–16; 2 Peter 2:15–16; Jude 11). This is simply evidence of Satan employing identical tactics against the church that he utilized against Israel in the Old Testament period, his purpose being to cast stumbling blocks (and thus failure) before that which God would bless toward bringing further blessing to the world.

The general lesson to be gleaned from the Pergamos era is that even when believers are faithful to Jesus' name and hold tight to sound doctrine, we must remain *separated* from the world, avoiding *all* compromise. To be in this world but not of it requires constant discipline and worship of Christ to combat the wiles of the devil, whether he attacks as blatantly as a roaring lion or subtly as a deceiving angel of light.

Bread of Heaven

In reference to Christ's challenge, *hidden manna* and a *white stone* are mentioned (Revelation 2:17). Hidden manna is the spiritual sustenance provided in the Word of God that is to be *individually* sought and gathered, just as the Israelites had to individually seek and gather the heavenly food he sent them in the wilderness (Exodus 16:4–5, 15–18).

A great mystery was revealed when Jesus proclaimed himself as the Manna that "gives life to the world" (John 6:33, 51). In essence, then, true believers, i.e., overcomers, are to seek for Christ in his Word in that he *is* the Word, and only in him can he be found by those who truly seek (John 1:1–4).

The white stone most certainly alludes to our *assurance* in the righteousness of God. White may symbolize *purity* as opposed to the "filthy rags" of the followers of Balaam and the Nicolaitans. Another allusion the white stone may signify is that of the stones in the garment of the high priest, worn as the priest would go before the Lord. Still another possibility rests with the idea of a white stone meaning *acquittal*; in ancient days, jurors would reveal their vote of "guilty" with a black stone and "not guilty" with a white stone.

Paper Victory

An interesting historical note exists in that Pergamos was home to a library that rivaled that of Alexandria, Egypt. Furthermore, in response to Egypt's elitist ban on papyrus exports to the Asian city, Pergamos was also home to the invention of *parchment*, a.k.a. vellum. The reason for the ban was due to Ptolemy of Egypt's distaste for Eumenes, the third-century king of Pergamos, for Eumenes persuaded Alexandria's librarian, Aristophanes, to relocate to Pergamos. However, Ptolemy imprisoned Aristophanes before he departed and imposed an embargo on papyrus exports to Pergamos, which led to Pergamene scholars inventing the far superior (and historically victorious) vellum.

THE CHURCH OF THYATIRA—PAPAL/PAGAN CHURCH: REVELATION 2:18-29

> *Commendation*: Good works, love, service, faith, patience.
>
> *Condemnation*: You allow Jezebel to teach idolatry and compromise.
>
> *Counsel*: Hold fast what you have until I return.
>
> *Challenge*: "To him who overcomes . . ." I will give millennial leadership and the Morning Star.

Thyatira was a city dominated by trade guilds and a happening social scene where religion was worn as casually as an ornament, though the guilds were each dedicated to a particular deity and to become a member (and successfully make a living) one had to swear loyalty to the deity of the guild with which they were employed. The prominence of trade (in pottery, for example) is possibly the reason for Jesus' speaking of nations being "dashed to pieces like the potters' vessels" (Revelation 2:27).

The word *thyatira* is formed by two Greek words: *thuo*, meaning "sacrifice," and *ateires*, meaning "unweary, or continual." Thus the idea of "continual sacrifice" agrees with the nature of the city per its multiplicity of Roman religious rituals and celebrations. Offering sacrifices had become a recreation.

In Revelation 2:19 Jesus commends the fact that the church's latter works exceeded the first, implying progress and genuine spiritual maturation after initial stagnation. It is not enough for one to commit to following Christ only to maintain a pretense of discipleship absent consistent growth. When met with life's challenges, rather than persevere in-step with the Spirit, we often regress or proceed with equal or less energy.

The Interpreter's Bible explains that stress and strain had ideally led Thyatiran Christians to press forward and not retreat. "It is a rich experience to meet a man after a few years' absence and to find that his touch upon life is surer, his understanding deeper, and his actions finer."[23] This was likely the case with Lydia, an eminent Thyatiran tradeswoman who lived in Philippi (Acts 16:14–15, 40), perchance she visited her homeland post-conversion!

Disciples Without Discipline

In Thyatira persecution was barely a threat. Christian living was easier and more affected by social and carnal indulgence, begging the question: How far will a Christian compromise with the world?

William Barclay offers warning:

> A church which is crowded with people and which is a hive of energy and a dynamo of activity is not necessarily a real church. It is quite possible for a church to be crowded, because its people come to it to be entertained instead of instructed, and to be soothed and petted instead of to be challenged and confronted with the fact of sin and the offer of salvation. A church may be so full of energy that it becomes a restless ferment instead of a haven of peace. A church may be packed with many activities, but in the abounding energy the centre may have been lost, and it may be a highly successful Christian club rather than a real Christian congregation.[24]

While true that Christ commended the Thyatiran church on a number of levels, his condemnation brought to light the lack of both evangelistic zeal and adherence to sound doctrine. This was betrayed by the church allowing the teaching of false doctrine by "Jezebel," and the church's failure to repent of heretical compromise. In all likelihood there was a particularly influential woman or female/priestess cult who sowed seeds of heresy in this first-century church.

Jesus references the Old Testament in his use of the name Jezebel (daughter of Ethbaal, king of Sidon; and pagan wife of King Ahab) who

---

23. Harmon, *The Interpreter's Bible*, vol. XII, 387–88.
24. Barclay, *The Revelation of John*, vol. 1, 129.

corrupted the nation of Israel by introducing Baal worship, i.e., spiritual adultery (1 Kings 16:30–33). This reference acts as a parallel for those who were bringing pagan practices and self-edification into the church. Even today ancient paganism is alive and well across Christendom, regardless of denominational or theological leaning. In the tradition of the Pharisees, unscriptural doctrine and human laws are *added* to God's Word and given divine gravity. In the tradition of the Sadducees, only the law of Moses and democratic church policy are edified as large portions of Scripture are ignored or *subtracted*. Consequently, the church ceases to serve Christ as Head and, intentionally or not, serves itself. The most negatively affected areas include the church building, the order of worship, the sermon, the pastor, Sunday attire, worship music, tithing, salaried clergy, baptism, the Lord's supper, biblical literacy, Christology, Christian education, and academic versus relational theology.[25]

The level of heresy to which the church had fallen is portrayed in the phrase "the depths of Satan" (Revelation 2:24). Such depths are exactly what Barclay's quote above is detailing. When Jesus' standards of Christian living and witness are abandoned for a personal standard of the same, one has ceased serving God and is choosing to serve self by placing one's own interests above Christ's.

Today many nominal Christians claim that Jesus is either one of many saviors or perhaps the chief of saviors, but they reject that he is the *only* Savior. This leads to a heart full of idols, of which Jesus becomes merely one among other gods, which leads to a life lived scarcely different from the heathen.

The grace of God is on full display when Christ says, "And I gave her [Jezebel] space to repent of her fornication [spiritual adultery]; and she repented not" (Revelation 2:21). Plainly, no change of mind took place, so Christ issued a warning of impending judgment by confinement to a "sickbed" for Jezebel and her "lovers." He then proclaimed death to her "children" so that all churches would know Christ for who he is (Revelation 2:22–23).

The *sickbed* signifies a long-term illness (strong delusion) brought about by association/fornication with Jezebel, who is a prophetic foretaste of the whore of Babylon detailed in Revelation 17–18. The *children* in this context would be the *deviant versions* (not all versions) of Roman

---

25. For meticulously thorough research into this revealing truth, see Viola/Barna, *Pagan Christianity? Exploring the Roots of Our Church Practices* and Wills, *Why Priests? A Failed Tradition*.

Catholic, Orthodox, and eventual Protestant and Independent denominations (offspring) spawned from the teaching of false doctrine.

Jesus' exhortation to "hold fast till I come" makes plain the idea that the message to Thyatira is not only intended for this historically specific congregation but is likewise intended for the church universal (Revelation 2:25); that message being to hold fast to truth, endeavoring to preserve its light in a dimming world.

Cross-Examination

The age of spiritual darkening that began with Pergamos continued through Thyatira, further damaging the church's spiritual integrity. Two common pagan practices that infiltrated Christianity during this era were *chanting* and use of the *crucifix*. Priests began to chant during services and individuals who prayed would often do so by reciting a word or phrase repeatedly, regardless of whether the meaning of said words or phrases was known or unknown to the speaker. This contrasts harshly with Jesus' words in Matthew 6:7 where he warned: "When you pray, do not use vain repetitions as the heathen do. For they think that they will be heard for their many words." Of course, the context of chanting referenced here does not include the uplifting and genuine praise found in the Latin hymns and canticles of old.

The crucifix itself is meant to evoke Christ's "continual sacrifice." But Christ died only *once for all* (he is not still dying) and in his own words he says, "It is finished." Moreover, in Revelation 1:18 he proclaims, "I am he who lives, and was dead, and behold, I am alive forevermore."

An obvious difference between Catholics and Protestants is the cross used to symbolize their faith. Whereas the Catholic cross often displays Christ in perpetual remembrance of his "continual sacrifice" for our sins, the Protestant cross is empty, heralding the fact that Jesus died for our sins, was buried, and rose in victory over death on the third day (1 Corinthians 15:3–4).

In addition to the impious crucifix there is an ongoing trend in the Church of Rome toward deifying Mary, earthly mother of Jesus. Media reports show that millions have petitioned the Pope to pronounce her as a member of the triune Godhead![26] Officially, prayers are encouraged to be directed to Mary; she has also been considered as a giver of salvation,

---

26. Lahaye, *Revelation Unveiled*, 67.

in direct blasphemous contradiction to the teaching of Scripture (John 14:6; Acts 4:12).

Compromise led to spiritual blindness for Thyatira, but there were yet those few who remained obedient and strived to "hold fast" until Christ returned, doing so by refusing to acquiesce to the disintegration and ill teachings of the fattening, politicized ecclesia, and opting to take the light of truth into "hiding" until it would be rekindled in full flame at the Reformation/Protestant transition. This was accomplished by the development of monasteries, scriptoriums, and individuals intent on perfectly preserving (by pen and inkwell) the Holy Scripture in its raw uncorrupted state so that the common person would eventually be able to experience God through his Word directly, rather than through priestly proxy. This development was assisted immensely by the divinely appointed invention and perfection of the printing press.

The Lord's counsel to Thyatira was surely meant for the faithful remnant of such a darkened time. And to such faithful individuals will be awarded positions of authority during the millennial reign of Christ on earth, and to such will also be given the Morning Star—revealed in Revelation 22:16 to be Jesus Christ himself!

Since the Thyatira era continues the unfortunate trend of compromise, the following list of adopted pagan-based changes and doctrines furthers the history of the church where we left off in Pergamos:

AD 709—Kissing the Pope's foot

786—Worship of icons and relics

850—Use of "holy water" begins

995—Canonization of dead saints

1079—Celibacy of the priesthood

1090—Prayer beads

1184—The Inquisition

1190—Sale of indulgences

1215—Transubstantiation, i.e. sacraments "magically" become Christ's body/blood

1220—Adoration of the wafer (bread/Host)

1229—Bible/Holy writings forbidden to laity

1414—Cup forbidden to laity at Communion

1439—Doctrine of purgatory and seven sacraments decreed

1534—Jesuit order founded

1545—Church "tradition" granted equal authority with Bible

1546—Apocryphal books added to Bible

1870—Infallibility of Pope declared

1965—Mary proclaimed Mother of the Church[27]

THE CHURCH OF SARDIS—REFORMED/ DEAD CHURCH: REVELATION 3:1-6

Commendation: Works, reputation of being "alive."

Condemnation: You are dead, your works are not complete.

Counsel: Watch, strengthen the things which remain, hold fast and repent.

Challenge: "To him who overcomes . . ." will be clothed in white, name not blotted from Book of Life.

Sardis, a city of commerce, industry, and the death cult of Cybele, simultaneously boasted strength and weakness. Enjoying the status of one of the world's mightiest cities in the sixth century BC under King Croesus (better known as the Greek King Midas), the progressive history of Sardis fell to repetitive conquest. Cyrus the Great of Persia overthrew Croesus; Alexander the Great conquered without bloodshed; Antiochus the Great later won the city; and in AD 17 the city fell to an earthquake but was restored by Roman emperor Tiberius Caesar, then definitively sacked by Tamerlane in the early fifteenth century AD.

Like the city, the church in Sardis displayed both strength and weakness. First, it was recognized for its works and its reputation for being "alive." Second, Christ condemned it as being "dead," in that its works were not complete, thus Sardis' ministry was illusory at best.

Prophetically, Sardis represents the condition of Christendom just prior to and transitioning into the Reformation. The Protestant Reformation itself was a response to the papal church's adoption of and continual emphasis on pagan doctrines (see Thyatira) rather than strict emphasis

---

27. Boettner, *Roman Catholicism*, 8–9.

on Scripture. The local church in Sardis must have offered an enticing ministry on the surface, but at its heart possessed no true power and suffered from spiritual want.

William Barclay offers commentary concerning *dead churches*:

> The church at Sardis was untroubled by any heresy . . . It was troubled neither by heathen attack and persecution, nor by Jewish slander and calumny. The truth was that the church in Sardis had ceased to matter.[28]

This brings to mind Paul's exhortation to Timothy that there would be souls who would have a form of godliness but would deny its power by refusing to live by the Spirit (2 Timothy 3:5). Also worth noting is Jesus' warning, "Woe to you when all men speak well of you!" (Luke 6:26).

A State of Death

The Reformation church earned the Lord's condemnation of being "dead" for two reasons: 1) They became state churches, seeking approval from political personas and the government rather than the approval of God; 2) the Reformation churches, though starting off well-intentioned, did not *sufficiently* change or sever pagan-infested customs, rituals, and doctrines of the Roman Church.

This failure led to many eventual divisions within the Protestant movement, such as the splintering legacy of the Anglican Church of Henry VIII and the Elizabethan Settlement, bogged down as they were with the burden of ultra-legalism. The infamous date of October 31, AD 1517, when Martin Luther nailed his 95 Theses on the door of Wittenberg Church in Germany, surely heralded an era of encouragement and spiritual liberty (due to widespread circulation of Holy Scripture), but the battle for *spiritual* liberty sadly dissolved into a battle for *political* liberty, primarily for Christians anxious to escape the political "beast" that the Roman Church had become. This reality stunted the far-reaching vision that originally sparked the Reformation.

Though Reformation leaders initiated the movement with ideal intentions, the work of actually "reforming" the church fell far short of the biblical ideal, revealing the human tendency to rely on its own understanding, thus forsaking the guidance of the Holy Spirit. This

---

28. Barclay, *The Revelation of John*, vol. 1, 148.

incompetence resulted in Christ counseling the church to wake up from its spiritual stupor, to be watchful as to its true condition, to strengthen the failing areas, to remember righteous practices and the "first love," to hold fast to truth, and to repent of apostasy so that a true *reordering* of the church could be manifest (Revelation 3:2–3).

Furthermore, Jesus warned that if the church did not wake up, or was not watchful, he would appear to them as a thief, unexpectedly, in judgment. For the repentant, this admonition to be watchful so as to not become complacent or dead was encouragement toward anticipation of Christ's return! And since the Reformation legacy has produced ever-increasing liberal theology and clerical compromise, the institutionalized churches of the modern era will be largely caught unawares when Christ appears in the clouds to gather his true church unto him.

Dead Disciples Walking?

Consider that as we are watchful for Jesus, he is watching us. We routinely petition him for his strength, comfort, and direction; yet he expects our love, loyalty, and service. Are we lenient or decisive in our discipleship? Do we act righteously one day and unrighteously in pride the next? Are we selfless for a season and selfish for the next? If we indeed love and are loyal to Jesus Christ, then we will joyfully serve him in season and out of season. If we do any less, then our devotion and Spirit-drivenness are suspect (1 John 3:6, 9; 5:18).

The true Body of Christ certainly has some of its numbers scattered amidst the Papal, Protestant, Orthodox and modern trends of institutionalized ecclesia; however, the predominant assemblies of worship encompassing the true church exist independently and in often unorthodox circumstances (as compared with mainstream denominationalism), not unlike the first-century church which operated as smaller home and communal groups. Also, the strongest disciples are predominantly found in areas of the world where believers are under fiercely violent and continual physical persecution, a foreign concept to the "soft" existence experienced in North America and other western nations, though completely in keeping with how the church was born and flourished (see Ephesus, Smyrna, and Philadelphia).

Despite the "deadness" of Sardis, a small remnant in this church is noted as not having "defiled their garments" (Revelation 3:4; James

1:27), meaning that they have not turned their hearts and ears to apostate teaching and doctrine. In light of this it is interesting that Sardis, literally *sardeis* in Greek, means "escaping ones, or remnant."

This remnant that "overcomes" will be "dressed in white," signifying Christ's righteousness, and will not have their names struck from the Book of Life (Revelation 3:5; Daniel 12:10). This assures believers of the security of being saved from spiritual death and eternal torment (Revelation 20:11–15).

Note: There are two books of life—the Book of Life, which is a record of all who have ever been born (Revelation 3:5), and the Lamb's Book of Life, a record of all who have called upon the name of Jesus Christ for salvation (Revelation 13:8; 21:27).

Burning the Midnight Oil

The parable of the ten virgins (Matthew 25:1–13) offers a striking circumstantial evaluation of the church today. The ten virgins represent the kingdom of heaven (represented by the church on earth), their lamps represent the Gospel—the light of the world—as well as "watchfulness," and the Bridegroom they are desirous to meet is Christ himself.

The five foolish virgins who awaited the Bridegroom did not carry a surplus of oil for their lamps should he tarry. Tarry he does, and so the wise virgins, well into burning their surplus oil, are prepared when a cry announces the arrival of the Bridegroom. As the ten virgins awake from their slumber and prepare to meet him, the wise rebut the foolish for neglecting to be vigilant, as their lamps have gone dark.

Straightaway the foolish ones endeavor to purchase more oil, yet while they are away the Bridegroom arrives and the wise who were prepared went away with him to the marriage "and the door was shut." Upon discovering their misfortune, the foolish virgins petition the Lord to let them in also. His reply is "Nay, I know you not."

The true church, the Body of Christ, are the *wise* virgins who keep their lamps lit and are always watchful and prepared for the arrival of Christ in the clouds to catch them away to the Judgment Seat and marriage supper of the Lamb. The Papal/Catholic and Reformed/Protestant institutionalized churches are the *foolish* virgins who have lost their zeal for his arrival, tending primarily to their own affairs to which they are more faithful than they are to their Lord. Again, I will note that members of the true church are indeed to be found within these denominational institutions and churches; it is the *overall* spiritual blindness of the institutions themselves that renders them "dead."

At the rapture of the church, the mainstream ecclesiastical institutions (and likely much of their clergy) will be largely left intact (left behind) and will begin the polarizing shift toward apostate consolidation at the behest of the False Prophet's unitarian ecumenical push toward a one-world religion.

A developing case of such apostasy is the Catholic-Muslim Interfaith Council that began to get marked attention in 2019 when Pope Francis announced a 2022 opening of the "Chrislam" headquarters in the United Arab Emirates. In February the same year, the pope met with Sunni Muslim leader Sheikh Ahmed al-Tayeb in Abu Dhabi (UAE) and the two men signed a global *peace covenant* titled the Document on Human Fraternity for World Peace from which a Higher Committee of Human Fraternity will administer covenant protocols purposed to *unite all world religions/ faiths*. On the surface it may seem innocently misguided in the name of goodwill to all, but attentive research will reveal the sinister underbelly of the global politics of religion and false peace.

Of course, there is sure to be a vast number of new believers who genuinely repent upon missing the rapture, realizing that their prior presumptive faith was merely a fleshly hope born more of a desire to escape hell than to love and serve God. It is such souls who will largely become the multitude of "tribulation saints," killed for their zealous testimony of Jesus Christ (Revelation 7:14).

THE CHURCH OF PHILADELPHIA—MISSIONARY CHURCH: REVELATION 3:7-13

Commendation: Works, missions, little strength, kept my word, have not denied my name.

Condemnation: none given

Counsel: Hold fast what you have.

Challenge: "To him who overcomes . . ." I will make him a pillar in the temple of God.

Reversing the "death" of Sardis' circumstance, the church at Philadelphia became truly "alive" in its dynamic and faithfulness. Reflecting this is the fact that while Sardis received the extremely harsh condemnation of being spiritually dead, Christ offered *no condemnation* whatsoever toward Philadelphia. Essentially getting back to basics, this church's missionary focus brought a spiritual weight and reward that far surpassed Sardis despite Sardis' much larger congregational size.

Well known is the meaning of the word *philadelphia*, "brotherly love." The reason behind the city's name rests in its historical origin. Philadelphia was founded around BC 150 by Attalus II Philadelphos, a former king of Pergamos, and it was due to his deep love and commitment to his brother, Eumenes (an eventual king of Pergamos) that the city gained its name.

In AD 17 an epic earthquake annihilated Philadelphia and Sardis, but soon both were restored by the Romans. By the latter end of the first century, a solidly Christian congregation existed and Philadelphia remained a Christian city until the late fourteenth century when it was conquered by the Ottoman Turks.

Mission Accomplished

The Philadelphia church era witnessed a revival of truth amidst and following the Reformation in Europe, then Britain, then eventually in the Americas which led to a worldwide Christian missionary offensive. Two factors merited this missionary zeal.

First, there was the mass production/printing of the Bible into common and multiple languages so that every individual could experience the "simplicity that is in Christ" (2 Corinthians 11:3); for example, when one read the Lord's command to "Go into all the world and preach the good news to all creation," one was inclined to obey it, literally (Matthew 28:19–20).

Second, in part due to greater availability of the Bible, there was a resurrection of study concerning the Lord's second advent, for it had all but disappeared by the end of the third century. The doctrine of the Lord's return, when taught properly in its prophetic and scriptural context, will *always* result in a consecrated church that is "in the world but not of it," ever increasing in zealousness for evangelism and missionary outreach toward fulfilling the Great Commission.

The Seven Churches 47

Revelation 3:7-8 conveys Jesus having the "key of David" (Isaiah 22:22) and setting before the church an "open door." Keys represent *authority* in prophetic Scripture and the open door signifies *opportunity* (1 Corinthians 16:9; 2 Corinthians 2:12; Colossians 4:3) or perhaps Jesus himself (John 10:9). Jesus' absolute authority enables us, the church, to accomplish his will as we look to him to open the doors he would have us go through. Too often we *assume* divine direction in the opportunities we pursue, sometimes pushing through doors that should remain shut. Jesus' yoke is easy only when we submit to his lead, and his burden is light only when we bear with him those burdens meant exclusively for us (Matthew 11:30; Acts 16:6-10). The door may also signify entrance into heaven or the kingdom of God (Acts 14:27; Revelation 4:1-2).

Revelation 3:8 records Christ's commendation, including the mention of the church having "a little strength." This is not intended as conveying any sort of weakness, but refers to the initial minority status of believers in Philadelphia in that the Philadelphia church era is to be characterized by small though powerfully strong congregations that rely on the Holy Spirit, and thus little human strength "lest anyone should boast" (Ephesians 2:8-10).

A modern trend often belittles the smaller church while praising the megachurch; however, as churches increase in size (at times beyond what is effectual) so too often does the ego of their leaders. Indeed, a growing church is a blessing, but not when its discipleship, dynamic, and effectiveness are sacrificed for numbers. Tim Lahaye has stated: "There is a tendency to compromise in order to gain opportunities, whereas in truth it is our responsibility to do right and God's responsibility to open the doors of opportunity."[29]

Revelation 3:9 speaks of the "synagogue of Satan" and Jewish pretenders—the same stock we saw in Smyrna (Revelation 2:9). This is a warning of law-worshiping legalists who will attempt to infiltrate the church with the heretical teaching of salvation by works, negating the "free gift of God" (Ephesians 2:8-9). But Jesus promises eventual full vindication (Isaiah 60:14).

Note that both the Smyrna and Philadelphia churches suffered hard persecution by these apostate Jews, and both churches thrived! Also, the spiritually dead church at Sardis outwardly appeared to be alive but endured little to no persecution. This evidences that a truly living church

---

29. Lahaye, *Revelation Unveiled*, 80.

will be under constant attack. Jesus said, "Woe to you when all men speak well of you" (Luke 6:26). From some people it is better to receive enmity and criticism than friendship and praise, for when opposition dies compromise flourishes.

Interpretive Logic

Revelation 3:10 buttresses our faith with Jesus' words, "Because you have kept my command to persevere, *I also will keep you from the hour of trial which shall come upon the whole world, to test those who dwell on the earth*" (emphasis mine). The trial referenced here is distinct from the limited local testing of the Smyrna church (2:10), proven in that this trial is to affect "the whole world, to test those living on the earth."

The "hour of trial" (or "hour of temptation") is equivalent to the time of Jacob's trouble (Jeremiah 30:7), the seventieth week of Daniel (Daniel 9:24–27), and the time of future "great tribulation" that Jesus spoke of in Matthew 24:9. This period of judgment is particularly detailed in chapters 6–18 of Revelation and is intended specifically for the hard-hearted unbelievers who "dwell on the earth," including those Jews who have yet to recognize Jesus Christ as their Messiah. We will cover this extensively in later chapters.

Those who "dwell on the earth" in this context are those who will be left behind when Christ gathers his church unto himself in the clouds at the rapture. The Lord God will edify specific individuals (144,000 witnesses; Revelation 7:4) during this time of judgment and there will also be many worldwide who come to know Christ as their Savior. However, these Tribulation saints are not exempt from suffering the effects of judgment and martyrdom (with the exception of those whom Jesus supernaturally protects for specific purposes, such as his preservation of the 144,000 witnesses and the Jewish remnant against genocide so that there will indeed be a *believing remnant* to become a reinstated priesthood among nations).

The prominent unbelieving population during the Seventieth Week (Tribulation) will echo Pharaoh's response to the judgments of God in that their hearts will harden ever deeper as the judgments intensify. The purpose of this judgment, however, is to provoke repentance—but "they blasphemed God, and did not repent of their deeds" (Revelation 16:11).

There need not be any difficulty in comprehending the precise meaning of the "hour of trial" that shall befall the whole earth, for *"the Lord knows how to rescue the godly from trials, and to keep the unrighteousness under punishment until the day of judgment"* (2 Peter 2:9 ESV).

In other words, there will be no wrath for Christ's bride. Yet numerous commentators often assault this premise by refuting the reality of the "catching away of the church" prior to the Day of Judgment, insisting that the church—per final purification—will remain on earth to suffer the wrath of God detailed in Revelation (or else be immune to it).

Unfortunately, commentators sometimes fall into a herd mentality in their assumptions that common and/or long-standing postulations are incontestable. Their argument against a pre-tribulation rapture of the church often rests in John 17:15, which reads, "I do not pray that you should take them out of the world, but that you should keep them from the evil one." Context is key.

Here Jesus beseeches his Father toward strengthening the disciples against Satan in their immediate discipleship context while they are *yet in the world*, thus promoting spiritual growth in resisting the devil and temptation *during their earthly lifetime* (pre-rapture). Jesus' prayer was not an appeal to negate the rapture, nor is it proof that the church will suffer the Seventieth Week. Rather, we are encouraged to endure—with Christ's help—the tribulations of life in a hostile world, but can anticipate an imminent hope that Christ will appear in the clouds to gather his bride to himself and then take her to his Father's heavenly house before his Father's wrath falls on a hateful planet (John 14:2–3). The tribulations of life and God's wrath are not the same.

What is presumptively implied by some interpreters is that since Jesus prayed on behalf of the disciples for divine protection from the devil, then divine protection (or immunity) would likewise be afforded the faithful during the Tribulation judgments, thereby "proving" the rapture to be either late in the Tribulation or outright fiction. Yet is not the rapture itself divine protection from judgment? Just as with believers through history, believers who come to faith during the Tribulation *will in fact experience suffering and martyrdom*, negating the implication of immunity outright (Revelation 6:9–11; 7:9–14; 11:7–10; 12:11; 14:1–3; 15:1–3). Also, believers during the final last-days judgment are not church age saints (Pentecost to rapture), they are Tribulation saints, as will also be clarified in later chapters of this study.

Further clarity is gained by utilizing interpretive logic. In the John 17 passage the disciples were already subject to the wiles of the devil, just as they had been *prior* to becoming disciples, placing the context of Jesus' prayer in their immediate sense relative to the *historical time* of his prayer. And relative to the time of his prayer, the rapture and judgments of Revelation were *still* in the future, as they yet remain at the time of this writing. Hence, the situation of being "in the world but not of it" is alluded to as Jesus' prayer continues (John 17:16–19), further illuminating the context of immediacy that shall endure while the disciples are *in the world* that they have now been sent out into by Jesus himself.

It is a fantastic stretch to force the context of God's wrath at the end of the age into the clear context of everyday discipleship Jesus communed with his Father about on behalf of his disciples (John 17). Moreover, in light of the previous information, Jesus prayed that his Father would keep the disciples from the *evil one* (Satan), not from last-days *trials and wrathful judgment* that will in actuality be sent and/or permitted by God himself and thus *not* of satanic origin. Said judgment cannot be identified as "evil" or "of the evil one" since the Lord God sends his wrath so that "the inhabitants of the earth will learn righteousness" (Isaiah 26:9).

It is further notable that Jesus specifies the "hour of trial" (Revelation 3:10) as being sent for the benefit of "those who dwell on the earth" as opposed to the church he is actively assuring will be *kept* from said "trial," clearly implying that the church will not be on the earth during the final Day of Judgment, having "now been justified by his blood, *we shall be saved from wrath through him*" (Romans 5:9).

The Blessed Hope

Revelation 3:11 proclaims "Behold, I am coming quickly!" This is the only church message (of the seven) that carries such an announcement. Former messages speak of preparation and watchfulness, but Philadelphia alone holds the promise of Jesus' soon return, paralleling Revelation 22:7. The prophetic significance of this invites unequaled anticipation for the Philadelphia church era in that it is viably our *present circumstance*; and modern believers have reason for a "blessed hope" soon to be realized! The day or hour of rapture cannot be known (Mark 13:32), but the nearness is perceived by those who have an "ear to hear what the Spirit is saying to the churches."

The Seven Churches

In Revelation 3:12 Jesus proclaims to spiritually victorious souls that he "will make them pillars in the temple of God," conveying a position of strength and honor in God's family. Paul likewise utilized this effective metaphor in Galatians 2:9 and 1 Timothy 3:15. Also in 3:12 Jesus relays that he will write on his "living pillars" the name of God and the name of his holy city, the New Jerusalem. This reflects the ancient (and modern) practice of inscribing personal ownership and honor memorials upon foundational constructs of importance.[30]

It is of peculiar interest that the Philadelphia church is given only commendation, praise, and encouragement with no condemnation at all, while the Laodicean church (the last of the seven churches) receives only condemnation and no commendation. This then reveals that Laodicea is none other than the apostate church of the Tribulation, filled with foolish virgins and lamps with no oil.

THE CHURCH OF LAODICEA—APOSTATE/ LUKEWARM CHURCH: REVELATION 3:14-22

Commendation: none given

Condemnation: You are lukewarm, wretched, miserable, poor, blind, and naked.

Counsel: Buy from me gold and white garments, anoint your eyes, be zealous and repent.

Challenge: "To him who overcomes . . ." I will grant to sit with me on my throne.

Laodicea was named after Laodice, the wife of (though he later divorced her) Antiochus II who founded the city circa BC 260. The city was liberated by the Romans in BC 129, eventually blossoming into a very influential city of material prosperity, offering upper-scale commerce and recreation, nearby hot springs, a popular medicinal eye salve, and a rich wool industry. Prosperity of this caliber naturally birthed metropolitan pride, but a spiritual pride also developed within the Laodicean church, inviting Christ's distinct condemnation concerning their adherence to worldly wealth and empty religion rather than his righteousness.

---

30. Weima, *Sermons to the Seven Churches*, 216–18.

Of course, the spiritual pride and apathy of the Laodicean church percolated for decades. Thirty years prior to Jesus' revelation to John we see the apostle Paul writing to the neighboring church in Colossae, specifically admonishing a church shepherd named Archippus to fulfill his ministry and guarantee that the Colossian epistle is likewise read in Laodicea (Colossians 4:16–17). Archippus eventually became the first bishop of the Laodicean church, for better or worse I cannot say; but Paul certainly took note of any seeds of compromise and sought to root them out.

Again, prophetically appropriate meaning is found in the Greek definition of *laodicea*, derived from two words: *laos* (people) and *dike* (judgment)—judgment of the people.

I Will Vomit You Out of My Mouth!

Jesus' comment in Revelation 3:15–16 that the Laodicean church is neither cold nor hot but lukewarm carries two possible yet complementary interpretations. First, that Jesus would have us be boldly for or against him rather than wallow in noncommittal cowardice, having a form of godliness but denying the power thereof (2 Timothy 3:5); let your *yes* be yes and your *no* be no, so that you will not fall under condemnation (James 5:12; also Matthew 5:37). Consider, too, the cold to hot conversion of Saul of Tarsus (Acts 9:1–22).

Second, a trifecta of the proximate cities Laodicea, Hierapolis, and Colossae may be intended, for their churches were closely connected in ministry and location led by Epaphras (Colossians 4:12–16). Hierapolis was known for its healing hot springs and Colossae for its refreshing cold springs. Laodicea, however, received its water supply via aqueduct from a hot spring nearly five miles away, wherein the water cooled to a lukewarm state by the time of its arrival. Both hot and cold water are useful for healing and drinking respectively. But lukewarm water is deemed useless.[31] Therefore, Jesus offers the graphically terse analogy of "vomiting" from his mouth those who would either vacillate between decisions or practice an illusory piety.

Consider that Jesus himself voiced each message to each church—the blessings and the curses! Yet he had *nothing good* to report of Laodicea. Many who would call themselves Christian today cannot bear the thought that Jesus would utter one harsh word to anyone or that he

---

31. Weima, *Sermons to the Seven Churches*, 239–40.

would let anyone end up in hell, particularly if they held good intentions (though left undone). Souls such as these distort, dismiss, or ignore Jesus' hard truths that would require the commitment, travail, and sacrifice of actual discipleship. And it is to souls such as these that condemnations such as that leveled against the Laodicean church are intended.

Jesus said, "Apart from me you can do nothing" (John 15:5). Paul explained that without the Spirit nothing of God can be discerned, and that to such a soul the things of God appear foolish for lack of understanding (1 Corinthians 2:14; Ephesians 4:14–15).

From the 1940s to today the western church has become more about branding, building campuses, committees, programs, and organizations than about building God's kingdom. It has also largely forsaken the relational Christlike example of discipling, exchanging it for the conveniently impersonal aspects of social groupthink. Discipleship is no longer understood as a way of life but rather a compartmentalized hobby or short/long term study one may complete and be done with. Attending classes and church services has replaced actually *living* for Christ.

True worship in spirit and in truth has been redefined toward an emotional salve that entertains and indulges the worshiper (rather than God) via emulation of worldly music shows. Corporate prayer for *theocratic* revelation by the Spirit has been substituted with restrictive planning by strictly *democratic* rule. Individual prayer has become tainted with selfish appeals to an aloof god of the imagination as one hopes for the best (James 4:3). The Holy Spirit has been replaced with endless resources dumped on our culture by an often not-so-Christian industry, leading to an accumulation of information devoid of spiritual transformation. And biblical policy has been displaced by church politics.

In sum, though there is neither male nor female in Christ Jesus (Galatians 3:28), the western church has been emasculated—there is no power. Truly there are real followers of Jesus in the West, but North American mainstream Christianity is falling fast into the Laodicean apostasy that will characterize a rapture-stricken global church that will cry, *"Lord, Lord, have we not prophesied in your name, cast out demons in your name, and done many wonders in your name?"* To which Jesus will reply, *"I never knew you; depart from me, you who practice lawlessness!"* (Matthew 7:22–23)

The Doom of Self-Deception

As the Sardis church era represented a dead church transitioning toward enlightenment, so the Laodicean church era represents a once enlightened church transitioning back toward death. This results in Jesus proclaiming his love for all, including those he rebukes and chastens, for he offers abundant (but not unlimited) grace even for those who would deny him (Revelation 3:19).

The gold, white garments, and eye salve that Christ offers are representative of spiritual wealth, righteous purity, and the ability to discern truth (Revelation 3:18). The offer, however, is refused out of Laodicea's perception of self-sufficiency. James 5:2–3 (ESV) speaks to such pride:

> Your riches have rotted and your garments are moth-eaten. Your gold and silver have corroded, and their corrosion will be evidence against you and will eat your flesh like fire. You have laid up treasure in the last days.

"For mixing together the seed of the divine word with the thistles of wealth, you have become unaware of your poverty in spiritual matters and of the blindness of your spiritual eyes and of your nakedness in good works."[32] The endgame of this church is evident in the coarse fact that *no commendation* is offered by Christ, underscoring the need for watchfulness and sound doctrine on behalf of the true church as the path toward *doctrinal defection* (a.k.a. apostasy) becomes more heavily trod.

Though truly faithful Christians are indeed scattered throughout modern Christendom, the Laodicean church era solidifies and ushers in a haughty, compromised, and spiritually blind church that is nothing more than an empty religious shell that will act as a conduit for the rise of the great whore of Babylon (one-world religious system; Revelation 17) until the Antichrist no longer needs her "charms" (realpolitik) and demands worship of himself which provokes the final push toward Armageddon and Christ's second advent (Revelation 17–19).

Being that the Laodicean church receives only condemnation it is logical to ask whether or not this is due to an absence of *all* true believers, for Jesus does not reference (as he did for previous churches) even a small percent within this church that yet "hold fast" to truth (Revelation 3:19–20).

---

32. Andrew of Caesarea, *Commentary on the Apocalypse* 3.16–17.

Recalling Jesus' warning to remove a church's lampstand when his authority is no longer recognized as sufficient (Revelation 2:5), we see that the Laodicean church indeed suffered this fate. Though the Laodicean lampstand is not mentioned as being taken away, Jesus standing *outside* the church is proof enough (Revelation 3:20). J. B. Smith observes, "Next to Calvary this is one of the most pathetic and heart-rending scenes in the entire Bible."[33]

What can we learn from this stark and sad scene? The image of Christ standing and knocking at the door is simultaneously an invitation (to receive him as personal Savior) and a warning of his soon return to receive/rapture his church unto himself and take her back to his Father's house.

The church overall having rejected Christ as Head, and with few to none faithfully proclaiming his Gospel, Jesus personally makes appeals to the *individual*: "If any *one* hears my voice and opens the door, I will come in to him and dine with him" (Revelation 3:20). The picture of Christ dining with the one who opens their heart to him conveys *fellowship* via the indwelling Holy Spirit and foreshadows the marriage supper of the Lamb that takes place in heaven following the rapture of the church and before Jesus' return to earth.

The church in this Laodicean state is unaware of its wretchedness, nakedness, and blindness and therefore continues its unholy revelry oblivious to the fact that Jesus Christ and his Holy Spirit have exited the church outright. Jesus cannot abide in the hearts of the disobedient and worldly:

> Why do you call me "Lord, Lord," and do not do the things which I say? . . . For whoever is ashamed of me and my words, of him the Son of Man will be ashamed when he comes in his own glory, and in his Father's, and of the holy angels (Luke 6:46; 9:26).

Following his rebuke Jesus counsels the guilty (Revelation 3:18) to purchase (i.e., surrender in humility and sacrifice) from him spiritual riches—*refined gold* (salvation, trials; Job 23:10), *white garments* (Christlikeness; 1 Peter 1:19), and *eye salve* (spiritual discernment of truth; John 9:39; Ephesians 1:17–18). Then he admonishes zealous repentance before it is too late (Revelation 3:19).

---

33. Smith, *A Revelation of Jesus Christ*, 95.

Anyone prayerfully surveying church history from its beginning through to the present will discern the trends forecast in Jesus' letters to the seven churches, including the clear and present danger of the Laodicean tragedy. Indeed, the Laodicean church is a prophetic shadow revealing the destiny of the Papal/Catholic, Orthodox, Reformed/Protestant, and even some Independent evangelical churches as they trend toward apostasy and ultimate judgment as a result of emulating worldly systems and neglecting their lamps and oil supply.

Jesus' messages to each of the seven historical churches close with wise counsel: *"He who has an ear, let him hear what the Spirit says to the churches."*

This reveals that the messages are not limited to their particular time/place in history, but in fact are prophetic, systematically revelatory, and eternal. Therefore, the Christ who walked amidst their lampstands is the Christ who is still alive today walking amidst ours.

4

The Rapture
No Wrath For His Bride

> "The things which will take place after this..."
> —REVELATION 4–22

AFTER THESE THINGS I looked, and behold, a door standing open in heaven. And the first voice which I heard was like a trumpet speaking with me, saying, "Come up here, and I will show you things which must take place after this." Immediately I was in the Spirit; and behold, a throne set in heaven, and One sat on the throne (Revelation 4:1–2).

A new order of "things" is indicated at the completion of the seventh and last letter to the churches. This is the third and final class of things Jesus commanded John to write (Revelation 1:19).

"The things which will take place after this," i.e., *after* the church age, do not concern the church on earth, for it will be in heaven as the Tribulation era unfolds on earth and will remain there until it returns to earth with Christ at his second advent (Revelation 19:11–21). Indeed, an interval of time (seven years) is necessary between the rapture and second advent to accurately facilitate many biblically predicted events concerning the church, Israel, and the world. Omitting or distorting this time interval leads to poor hermeneutics and bad theology.

John MacArthur summarizes the distinction between the rapture and the second advent:

> Scripture suggests that [Jesus'] second coming occurs in two stages—first the rapture, when he comes *for* his saints and they are caught up to meet him in the air (1 Thessalonians 4:14–17), and second, his return to earth, when he comes *with* his saints (Jude 1:14) to execute judgment on his enemies. Daniel's seventieth week must fall *between* those two events. That is the only scenario that reconciles the imminency of Christ's coming *for* his saints with the yet unfulfilled signs that signal his final glorious return *with* the saints.[1]

AN OPEN DOOR

It was no coincidence that the first thing to happen after John had described the seven churches is his *hearing a voice like a trumpet and then being taken up into heaven where he then sees the church* represented by twenty-four elders. As John was the last remaining apostle and a part of the church, his hearing a trumpet-like voice and being taken up into heaven conveys the rapture of the church prior to the final judgment of the earth.

Although the "catching away of the saints" is not specifically taught here in chapter 4 of the Revelation, the applicable conveyance of such is particularly identified by anyone familiar with *all* of previous Scripture, lending to the expectation of readers of the Revelation of Jesus Christ to have an intimate comprehension of prophetic application concerning the *entire* Word of God. Amidst our worshipful study and humility, the Spirit of God lovingly and intricately weaves together the personality, wisdom, and experience of both human finitude and divine infinity so that a living tapestry emerges showcasing our interactive place within the core of the Godhead's creative revelation (Genesis 1:26—2:24). When we give more of ourselves to God, he gives more of himself to us. Imagine the latent mysteries opened to John as his scriptural knowledge blazed to new life as never before—Revelation's 404 verses carry 518 prior Scripture references!

John looked and saw "a door standing open in heaven." Consider that Jesus identified himself as the Door through which one must pass to

---

1. MacArthur, *The Second Coming*, 87. Emphasis in original.

be saved from damnation (John 10:7-9). Then John heard a voice like a trumpet (Revelation 4:1) identical to that he previously heard (1:10-13). Both instances confirm Jesus as the speaker and therefore connect Jesus directly with the "trump of God" contexts heralding the coming of the Lord in the clouds at the rapture. Refer to the following biblical passages for further insight: 1 Thessalonians 4:13-18; 2 Thessalonians 2:1; 1 Corinthians 15:50-57; Titus 2:13; 1 John 2:28—3:2; Philippians 3:20-21; Matthew 25:1-13; John 14:2-3; James 5:7-8.

Again, it is important to note that the rapture is *not* the second advent. At the rapture, the Lord appears in the clouds to believers only, who are called up to meet him (John 14:2-3). He does not set foot upon the earth at this time. His return at the *end* of the seven-year Tribulation, however, will be seen by *all*, believer or not, and Christ will literally set foot upon the earth, specifically onto the Mount of Olives in Israel just outside the city of Jerusalem (Zechariah 14:4). Then, following his adjudication, he will begin establishing his earthly kingdom (Matthew 25:31-46). To further examine the distinction between these two events, compare the apostle Paul's description of the rapture in 1 Thessalonians 4:13-18 to Jesus' description of his second advent in Matthew 24:27-31.

One can plainly see that the scriptural placement of John being taken into heaven indicates the rapture in that 1) Revelation chapters 4 and 5 present a vision in heaven, while chapter 6 introduces the final judgments on earth, providing juxtaposing perspectives; 2) there are nineteen references to the church (Gk. *ekklesia*) in chapters 1-5 yet chapters 6-18 do not mention the church once (it having been "caught away" from the earth, only reappearing again in chapter 19 as a bride *returning to earth with Jesus*); and 3) the extensive use of Old Testament language via specific symbols and typology in chapters 6-18 indicates *Israel* as the focus, not the church. This is further understood by the fact that the church age (present age) is the "time of the Gentiles," and the Tribulation era is the "time of *Jacob's trouble*" determined by God for his final judgment of Israel (Jeremiah 30:7; Luke 21:24).

THE GOOD NEWS

Thus there is good news that should give cause to rejoice—an *escape* from the Day of God's Wrath (the Tribulation, Seventieth Week, Day of the Lord) awaits the generation of Christians that would see the judgment of

Israel and an unbelieving world (Luke 21:36). This is not escapism. The plain sense of Scripture undeniably presents a pre-tribulation rapture of the church, despite deviant ideologies. In fact, a pre-tribulation rapture was taught and preached by most of the ante-Nicene Fathers throughout the first four centuries of the church,[2] and was not widely challenged until after the marriage of the church to the state as initiated by Constantine's Edict of Milan in AD 313 whereupon humanism and liberal theologies began the trend toward the eventual spiritual dark age.[3]

Even the antediluvian prophet Enoch received knowledge from God concerning a pre-tribulation rapture, despite the church being a mystery at the time:

> And the righteous shall arise [be raptured] from their sleep [death, sin], and wisdom shall arise and be given to them [sanctified by Christ]. And after that the roots of unrighteousness and those who plan violence and those who commit blasphemy shall be cut off [turned over to God's wrath], and the sinners shall be destroyed by the sword [God's righteous Word] (Enoch 91:10–11).

History shows that wherever the truth of the imminent appearance of Christ in the clouds to "catch away" his church has been presented it has resulted in the same effect that first-century believers experienced—a continual zeal for spreading the Gospel, a desire to be ever closer to God, and a desire for holy living in an unholy world. Jesus himself expressed imminency (Revelation 3:11; 22:7, 12, 20).

Notably, the term "rapture" is not found in the Bible, though it is an expression for the Latin words *rapere* and *rapturo* as well as the Greek words *harpazo* and *rhuomai*, each meaning "to be caught up," "snatched away," or "delivered."

The rapture is an imminent event and there are no specific signs that must precede it; although, the rapture event itself shall be a crucial sign for every soul left behind! Jesus appears in the air (again, this is *not* the second advent) and calls all *believers* to him in an instant, dead and living. The dead, whose spirits have been with the Lord since death, receive incorruptible perfect bodies, while the *living* at the time of the rapture instantly experience a bodily transformation into perfection:

---

2. See Appendix B Expanded Commentary #3.
3. Oden, *Classic Christianity*, 809–10.

> Behold, I tell you a mystery. We shall not all sleep [die physically], but we shall all be changed, in a moment, in the twinkling of an eye, at the last trumpet. For the trumpet will sound, and the dead will be raised imperishable, and we shall be changed. . . . Death is swallowed up in victory (1 Corinthians 15:51–54 ESV).

Believers will be "*caught up* in the clouds to meet the Lord in the air," and so we shall always be with the Lord (1 Thessalonians 4:17). First Thessalonians 4:18 admonishes us to "comfort/encourage one another with these words."

THE BAD NEWS

It is unfortunate that many do not comfort others with these words because they feel that topics like the rapture are confusing or controversial. This is disappointing when it is so clearly and simply taught in Scripture. Apparently some do not believe previously hidden mysteries to have yet been revealed, in contrast to passages such as that above where mysteries are *explicitly* being revealed!

Attempts to complicate doctrine are often made when a dominant understanding of it does not suit one's purpose or interpretive belief system (hermeneutic). For example, some deny any form of rapture while others assert a rapture of the church at either the midpoint or end of the seven-year Tribulation, just prior to the return of Christ to earth (i.e., mid- and post-tribulation). The reason behind this vein of thought is that a pre-tribulation rapture would deny the church those purifying trials and suffering which are expected in the lives of believers. To this odd conjecture I suggest that most if not all Christian lives indeed *do* carry a fair volume (or more) of purifying trials and suffering, just as Jesus and Paul predicted (John 16:33; Romans 5:3–5). Regardless, an escape from God's final wrath does not make sense to adherents of this reasoning due to an unbiblical presumption that believers in the last days are required to pass through the ultimate calamity at the end of the age.

My argument against this unscriptural belief challenges the failure of that presumption to explain why end-time believers—the church—should suffer *God's wrath* when no other church age generation has suffered the same. Again, there is no scriptural evidence suggesting that all those believers who have died since Pentecost will be placed back on the earth with the solitary purpose of suffering through the seal, trumpet, and bowl judgments of Revelation. And to dismiss every other generation as exempt simply because they are not alive during the "tribulation generation" is childish reasoning.

Furthermore, it is blatantly unbiblical for multitudes of true believers living in any generation to believe that the next prophetic event they may experience is a seven-year era of tyrannical anti-Christian rule, unprecedented global war, and God's wrath, rather than a Bridegroom arriving in the clouds to take his church home to his Father's house where he has prepared a place for them (John 14:2–3). Such a darkness on the horizon would depress any soul, diminish zealous evangelism, and render pointless the "blessed hope" like that found in Titus 2:11–13 (ESV):

> For the grace of God has appeared, bringing salvation for all people, training us to renounce ungodliness and worldly passions, and to live self-controlled, upright, and godly lives in the present age, waiting for our blessed hope, the appearing of the glory of our great God and Savior Jesus Christ.

MORE GOOD NEWS

Additional hope—the engine of discipleship—is offered through examples of prophetic foreshadowing that indicate the rapture:

1. God saved Noah and his family as he brought a flood judgment upon all the world (Genesis 7:5–7).
2. God saved Lot's family as he turned the cities of Sodom and Gomorrah into ash (Genesis 19:29).
3. God raptured the prophets Enoch and Elijah *alive* into heaven (more on them later; Genesis 5:18–24; Hebrews 11:5; 2 Kings 2:7–13).
4. Jesus' bodily resurrection, translation, and ascension into heaven (Mark 16:19). And Paul's experience (2 Corinthians 12:2–4).
5. Philip was instantly and bodily translated/raptured, not to heaven, but from one physical location to another twenty miles distant (Acts 8:39–40).
6. The public rapture of the two witnesses in Revelation 11:3–13.

In ancient times just as in our own, a nation's ambassadors were called home prior to declarations or acts of war. According to 2

Corinthians 5:20, believers are called "ambassadors for Christ." Thus, God will call his ambassadors home prior to leveling war on the world, for *the Lord knows how to deliver the godly from trials, and to reserve the ungodly under punishment until the day of judgment* (2 Peter 2:9).

In addition to the rapture of the church, there will indeed be a few additional "raptures" that occur during and after the seven-year Tribulation, each to be later discussed at length. These additional raptures have nothing to do with the church but clarify Paul's meaning in 1 Corinthians 15:20–23 (ESV) when he says, *"But each in his own order: Christ the firstfruits, then at his coming those who belong to Christ."*

1. Revelation 11:3–13 details the public rapture of the two witnesses/prophets near the midpoint of the Tribulation.
2. Revelation 6:9–11; 7:9–17; 15:2–4; and 20:4 address the martyrdom of and eventual resurrection of the Tribulation saints at Christ's return.
3. Daniel 12:1–2 and Isaiah 26:19–21 reveal that all believers of the Old Testament—pre-Christ—era will be resurrected and rewarded at the second advent.

Recall that those martyred for Christ during the Tribulation are not part of the church and therefore are not required to be present in heaven at the Judgment Seat and marriage supper of the Lamb, which are specifically for the church (2 Corinthians 5:10). The "refining by trial and suffering" for Tribulation believers occurs via faithfully enduring both persecution and the effects of a world being judged. This truth holds for those martyred *and* for those who survive to usher in the millennial kingdom after Jesus returns to earth and establishes his authority (Matthew 25:31–46; Revelation 20:4–6). It is the multitudes of persecuted and martyred Tribulation believers that are often mistaken for the church during the final seven-year time of Jacob's trouble, but they are a distinctive class of citizens who also inherit the kingdom as we shall see in later chapters.

NO WRATH FOR HIS BRIDE

It is necessary to here include supplemental details showcasing the *biblical view* of the rapture rather than getting lost in the plethora of man's contradictory traditional views.[4]

---

4. For excellent and extensive treatment of both the biblical and varying traditional views of the rapture, see Hitchcock, *The End*, 121–201; Hampson, *The End Times*,

Many are surprised to discover that both the apostle Paul *and* Jesus taught the rapture; however, Jesus' teaching of such was veiled by parable and allusion (Matthew 25:1–13; John 14:2–3) until Paul unveiled the mystery (1 Corinthians 15:51). Understanding the rapture event correctly will bring newfound confidence in one's discipleship to Jesus Christ, as well as rekindled hope in one's future and the zealousness required to effectively live and share the Gospel.

Two factors merit missionary zeal. First, the availability of the Bible in common and multiple languages allows every individual to *personally* experience "the simplicity that is in Christ" (2 Corinthians 11:3). For example, when one reads for themselves the Lord's command to "Go and make disciples of all nations," one is inclined to literally obey it. Furthermore, hearing from God directly from his Word guarantees intimate communion with him through his Spirit.

Second, and as previously stated, the past few hundred years have witnessed a resurrection of study regarding Jesus' appearance in the clouds to gather his bride and then his subsequent return to earth, for the topic had all but disappeared by the end of the fourth century AD. The doctrine of the Christ's return, when taught properly in its scriptural and prophetic context, will *always* result in a consecrated church that is "in the world but not of it," ever increasing in ardent passion for evangelism and mission outreach toward fulfilling the Great Commission (Matthew 28:19–20).

As we shall see, the biblical view of the rapture is plainly pre-tribulational in that the church and Israel necessarily remain *separate* entities with God's wrath to be poured out on an unbelieving Israel (and world) for seven years as a raptured church is spared the same, for *Jesus has delivered us from the wrath to come* (1 Thessalonians 1:10).

THE BRIDE OF CHRIST IS THE TRUE CHURCH

To wholly understand the rapture one must grasp *who* and *what* the church is. The New Testament utilizes two senses of "the church": 1) the *universal* church (the Body of Christ) which includes all believers (even Jews who have received Christ) from Pentecost to rapture; 2) the *local* church which is geographically and temporally limited yet is a visible and practical manifestation of the church universal.

61–83; Lahaye, *Rapture Under Attack.*

Herein, the church exists *because of* Christ, *for* Christ, and to reign *with* Christ, a verdict rooted in Scripture since the Father of glory put all things under Christ's feet and gave him to be head over all things to the church, which is his body (Ephesians 1:22-23).

Thus the passion of the Christ necessitates the passion of the church, for the church has been saved and sanctified by him (Ephesians 5:25-29), purchased by him (Acts 20:28), founded on him (Ephesians 2:19-20), built by him (Matthew 16:18), is subject to him (Romans 7:4), and is loved by him (Ephesians 5:25).

> Let us be glad and rejoice and give him glory, for the marriage of the Lamb has come, and his wife has made herself ready. And to her it was granted to be arrayed in fine linen, clean and bright, for the linen is the righteous acts of the saints (Revelation 19:7-8).

The Lamb, of course, is Jesus Christ (Revelation 5:12). The Lamb's wife is the church (Ephesians 5:22-23). Though *Israel* had been metaphorically referenced as the "wife of Jehovah" in the Old Testament (Isaiah 54:5-8), she was consistently unfaithful and eventually "cut off" (rejected), leading to the Gentiles (non-Jews) being "grafted in" to the Root/Christ (Romans 11:11, 20), thus bringing salvation to the world.

Therefore, Israel cannot be the wife of the Lamb since the remnant of Israel, and thus *all* Israel, will not be saved until they see him at his return, *accompanied by his church/wife* (Revelation 19:7-8, 14). Only then will Israel see him as the true Messiah and be consequently "grafted back in" from whence they were cut off (John 15:1-8; Romans 11:23, 25-27), being restored to a highly blessed position of authority beside Christ *and* his church.[5]

THE RAPTURE OF THE CHURCH AND MARRIAGE OF THE LAMB

Keen awareness of ancient Jewish marriage customs lends to greater comprehension and appreciation concerning the rapture and the Lamb's wedding celebration, for Jesus often alluded to three aspects of Jewish marriage as a reference point for his instruction, a method employed to introduce new teaching through familiar means:[6]

5. See footnote #10 concerning replacement theology.
6. For insightful study on the prophetic implications of ancient Jewish marriage

- The parents of both bride and groom formed a marriage contract, with the parents of the groom paying a dowry to the parents of the bride. A betrothal ceremony expressed the agreement that the couple were now man and wife and were expected to act faithfully, though they would not live together for nearly a year. This was the legal marriage.
- After about a year, the groom, accompanied by his friends, would proceed to his bride's house at midnight by way of a parade of torches and lamps. The bride would be expecting him and would have made herself ready with her maidens. She and her maidens would then join the procession and return with the groom to his house for the marriage supper/celebration.
- The marriage supper was a celebration consisting of all friends and family involved with the bride and groom and could last for several days, as seen at the wedding in Cana (John 2:1–12).

The first aspect, the betrothal ceremony, is consummated on earth when an individual places his/her trust in Jesus Christ as Savior, the dowry having been paid by Christ's own blood. The unfaithfulness of a believer is spiritual adultery in that such would violate the betrothal/promise to Jesus Christ.

The second aspect of the marriage is illustrated through the rapture of the church when Christ appears in the clouds *to claim his bride and take her with him to his Father's house* in heaven (John 14:2–3) where she is found worthy to be his bride and is granted to be arrayed in righteousness (as refined by the Judgment Seat of Christ; 2 Corinthians 5:10; Psalm 17:15; Revelation 19:8). Also examine the parable of the ten virgins in Matthew 25:1–13 for a striking circumstantial evaluation of the present-day church and the importance of being ready and watchful for Jesus' arrival in the clouds.

The third aspect, the marriage supper, is announced in Revelation 19:9 and commences *in heaven* following the bride being judged and made ready by adorning the fine white linen which represents "the righteous acts of the saints" (Revelation 19:8), offering further proof that the bride is the church.

---

tradition, see Brant Pitre, *Jesus the Bridegroom: The Greatest Love Story Ever Told*, (Image, 2017). Also Hitchcock, *The End*, 225–29.

Succeeding the marriage supper in heaven is the preparation for the *return to earth* with Jesus Christ and the heavenly hosts (Revelation 19:14). And in light of all this it is grandly significant to recall that the church has been *in heaven* experiencing these events while God's wrath (Revelation 6–18) has poured onto the earth—therein exempting the church from such judgment for *Christ himself suffered his Father's wrath in his wife's stead when he endured the cross* (2 Peter 2:9; Revelation 3:10).

TWO SHALL BECOME ONE FLESH

"Wives, submit to your own husbands, as to the Lord. For the husband is the head of the wife even as Christ is the head of the church, his body, and is himself its Savior. . . . Husbands, love your wives, as Christ loved the church and gave himself up for her . . . [for] we are members of his body. Therefore a man shall leave his father and mother and hold fast to his wife, and the two shall become one flesh. This mystery is profound, and I am saying that it refers to Christ and the church" (Ephesians 5:22–32 ESV).

In his letter to the church in Ephesus, Paul accentuates the mysterious yet practical correlation between human marriage and the church's relationship to Christ, particularly the prime detail of "two becoming one flesh," further reinforcing the fact that the church *will not* suffer God's wrath at the end of the age, for we *"having now been justified by his blood, shall be saved from wrath through him"* as *"there is therefore now no condemnation for those who are in Christ Jesus"* (Romans 5:9; 8:1).

This truth would be reinforced by Jesus' brother James, the apostle Peter, the writer of the book of Hebrews, and Jude (James 5:7–9; 1 Peter 1:13; Hebrews 9:28; Jude 21). The same would later be echoed by Jesus himself to the church in Philadelphia:

> Because you have kept my command to persevere, I also will keep you from the hour of trial which shall come upon the whole world, to test those who dwell on the earth (Revelation 3:10).

THE JUDGMENT SEAT OF CHRIST AND THE MARRIAGE SUPPER OF THE LAMB

After the initial rejoicing and reunion with loved ones in heaven following the rapture, Jesus will commence with decrees from the Judgment

Seat. This judgment is only for raptured believers of the church age (Pentecost to rapture)—the dead in Christ and those who are alive when raptured—each individual being judged according to his/her service and ministry while on earth (2 Corinthians 5:10; Hebrews 4:13).

Jesus will examine our works and motives (1 Corinthians 4:5; Matthew 6:1–2; 12:36; Enoch 45:3), exposing our sincere, reluctant, obligatory, or proud motivation, revealing whether or not the works we accomplished were done in the name of Jesus Christ. However, this judgment is not to determine one's salvation, nor is it a judgment for sins committed prior to one's salvation.

This judgment determines the rewards which believers will receive for faithful service after salvation (1 Corinthians 3:11–15). If one's works "withstand the fire," rewards will be received; if one's works "burn away," no reward will be received save the sole reward of salvation, thus having been saved "through fire" or "by grace."

The New Testament offers five examples of rewards or crowns:

1. The Imperishable Crown—for those who consistently practice self-discipline and self-control (1 Corinthians 9:24–27).

2. The Crown of Righteousness—for those who eagerly look for the Lord's return and live righteously as a result (2 Timothy 4:8).

3. The Crown of Life—for those who faithfully endure and persevere under the trials and tests of life (James 1:12; Revelation 2:10).

4. The Crown of Rejoicing—for those who win people for Christ (1 Thessalonians 2:19).

5. The Crown of Glory—for church shepherds and leaders who lovingly and graciously comfort, counsel, and direct God's flock (1 Peter 5:1–4).[7]

Upon receiving their rewards, of which there may be many others not recorded, the redeemed will humbly cast their crowns at the feet of their Redeemer, saying, "You are worthy, O Lord, to receive glory and honor and power; for you created all things, and by your will they exist and were created!" (Revelation 4:10–11)

Following the Judgment Seat, the celebration of the marriage of the Lamb and the wedding supper begins and continues through the second advent and into the millennial kingdom (Revelation 19:7–10). The

---

7. Edited from Hitchcock, *The Complete Book of Bible Prophecy*, 52.

events of the Judgment Seat, the marriage of the Lamb, and the wedding supper celebration take place in heaven and last for the duration of the final seven years of tribulation on the earth. The following thousand-year kingdom will be the celebratory honeymoon.

At the end of the seven years, all raptured believers will have been sanctified and purified and will prepare to descend to earth with Jesus Christ and the hosts of heaven to judge the world and its inhabitants (Revelation 20:14). The surviving Gentile population on earth will be divided between believer and nonbeliever—the separation of the "sheep and goats" (Matthew 25:31–46). The believers will then enter into the new millennial kingdom in their natural bodies to live, farm, build, and bear children with longevity of life restored (Isaiah 65:21–23); the unbelievers will be sent to hell. This specifically vital judgment *after* Jesus' return would be impossible if the rapture occurred *at* his return, for then there would be no believers on earth to separate.

5

The Throne of God

> Immediately I was in the Spirit; and behold, a throne set in heaven, and One sat on the throne. And he who sat there was like a jasper and a sardius stone in appearance; and there was a rainbow around the throne, in appearance like an emerald.
>
> —REVELATION 4:2–3

THE THRONE OF GOD is the central object in heaven and appears to be a fixed point with all things in heaven located in relation to it, evidenced by phrases such as "before the throne," "about the throne," "out of the throne," and "in the midst of the throne."

That John saw a throne *set* in heaven indicates a contextual specificity, here being the purpose of executing the judgments of the Tribulation that are about to be revealed. This opens the probability of different—but equally authoritative—thrones of God with various roles defined by active contexts. Consider that John later sees a great white throne that is clearly distinguished from the aforementioned throne in that it is "great" and "white" and is of strikingly different purpose in that Jesus himself is seated on it (Revelation 20:11); this throne is also distinct from the Judgment Seat of Christ (2 Corinthians 5:10).

Various heavenly thrones of God in no way diminishes his eternal sovereignty, but rather serves to emphasize the eternality of his omnipresent authority by highlighting specific and multitudinous aspects of such according to the particular visionary revelations given to a particular individual (John) in history that we now encounter in Holy Scripture.

Also noteworthy is the fact that before Israel rejected God from reigning over them, he dwelt upon the mercy seat (throne) between the cherubim (of the Ark of the Covenant) and communicated directly with his people (1 Samuel 4:4; 8:7; Exodus 25:18, 22). Scripturally there is no mention of God having his throne elsewhere during this time. He indeed retained his heavenly throne, but the contextual omission serves to emphasize God dwelling in Israel's midst, prophetically pointing to Immanuel (Matthew 1:23).

The fourth chapter of Revelation presents seven specific characteristics of God's heavenly throne:

The Triune God (Revelation 4:2–3)

John's statement, "Immediately I was in the Spirit," is a reference to the Holy Spirit. Though Christians, like John, are filled with the Holy Spirit, there are circumstances when God "moves" upon people as he "moved" upon the prophets and apostles in a special revelatory sense during proclamations and the times of divinely inspired writing of the Holy Scripture (2 Peter 1:20–21). Simply put, upon the indwelling of the Holy Spirit at Pentecost, such moving was afterward termed as being "in the Spirit."

Revelation 4:2 indicates Someone sitting on the throne. Both God the Father *and* his son Jesus Christ are present here as the actual throne is occupied by the Father, and, as taught in numerous passages of Scripture, the son is "seated at the right hand of God." The Holy Spirit's presence is implied as John is "in the Spirit," showing the powerful reality of God's triune omnipresence. However, the Spirit is explicitly described in verse five as "seven lamps of fire burning before the throne."

The one seated on the throne appeared as the precious stones sardius and jasper, which were the *first and last* stones in the breastplate of the High Priest (Exodus 28:17–20). H. A. Ironside elaborates: "As these stones bore the names of the tribes of Israel, arranged according to the births of the twelve patriarchs, the one would suggest at once the name Reuben, 'behold a son,' and the other Benjamin, 'son of my right hand.'"[1]

Therefore, Jesus Christ and his redemptive work are exalted by the very colors that illuminate from the throne! And the rainbow that surrounds the same in emerald glory evokes God's faithfulness by its iteration of the Noahic covenant. This vision of God in terms of light corresponds soundly to the psalmist's description of God covering himself with light as a garment (Psalm 104:2), and Paul's comment that God dwells in "unapproachable light" (1 Timothy 6:16).

The Twenty-four Elders (Revelation 4:4)

These are twenty-four redeemed *men* representing the glorified saints of the church age—the whole heavenly priesthood. The idea that the twenty-four may be angels is dismissed as angels are never seen wearing crowns or sitting on thrones, nor are they promised such. Men are promised both throughout Scripture (Matthew 19:28; 1 Corinthians 9:25; 2 Timothy 4:8; Revelation 2:10; 3:21). Also, the term "elder" is never applied to angels or any other entity except man. Additionally, Revelation 5:9 indicates the twenty-four elders as having been *redeemed by Christ's blood*, a circumstance no angel can claim.

This dynamic of "twenty-four" representing a larger body was first manifested in 1 Chronicles 24:1–9, during David's time, when twenty-four individuals presided over the entire priesthood of Israel. Some well-meaning students of the Bible suggest that the significance of the number twenty-four rests in a representation of the twelve tribes of Israel *and* the twelve apostles of the Lamb, both of which are referenced concerning the New Jerusalem in Revelation 21:10–14. Even so, in considering Israel's forfeiture of her priestly function (Exodus 19:5–6) as a result of her disobedience and rejection of her Messiah, we can better understand Peter's claim that the church is "a royal priesthood, a holy nation . . . who once were not a people but are now the people of God" (1 Peter 2:9–10). This is not replacement theology, nor does this negate the fact that "all Israel shall be saved" at the second advent (Romans 11:26). This simply means that stewardship of the kingdom was taken from Israel and given to the church.

---

1. Ironside, *Revelation*, 50.

The Throne of God

Jesus said, "Assuredly I say to you, that in the regeneration [millennial earthly kingdom], when the Son of Man sits on the throne of his glory, you [disciples/church] who have followed me will also sit on twelve thrones, *judging the twelve tribes of Israel*" (Matthew 19:28; Luke 22:30). J. B. Smith explains further:

> This subordinate position of Israel as compared with the regal and sacerdotal ministry of the church "in the regeneration" and the coming kingdom as well as the uniform position of the twenty-four elders encircling the throne, is in direct opposition to the view that twelve of the throne sitters represent the church and another twelve Israel. *It is altogether improbable that Israel would have equal rank with the church in heaven and afterward be judged by the church during the kingdom age.*[2]

Additional interpretive logic showing that Israel is not represented among the glorified elders in heaven concerns the chronological flow of prophetic revelation that John recorded, wherein Israel as a nation will not yet have received Jesus as Messiah at the time of the rapture. The church will be in heaven, represented in the heavenly tabernacle by the twenty-four elders, while a still unbelieving Israel remains on earth to endure the final judgment toward an eventual remnant being saved.

Israel will indeed be a separate people from the church in the thousand-year kingdom, sharing in kingdom duties and privilege, yet still shall be "judged by the church." This fact alone proves replacement theology as erroneous.

In sum, the elders are simply twenty-four individuals chosen to represent the church, having been exalted to a specific office in which to worship and serve Almighty God, first in heaven as he executes judgment on the earth, and then in his earthly kingdom. Scripture does not definitively indicate who the twenty-four elders may be, thus any attempt to identify them is mere speculation. There were 120 original apostles, including women, who met in the upper room to await the arrival of the Holy Spirit on Pentecost (Acts 1:13–17, 21–26). The Twelve were set apart for specific church leadership roles, as were Paul, Apollos, Barnabas, Aquila and Priscilla, and many others (Acts 13; 18; 1 Corinthians 3:5; 4:6). And there has been nearly two thousand years of church history saturated with possible souls to occupy such thrones. Fortunately, Jesus will assign such authority in accord with his infinite wisdom.

---

2. Smith, *A Revelation of Jesus Christ*, 106. Emphasis mine.

These twenty-four elders are mentioned twice more in Revelation. In 11:16 we see them fall prostrate and worship God in heaven as divine judgment continues on the earth. In 20:4, after Jesus' return to earth "in power and great glory" (Revelation 19:11), the Seventieth Week judgment is complete and judicial authority is given to the twenty-four elders toward establishing Christ's millennial rule on earth (1 Corinthians 6:2).

The Signs of Judgment (Revelation 4:5)

Lightning, thundering, and voices. Such is representative of God throughout Scripture, as seen in Exodus 19:16; Job 37:4; Psalm 77:18; and Ezekiel 1:13. Therefore, since these issue from the throne it is logical to conclude that they are a prelude (in this context) to the judgment about to fall upon the earth as recorded in Revelation 6–18. Similar and more violent preludes to specific aspects of God's wrath appear in Revelation 8:5; 11:19; and 16:18.

The Seven Spirits of God (Revelation 4:5)

Previously referenced in Revelation 1:4, John may have been referring to the sevenfold attributes/ministrations of the Holy Spirit revealed in Isaiah 11:2–3:

- the Spirit of the Lord
- the Spirit of wisdom
- the Spirit of understanding
- the Spirit of counsel
- the Spirit of power
- the Spirit of knowledge
- the Spirit of the fear of the Lord

Since these attributes are eternal qualities of God, when one becomes filled with the Holy Spirit upon salvation one should display not only each of these seven attributes but also the fruit of the Spirit as revealed in Galatians 5:22.

It may also be that the seven spirits are identified with the seven angels of the seven churches (Revelation 2–3). The apostle Peter informs us of the angels' desire to examine the sufferings, salvation, and future glories of Christ (1 Peter 1:10-12). And the apostle Paul announces that formerly hidden mysteries of God would be made known by the church to the principalities and powers in the heavenly places—to angels both dark and light (Ephesians 3:8-11).

The Sea of Glass (Revelation 4:6)

Being a part of the heavenly tabernacle, the sea of glass is undoubtedly a literal sea of crystalline substance, for it is "before the throne" and soon to be full of a multitude of believers standing on it. Here in Revelation 4:6 it is unoccupied, but in Revelation 15:2-4 it is occupied by the great multitude of martyred Tribulation saints as they worship and sing praise to the Lord God—said saints having received their incorruptible bodies once their "number was completed" (Revelation 6:11). The sea of glass is the epitome of the bronze sea that Solomon made for the temple to replace the laver for ritual cleansing in the mobile tabernacle (1 Kings 7:23-26; 2 Chronicles 4:2-6). When the martyred multitude later stand upon this glassy sea in worshipful awe of God, they will be made forever clean.

Imagine the reflective nature of this glassy sea. Everything from God's glory to worshiping hosts will be heightened toward an atmosphere of pure joy and awe unlike anything yet experienced!

The Four Living Creatures (Revelation 4:6-8)

In some translations these creatures are referenced as "beasts" from the Greek *therion*, which means "wild beast." While *therion* is commonly used in later chapters of Revelation, the Greek *zoa* is used in chapter 4, meaning "living creature." They are comparable to (if not in fact are) the seraphim of Isaiah 6:1-4, described as being full of eyes (denoting wisdom), having six wings (denoting swift service), never resting, and possessing characteristics *like* a lion, a calf, a man, and a flying eagle, crying "Holy, holy, holy, Lord God Almighty, who was and is and is to come!" It is clearly evident that these creatures are initiators of worship, perpetually drawing attention to the holiness of God.

The Heavenly Worship of Christ (Revelation 4:9–11)

Upon the initiation of worship by the four living creatures, the twenty-four elders cast their crowns before the throne and voice their praise, plainly focusing their worship onto the triune Godhead in response to his creative power and purpose.

THE SEVEN-SEALED SCROLL AND THE LAMB

"And I saw in the right hand of him who sat on the throne a scroll written inside and on the back, sealed with seven seals. Then I saw a strong angel proclaiming with a loud voice, 'Who is worthy to open the scroll and to loose its seals?' And no one in heaven or on the earth or under the earth was able to open the scroll, or to look at it" (Revelation 5:1–3).

This scroll (or book) has three characteristics: it is in the right hand of God, it is written on both sides, and it is sealed with seven seals. It is also the same scroll/book Daniel was instructed to "seal up" until the time of the end (Daniel 12:4).

It is apparent that even angels are excluded from opening the scroll, evidenced by the fact that a "strong angel" is searching for Someone to open it and break its seals. The angel here is likely Gabriel in that his name means "strength of God" and he was the informing angel who ordered Daniel to seal up the scroll.

It is significant that the sealed scroll does not make its appearance in the book of Revelation until *after* the completion of church history that was detailed in the letters to the seven churches. Moreover, what the Spirit said to the churches was not included in the sealed scroll referenced in Daniel 12, for Gabriel revealed to Daniel that it documents that which shall befall Israel (not the church) in the latter days, i.e., the time of Jacob's trouble (Jeremiah 30:7; Revelation 6–18).

As shall be seen, the scroll is intimately related to humanity and humanity's relationship to earth. The importance of the scroll is underscored by the fact of John's weeping when no one was found worthy to open it or look inside it (Revelation 5:4). But alas! There is Someone worthy who has prevailed to open the scroll and loose its seven seals—the Lion of the Tribe of Judah, the Root of David (Revelation 5:5; 22:16)!

Jeremiah 32:6–15 presents a series of events foreshadowing the scene John witnesses in heaven. Concerning the right to own property, God promised through Jeremiah that Israel would go into captivity for seventy years but would one day return to the land. To prove to Israel that they would indeed return, God had Jeremiah perform a peculiar thing. Jeremiah's cousin, Hanamel, owned a piece of property he knew would be worthless once Nebuchadnezzar captured Jerusalem. God had Hanamel contact Jeremiah, offering him the property. Jeremiah bought the land, signed and *sealed the deed*, had it witnessed, and gave the deed of purchase to Baruch son of Neriah in the presence of Hanamel, the witnesses, and the Jews in court.

Jeremiah then instructed Baruch, who acted as secretary, to place the sealed scroll/deed in a clay jar, preserving it for his heirs. Other documents were preserved along with the deed which verified the legal owners of the property. Thus it was that Jeremiah never lived to experience the day Israel returned to the land, but his legal heir could one day appear before the proper authorities and, on the basis of his kinship to Jeremiah, "prove that he was worthy to open the scroll" and own the property.

This parallels the scene in heaven in that the seven-sealed scroll can be understood as (though in fact is not) the *title deed*[3] to earth, given by God to Adam, who lost it through disobedience. As a result and by forfeit, Satan gained control (not ownership) of the world and shall have such control until the second advent.

> And I looked, and behold, in the midst of the throne and of the four living creatures, and in the midst of the elders, stood a Lamb as though it had been slain, having seven horns and seven eyes, which are the seven Spirits of God sent out into all the earth. Then he came and took the scroll out of the right hand of him who sat on the throne (Revelation 5:6–7).

When Jesus finished the work of atonement/redemption at the cross, he proved his claim to rule over the earth and universe, restoring humanity's right to the earth *through* him. Hence, *only* Christ is worthy and able to open the scroll. One of the elders refers to Christ as the Lion of the Tribe of Judah, indicating his might and authority, but John, through the eyes of faith, sees him as a sacrificial Lamb.

The "seven horns" prove that the Lamb is not weak, as a "horn" in Scripture signifies power and authority (e.g., the "little horn" of Daniel 7; Zechariah 1:18–21). The "seven eyes" are specifically explained in the

---

3. Both H. A. Ironside and Tim Lahaye use the "title deed" analogy for the seven-sealed scroll in their writing.

passage as being the seven spirits of God (Isaiah 11:2; Revelation 4:5), denoting omniscient wisdom and spiritual sovereignty.

In Matthew 28:18 Jesus says of himself, "All authority has been given to me in heaven and on earth." Thus the taking of the scroll from he who sat upon the throne shows a transfer of authority from the Father to the son, whereupon Jesus commences with opening the scroll's seals (Revelation 6:1), the contents of which are revealed in Revelation 6:1—8:1. The time has arrived for Jesus Christ to put his enemies under his feet (Psalm 110:1; 1 Corinthians 15:24-28). The things "written within" are revealed later (Revelation 5:1; 8:6—22:20).

Therefore, the scroll is not a title deed, but is a *Book of Judgment*, as the opening of the seals officially begins the seven-year Tribulation. Proof of the chronology of Revelation is further evidenced here as Jesus does not proceed to open the sealed scroll until *after* he is proclaimed worthy to do so, with the subsequent opening of each seal then releasing specific judgments associated with the same.

Revelation 5:8-14 displays universal worship toward God and the Lamb; songs of praise for the worthiness of the Lamb to open the scroll and offer redemption through his blood; and shows the redeemed being prepared to reign on the earth.

6

The Time of Jacob's Trouble

> Alas! For that day is great, so that none is like it; and it is the time of Jacob's trouble, but he shall be saved out of it.
>
> —JEREMIAH 30:7

BEFORE EXPOUNDING THE SPECIFICS of Revelation 6 and beyond, some historical context is necessary toward a more thorough comprehension of the events to be examined. As aforementioned in this study, the book of Revelation is chronological but includes parenthetical portions with essential background information, much like Genesis 1–2 presents a sweeping account of creation then follows with a more detailed tally of creation specifics. This is a trait common in Semitic literature.

I will again stress the importance of a literal interpretation, as some schools hold that the events of Revelation 6–18 have already come to pass historically. Such have missed the entire point of the book of Revelation.

As the reference to the time of Jacob's trouble conveys, the judgments at the end of the age are especially directed toward Israel (Jeremiah 30:5–9; Daniel 9:24–27); a more concentrated proof of this rests in the systematic dealing of Israel outlined in the Seventieth Week of Daniel (to be examined below). This "time of trouble" is referenced over fifty times in the Old Testament by the expressions "the day of wrath," "the day of calamity," "the day of the Lord," "the day of the Lord's wrath," "the day of the vengeance of our God," et al.

In every case Israel is the focus of judgment. This "hour of judgment" (Revelation 3:10) is also mentioned (in similar terms) in over a dozen instances in the New Testament, in which the term "tribulation" was used by Jesus himself to describe this future time of trial (Matthew 24:21).

A PROPHETIC STRUGGLE

Genesis 32 describes Jacob's return home from the house of Laban. At the Jabbok River, Jacob encounters an angel and wrestles with him. When the angel does not prevail (for instructive purposes) he strikes Jacob on the hip and cripples him. Jacob realizes that the angel is God himself (pre-incarnate Christ) and feels fortunate to have survived! God changes Jacob's name to *Israel*, for he has "strived with God" and prevailed.

Likewise, national Israel has striven with God perpetually and the Seventieth Week will be Israel's final wrestling match, though not just with God but also with the devil and pride. Satan's deceptive work and warring against the Lord God will reach maniacal levels during this last-days judgment and will revolve around two individuals. The first individual is the Antichrist, called the "beast" in Revelation 13:1–10 and "the prince who is to come" in Daniel 9:26.

Tremendous power will be given to Antichrist by Satan (Revelation 13:2) and this power will be used politically toward becoming the dominant authority in the world (13:7). Such power will also be used ecclesiastically (religiously) toward becoming the object of world worship (13:8), yet this will be nothing less than worship of Satan himself: "So they worshiped the dragon [Satan] who gave authority to the beast [Antichrist]" (13:4).

The second individual is the False Prophet, referred to as "another beast" (13:11), who will assist the Antichrist by performing "miracles" (via occult power) which will cause the world to worship Antichrist (13:12–14); and when the world as a whole does not acquiesce, the False Prophet demands such worship, or death (13:15).

Jesus prophesied that lawlessness will abound during this time: "And because lawlessness will abound, the love of many will grow cold" (Matthew 24:12). Multitudes will die and those who come to believe

The Time of Jacob's Trouble

in Christ will be persecuted and hated: "Then they will deliver you up to tribulation and kill you, and you will be hated by all nations for my name's sake" (24:9).

As frequently stated, the tribulations of this era will be a time of terrible distress for Israel: *"Alas! For that day is great, so that none is like it; and it is the time of Jacob's trouble, but he shall be saved out of it"* (Jeremiah 30:7).

Revelation 6 initiates God's vindicating judgment that is recorded in chapters 6–18. Nowhere else in Scripture can we see such an ascending escalation of judgment (Amos 5:18). Neither the great flood of Noah's day, the destruction of Sodom and her sister cities, nor the plagues of Egypt compare to the divine wrath that will consume the earth for seven years (Matthew 24:22).

Let us consider a few common questions:

Will Jacob's trouble, i.e., the Tribulation, begin immediately after the rapture?

Perhaps. Yet there may be an unspecified period of time between the two events in light of the prophecy recorded in Ezekiel 38–39, which may in fact be the prelude to the Tribulation wherein God supernaturally saves Israel from annihilation by destroying her enemies. This saving act will resonate around the world for *seven months* (Ezekiel 39:12–13) as Israel and the nations come to terms with Almighty God acting in such a powerful and obvious way (Ezekiel 38:23; 39:7).

A soul harvest will certainly result as many people—Jew and Gentile—turn to Jesus Christ in true humility. Meanwhile, the geopolitics of the world will have been transformed instantly and much will swiftly happen on the global stage, particularly the eventual swift rise of Antichrist and a long-awaited peace covenant between Israel and her moderate Islamic neighbors, made possible as all radical Islamic archenemies will have been neutralized by supernatural earthquakes, confusion, and a massive firestorm (Ezekiel 38:18–22). The fourth chapter of my book *Firestorm: America, Israel, Iraq and Their Prophetic Future* offers expansive insight on this very event.[1] It may seem odd that God would save Israel from obliteration only to then systematically judge his chosen

---

1. Birch, *Firestorm*, 142–77. An updated report can be found at jonbirch.com or veritasunum.org, weblog entry "Distant Thunder: Firestorm on the Horizon." Also see Rosenberg, *Epicenter*, 162–70, 245–60; Hitchcock, *The End*, 293–310.

nation (and world) for seven years. Wisdom results in understanding God's grace and will for Israel, the world, and all who would worship him, for his merciful chastisement precedes a final and just reckoning for all unto salvation or damnation (Deuteronomy 8:5; Proverbs 3:11; Isaiah 26:9; 1 Corinthians 11:32; Hebrews 12:11; Revelation 3:19).

The rapture may happen long before, just prior to, or sometime during the season between the firestorm and signing of the peace covenant that officially begins the seven-year Tribulation (Daniel 9:27). Antichrist is thought to be (and no doubt presents himself as) a possible political messiah and peace-bringer for the world, which explains why Israel would accept such a brokered treaty (some perhaps viewing him as the Jewish Messiah). The lack of opposition to the peace accord between Israel and the Antichrist's faction suggests that the church has been raptured by the time of the striking of the covenant, a circumstance lending further urgency to an already tumultuous world wherein the nations shall desperately seek peace at any cost (2 Thessalonians 2:3–4). This "peace" turns out to be false (Daniel 9:27).

The rapture being an imminent event means there is no sign or warning that must preface the catching away of the church. However, for those left behind, the rapture itself will be a sign that the Tribulation to follow is imminent (2 Thessalonians 2:1–12).

The recent Abraham Accords of 2020 joined by Israel and several moderate Islamic nations (with more to follow) is a grand and necessary development toward peace.[2] It is, I believe, a primary political avenue the Antichrist will highjack and pervert toward his own ends upon his public arrival in the global theater.

Will the Tribulation be worldwide?

Yes, although Scripture is clear that the Antichrist will not rule over the entire world in that there shall be some nations (and many individuals) that rebel or refuse his authority (Daniel 7:15–25; Revelation 13:4). Also, most of the trumpet and bowl judgments are revealed as affecting a third or fourth part of the earth, including the seat (throne) of the beast, his kingdom, and those bearing the mark of the beast. The cumulative affect

---

2. For world-class analysis on this contemporary development, see Rosenberg, *Enemies and Allies*. For daily updates on Israel and the Middle East, visit allisrael.com and allarab.news.

of the series of judgments will result in more than half of the global population being killed. Add to this the number of martyrs who will die for their faith in Christ. Therefore it is a surety that the entire world will be affected in some way even supposing the core of judgment falls only upon the Middle East, Near East, North Africa, Europe, and Eurasia.

How long will the Tribulation last?

From the signing of the covenant between Antichrist and Israel to the second advent of Christ will be a span of *seven years*, about which the Bible has more to say than any other prophetic timespan. This seven-year period is divided into two periods of three and one-half years. The first half of the seven years will entail the seven seal judgments, the appearance of the 144,000 witnesses, and the appearance of two distinctive witnesses whom shall prophesy in Jerusalem against Antichrist.

The midpoint of the seven years will witness the death of Antichrist, the indwelling or reanimation of the Antichrist's body by Satan, the breaking of the Antichrist-Israeli covenant and desecration of the Jewish temple/tabernacle, and the public death and resurrection of the two witnesses.

Lastly, the second half of the seven years consists of the seven trumpet and seven bowl judgments, the destruction of Babylon, Armageddon, and the return of Christ. These last three and one-half years are termed "the great tribulation" as the judgment shall be more severe upon Israel than the previous three and one-half years.

The Seventieth Week time frame of seven years is often referred to in segments as opposed to the whole. To clarify, the truncated references are listed:

- Each half of the Week totals three and one-half years, also referenced as "a time, times, and half a time" (Daniel 7:25; 12:7; Revelation 12:14).
- The entire Week consists of 2,520 days; half of which is 1,260 days, or three and one-half years.
- The entire Week totals 84 months; half of which is 42 months (Revelation 11:2; 13:5).

Now we shall examine in detail this "seven years."

THE SEVENTY WEEKS OF DANIEL

Referenced in Daniel 9:24–27, seventy weeks literally means "seventy sevens" of years. If this designation of time were meant to be *days*, as in Daniel 10:2–4, it would have been so expressed. The designation is clearly *years*, as seen in Daniel 9:2 referencing Jeremiah's prophecy concerning the "number of years specified." Daniel 9:27 also reveals that the seventieth, or last, "week of years" is divided into two parts of three and one-half years each, each half described in Daniel 7:25 as "a time and times and half a time." The sum of the "seventy sevens" equals 490 years, as they are determined apart from any other years of Israel's history (Daniel 9:2, 24). Daniel 9:24 (ESV) reveals the purpose of the Seventy Weeks to be sixfold:

1. *"To finish the transgression."* The "transgression" is Israel's rebellion against God. The Law served as a guide toward both morality and Christ who was the Seed to come (Galatians 3:17–25). Israel failed to receive her Messiah and was thus cut off from God's favor as a result of unbelief. Her restoration will not be complete until Jesus Christ returns to earth and establishes his kingdom.

2. *"To put an end of sin."* This will not occur until *after* both the second advent and Jesus Christ's thousand-year kingdom on earth (Zechariah 14:1–21).

3. *"To atone for iniquity."* Atonement was accomplished at the cross for every soul, though national Israel has not yet claimed such victory and will not until the second advent (Zechariah 13:1–7; Romans 11:25–27).

4. *"To bring in everlasting righteousness."* After the three previous mentions have been realized, then the ushering in of everlasting righteousness shall commence (Matthew 25:31–46).

5. *"To seal both vision and prophet [prophecy]."* This will put an end to the need for inspired prophets commissioned to rebuke Israel (or anyone) to repentance, for the entire nation shall know the Lord.

6. *"To anoint a most holy place [i.e., Most Holy]."* The Most Holy is *not* a reference to the Lord God, but to a place, as this is a reference to the cleansing of the holy of holies, the temple, and Jerusalem from the desecration committed by the Antichrist and Gentiles. The two-word conjunction "Most Holy" is never *by itself* used to designate a person in Scripture, and further supporting this is the fact that

in Daniel 9:25 the Messiah is doing the anointing. It would here be contextually illogical to anoint himself, as he is already holy.

DETERMINING THE SEVENTIETH WEEK

Admittedly, the topic of this section is a bit technical; however, prayerful consideration as you read will bring the joy of comprehension and wonder at God's perfect Word as we study to show ourselves approved unto him.

Daniel prophesied that seventy weeks would be determined for Israel, specifically for the aforementioned sixfold purpose. Within the context of biblical prophecy and Hebrew tradition a prophetic "week" is a period of seven years, each prophetic year consisting of 360 days (12 months of 30 days each).

In complex contrast to our solar year, the common Jewish lunar-solar calendar yields 12 months of 29 or 30 days each, totaling 353, 354, or 355 days a year. A thirteenth month of 30 days is added every two or three years over a nineteen-year Metonic cycle, resulting in Jewish leap years consisting of 383, 384, or 385 days.[3] This is done to remain in sync with astronomical seasons as well as with the West's Gregorian solar calendar of 365 days per year (and simpler leap years!).

As noted above, the Seventy Weeks comprise 70 "weeks" of 7 years, equaling 490 years. These 490 years are divided into three distinct periods, two periods having been fulfilled and the third and final period as yet unfulfilled.

Daniel 9:25 lists the first two periods: "From the going forth of the command to restore and build Jerusalem until Messiah the Prince, there shall be *seven weeks* and *sixty-two weeks*; the street shall be built again, and the wall, even in troublesome times."

"Seven weeks," or seven sevens, equals 49 years. "Sixty-two weeks," or sixty-two sevens, equals 434 years. Thus far the total is 49 + 434 = 483 years, or 69 weeks. Daniel 9:26 goes on to say, *"And after the sixty-two weeks Messiah shall be cut off, but not for himself."*

"Cut off" is a reference to the culmination of the Jews' unbelief, i.e., the crucifixion of Christ. It is at this point where God turned his attention toward the Gentiles so that Israel would be provoked unto jealousy

---

3. See Jewish traditional writing *Seder Olam* (Order of the World); and Rabbi Nathan Bushwick, *Understanding the Jewish Calendar*, (Moznaim, 1989).

(Romans 11:11). Some see this as the temporary cessation of God's prophetic time-clock for Israel.[4]

Isaiah 61:1–2 (ESV) professes, *"the year of the Lord's favor, and the day of vengeance of our God."* Since the ascension of Christ after his resurrection we have been living in the age of grace or "year of the Lord's favor." The mention of "the day of vengeance of our God" entails the Seventieth Week—the seven-year Tribulation—which shall commence sometime following the rapture. The rapture event itself effectively ends the year of the Lord's favor, for God shall return his focus toward the judgment and full restoration of Israel. Hence, we are left with the final "week of years" (7 years) yet unfulfilled, bringing us to the equation 483 + 7 = 490 years.

The scriptural record of the three divisions are as follows:[5]

Division One—Seven sevens/weeks, or 49 years.

During this season, Jerusalem's streets and walls were to be rebuilt, "even in troublesome times" (Daniel 9:25). In all, there were three decrees for restoring the holy city. The first decree came during the first year of the reign of the Persian king Cyrus (Ezra 1:1–4; 3:8; Isaiah 44:28). But during the reign of Cyrus' son, Cambyses, work on the city and temple ceased (Ezra 4:1–24).

Afterward, Darius I came to reign and in his second year he reconfirmed the decree made by Cyrus (making it the second decree). Thus, work began again and the temple was finished in Darius' sixth year, but the city remained unfinished although fifty-seven years had passed since the first decree by Cyrus (Ezra 6:1–15).

Xerxes then reigned twenty-one years during which the city remained unfinished (Daniel 11:1–3). Artaxerxes followed and reigned twenty years then gave the third decree to Nehemiah to restore Jerusalem unto the Messiah (Nehemiah 2:1—6:19; Daniel 9:25–26). The walls were restored in only fifty-two days upon Nehemiah's arrival in Jerusalem; but this still was not the full restoration, as the *city* was not yet rebuilt (Nehemiah 7:4). Also, neither the wall nor the city had yet been dedicated (Nehemiah 12:27—13:30). The *full* restoration occurred 49 years *after the third decree*, which was given circa BC 452.

---

4. Smith, *A Revelation of Jesus Christ*, 5; Walvoord, *Every Prophecy of the Bible*, 258–59; Hampson, *The Book of Revelation*, 54–57.

5. See also Lahaye, *Revelation Unveiled*, 135–36; Ironside, *Daniel*, 90–93.

Notably, more than 49 years elapsed from the first decree to the third, therefore the exactness of prophetic fulfillment, requiring only 49 years, must be understood as encompassing specifically the 49 years *following the third decree.*

Circumstantially, three decrees proves that the city was not completely restored until *after* the third decree—the third undoubtedly being the "command to restore and build Jerusalem until Messiah" comes (Daniel 9:25). Moreover, the same passage records that restoration would happen during "troublesome times," and the only other Scripture passage recording such troublesome times under any of the three decrees occurs in Nehemiah 4:1—6:14 which is under the third decree. Thus we see that Ezra dealt with restoring the *temple* and Nehemiah dealt with restoring the *city*.

Division Two—Sixty-two sevens/weeks, or 434 years.

This period began immediately after the first period of 49 years and proceeded uninterrupted until the Messiah was "cut off," from the Hebrew *karath* which means precisely "to cut off in death."

As mentioned above, the total years of the "seven sevens" and "sixty-two sevens" equals 483 years, leaving the final "seventieth week" of seven years to be fulfilled long after the crucifixion and following the completion of the "year of the Lord's favor" (Isaiah 61:2).

Division Three—One week of seven, or 7 years.

This is the Seventieth Week, a.k.a. the Tribulation or Jacob's trouble. After being broken off in unbelief and their city destroyed (Daniel 9:26; Matthew 21:43; 24:2; Acts 13:45-49; Romans 11) the sixty-ninth "week of years" ended God's specific focus upon Israel. Nothing of the sixfold purpose of the Seventy Weeks of Daniel has yet been fulfilled (each one pertaining to Israel), and yet it *shall be* fulfilled amidst the events of Revelation 6:1—19:21 as revealed to the apostle John.

Though Daniel received revelation of this final Week, he did not receive the level of detail given to John. And to reiterate, it is between the sixty-ninth and seventieth weeks that the church age exists, book-ended, so to speak, by the Lord God's dealing with Israel.

It may cause one to wonder that had the Jews accepted their Messiah initially, there would be no need for a Seventieth Week of wrath and judgment, dramatically altering world history. But the waywardness of humanity and the consequence of choice determined that Almighty God would have a most merciful plan born of his love. Amen!

TRIBULATION AND *THE* TRIBULATION

The New Testament confirms that believers throughout the church age will experience trials and tribulations. Jesus said, "In the world you will have tribulation; but be of good cheer, I have overcome the world" (John 16:33). The apostle Paul added, "Indeed, all who desire to live a godly life in Christ Jesus will be persecuted . . . but we rejoice in our sufferings, knowing that suffering produces endurance" (2 Timothy 3:12; Romans 5:3 ESV).

Yet the worldly persecution, trials, and tribulations of the church in the current age are *not* the wrath of God (as outlined in chapter four). Rather, as we have seen in this present chapter, an as yet unfulfilled seven-year interval of God's wrath—*the* Tribulation—will befall Israel and an unbelieving world. Jesus assured his disciples that prior to both his return and the kingdom age, "There will be great tribulation, such as has not been since the beginning of the world until this time, no, nor ever shall be. And unless those days were shortened, no flesh would be saved" (Matthew 24:21–22).

Jesus' reference to *the* Tribulation is determined by the context of Matthew 24:5–39, which is specifically the end of the age and his return to earth in accord with the disciples' inquiry (Matthew 24:3).

Some Old Testament passages foretelling the dreadful Day of God's Wrath include Deuteronomy 4:27–31; Isaiah 2:12–22; 24:1–23; 26:20–21; 34:1–8; Daniel 12:1; Joel 1:15–20; 2:1–11, 30–32; Amos 5:18–20; Zephaniah 1:14–18; 3:8; Zechariah 13:7–9; 14:1–21; and Malachi 4:1–6.

Additional New Testament passages expanding our understanding of the Tribulation include Mark 13; Luke 21:7–28; 2 Thessalonians 2:1–12; and Revelation 6–19.

7

The Breaking of the Seals

> Now I saw when the Lamb opened one of the seals; and I heard one of the four living creatures saying with a voice like thunder, "Come and see!"
>
> —REVELATION 6:1

AFTER TAKING THE SCROLL from the right hand of his Father, Jesus prepares to open it, but must first break the seven seals on the outside of it, an act that begins the systematic judgment of Israel, unbelievers, and the earth. It is notable that the seal judgments are the very judgments that Jesus predicted would befall the world at the end of the age (Matthew 24–25; Mark 13:6–25; Luke 21:9–26).

One must mark the observation that Christ is *in heaven* as he initiates the judgment that befalls *the earth*; hence, there is a direct correlation between the two distinct places in that heavily symbolic but literal acts in heaven unleash steadily increasing judgment on the earth that is itself both heavily symbolic *and* literal.

Also, upon exposure to the truth in the Revelation of Jesus Christ (and indeed the entire Bible) one must be disciplined in practicing *exegesis* as opposed to *eisegesis*. These Greek terms express the proper and improper way to approach scriptural interpretation. *Exegesis* means "reading from"—to be understood as reading from God's Word *as it is written*, i.e., What is God saying to us? *Eisegesis* means "reading into"—to be understood as reading into God's Word what one may wish God to mean so that a particular human-devised theory or theology can thus be "proven," i.e., Humanity tells God what he means regardless of what he is saying.

Whitewashing prophecy with the allegorical, mystical, emotional, presumptive, and overtly historical brushes leads to more confusion and quandary than is necessary. It cannot be stressed enough that the literal understanding of even the most difficult passages leads to greater understanding and a more thorough appreciation of both the Word of God and its Author.

THE FOUR HORSEMEN OF THE APOCALYPSE

The first four seals offer striking imagery of horses and riders bearing progressively grave circumstances in their wake. Careful study of the context indicates that this is a *symbolically* stirring and visually dramatic presentation of *literal* events. Through these "horsemen" God conveys and systematically unfolds future world conditions.

Horses in Scripture signify strength, conquest, warfare, and terror (Job 39:19–25; Isaiah 31:1). A foreshadowing of the four horsemen that John sees is found in Zechariah 6:1–8. Zechariah's vision reveals four *riderless* horses drawing chariots—representing judgment by the "four spirits of heaven," i.e., agents of wrath—which are set loose upon the earth to deal out vengeance on Babylon, Egypt, and other nations that have oppressed God's people. Zechariah's post-exilic prophecy is a general reminder to Israel of God's sovereign protection against any nation that would seek to destroy her, looking simultaneously to Israel's past, present, and future in light of being newly restored to the land after seventy years of Babylonian captivity.

THE FIRST SEAL: WORLD CONQUEST

"Now I saw when the Lamb opened one of the seals; and I heard one of the four living creatures saying with a voice like thunder, 'Come and see.' And I looked, and behold, a white horse. And he who sat on it had a bow; and a crown was given to him, and he went out conquering and to conquer" (Revelation 6:1–2).

The Breaking of the Seals

This is the rise of Antichrist. The rider of the white horse in Revelation 6:2 is *not* the Rider of the white horse in Revelation 19:11, for the former is not named and the latter is named "Faithful and True . . . the Word of God . . . King of kings, and Lord of lords." The former has a bow and is followed by war, famine, and death; the latter has a sword and treads the winepress of the fierceness and wrath of Almighty God, and is followed by the armies of heaven also on white horses. The former is given a crown; the latter already possesses many crowns. The two riders share no similarities beyond the white horse.

It is important to identify this first rider as a key toward understanding the following three. As world conditions trend toward increasing global chaos, eventually to reach a crescendo perhaps as a result of the fulfillment of Ezekiel 38–39 and/or the consequences of the rapture, a point will be reached wherein the world seeks for answers to the upheaval and uncertainty. World leaders will wrestle for positions, comprehension of events, and global control. This particular time in history will call for a calm, charismatic, intelligent, and persuasive (or coercive) individual to whom the fearful planet can turn for explanation and solution. This individual will certainly be both politically and militarily savvy.

Throughout Greek and Roman history the symbolism of riding a white horse into a particular territory or city conveyed the might and authority of a conquering military leader. The passage above describes the rider on the white horse as having a bow and a crown, yet no arrows are mentioned. This probably denotes a swift, political, largely diplomatic rise onto the global stage (hence the crown) rather than a militant rise to power; however, the possession of a bow still proves military backing and ability, as bows represent martial might (Psalm 46:9; Jeremiah 49:32; 51:56).

Notably the crown is *given*, not taken. This proves God's sovereignty as he allows events to unfold at his specific disclosure. A later reference to this same individual asks, "Who is like the beast? Who can make war against him?" (Revelation 13:4). This "man of lawlessness" (2 Thessalonians 2:3) will "confirm a covenant with many for *one week*" (Daniel 9:27), meaning he will strike a peace deal between Israel and her neighbors for a duration of seven years (or "week" of years). The first three and one-half years will be generally peaceful for Israel as the covenant is observed, though it is a false peace, and shall be broken "in the middle of the week" (Daniel 9:27).

The fact that this persona will go out "conquering and to conquer" suggests that his rise and hold on power may not be completely unchallenged (Daniel 7:15–25; Revelation 13:4). Further evidence of this is supplied by the breaking of the second seal.

THE SECOND SEAL: WAR

"When he opened the second seal, I heard the second living creature saying, 'Come and see.' And another horse, fiery red, went out. And it was granted to the one who sat on it to take peace from the earth, and that people should kill one another; and there was given to him a great sword" (Revelation 6:3-4).

The red horse and rider symbolize war and bloodshed, for he is *given* power to "take peace from the earth that people should kill one another." This rider is also *given* a sword, another scriptural symbol for war and judgment (Matthew 10:34; Revelation 19:15).

During the Antichrist's campaign for world conquest, some rulers, nations, and regions will rebel or hesitate in their pledging of allegiance to him, resulting in the Antichrist removing their authority by force (Daniel 7:7-8, 15-21, 23-25; Revelation 13:4).

The Antichrist comes to power politically, but will remain in power (for a season) militarily. The opening of the next two seals reveal that war will be terrible and far-reaching.

THE THIRD SEAL: FAMINE

"When he opened the third seal, I heard the third living creature say, 'Come and see.' And I looked, and behold, a black horse, and he who sat on it had a pair of scales in his hand. And I heard a voice in the midst of the four living creatures saying, 'A quart of wheat for a denarius, and three quarts of barley for a denarius; and do not harm the oil and the wine'" (Revelation 6:5-6).

The color black is used elsewhere in Scripture to signify famine, particularly in Jeremiah 4:28 and Lamentations 4:8–9. Famine often follows war, as it did in the aftermath of World War I, resulting from suddenly limited resources due to destruction of produce and personnel coupled with severely limited inroads of replenishment of the needed resources. God also threatened the judgment of famine as a consequence to those who are disobedient (Leviticus 26:26; Ezekiel 4:16), once proclaiming to Ezekiel, "I will break the supply of bread in Jerusalem. They shall eat bread by weight and with anxiety, and they shall drink water by measure and in dismay" (ESV).

Inflation is a direct consequence of widespread famine. The pair of scales (or balances) in the rider's hand indicates the scarcity of food, and the reference to a *denarius* (or a day's wages; Matthew 20:10) indicates that the common people will be hit hard by economic turmoil and food shortages. However, the lack of harm to the "oil and wine" demonstrates the injustice of humanity to the fellow man in that these products are often possessed by the wealthier classes that will likely see lesser degrees of suffering at this time. A sad day indeed when necessities are scarce and luxuries plentiful.

THE FOURTH SEAL: DEATH

"When he opened the fourth seal, I heard the voice of the fourth living creature saying, 'Come and see.' And I looked, and behold, a pale horse. And the name of him who sat on it was Death, and Hades followed with him. And power was given to them over a fourth of the earth, to kill with sword, with hunger, with death, and by the beasts of the earth" (Revelation 6:7–8).

The pale horse signifies the ashen pallor of disease and death. The circumstance of Hades (hell) following Death is a clear indication that a majority of those who die specifically as a result of these events will be unsaved (nonbelievers). The fighting, famine, and death are results of the wars that shall carry well into the seven years of judgment, affecting one quarter of the earth's population. The "beasts of the earth" will be a factor in population loss as well. Animals may begin to hunt humans for food and may become more aggressively violent due to the calamitous situation.

Note again that power was *given* to Death and Hades, indicating that even this tragic scenario falls under God's sovereign purpose. That their power was over "a fourth of the earth" reveals the surety of God's permissive will and his still active mercy concerning a remnant of souls being given space to repent (Ezekiel 14:21–22).

THE FIFTH SEAL: MARTYRS

"When he opened the fifth seal, I saw under the altar the souls of those who had been slain for the word of God and for the testimony which they held. And they cried with a loud voice, saying, 'How long, O Lord, holy and true, until you judge and avenge our blood on those who dwell on the earth?' And a white robe was given to each of them; and it was said to them that they

should rest a little while longer, until both the number of their fellow servants and their brethren, who would be killed as they were, was completed" (Revelation 6:9–11).

Here John sees an altar in the heavenly tabernacle, and beneath it he glimpses the slain souls of Tribulation believers killed for their testimony (Leviticus 4:7; 17:11). These martyred dead are seen in heaven calling out in inquiry as to how long it will be until they are avenged, to which they were given white robes (of righteousness) and encouraged to wait a little while longer until their number (of those to be martyred) was completed—another encouraging example of God's sovereignty (Genesis 4:10; Hebrews 11:4). Enoch prophesied of this very moment:

> In those days the prayer of the righteous shall have ascended, and the blood of the righteous from the earth shall be before the Lord of spirits. In those days the holy ones who dwell above in heaven shall unite with one voice and supplicate and pray and praise, and give thanks and bless the name of the Lord of spirits on behalf of the blood of the righteous which has been shed, that the prayer of the righteous may not be in vain before the Lord of spirits, that they may have justice, and that they may not have to wait forever (Enoch 47:1–2).

This company of slain saints will receive their resurrection bodies near the end of the seven years in preparation for returning to earth with Jesus, the church, the Old Testament saints, and the heavenly hosts. This event will be detailed later (Revelation 7:9–17; 15:1–4).

At the beginning of the Seventieth Week, sometime following the rapture, 144,000 Jews will be sealed by God (Revelation 7:3–8), effectively becoming the "lampstand" of the world since the church will have been taken from the earth. Their subsequent witness to the truth of Jesus Christ will initiate a progressive soul harvest that will continue through the Tribulation.

Those who become believers in Christ during this time will be the saints of their age—Tribulation saints—for they "are the ones who come out of the great tribulation, and washed their robes and made them white in the blood of the Lamb" (Revelation 7:13–14). They will experience great personal persecution and even martyrdom (death) because of "the word of God and for the testimony which they held."

The last three and one-half years of the Tribulation will be exponentially worse than the first three and one-half years, for the seven-year covenant will be broken by the Antichrist "in the middle of the week" (Daniel

9:27). He will then reveal his god-complex and total war will be declared against all who oppose him, particularly the Jews and subsequently anyone who proclaims Christ as King or simply rejects Antichrist's usurped authority (Matthew 24:9–10; Luke 21:12–17; John 16:2).

THE SIXTH SEAL: CATASTROPHIC JUDGMENT

"I looked when he opened the sixth seal, and behold, there was a great earthquake; and the sun became black as sackcloth of hair, and the moon became like blood. And the stars of heaven fell to the earth, as a fig tree drops its late figs when it is shaken by a mighty wind. Then the sky receded as a scroll when it is rolled up, and every mountain and island was moved out of its place.

And the kings of the earth, the great men, the rich men, the commanders, the mighty men, every slave and every free man, hid themselves in the caves and in the rocks of the mountains, and said to the mountains and rocks, 'Fall on us and hide us from the face of him who sits on the throne and from the wrath of the Lamb!' For the great day of his wrath has come, and who is able to stand?" (Revelation 6:12–17).

This seal judgment extends into the second half of the seven-year Seventieth Week. After reading the above passage, one is easily awestruck by the absolute terror that will be kindled in humanity as almost unimaginable events become reality.

A planet-shaking earthquake, volcanism, meteor bombardment, and indescribable displays of destruction will force fear into human hearts. Yet the rebellious and stubborn nature of humanity will thwart repentance in most (Jeremiah 8:20; Hosea 10:8), and instead of turning to God multitudes will hide in mountains and caves, wanting to die, saying to the rocks and mountains, "Fall on us and hide us from the face of him who sits on the throne and from the *wrath of the Lamb!*"

Normally, we would not associate wrath with the Lamb of God, Jesus Christ, for we know a lamb signifies gentleness and kindness. Yet, William Barclay indicates that

> there is laid down the great fact that the wrath of God is the wrath of love. God's wrath is not the sheerly destructive wrath of hatred, which is out to blast and to destroy. God's wrath is the

wrath of love, which even in anger is out to save, to amend and to redeem the one it loves.[1]

The volume of imagery in the sixth seal text should not be minimized or dismissed as ambiguous symbolism. The comparative articles "as" and "like" create a bridge (simile) between something familiar and something fantastically indescribable but still literal; the *absence* of such articles in a text denotes literal/actual events that are easier to describe with little or no symbolism.

For instance, John looked and "there *was* a great earthquake" and "every mountain and island *was* moved out of its place." There is no use of simile for the mountains and islands; therefore John witnessed an actual earthquake and actual topographical displacement! Then "the sun became black *as* sackcloth of hair, the moon became *like* blood . . . the stars of heaven fell to the earth *as* a fig tree drops its late figs when it is shaken by a mighty wind . . . the sky receded *as* a scroll."

For the heavenly descriptions the comparative articles introduce familiar comparisons to literal and actual events that are basically indescribable. Perhaps a planetary axial shift brings about these horrendous conditions.[2] Circumstances become so dire that every strata of society is affected. Even the most powerful of men will recoil in fear, knowing from whom this judgment proceeds (John 5:22).

"For the great day of his wrath has come" is an intentional identifier of the heavily prophesied Old Testament references to the "day of the Lord," "time of Jacob's trouble," et al. God has long foretold that he would shake the heavens, the earth, the sea, and the nations (Isaiah 34:4; Haggai 2:6–7), with the earth moving out if its place (Isaiah 13:13; Jeremiah 4:24; Nahum 1:5) and the sun turning black while the moon turns blood-red (Joel 2:31).

Now the time has arrived for humanity's greatest fear: God's judgment of all evil! Moreover, God becomes a witness against the sins of Israel and levels his judgment in full (Micah 1:1–5).

Christians know that Almighty God is a God of both justice and love, for justice flows from his love. Even John 3:16–18 indicates the dual aspect of God's interaction with humanity—if one believes and calls on the name of Christ in humility, then one's soul shall enjoy eternal unity

---

1. Barclay, *The Revelation of John*, vol. 2, 20.
2. See Appendix B Expanded Commentary #4.

with God; if one does *not* believe, then one dies and suffers eternal separation from God.

Yet, as the age of grace continues to unfold, humanity is swift to forget or trivialize God's perfect justice. And in regard to the Lamb being the Executor of divine wrath, J. B. Smith states, "He is now not the Lamb of sacrifice but the Executor of justice upon those who have spurned his overtures of grace."[3]

Before progressing to the seventh seal, there is a parenthetical aside, or interlude, that describes the 144,000 witnesses of Israel and also an innumerable multitude of Tribulation saints. The purpose of such an interlude is to further detail or add supplemental matters toward a richer comprehension and clearer interpretation of events either retrospective (referencing things already mentioned in Revelation) or prospective (pertaining to things to come). There will be a few of these parenthetical revelations as we continue. I like to think of them as the "extra features" in Jesus' revelation to John.

This interlude records two visions. In the first (retrospective), John sees 144,000 Jewish men sealed by an angel in preparation to act as prophet-evangelists. In the second (prospective), John watches a vast multinational multitude of martyrs worshiping the Lamb and being prepared to serve him as he initiates his millennial kingdom on earth.

---

3. Smith, *A Revelation of Jesus Christ*, 127.

8

Prophets and Martyrs
Parenthetic Revelation I

AFTER THESE THINGS *I saw four angels standing at the four corners of the earth, holding the four winds of the earth, that the wind should not blow on the earth, on the sea, or on any tree. Then I saw another angel ascending from the east, having the seal of the living God. And he cried with a loud voice to the four angels to whom it was granted to harm the earth and the sea, saying, "Do not harm the earth, the sea, or the trees till we have sealed the servants of our God on their foreheads." And I heard the number of those who were sealed. One hundred and forty-four thousand of all the tribes of the children of Israel* (Revelation 7:1–4).

Four angels are seen standing at the four corners of the earth, holding the four winds of the earth that the wind should not blow on the earth, on the sea, or an any tree. The "winds" and "wind" in this passage are synonymous with judgment as revealed in Revelation 7:3 when "another angel ascending from the east, having the seal of the living God" admonishes the trumpet-bearing angels *not to harm* the earth, the sea, or the trees (Daniel 7:2; 8:8; Zechariah 2:6). The wind (trumpet judgments) will be held in check until after the breaking of the seventh seal.

The image of restraining angels of judgment recurs in Jewish literature, as when angels of the waters are commanded by God to hold the flood torrents in check until Noah had constructed the ark and was secure inside with his family and the flora and fauna (Enoch 66:1–2).

These angels of the winds in Revelation are plainly agents of divine retribution, for they have "the seal of the living God" and have "sealed the servants of our God." The four angels are also the first four of the seven trumpet-wielding angels to whom are given power to harm the earth, the sea, and the trees.

A striking line in the apocryphal book of Ecclesiasticus describes the Tribulation, and while the *Apocrypha* is not inspired biblical canon, this particular line may have been taken from (or inspired by) biblical sources:

> There be winds that are created for vengeance, and in their fury lay on their scourges heavily; in the time of consummation they pour out their strength, and shall appease the wrath of him that made them. Fire, and hail, and famine, and death, all these are created for vengeance; teeth of wild beasts, and scorpions and adders, and a sword punishing the ungodly unto destruction.[1]

Of further interest is the fact that this passage was written centuries prior to the divinely inspired penning of the book of Revelation, and of particular note is the reference to "winds that are created for vengeance," evoking exactly the imagery of what befalls the earth after the sounding of the first trumpet.

The four angels are commanded not to harm the earth, the sea, or the trees *until* the sealing of the servants of God. The seal on the servants' foreheads will be God's written name (Revelation 14:1) and will afford them supernatural protection from judgment (9:4), but also implies godly possession and godly service. It will, however, be a literal and visible seal, for the demonic locusts from the Abyss will be able to see it (9:4). A parallel reference to setting a seal upon the forehead can be found in Ezekiel 9:4, though in this instance those sealed are godly men and not angels.

THE 144,000

The number of those sealed is 12,000 from each of the twelve tribes of Israel, totaling 144,000 (Revelation 7:4–8). The time of their sealing will occur after the rapture of the church and before the trumpet judgments begin, though whether this will be immediately after the rapture or at some point amidst the breaking of the seal judgments is not revealed. However, with the catching away of the church there will cease to be a

---

1. *The Apocrypha*, "Ecclesiasticus," 108, column b, (Oxford University Press, 1913). Being the 1611 version, revised 1894.

"lampstand" of truth on the earth, lending to the likelihood of the 144,000 witnesses being sealed sooner than later in the Tribulation.

That these are Jewish *men* is proven in Revelation 14:4, thereby negating the wayward notions and heinous theologies insisting upon the 144,000 being a symbolic or allegorical representation of the church (a.k.a. New Israel) or any particular cult.

The repeated descriptions of who these sealed ones are cannot be written off and can only be fully understood in a literal sense. The fact of 12,000 *Jewish male virgins* (Revelation 14:4) being sealed from twelve tribes of Israel proves there is no connection with the church for there is never any tribal identity concerning the church, even for those fulfilled Jews saved in the church age. Moreover, as discussed previously, Israel's prominence during the time of Jacob's trouble indicates strongly that the church age will be over.

Scripture reveals via Daniel's revelation of the Seventy Weeks (Daniel 9:24–27) that the era of the church and the times appointed to Israel cannot overlap. Israel, having been "cut off" from the Root of Jesse prior to the church's origin on the day of Pentecost when the Gentiles were "grafted in," will not be grafted *back* in until the "fullness of the Gentiles" has been completed (Romans 11:5–26). Furthermore, proof that Israel remains cut off and is awaiting the process of being grafted back in rests in Revelation 14:4 wherein the 144,000 are called the "firstfruits unto God"—for they shall be the first Jews of the Tribulation to recognize Jesus as Messiah—indicating the initiation of the grafting back in of Israel. And it is not until all national Israel (the remnant; those which are left) looks upon him whom they have pierced that they will be saved (at the second advent).

TRIBAL NUANCE

In regard to the list of the twelve tribes of Israel (Revelation 7:5–8), there are 29 tribe lists to be found in all of Scripture, each differing from others. Such prominence in the Bible implies an importance that is not to be dismissed or diminished by spiritualizing the variances.

In Revelation 7:5–8 the names of Dan and Ephraim are not present, their places being taken by Levi and Joseph. Since Joseph had two sons, Ephraim and Manasseh, it appears that there are *thirteen* tribes of Israel, but the tribe of Levi was not considered one of the twelve tribes for it consisted of the priests that lived off the tithe of the twelve tribes proper (Joshua 14:3–4; Numbers 1:47–50; 18:21–24). Joseph's name is substituted for Ephraim while Manasseh remains on the list of focus, not an unusual occurrence since there are numerous times in the Old Testament when Joseph replaces either of his two sons in tribal tallies. Passages concerning the New Jerusalem include Levi and Joseph because they were of the twelve original sons of Jacob, while Ephraim and Manasseh, being sons of Joseph, were not (Ezekiel 48:30–35; Revelation 21:12).

Considering this information, we see then that the one notable omission from the tribal list is the tribe of Dan. Jacob's original twelve sons included Joseph and Dan, but Dan eventually betrayed the house of Jacob/Israel by being the first to fall into idolatry and pride (Judges 18:14–31; 1 Kings 12:28–33), which was foretold by Jacob himself in that Dan would not live up to his calling to judge his people, for "Dan shall be a serpent in the way, a viper by the path, that bites the horse's heels so that his rider falls backward" (Genesis 49:16–17 ESV).

Also, Deuteronomy 29:18–21 required that anyone who introduced Israel to idolatry would have their name blotted out from under heaven and would be separated from all the tribes of Israel according to the curses of the covenant.

Joseph, however, received a double-portion blessing through his two sons, perhaps as a remedy to Dan's apostasy. This, too, was anticipated by Jacob when he declared that "Joseph is a fruitful bough, a fruitful bough by a spring; his branches run over the wall" (Genesis 49:22 ESV). As mentioned before, it is not an unusual occurrence for Joseph to be substituted for either of his sons in the tribal lists, as he stands in for Ephraim in Revelation 7:8.

The list of tribes in Revelation 7 intentionally begins with Judah, the tribe of Messiah who judges all. Dan, formerly at the judgeship position, is excluded outright from being represented among the 144,000 and parallels the exclusion of Judas from the twelve disciples as a result of his betrayal. And whereas Judas was replaced by Matthias (Acts 1:26), it appears that Dan is replaced by Levi (Revelation 7:7). Nevertheless, and by God's abounding grace, we see Dan restored at the *top of the list* for the inheritance of land allotments during the thousand-year kingdom (Ezekiel 48:1).

Altogether, the 144,000 Jewish evangelists will be a formidable witness to truth during the darkening hour of trial upon the earth, possibly even speaking to the world against the political advance and eventual militant rise of Antichrist, though *two* witnesses in particular will purpose to reveal Antichrist's demonic identity to Israel.

As to where these 144,000 witnesses will be located geographically is determined when one considers the dispersion of the Jews in the wake of their temple's destruction in AD 70. God's chosen people have been scattered among the nations and though many are currently returning to their homeland in fulfillment of prophecy (Ezekiel 36:16–38; 39:23–28), there will remain large numbers throughout the world as positioned by the Lord God toward his purpose, for 144,000 evangelists crammed into one small plot of real estate (Israel) would not fulfill the Great Commission (Matthew 28:18–20). To this end, the 144,000 will be strategically located around the world. The late prophetic hour hints that they already are!

THE MARTYRED DEAD IN HEAVEN

The previous record of the 144,000 witnesses was of a retrospective nature while the following record that concerns the martyred dead is prospective as it looks forward to the end of the Tribulation and beyond (Revelation 7:9–17). The martyred dead of this passage include those previously mentioned in Revelation 6:9–11, though here in chapter seven their prophetic destiny is revealed (7:15–17).

> After these things I looked, and behold, a great multitude which no one could number, of all nations, tribes, peoples, and tongues, standing before the throne and before the Lamb, clothed with white robes, with palm branches in their hands, and crying out with a loud voice, saying, "Salvation belongs to our God who sits on the throne, and to the Lamb!" All the angels stood around the throne and the elders and the four living creatures, and fell on their faces before the throne and worshiped God (Revelation 7:9–11).

Unlike the 144,000, this multitude cannot be numbered and neither are they of only one ethnicity, but come from all nations, tribes, peoples, and tongues who have come to believe in Christ during the "day of vengeance of our God," and have paid the penultimate price for their new faith. These souls have "come out of the great tribulation" and have "washed their robes and made them white in the blood of the Lamb," having been martyred following their salvation (7:14).[2]

---

2. The blood of Jesus Christ. William Barclay expounds, ". . . when the New

The palm branches in their hands convey victory and rejoicing as they glorify their Savior (John 12:13). The innumerability hearkens back to God's promise to Abraham that his descendants (physical and spiritual) would one day be numbered as the stars in heaven and as the sand of the seashore (Genesis 15:5; 32:12).

Some believe this martyred multitude to be or to represent the entire church body of believers, this by default requiring either a later rapture for the church (at the middle or end of the Tribulation) or none at all. This reckoning ignores the context of Revelation 7:14 (which specifies exactly who the martyrs are) and confuses a coherently ordered understanding of John's record. Not every member of the universal church body has been martyred. And recall that the church was "kept from the hour of trial" while this multitude has "come out of" it.

Also, in representing the church in heaven, the twenty-four elders are *seated* on thrones and *crowned* as kings and priests to *reign with Christ* in his kingdom. This multitude in Revelation 7:9–14 is *standing uncrowned* and ready to *serve Christ*. The differences are not diminutive, only distinctive.

Another reason this multitude cannot be the church rests in the fact that John would have recognized them as such, dispelling the need for the angel to instructively ask John who they are (Revelation 7:13). What is more, the church Body is later seen as the Bride of Christ preparing to return with him at his second advent (19:7–16), having been *with him in heaven* for the duration of the Seventieth Week.

Now consider Revelation 6:9–11 and "the souls of those who had been slain for the Word of God and for the testimony which they held." The souls under the altar waiting for their number to be complete appear to be identical with (and at least include) the innumerable multitude of martyrs in Revelation 7:9–17, for their number is increasing! It may be that their number is nearly complete for in 7:9 they are standing before the throne in worship rather than resting beneath the heavenly altar.

We see them a third time in Revelation 15:2–4 proclaiming and praising the last of God's judgments in preparation for their resurrection to glory (by receiving their resurrection bodies). Here their number has multiplied still further in proportion to the exploding persecution

---

Testament speaks about the blood of Jesus Christ, it means not only the death of Christ; it means everything that Jesus did in his life and in his death. We cannot separate the life and death of Jesus; they go together; his death would lose its value without the life which went before and after it" (*The Revelation of John*, vol. 2, 37).

resulting from the implementation of the mark of the beast (Revelation 13:16–18).

In light of divine wrath, I reiterate that the church is never the object of such, but is only and ever the object of God's love. The church is indeed rebuked and disciplined during her sojourn on earth (Revelation 3:19), but she will not suffer divine *wrath*, for Jesus Christ endured the same when the Father poured it on his son as he hung upon the cross (Isaiah 53:1–12; Hebrews 9:24–28).

As discussed earlier, the time of Jacob's trouble is reserved for an unbelieving Israel and an unbelieving world, but "there is therefore now no condemnation for those who are in Christ Jesus" (Romans 8:1).

THE SEVENTH SEAL

The parenthetical chapter 7 of Revelation now concludes and the chronological list of events reconvenes in Revelation chapter 8. Referring back to the seven-sealed scroll, we see that the breaking of the first four seals introduced successive judgments, the fifth being subsequent to the initial four in revealing a census of the slain, and the sixth seal showing signs in the heavens and on earth of far worse judgment to come as the wrath of the Lamb prepares to be unleashed through the trumpet and bowl judgments.

> When he opened the seventh seal, there was silence in heaven for about half an hour. And I saw the seven angels who stand before God, and to them were given seven trumpets. Then another angel, having a golden censer, came and stood at the altar. And he was given much incense, that he should offer it with the prayers of all the saints upon the golden altar which was before the throne. And the smoke of the incense, with the prayers of the saints, ascended before God from the angel's hand (Revelation 8:1–4).

The silence in heaven and the activity that follows evokes Jewish temple liturgy. After the slaughter of a sacrificial lamb, the altar of incense was prepared (Leviticus 16:12; Numbers 16:46). This was followed by two priests relighting the lamps of the golden lampstand with burnt coals and ashes taken from the golden altar upon entering the holy place. One priest would then fill the golden censer with incense as the other would put burning coals into a golden bowl. *A solemn silence permeated the ceremony.*

This silence in heaven could also be described as the deep breath before the plunge, a time of worshipfully weighing the theistic gravity of the moment and what is to come. Also see Zephaniah 1:1–7; Zechariah 2:12–13; and Habakkuk 2:20.

The angel with the golden censer offering the incense with the prayers of the saints illustrates that the prayers of the faithful, like the smoke of incense, continuously ascend to Almighty God. Unanswered prayers are thus "stored" in heaven awaiting their fulfillment. For example, Psalm 122:6 advises us to pray for the peace of Jerusalem; however, absolute and lasting peace will not become reality in Jerusalem *until* Jesus himself is on the throne. Likewise, believers have prayed unceasingly for Christ to return since his ascension into heaven following his first advent, and such prayers will continue to ascend before the throne *until* he sets foot once again upon the earth.

Yet the Word of God assures us of coming justice and final peace, encouraging our perseverance and strengthening our faith. Remember that God's love is the foundation of justice, which includes the judgment of the wicked and reward of the righteous. God does not condemn and judge out of enjoyment but out of necessity:

> Though he cause grief, he will have compassion according to the abundance of his steadfast love; for he does not afflict from his heart or grieve the children of men (Lamentations 3:32–33 ESV).

Notice that the breaking of the seventh seal does nothing to the earth, it simply introduces the trumpet judgments (just as the seventh trumpet will introduce the bowl judgments).

9

The Blowing of the Trumpets

> Then the angel took the censer, filled it with fire from the altar, and threw it to the earth. And there were noises, thunderings, lightnings, and an earthquake. So the seven angels who had the seven trumpets prepared themselves to sound.
>
> —REVELATION 8:5–6

JOHN OBSERVES THE ANGEL with the censer of prayers filling it with fire from the altar (the brazen altar of judgment; 2 Chronicles 1:5–12). The angel then casts the fire to the earth, indicating that "the prayers which ascended to heaven would be followed by judgments descending upon the earth."[1] This picture reflects the vision of Ezekiel wherein a linen-clad man takes hot coals from between the cherubim and is commanded to scatter them over Jerusalem (Ezekiel 9–10:2).

The stage is now set for further systematic divine retribution; thus, the seven angels with the seven trumpets prepare to sound (Revelation 8:2, 6; Enoch 20). Notably, the sounding of trumpets in Scripture has always heralded strikingly pivotal events; for example, the successive sounding of trumpets at the giving of the Law (Exodus 19:16–19; 20:18);

---

1. Smith, *A Revelation of Jesus Christ*, 138.

the Jubilee (Leviticus 25:9); victory in battle (Joshua 6:5, 20; Judges 7:18; 2 Samuel 2:28; Nehemiah 4:20); at feast days (Psalm 81:3); impending judgment (Hosea 8:1; Joel 2:1); and at the rapture of the church (1 Corinthians 15:51–52; 1 Thessalonians 4:16).

In the book of Revelation a new succession of seven trumpets heralds heightening doom, commencing at or near the middle of the Seventieth Week as evidenced by Revelation 6:17 in that "the great day of his wrath has come," whereas the seven seal judgments (transpiring over the first three and one-half years of the Tribulation) will have just concluded. The last three and one-half years of the Tribulation are also known as the "great tribulation," for judgment steadily intensifies as Satan attempts to consolidate his control over the world (Matthew 24:21; Revelation 7:14). Furthermore, Jacob's trouble intensifies exponentially from this point since it is in the middle of the seven-year Week that Antichrist breaks the covenant made with Israel, desecrates the temple/tabernacle, and declares war on the Jews, resulting in a mass exodus of Jews out of Jerusalem in search of refuge (Revelation 12:6).

An intriguing parallel is found in the fact that much of what befell Egypt as it suffered the plagues prior to the Exodus will also befall Israel during the last half of the Seventieth Week. This is not accidental, as there is nothing new under the sun (Ecclesiastes 1:9), and serves as a template toward understanding that what has happened literally in the past will also happen literally in the future.

Expositors attempting to allegorize prophetic Scripture, thereby explaining the same as entirely nonliteral, do a better job of (unintentionally) obscuring the truth than expounding it. Attempts to soften the harshness of what is written and/or to dilute occasionally unimaginable imagery through overt rationalization often leads to bad theology. Alternately, by faith, it is not difficult to accept a *supernatural* aspect when one considers that the judgment revealed in Revelation involves *direct* involvement from the Creator, thus rendering moot any human rationale. When Genesis 1:1 is received by faith in humility, the disciple progresses beyond belief to genuine conviction, which allows true wisdom to take root.

As with the first four seals, the first four trumpets form a cohesive unit followed by the more distinctive fifth through seventh trumpets which themselves form a unit of three woes, or warnings of dreadful disaster upon humanity.

THE FIRST TRUMPET: HAIL, FIRE, BLOOD

"The first angel sounded: And hail and fire followed, mingled with blood, and they were thrown to the earth; and a third of the trees were burned up, and all green grass was burned up" (Revelation 8:7).

This displays similarity to the seventh Egyptian plague (Exodus 9:22–26), though the emphasis here is on vegetation while in Egypt vegetation, beasts, and men were affected. Agricultural industry will be thwarted after this. This judgment also recalls the firestorm that fell on Sodom and Gomorrah (Genesis 19:1–29), thus there is no reason to deny a literal event here. Also see Joel 1:15–20.

THE SECOND TRUMPET: A BURNING MOUNTAIN AND BLOOD SEAS

"Then the second angel sounded: And something like a great mountain burning with fire was thrown into the sea, and a third of the sea became blood; and a third of the living creatures in the sea died, and a third of the ships were destroyed" (Revelation 8:8–9).

Possibly this "burning mountain," as it appeared to John, is a very large meteor ablaze from atmospheric friction. The sea here is almost certainly the Mediterranean, as the judgment of the seals, trumpets, and bowls is foremost focused upon Israel and the area of the old Roman Empire—the epicenter of the known world at the time John received the Revelation. Further evidence suggesting that the sea mentioned is the Mediterranean rests in the fact of later judgment affecting *other* bodies of water. However, if the "sea" in this passage means the sum of the earth's larger bodies of water (oceans), then we may assume wider affectation. Consider also the tsunamis to result from such an impact on a large body of water, devastating coastlines well inland.

This judgment parallels the first Egyptian plague where the Nile and even potted water turned to blood (Exodus 7:20–25; Psalm 78:44; 105:29), but under this trumpet only a third of the sea becomes blood which will undoubtedly contribute to a third of the living creatures perishing therein.

A third of the ships on the sea being destroyed will effectively hinder maritime commerce. Just as Egypt's gods were struck by each plague, the world's gods will be struck by God's wrath. The doom of the waterways disables a vast portion of the world's economy and reminds mankind that

God remains in control, even concerning his purposes at sea—a truth immortalized in Samuel Coleridge's *Rime of the Ancient Mariner*.

Undoubtedly, a literal understanding of these events is difficult to reconcile from a naturalistic perspective, but is completely manageable upon accepting the supernatural aspect.

THE THIRD TRUMPET: WORMWOOD

"Then the third angel sounded: And a great star fell from heaven, burning like a torch, and it fell on a third of the rivers and on the springs of water; and the name of the star is Wormwood; and a third of the waters became wormwood; and many men died from the water because it was made bitter" (Revelation 8:10–11).

With the "burning mountain" falling on the sea (salt water), we now witness a "great burning star," possibly another meteor, falling on a third of the rivers and springs (fresh water) and making them bitter, effectively causing many to die from thirst or from drinking the bitter water. Compare this instance with the experience of Israel at Marah in Exodus 15:23–25 when God made bitter waters sweet. Hence, if God can literally make bitter waters sweet, can he not make sweet waters bitter?

Wormwood is a very bitter herb and seems to offer nothing more than simply being an appropriate name given to the "burning star" in light of its purpose. John understood the significance of the name as he would have expectedly had knowledge of the herb and its chemical effect, along with the fact that wormwood symbolized divine punishment (Jeremiah 9:15; Amos 5:7).

A few other possibilities exist concerning the burning star and burning mountain. Many suggest the idea of nuclear weaponry and its resulting destruction and radioactive fallout poisoning the waters. Had John witnessed nuclear warfare in the vision, he undoubtedly would have found it difficult to put into first-century terminology what he saw. However, I propose that if the burning objects are not meteors or weaponry of some sort, plausibly they are *angels of judgment* sent by God to strike the specific waters, as when an angel of death was sent to strike the Egyptian firstborn and the might of the Assyrian army (Exodus 12:23; 2 Kings 19:35), and angels of destruction were unleashed upon Egypt (Psalm 78:49). Recall that angels are often referenced as stars in Scripture (see chapter two) and in Jewish thought (Enoch 86:1; 88:1).

And lastly, in keeping with prophetic allusion, we must consider the use of comparative articles (e.g., like/as). John may have been shown a dramatically symbolic image of burning objects that instantly explained a severely *literal consequence* of judgment while obscuring the *exact means* (other than supernatural divine decree), as when Daniel explained Nebuchadnezzar's symbolic dream of a great gold, silver, bronze, iron, and clay image of a king that was crushed to dust by an uncut stone and then blown away in the wind as the stone grew into a mountain that filled the earth (Daniel 2:25–45). Prophetic dreams and visions often contain heavy symbolism that *always* points to specifically literal/actual meanings and things. Therefore direct revelation from God is necessary for interpretation, though he may still keep portions obscure for his own purposes.

THE FOURTH TRUMPET: SUN, MOON, STARS STRUCK

"Then the fourth angel sounded: And a third of the sun was struck, a third of the moon, and a third of the stars, so that a third of them were darkened; and a third of the day did not shine, and likewise the night" (Revelation 8:12).

The darkening of a third of the sun, moon, and stars is either supernatural or a physical result of the first trumpet's burning of a third of the vegetation by fire from the sky, as dense smoke would begin to widely taint the atmosphere. Notice the connection here with the sixth seal and fifth bowl judgments. There is further connection with the ninth plague of Egypt, though the Egyptian plague of supernatural darkness was total and could be *felt* and lasted for three days (Exodus 10:21–23). It is unspecified as to how long the fourth trumpet effects last.

Thus far we see that the first four trumpet judgments affect material creation, the last three will directly affect moral creation, i.e., humanity.

A Warning!

"And I looked, and I heard an angel flying through the midst of heaven, saying with a loud voice, 'Woe, woe, woe to the inhabitants of the earth, because of the remaining blasts of the trumpet'" (Revelation 8:13).

Some Bible translations render the flying *angel* as an *eagle*. This has been considered by a majority of scholars, interpreters, and theologians to be an unintentional mistranslation in that scriptural evidence is stacked against the use of "eagle," for whenever God announces great events or plans he uses *angels*. There is no other instance in Scripture where God has done otherwise (Balaam's talking donkey does not apply as such was a sanctioned personal appeal in response to disobedience, not a divine pronouncement; Numbers 22:21–35). Although whether it is an angel or eagle that heralds doom, people will surely notice!

Since the angel's message is to the "inhabitants of the earth" it is logical to conclude that the "heaven" through which the angel is flying is the earth's atmosphere. If this is not the case, then the message is simply an announcement of divine intent made in the heavenly tabernacle.

The three "woes" are also translated as "trouble," indicating calamitous doom and reflecting indirectly Isaiah's pronouncement, "Woe is me, for I am ruined!" after setting his eyes upon the Lord of hosts (Isaiah 6:5). The three woes are actually the fifth, sixth, and seventh trumpet judgments, evidenced by the warning angel to be much worse than anything prior. The rebellion of humanity against the Lord God worsens progressively, as do God's judgments in response.

The three woes are:

1. Demon locusts from the Abyss
2. Demon horsemen from the Abyss
3. Preparation for final judgment

THE FIFTH TRUMPET/FIRST WOE: DEMON LOCUSTS

"Then the fifth angel sounded: And I saw a star fallen from heaven to the earth. And to him was given the key to the bottomless pit. And he opened the bottomless pit, and smoke arose out of the pit like the smoke of a great furnace. And the sun and air were darkened because of the smoke of the pit. Then out of the smoke locusts came upon the earth. And to them was given power, as the scorpions of the earth have power . . . And they had as king over them the angel of the bottomless pit, whose name in Hebrew is Abaddon, but in Greek he has the name Apollyon. One woe is past. Behold, still two more woes are coming after these things" (Revelation 9:1–12).

The "star" that falls to the earth is clearly a figurative reference since it is then referenced as "him" when given the key to the bottomless pit, and "he" when opening the same. Stars are often used as symbols for angels (Revelation 1:20; Job 38:7; Enoch 86:1; 88:1) and Revelation 20:1 indicates an angel coming down from heaven with the *key to the bottomless pit* (or Abyss) and a great chain in his hand, with which he binds Satan who remains imprisoned in the Abyss for one thousand years (this occurs after the second advent). The star of 9:1 and angel of 20:1 are likely the same being, one of God's own heavenly agents, not a fallen angel.

The Abyss

The smoke rising out of the pit like a great furnace and darkening the sun and air denotes a literal smoke rising from a literal burning. This is a "smoke of torment" that we see reflected in the destruction of Babylon (Revelation 18:9, 18). We know there is torment in Hades, for a certain rich man testified from there, "I am tormented in this flame!" (Luke 16:24).

The Abyss (a.k.a "the pit") is not Hades or hell itself but may be the great gulf (or chasm) that is fixed between the place of torment (hell, Hades) and the place of comfort (Paradise). Jesus describes this place in Luke 16:19–31. The historical book of Enoch carries the most detailed descriptions of the Abyss; the biblical books of 2 Peter and Jude only reference it. It is a wasteland at the end of heaven and earth that has become a prison for those fallen angels which transgressed God's prohibitions (2 Peter 2:4; Jude 1:6; Enoch 18:12–16). It is a horribly chaotic dimensional void where incarcerated angels are bound together in flames that burn and blaze, "and the place was cleft as far as the abyss [could be seen], full of great falling columns of fire" (Enoch 21:1–10).

J. B. Smith adds a very disconcerting consideration for the damned souls of the future: "If then smoke issues from the torment of the doomed, one need not wonder that the sun and the air will be darkened by reason of the smoke accumulating in the pit from the days of Cain unto that future occasion."[2]

The Destroyer

Revelation 9:11 reveals the name of a king ruling over the demon locusts that are released from the pit. This king's name is given in both Hebrew (*Abaddon*) and Greek (*Apollyon*) so as to instruct both the Jew and the Greek (non-Jew) of his identity. Some interpreters claim that this king, whose names mean "destroyer," is either Satan himself or the angel to whom is given the key to the bottomless pit. This is refuted by the fact

---

2. Smith, *A Revelation of Jesus Christ*, 143.

that Satan is never equated with the name Destroyer in the Bible and that, following the contextual flow, the king over the demon locusts is referred to as an angel *of* the bottomless pit, and is not *loosed from* the pit until the angel with the key opens the pit. Satan has clearly not been in this prison, he has been freely prowling the earth for millennia like a lion seeking whom he may devour (1 Peter 5:8).

Further, it would not be in keeping with God's sovereignty to entrust to Satan or any fallen angel the key and authority with which to wield such command and allowance as he ordains. Indeed, God's heavenly agents that remained loyal are thus utilized toward carrying out his divine will—an aspect of their created purpose.

The Swarm

Revelation 9 boasts the most frequent and concentrated use of the comparative articles "like" and "as" than anywhere else in Scripture. Recall that such uses signify *similarity* rather than identity when conveying literal/actual events. The comparisons only appear in the *description* of the demon locusts, not when relaying the certainty of their master, their purpose, or the outcome of the judgment.

Upon reading the text surrounding the fifth trumpet judgment one is reminded of the eighth plague of Egypt when locusts appeared (Exodus 10:12–15). Through the loosing of these demon locusts of judgment the prophetic words of Joel 1:1–4 and 2:1–11 are finally realized as the Day of the Lord has come at last.

They will not harm the greenery of the earth (unlike natural locusts) as it had already been judged in Revelation 8:7, nor will they harm those who have the seal of God on their foreheads. The sealed will include the 144,000 of 7:4 and may include those who come to know Christ during the Week of Judgment, though it is not specified. It is specified, however, that those *not* having the seal of God will be targeted for severely painful judgment to last for five months, paralleling the same length of time that natural locusts would appear over the land (May to September). The act of God's supernatural protection of "the sealed" parallels the act of God's supernatural protection of Israel in Goshen during the Egyptian plagues.

Revelation 9:4–11 details the ability and appearance of the demon locusts from the bottomless pit. Despite their purpose of terror it is evident that their authority is subject to God's sovereignty as *he* commands them (9:4) and limits their terror (9:5). The appearance of the demon locusts is beyond direct description, lending to John's heavy use of symbolism via comparative articles and phrases.

There is a tendency to equate the imagery of the fifth and sixth trumpets with modern tools and mechanics of war, but this understanding is loosely founded. The supernatural but literal factor cannot be dismissed as the demon locusts are actually loosed from the bottomless pit by an angel at God's behest (9:2) and have a fallen angel as king over them (9:11). The pit itself is an actual place from which smoke pours forth and darkens the sun and air (9:2). The parameters of torment are too precise for a large modern mechanized air or ground force under human command to uphold (9:3–5). For men to seek death at the appearance and threat of such beings demands a more fearsome enemy than the too-familiar human methods of warcraft; and death itself will be kept from those seeking it. Apparently even suicide will be checked by supernatural means (9:6), at least until the sixth trumpet judgment when additional mounted demons are loosed and allowed to kill.

The "Giant" Void in Christian Doctrine

So who or what are these demon locusts, and where did they originate?

> There were giants on the earth in those days, and also afterward, when the sons of God came in to the daughters of men and bore children to them. Those were the mighty men who were of old, men of renown (Genesis 6:4).

Scripture identifies two classes of demons: 1) those disembodied wicked spirits seeking to indwell the bodies of people or animals so as to interact directly with the physical realm (Matthew 12:43–45; Luke 8:26–33; Acts 19:13–16; Enoch 15:8–12; 16:1); and 2) fallen angels (Isaiah 14:12–15; Daniel 10:10–20; Ephesians 6:11–12), some of which are imprisoned in chains of darkness and reserved for the day of judgment (2 Peter 2:4; Jude 1:6; Revelation 9; Enoch 1:3–9; 18:10—19:2).

The imprisoned ones are in confinement for the abomination they committed against Almighty God and his creation in Genesis 6:1–7, an act that simultaneously placed heightened enmity between fallen angels and humans due to its reprehensible violation—an enmity which originated when Lucifer provoked the fall of humanity as recorded in Genesis 3.

The following information illuminates much toward identifying the demon locusts, their origin, purpose, and destiny. Also clarified are many historical enigmas, theological gray areas, and misconceptions regarding God's character throughout the Old Testament.

The Nephilim *and* Rephaim

Genesis 3:15 was the first messianic prophecy given, stating that the *Seed of the woman* (proving Divine involvement through a virgin birth) would eventually conquer the seed of the serpent by bruising the serpent's head. The significance of the Seed of the woman rests in that it is physiologically the seed of the *man* that is needed to fertilize the female egg; also the seed of the man determines the sex of a child. Thus, a divine human Savior would be miraculously born into the world through a human vessel to restore what humanity could not restore to itself.

At the issuance of this prophecy, fallen archangel Lucifer/Satan (the serpent) straightaway set to work on a diabolical strategy to negate the Seed's entrance into the world. Genesis 6 gives insight into this satanic tactic: Certain fallen angels procreated with human women (or performed some manner of genetic engineering) to corrupt the human seed (genome), thereby corrupting the image in which mankind had been created and nullifying the avenue through which a Savior had been promised to arrive (Enoch 6—10:16). The generational bloodline of Abel and Seth were specifically targeted—via genetic corruption and murder—per the blessing of the messianic prophecy, but the descendants of Adam and Eve's "many other sons and daughters" would have suffered likewise as evil progressively covered the face of the earth and polluted almost all flesh (Genesis 5:4; 6:1–12).

Ultimately, only several individuals were left untainted. Abel was murdered and most of Cain's cursed lineage were bred out or given to evil; likewise with Seth's line. After 1,600 years (from creation) only eight genetically pure humans remained of Seth's blessed lineage. Then Almighty God responded to the demonic saturation of his creation by way of a great deluge, thus destroying the genetically spoiled and evil-bent humanity and saving only eight souls (Genesis 7:13; 1 Peter 3:20; Enoch 10:2, 22).

The question arises as to whether all the *righteous* genetically pure God-followers from Seth's line (and other's) were corrupted or killed prior to the flood, for it would seem unjust for them to be destroyed by God's judgment while only Noah's family was saved. The ancient book of Jasher (or Book of the Upright)[3] offers insight into God's grace:

> And all the sons of men who knew the Lord died in that year before the Lord brought evil [the flood judgment] upon them; for the Lord willed them to die, so as not to behold the evil that God would bring upon their brothers and relatives, as he had so declared to do (Jasher 5:21).

The Jasher text explains that many righteous souls did in fact turn to evil, while many other righteous were brutally killed for their belief in the Lord God. But God's graciousness led to peaceful deaths for his own who survived in that year before the flood judgment came—one of whom was Enoch's son, Methuselah (Genesis 5:21–27; Jasher 5:34–36).

Noah, Ham, Japheth, Shem, and their wives survived the flood via the ark, and being of the godly line of Seth, they preserved the messianic bloodline (from Adam to Christ) required for the eventual fulfillment of Genesis 3:15. The references in Genesis 6:9 and 7:1 that Noah and his household were "perfect" and "righteous" in his/their generations are not acclamations of personal, mental, or spiritual perfection; rather, these proclamations from God are referencing Noah and his household's *genetic perfection*, being fully human and uncorrupted by the "seed of the serpent."

The offspring of the fallen angels that initiated the unholy union between themselves and human women are called "giants," or *Nephilim* in some Bible translations (Genesis 6:4), meaning "the fallen ones" from the Hebrew word *naphal*, itself meaning "to fall." The fallen angels themselves, or progenitors, are often called the "sons of God" because they were originally a part of the heavenly host of created angels, until their rebellion under Lucifer (Genesis 6:1–2; Job 1:6; 2:1; 38:7; Enoch 64:2).

The great author J. R. R. Tolkien borrows this truth and weaves it into the backstory of his Middle-earth moral epic.[4] *The Silmarillion* is Professor Tolkien's treatment of the creation story of Middle-earth and its earliest primeval ages wherein a mighty but fallen holy one (i.e., angel) named Melkor became envious of another created race—the Elves. Therefore, in his rebellion Melkor cloaked himself in shadow and worked against the One God, Ilúvatar:

---

3. See Appendix A.
4. See Appendix B Expanded Commentary #5.

> For who of the living has descended into the pits of Utumno [Melkor's fortress], or has explored the darkness of the counsels of Melkor? Yet this is held true by the wise of Eressëa, that all those of the Quendi [Elves] who came into the hands of Melkor, ere Utumno was broken, were put there in prison, *and by slow arts of cruelty were corrupted and enslaved; and thus did Melkor breed the hideous race of Orcs in envy and mockery of Elves*, of whom they were afterwards the bitterest foes . . . This it may be was the vilest deed of Melkor, and the most hateful to Ilúvatar.[5]

Notably, nearly every region worldwide has legends of giants dwelling in the land, and a flood that was divinely sent to destroy them and/or to cleanse the earth from various sorts of evil.

When "gods" Walked the Earth

The Nephilim are identified as "heroes/mighty men of old" and "men of renown" (Genesis 6:4). Why? Unions between the fallen angels and human women resulted in highly intelligent, large-statured, and supernaturally powerful "giants" who were esteemed as *gods*, though in reality they were demonic/human half-breeds, therefore possessing already damned spirits, and possibly in some cases, perverted animalistic spirits (Romans 1:18–32; Jasher 4:18). When these giants died, for they were not physically immortal, their condemned spirits wandered (and still wander) the earth in search of physical bodies to inhabit, even after the flood (Enoch 15—16:1). The clear and present danger of these evil spirits are the reason for many warnings and examples of Jesus' authority over all manner of evil (Matthew 12:43–45; Luke 8:26–33).

Indeed, one can readily imagine the antediluvian world so full of dark influences fast becoming overtly reprobate and wicked beyond redemption, leading to the situation wherein the Lord God regretted his creation of man and was so grieved in his heart (Genesis 6:5–7).

Genesis 6:4 reveals that after the flood the unions between human women and fallen angels continued: "There were giants on the earth in those days, *and also afterward [after the flood]*, when the sons of God came in to the daughters of men and they bore children to them."

Thus, after coming so close to succeeding in his attempt to breed out humanity, Satan must have felt a surge of confidence when God

---

5. Tolkien, *The Silmarillion*, 50. Emphasis mine.

promised to never again flood the earth (Genesis 8:21; Enoch 10:22). And so, Satan began anew with the same strategy, only this time, post-flood, his craftiness disclosed a tactical shift. Perhaps Satan knew or discovered slivers (never the whole) of God's plan and worked and re-worked his defiance accordingly.

Following the calling out of Abram (Genesis 12) it would seem that the slow pace of passing generations on earth would give Satan an edge. As God prepared to raise up a new class of people to be his chosen, Satan began to saturate Canaan, the Promised Land, with another breed of demonically spawned giants in order to contest God's claim on the land. This second wave of giants were called *Rephaim*, meaning "dead ones," after Rapha, their fallen angel forefather. Human kings of the region, including Abram, often fought against these violent giants (Genesis 14:5–16), lending to their existence in the deep histories of Babylonia, Egypt, Sumeria, and other ancient kingdoms of Mesopotamia and beyond. For example, the Sumerian pantheon consisted of seven prime overlords called the *Anunnaki*, which means "sky-gods," specifically "those who descended from the sky," i.e., fallen angels. These beings are referenced in various texts (e.g., *Enmerkar and the Lord of Aratta*) discovered near the Persian Gulf and date back to circa BC 2300.

There were many tribes and cultures of these giants that dominated ancient Israel and the surrounding region: Kenites, Kadmonites, Hittites, Amorites, Canaanites, Girgashites, Jebusites, Anakims, Emims, Zamzummims, and others. The land of Ammon was a land of giants (Deuteronomy 2:19–21). A valley of giants is mentioned in Joshua 15:8 and 18:16. Joshua 13:12–13 speaks of geographical boundaries for Israel's tribes, making reference to Moses' exploits with some of these giants. Moses also recalled that the Hebrews (and humanity) would contend with many *gods* post-Babel (Deuteronomy 4:15–20; 29:23–29; 32:16–24). There is the notorious instance when ten of the twelve spies of Israel fearfully noted the vastness of fortified cities and saw themselves as "grasshoppers" compared to the Anakim giants (Numbers 13:28, 32–33). Also see Deuteronomy 1:28–30; 2:10–11; 9:1–2; Joshua 15:14; 1 Chronicles 11:23; 20:4–8; and Amos 2:9–10.

The vile Rephaim commandeered many human cities by destroying them outright or intermingling themselves within human populations by domination, even eating the inhabitants (Numbers 13:32–33). Entire giant cultures were also established and became monumental powers in the region, as in Gath, Gaza, and Ashdod of Philistia (Joshua 11:21–23). The conquest of Canaan under Joshua and Caleb was purposed to eradicate the warring giant tribes and claim the land (Joshua 12:7—13:7; 14:12–15), but Israel's cyclical disobedience of "whoring after other gods" prolonged the conflict and led to God leaving intact several giant-occupied regions with which to test Israel (Judges 2:11—3:6). One can understand why then God would proclaim, "Whoever sacrifices to any god, other than the Lord alone, shall be *devoted to destruction* [damned; from Hebrew *kherem*]" (Exodus 22:20 ESV).

Centuries of war with these giant cultures commenced, giving rise to seemingly questionable practices Israel was commanded by God to perform toward ensuring total victory. However, understanding the unholy genetic makeup of these giants and their satanically-driven intent to destroy Israel helps one to more readily accept the instances in Scripture where God (who is holy) commands Israel's armies to destroy every last *man, woman, child, and beast* of these genetically profane societies, as they were beyond redemption—the beasts/livestock thereof being at times critically unclean for having been in the giants' possession (Deuteronomy 3:4-6; 1 Samuel 15:3). Herein, war is how God primarily extinguished the giants on the earth after the great flood, though he settled the issue by imprisoning the fallen angels specifically involved in the genetic desecration of humanity and forbade the remaining fallen from pursuing the task (Psalm 82; Jude 1:6; Enoch 12—14:7; 18:10–16).

Remaining giants did persist for many subsequent generations, however, as they migrated away from the Canaanite epicenter and sought prominence around the world. This was undoubtedly a devilishly designed flood of untruth intending to corrupt and dilute divine truth toward foiling God's grand purpose.

The Giant Tale We Know

By the time of King David, Israel was well-established in the land and in warfare. Rising national powers all around were of serious concern, whether enemy or ally. With fewer giants—and their days numbered—they were seen less seldom on the battlefield, thus becoming more political in their kingships and using human armies to fight their wars, accented by giant auxiliaries and champions (1 Samuel 21:10-15).

Notably, at just over nine feet tall, Goliath of Gath was one of these Rephaim champions (1 Samuel 17:4-7), as was Og, king of Bashan, who stood nearly eighteen feet (Deuteronomy 3:11). In David's latter years, he leads Israel in a war with Philistia where four of Goliath's vengeful brothers are killed (2 Samuel 21:15–22; 1 Chronicles 20:4–8). Intriguingly, 1 Samuel 17:40 records that a younger David, just before confronting Goliath in a duel to the death, gathered *five* smooth stones for his sling. Some have contended that David lacked faith in the accuracy of his sling shot, or that he believed it may have taken more than one stone to bring down the giant. I assert that David seriously considered the possibility that Goliath's *four* brothers would attempt to avenge their sibling's defeat immediately upon his death! One stone for each of them. David's faith was solid, in himself and in his God.

Moreover, there is a prophetic connection here with Genesis 3:15. Goliath was of the seed of the serpent (Rephaim), and David was of the seed of the woman (human messianic lineage). Goliath's scale armor and venomous words against Israel signified serpentine intent. David killed the giant with a stone to the head which he then cut off (1 Samuel 17:48–51), Goliath thus suffering the same fate as his god Dagon (1 Samuel 5:1–4). Thus the seed of the woman crushed the head of the seed of the serpent. In perfect prophetic symmetry, David's victory over Goliath portends Christ's victory over the devil.

The Giant Tales We May Not Know

As Israel grew in might and cunning, many remaining giants must have determined to seek glory elsewhere, for we see them establishing and reestablishing dominance within (if not originating) the superpowers of the region: Egypt, Babylonia, Assyria, the Hittite Kingdom, et al. This historical flow of nations fits perfectly into God's dealings with both Israel and world kingdoms (Daniel 2:21–22).[6]

It is highly probable that the Nephilim/Rephaim were in fact the gods of many ancient kingdoms like Egypt, the mountain kingdom of Urartu/Aratta, and the fabled Midas City in Asia Minor. They are most likely the Titans and Olympians of Greek mythology as well as the origin of the Roman Pantheon, considering that the Romans adopted and

---

6. For highly acclaimed and satisfying scholarship concerning the intricate histories of Israel and surrounding world kingdoms and nations, please enjoy the following volumes: *Ancient Post-Flood History,* Ken Johnson (biblefacts.org, 2010); *The Chronology of the Old Testament,* Floyd N. Jones; *The Exodus Case: New Discoveries of the Historical Exodus,* Lennart Moller; *The History of the Ancient World,* Susan W. Bauer.

reworked the Greek legends as their own. Rome itself has a colorful birth mythos involving twin boys named Romulus and Remus born to a virgin princess, Rhea Silvia, who claimed to have been raped by the god Mars.[7] Notably, the Greek biographer Plutarch records that the twins' appearance was "of more than human size and beauty."[8]

The great warrior Aeneas, a veteran of the Trojan War and cousin of the slain Hector, also bears striking *giant* characteristics. Virgil's epic *The Aeneid* expands on Homer's *Iliad* and *Odyssey* and chronicles Aeneas' sojourn from Troy to Italy where he settles in the heart of Latium just in time to help a neophyte Rome rise in both lawful and martial prowess, thus helping Rome find its identity. Unlike the individualistic and deadly Olympian Achilles, Aeneas is not bent on destroying cities but founding them for the betterment of the peoples both within and without their walls. Truly, such a cosmopolitan piety may seem odd for a Rephaim when one is aware of their origin. But with the imprisonment of those fallen angels who initiated the rise of the giants, coupled with thinning numbers due to successful wars fought against them, it is plausible that a tactical shift in survival philosophy would develop.

This thinking illuminates the plausibility of some actual truth behind the fantastical arcane legends. Early church voices such as Origen, Philo, and Justin Martyr offered comment on this sobering reality.[9] And since there were giants on the earth even *after* the flood, could not some have ended up in Egypt, Macedonia, Scandinavia, the Americas, or elsewhere?[10] This would associate mythical, religious, engineering, and architectural similarities between many civilizations despite geographical and chronological distance. Truth is often stranger than fiction, and in this case it actually is. And it makes more sense.

In sum, the imprisoned angels that kept not their proper domain, but rebelled and gave themselves over to sexual immorality in pursuit of strange flesh (humanity), have been held in reserve only to be unleashed upon the earth at God's command to be his hand of judgment on an unbelieving world prior to their own final doom (Jude 1:6–7). That these incarcerated angels are in fact the demon locusts and horsemen of Revelation 9 is proven in that nowhere else in Scripture do these imprisoned

---

7. Livy, *The Early History of Rome* 1.4, 37–38. Also Cotterell/Storm, *World Mythology*, 80–81.

8. Plutarch, *Romulus*, in *Plutarch's Lives*, vol. 1, 27.

9. Origen, *Contra Celsum* 4.92; Philo, *On the Giants* 6; Justin Martyr, *2 Apology* 5.

10. See Appendix B Expanded Commentary #6.

angels of Jude 1:6 make a post-detention appearance. Also, Revelation 9 reveals the macabre details of their duty as foreordained by God upon their confinement. One could not conjure imagery so dark as the nefarious savagery to be wrought by these vile beings upon their temporary future discharge into the world.

The events outlined above in tandem with the Scripture referenced serve to prove with finality that God's sovereignty cannot be removed or diminished, even when the world allies against him. Moreover, we find that the seed of the serpent, though not at all a divine miracle, was just as literal and supernatural as the truly divine miracle of the Seed of the virgin woman. However, Lucifer—a created being—is not on equal footing with God; he is not one side of a divine yin-yang. At the cross, Jesus Christ crushed the head of the serpent and fulfilled the Genesis 3:15 prophecy. It is finished.

Let us thank our awesome and loving God for sending us his son, Jesus Christ, to die in our stead so that we may spend our eternal lives *in peace* and *at peace* with him, rather than with the damned who shall suffer eternal oblivion, anguish, and separation from all that is good (John 3:16–21).

THE SIXTH TRUMPET/SECOND WOE: DEMON HORSEMEN

"Then the sixth angel sounded: And I heard a voice from the four horns of the golden altar which is before God, saying to the sixth angel who had the trumpet, 'Release the four angels who are bound at the great river Euphrates.' So the four angels, who had been prepared for the hour and day and month and year, were released to kill a third of mankind.

Now the number of the army of the horsemen was two hundred million . . . But the rest of mankind, who were not killed by these plagues . . . did not repent of their murders or their sorceries or their sexual immorality or their thefts" (Revelation 9:13–21).

The horned golden altar from which a voice proceeded is the same as mentioned in Revelation 8:3, connecting the coming judgment with the prayers of the saints (8:3–4). Blood sprinkled on the horns of the altar in the earthly tabernacle represented mercy toward those who had sinned in ignorance (Leviticus 4), but in the passage above mercy has become judgment for the rejection of Christ and willful ignorance.

The four angels to be released are fallen angels (holy angels are never bound), referring again to the fallen angels reserved for the day of judgment (Jude 1:6). The precision of the four angels' release being "prepared for the hour and day and month and year" discourages attempts at a non-literal understanding of the events revealed in the passage and proves God's historical and prophetic authority. The Lord God often uses wicked agents to fulfill his purpose—Pharaoh, Judas, fallen angels, etc., making even man's wrath ultimately praise God.

The significance of the Euphrates River is realized in knowing that it is the eastern border of Old Testament Israel, separating the Holy Land from her enemies, Babylon and Assyria, from whence came godly judgment on occasion. This parallel cannot be ignored as the judgments of Revelation are focused primarily upon an unbelieving Israel that routinely failed to be the "priesthood among nations."

There is no need to spiritualize the reference to this great river, for a literal meaning is proven in its mention as an actual place of imprisonment for the four fallen angels and as a place where the demon horsemen rally behind their four fiendish "generals" prior to setting out on their campaign to kill a third of mankind.

Being that such judgment comes from the east (Euphrates River) it is unspecified as to whether the third of mankind to be killed means a third of the population of the Middle East, North Africa, and Eurasia or a third of the population of the earth. Yet the text suggests that a third of *all* mankind is targeted, for at this point of the Tribulation the judgments worsen in severity and reach, as proven in Revelation 8:13 when the warning angel flies through the earth's atmosphere proclaiming, "Woe, Woe, Woe to the *inhabitants of the earth!*"

The impact of previous judgments will already have begun to affect the world at large—economically, civically, socially, emotionally, and physically at the very least. Recall that Revelation 6:8 records the slaying of a fourth of mankind. The demonic horsemen are charged with destroying a third of mankind—a third of what is left! One-fourth plus one-third of three-fourths equals one half. So by the fulfillment of the sixth trumpet one half of the earth's population will be slain.

Revelation 9:16–19 explains the 200 million horsemen's appearance and purpose. The analysis of the demon "locusts" of the previous trumpet judgment shows them to be literal supernatural demonic creatures. Likewise, the demonic "horsemen" are of the same origin (Abyss; the pit) with the same purpose of bringing judgment upon the moral creation.

However, while the demon locusts will *torment* humanity, the demon horsemen will actually *kill*.

The difference in assignment between the two groups also lends to their different overseers; the demon locusts have a king over them, while the demon horsemen have four "angel-generals" to lead them. This logistical ordering of hierarchy and mission even within the ranks of fallen angels testifies to the overall sovereignty of the Lord God as he orchestrates every aspect of his systematic judgment.

Revelation 9:20-21 states that the "rest of mankind, who were not killed by these plagues, did not repent." From this verse we may conclude that those killed by the demon horsemen will be individuals who have rejected Christ and his salvation, for the unrepentant will be systematically purged from the earth (*systematically* for the sole reason of expressing God's grace even amidst final doom). But even with space to repent, hundreds of millions of souls will die in their *chosen rebellion* against God. Their freedom of choice is proven in that space is given to repent, an unnecessary grace if the choice to repent were not an option. Worse still, the rest of mankind who were not killed by the demon horsemen remained unrepentant.

To this sad response, H. A. Ironside laments, "If the cross of Christ, with its marvelous exhibition of holy love, will not reconcile men to God, punishment will never avail to win their hearts either."[11]

Revelation 9:4 supports the idea of continued protection for those who are "sealed."

Clarifying the Context

Some expositors attempt to equate the 200 million demonic horsemen with the "kings from the east" of Revelation 16:12 since it speaks of the "great river Euphrates" being dried up in preparation for the eastern kings' advance on Israel.

This understanding is not sound in that Revelation 16 details the bowl judgments which are different from the trumpet judgments and "the way of the kings from the east" is only then *prepared* for their later passage (the Euphrates boasts a series of Russian built dams that make possible its "drying up" if not done supernaturally). Revelation 16:13-16 then reveals that Satan sends out unclean spirits (like frogs) to gather *"the*

---

11. Ironside, *Revelation*, 98.

kings of the earth and of the whole world" (including the kings of the east) to bring them together for the final battle of Armageddon at the end of the Tribulation.

The "kings of the east" are men, not demons. And these men will be moving toward the marshaling point in the valley of Esdraelon (the valley of Armageddon) where the push toward final confrontation will begin between Antichrist's army and those allied against him (Daniel 11:40–45).

Clearly, the role of the eastern kings of Revelation 16:12 is not to destroy a third of mankind for they themselves will be destroyed by Christ at the second advent (Revelation 19:19–21). Moreover, they are not referenced as being "released" as agents of judgment, only as being "gathered" for "the battle of that great day of God Almighty." Furthermore, the timing of the release of the four bound angels and the demon horsemen of the sixth trumpet is well prior to the drying up of the Euphrates (sixth bowl). And the drying up of the Euphrates is a direct result of an angel pouring out the sixth bowl judgment on the river itself, not the result of the bound angels and horsemen being released.

Previously, after discussing the sixth seal judgment and prior to analyzing the seventh seal, a parenthetical interlude was highlighted. Now, after examining the sixth trumpet judgment and immediately prior to examining the seventh trumpet, we again encounter supplemental material that enriches our comprehension and clarifies interpretation in both the retrospective and prospective contexts.

The proleptic character of passages will become more prominent through the remainder of the book of Revelation. *Proleptic* simply means that events of the future are expressed as though they had already taken place.[12] An example is seen in Revelation 6:17 with the proclamation, "the great day of his wrath has come, and who is able to stand?"

This peculiar use of tense occurs because John was shown future events as an eyewitness, being "in the Spirit" and actually present in the future contextual witness of history.

---

12. Smith, *A Revelation of Jesus Christ*, 149.

10

The Little Scroll and the Two Witnesses
Parenthetic Revelation II

I SAW STILL ANOTHER mighty angel coming down from heaven, clothed with a cloud. And a rainbow was on his head, his face was like the sun, and his feet like pillars of fire. He had a little book open in his hand. And he set his right foot on the sea and his left foot on the land (Revelation 10:1–2).

Revelation 10:1–4 describes "another mighty angel coming down from heaven" as having a majestic appearance, holding a little scroll (or book), setting his right foot upon the sea and his left upon the earth, and making an announcement resulting in the utterance of seven thunders. Clearly, the visionary scene has shifted from the heavenly tabernacle back to earth.

Though the angel exhibits majesty, it is not Jesus Christ, as some speculate, because this angel *descends from heaven* and nowhere does Scripture indicate that Jesus would return to the earth (even figuratively) before or during Jacob's trouble prior to his second advent. Also, the indication of this being "another angel" puts it in the contextual similarity of those other angels/messengers as utilized in previous tasks concerning the final judgments.

Notice, too, that John does not fall down and worship this angel. Jesus is never equated with or referred to as an angel in apocalyptic literature. Even the autonym "Angel of the Lord" is an Old Testament title for a pre-incarnate Christ, which has no bearing in the Apocalypse or for a resurrected Christ.

The angel indeed displays certain attributes of God that are meant to convey the surety of God's sovereignty over all of heaven and the earth, even amidst judgment. God's holiness is represented by the sunlike face; his mercy and covenant faithfulness are indicated by the rainbow; and just judgment is revealed by the descent from heaven clothed with a cloud coupled with feet like pillars of fire.

The placement of the angel's feet upon both sea and land simply signifies authority over creation, thereby proving the divine privilege to judge it. It may be that this stance, or claim, is in open defiance of Lucifer's attempted planetary consolidation under his own foul rule.

The scroll in the angel's hand is not the scroll of Revelation 5:1 (which was in Jesus' hand), and though no information is given as to its contents, it must represent the prophetic Word, as will be seen.

Upon hearing the utterance of the "seven thunders," John prepared to record their truth, but was forbidden to do so, paralleling a similar circumstance experienced by Daniel and Paul (Daniel 12:9; 2 Corinthians 12:4).

Amos 3:8 describes God's voice as that of a roaring lion and Psalm 29:3–9 displays God's voice as being thunderous and sevenfold—"the God of glory thunders." Other than echoing glory, consider that thunder is indicative of a coming storm; therefore, *seven* thunders would be anticipatory of coming *storms*, heralding further and harsher judgment. The angel utters the very voice of God. John does the same in his recording of the Revelation.

Revelation 10:5–6 describes the angel lifting his hand to heaven, making an oath to God (who is greater than the angel) and proclaiming there would be no further delay in the fulfillment of those things which must come to pass prior to the Lord's return. The oath to God would not be necessary if this angel were Christ himself.

Revelation 10:7 shows John being informed that when the seventh trumpet sounds "the mystery of God would be finished," as declared to the prophets. J. B. Smith states,

> The mystery of God is a general term, *signifying the sum total of all that it has pleased God to reveal to man concerning his counsel and purposes in the world.* The seventh trumpet includes all that God purposes still to reveal, by which is meant not that the end has come when the trumpet sounds, but that the *revelation* of the mystery will then be concluded.[1]

---

1. Smith, *A Revelation of Jesus Christ*, 160. Emphasis mine.

EATING THE WORD OF GOD

"Then the voice which I heard from heaven spoke to me again and said, 'Go, take the little book which is open in the hand of the angel who stands on the sea and on the earth.' So I went to the angel and said to him, 'Give me the little book.' And he said to me, 'Take and eat it; and it will make your stomach bitter, but it will be as sweet as honey in your mouth.' Then I took the little book out of the angel's hand and ate it, and it was as sweet as honey in my mouth. But when I had eaten it, my stomach became bitter. And he said to me, 'You must prophesy again about many peoples, nations, tongues, and kings'" (Revelation 10:8–11).

The command to John to eat the scroll is paralleled in Ezekiel 2:9—3:4 and Jeremiah 15:16–18. Again, this book must be the prophetic Word of God (Psalm 119:103). Eating it means to partake of its contents—the promises *and* the judgments—and to live by applying to one's life the truth of those contents. Speculating exactly what else this scroll may be is fruitless.

Notice that twice John is told to *take* the scroll in the angel's hand. It is not given to him. Even when John asks the angel to give him the scroll, he is instructed to take it. God's revelatory truth is never forced upon anyone; John (and we) must choose to taste and see the Lord's goodness (Joshua 24:15; Job 12:11; Psalm 34:8; 119:103; Hebrews 6:5; 1 Peter 2:3). William Barclay adds that "God's messenger must be in the end a willing messenger, not a conscript, but one who has put out his hand to the task."[2]

Eating the Word of God also suggests that before one can be a mouthpiece for him, one must *digest* the Word by meditating/feeding on it. The sweetness in the mouth followed by bitterness in the belly indicates the quality of God's Word. The sweetness comes to John (and us) in the promises of our Lord's blessings and his soon return; the bitterness comes as we are confronted with the fact that hard judgment must be enacted upon the earth and unbelievers.

Prophetic truth is often sweet, particularly to new Christians. But when such truth is contemplated and digested it leads to self-examination, self-discipline, sacrifice, and sanctification in the Spirit. This task is ever bitter due to the rebellion of our flesh. Yet God's truth demands discipline to hearken unto his will and thus receive power to walk in the blessedness of obedience (1 Samuel 15:22; 2 Corinthians 10:3–6).

---

2. Barclay, *The Revelation of John*, vol. 2, 69.

In one of his letters, John tells us that everyone who truly looks for the return of Jesus will purify themselves—via discipline toward Christlikeness—because Jesus' purity and fellowship is specifically sought, not just the reward of heaven (1 John 3:3). The hard truth of the true cost of discipleship either transforms people completely or hardens them into compromising waywardness, thereby searing their consciences with a hot iron and tempting either a designer discipleship of the flesh or an outright departure from the faith (1 Timothy 4:1–2).

The stark truth of the Revelation in concert with the hard realities of Christian persecution inspired and enabled the church to grow swiftly in its first few centuries, resulting in contagious holy fervor and the expansion of the heavenly kingdom on earth. However, when outward regional persecution diminished and the cares of the world began to crowd out deep love for Christ, Jesus' warnings to the church became—and remain, particularly in the West—dangerously urgent (Matthew 13:22; Revelation 2–3). Today, as radical relativism is touted religiously, the need for absolute truth concerning what is good and evil has never been greater. Only the incarnate Word of God, Jesus Christ, offers the absolute revelation that can absolutely save a soul.[3]

THE TEMPLE OF REJECTION

"Then I was given a reed like a measuring rod. And the angel stood, saying, 'Rise and measure the temple of God, the altar, and those who worship there. But leave out the court which is outside the temple, and do not measure it, for it has been given to the Gentiles. And they will tread the holy city underfoot for forty-two months'" (Revelation 11:1–2).

It is important to remember that the continued focus of the time of Jacob's trouble is expressly upon the *Jewish people and nation*. As such, look for repeated references to the holy city, the court, the temple, the altar, olive trees, lampstands, etc.

Revelation 11 is considered by some to be one of the most complex and confusing chapters in the book; but this only results with attempts to replace Israel with the church, thus forcing the church into a vision and historical/prophetic context where it does not belong, which also wrongly forces the church into many Old Testament prophecies. Performing this

---

3. For expanded discussion of this theme, see Horton, *The Portable Seminary*, 336–44.

injustice to Scripture attacks scriptural integrity and creates interpretive assumptions that are blatantly false, leading to deviant theologies that are founded on human reason and loose allegorical ideals and not on the truth of God's Word. The apostle Paul warned of such doctrinal trends and trickery (Ephesians 4:14–15).

Chapter 11, verse 1 describes John being given a reed to measure the temple, the altar, and those who worship there. This symbolic act historically parallels that performed by Ezekiel and Zechariah. However, here in Revelation 11 no measurement is given, alluding to the idea that both the temple and those who worship therein *fall short* in their purpose, as this rebuilt last-days temple/tabernacle (the first since AD 70) will be a "temple of rejection" since the reinstitution of the sacrificial system will be a Jewish declaration that Israel does not accept Jesus Christ as Messiah (though still intending to honor Yahweh).

That a temple/tabernacle will be constructed in Jerusalem in the last days is also indicated by Paul (2 Thessalonians 2:3–4). Moreover, this new temple/tabernacle will be built on the basis of a "covenant with death, and with hell," i.e., a treaty with the Antichrist (Daniel 9:27; Isaiah 28:15). Further proof that this will be a temple of rejection rests in the fact that there is no mention of the glory of the Lord filling the temple as he filled both the tabernacle in the wilderness and Solomon's temple upon its completion (Exodus 40:34; 2 Chronicles 7:1).

In contrast, Revelation 21:9–27 describes the New Jerusalem and its *exact measurements* via an angel that accompanies John. There is also no temple (in the former sense) in this perfect city—the New Jerusalem—for God Almighty and the Lamb are its temple (Revelation 21:22).

DOCTRINES OF REJECTION

Several theories place the writing of Revelation much earlier than AD 95, averring instead a date circa AD 64 *prior* to the fall of Jerusalem in AD 70, insisting that the destruction of the temple and surrounding chaos of that time fulfills most of John's prophecy. This thinking has also asserted that the temple of Revelation 11 is the one ruined in AD 70 because John could not have had a vision of a Jewish temple that did not exist. Truly? Consider the presumptive arrogance of such a belief that limits God to what he can or cannot reveal to his servants!

Schools of thought such as preterist, post-millennialism, and amillennialism dismiss a last-days Jewish temple or a prophetically significant modern state of Israel. The idea of John conveying a nonliteral "spiritual temple" is likewise popular. Indeed, these are efforts to avoid the inconvenient truth of most prophecies in Revelation being future-oriented—a point of contention for those who esteem their preferred personal doctrines higher than Scripture itself.

Theories of historical and biblical revisionism that replace Israel with the church, that redefine divine covenants, that deny a pre-wrath rapture of the church, and that allegorize nearly everything only serve to wreak havoc on a straightforward understanding of God's perfect narrative as *he* tells it throughout his Word. It must be stated, however, that such heresies (intentionally errant or not) often benefit the church in unintended ways, forcing the church to develop and articulate better theological orthodoxy—a thoroughly systematic statement of biblical revelation.[4] With this in mind, the near indisputable scriptural and traditionally accepted historical fact that the Revelation was written circa AD 95 cannot be ignored.[5]

The Bible itself reinforces that John prophesied of a yet future temple in that two previous prophets—Ezekiel and Daniel—also prophesied of a future temple when it was yet non-existent. Ezekiel was commanded to measure the temple in a vision long after it had been demolished by Nebuchadnezzar's armies (Ezekiel 40–44). Daniel predicted the temple's desecration while there was no temple standing in Israel (Daniel 9:26–27). Here then is biblical precedent for John to prophesy concerning events surrounding and affecting a literal future temple/tabernacle in Israel. Irresponsible theories and bad theology are doomed attempts to rob God of his sovereignty and sure Word of prophecy.

Revelation 11:2 is the angel's command to John *not* to measure the outer court, as it has been given to the Gentiles, and will be trampled (along with the holy city) for three and one-half years (forty-two months). As with verse 1, the context of verse 2 is the first half of the seven-year Tribulation, since the "fullness of the Gentiles has come in" and the church age of the Lord's favor upon the Gentiles (nations) has ended (at Israel's covenant with Antichrist).

---

4. Shelley, *Church History*, 3rd ed., 47.
5. See Appendix B Expanded Commentary #1.

THE TWO WITNESSES

"And I will give power to my two witnesses, and they will prophesy one thousand two hundred and sixty days, clothed in sackcloth.' These are the two olive trees and the two lampstands standing before the God of the earth" (Revelation 11:3-4).

Accompanying the 144,000 Jewish witnesses in their gospel mission throughout the earth during the Tribulation, two powerful witnesses will arise in Israel and will prophesy in Jerusalem against the Antichrist and his kingdom (Revelation 11:3-13). Two is the number of testimony (John 8:17; Exodus 31:18), and these two will prophesy for 1,260 days (forty-two months). Whereas the 144,000 will minister for the duration of the seven years of judgment, the two witnesses shall do so publicly for only the first three and one-half years. The two are clothed in sackcloth as they are in mourning over the travail of Israel and are determined to induce Israel to repent for her millennia of rejecting Messiah.

They shall have power to issue plagues and drought as often as they desire, and anyone trying to overtake them will be destroyed by fire from the witnesses' mouths. Whether the fire issues literally from their mouths or falls from heaven at their command is not explained, but the result is the same and evokes God's words to Jeremiah: *"I am making my words in your mouth a fire, and this people wood, and the fire shall consume them"* (Jeremiah 5:14 ESV).

Hyperbole is an effective teaching tool where exaggeration is used to illustrate a literal truth. The idea of fire-breathing prophets burns into one's mind the truth of God's judgment on those who reject him. Thus, fiery retribution rests in the mouths of the two witnesses who are given command of such by God. Jesus also used hyperbole (and humor) to express profound truth (Matthew 23:24; Luke 18:25).

This deathly display of judgment is fitting, however, for the two witnesses are the "two olive trees and the two lampstands standing before the God of the earth" (Revelation 11:4). Oil from the olive tree is what fuels the flames upon the temple lampstands, and the flames explicitly symbolize the Holy Spirit and his perfect judgment.

Zechariah saw in a vision these two witnesses being prepared in heaven for their future ministry against the Antichrist and a stiff-necked Israel: *These are the two anointed ones, who stand by the Lord of the whole earth* (Zechariah 4:11-14 ESV).

At the midpoint of the Tribulation the Antichrist (the "beast" of Revelation 13:1–10) has the two witnesses killed (God allows this; Revelation 11:7). Their bodies are shamefully displayed for three and a half days somewhere in Jerusalem, yet the entire world (via modern technology) will be able to watch what happens to those who oppose Antichrist. A victorious atmosphere will ensue as "those who dwell on the earth will rejoice over them, make merry, and send gifts to one another, because these two prophets tormented those who dwell on the earth" (Revelation 11:10).

Jerusalem is referenced as "the great city which spiritually is called Sodom and Egypt, where also our Lord was crucified" (Revelation 11:8). This calls to mind the rejection God has received from Sodom, Egypt, and Israel, reinforcing the just purpose of God's wrath being poured out.

After three and a half days the Spirit of God will enter the dead prophets' bodies and the world (and Antichrist) will witness their resurrection and ascension into heaven. Fear will fall on those who see this miracle and in the same hour a great earthquake levels a tenth of the city of Jerusalem, killing *seven thousand* and causing many who are unsaved (perhaps mostly Jews) to suddenly give glory to the God of heaven! This proclamation may seem suspect as a reaction under great duress, yet the context does not imply an insincere utterance. Rather, John's writing testifies that they *gave glory* to God, a response provoked by an understanding of salvation and an expressive heart of deep gratitude. This is entirely in keeping with the prophetic message of Isaiah 26:9 (ESV), "... when your judgments are in the earth, the inhabitants of the world *learn righteousness*."

WHO WILL THE TWO WITNESSES/PROPHETS BE?

The two witnesses will most certainly be Elijah and Enoch, two prophets from Old Testament history that warned of idolatry, corruption, false prophets, and the return of the King (1 Kings 17–19; Jude 1:14–15; book of Enoch). This is fitting since upon being sent back to earth they would be opposing the Antichrist and warning Israel not to see him as any type of messiah. Furthermore, both Elijah (a Jew) and Enoch (a Gentile) escaped death through bodily transportation into heaven (Genesis 5:24; 2 Kings 2:11), and since it is *appointed to men to die once* (Hebrews 9:27), their deaths would thus be fulfilled during Israel's final judgment (Seventieth Week) and their public resurrection into glory would indeed be a wondrous testimony and bookend to their earthly ministry! With God anything is possible, yet everything he accomplishes is done with perfect theological reason.

At their previous death-defying departure from earth into heaven—a foreshadowing of the rapture—neither Enoch nor Elijah received an incorruptible resurrection body, for such would negate Jesus himself being the "firstfruits" of those who die and are resurrected into glory (1 Corinthians 15:20–23). Therefore, *the only two individuals in pre-rapture history who have not tasted death are Enoch and Elijah.* These two men have been actively preserved in heaven in their natural bodies; the how of such a circumstance is certainly a divine mystery!

There is, however, a generation that will *never* taste death, due to the rapture, and is anomalous concerning the above reference in Hebrews. Titus 2:11–13 presents this "blessed hope" and the apostle Paul reveals to us the mystery of the rapture in that "we shall not *all* sleep [die physically], but we shall all be changed" from corruption to incorruption (1 Corinthians 15:51–54 ESV). If Enoch or Elijah had indeed received incorruptible resurrection bodies at their translation into heaven, then Paul would not have been revealing a rapture "mystery" at all and would surely have used such an example.

Some prominent and respectable prophecy scholars claim that Moses rather than Enoch will accompany Elijah in his end-time ministry. The certainty of Elijah as one of the two witnesses is supported by Malachi 4:5 (ESV) wherein God proclaims, *"Behold, I will send you Elijah the prophet before the great and awesome day of the Lord comes."*

With no such defining Scripture reference for Enoch, however, textual and mental gymnastics have surprisingly arisen in the considerations of many learned minds. The *absence* of an explicit passage proving Enoch as Elijah's compatriot in no way leaves room for wild speculation or dogmatic assertion. As such, just as the word "trinity" is not found in Scripture, the triune nature of God is undeniably evident and present as a foundational reality to anyone intimately involved with God's Word (Isaiah 48:16; Matthew 3:16–17; 28:19).

Oddly, the arguments for Moses being one of the two witnesses are decidedly vague and opinionated, as if out of a desire to maintain an outdated inferior view held by long-favored and honorable teachers. Although certainly not a salvation issue, and surely a topic for lively discussion and research, interpretive logic proves that Moses cannot be one of the two witnesses of Revelation 11, primarily due to the fact that Moses died physically and was buried in the land of Moab by the

Lord himself (Deuteronomy 34:5–8). And, via Michael the archangel, God protected Moses' body from defilement by the devil (but not from natural elements and decomposition), again refuting a bodily resurrection or translation (Jude 1:9).

If Moses were one of the two witnesses he would thus die twice. The fact that Lazarus of Bethany died and was resurrected to live and then again die a physical death does not support the case of Moses being a last-days witness in that Lazarus was only dead four days and his body had only begun to corrupt, then being healed anew by Jesus but not given an immortal body (John 11:38–44). Moses' body ultimately was buried and decomposed entirely, his spirit now having been in heaven for several millennia without the resurrection body he awaits.

Finis Dake, addressing Matthew 27:51–53, states,

> It is true that a few have been raised from the dead temporarily, to show the glory of God, but *no such person has ever seen corruption [entirely decomposed] nor has he ever undergone his appointed death and lived again* in this life to die the second time.[6]

Some believe Moses and Elijah are the only two prophets who performed the powers to be displayed by the two witnesses, but this is incorrect and particularly so in that Elijah's disciple Elisha was blessed with a double-portion of Elijah's ministry (2 Kings 2:8–15). A prophet does not *possess* power to perform miracles, it is God's power impartially expressed through a chosen (and humble) vessel.

Others believe that Moses and Elijah's appearance at Christ's transfiguration (Matthew 17:1–4) vouches for them being the two witnesses; but this too is false and based on a presumptively forced context, for Moses' presence in tandem with Elijah in no way proves him to be the second witness of Revelation 11.

Moses' spirit would indeed be identifiable via the Holy Spirit, proven by Peter's reaction (despite their having never met), but Moses' appearance at the transfiguration strictly represented the Law while Elijah represented the Prophets, perfectly capturing the fulfillment of all Old Testament statutes and prophecies concerning the life and ministry of Jesus (Luke 24:44). Such powerful symbolism pointing to literal fulfillment was not lost on Peter, James, and John.

In reference to symbolism, many commentators both past and present believe the two witnesses to represent the church, arguing that

---

6. Dake, *Revelation Expounded*, 110. Emphasis mine.

the book of Revelation is mostly symbolic and thus the two witnesses should not be taken literally.[7] Per contra, as discussed throughout this study, symbols in Scripture are never ambiguous and always point to specifically literal things with absolutely definitive reason. The biblical cross-testament and prophetic contexts of the two witnesses evinces two individual men with a distinct purpose at the end of the age who have no affiliation with the church.

Consequently, when all of Scripture is weighed, and considering what we know of Enoch in light of Hebrews 9:27, it makes sublime sense that Enoch will accompany Elijah to fulfill a spectacular God-ordained mission in the first half of the time of Jacob's trouble. The early church father Oecumenius adamantly taught this understanding; in fact, "From the second century onward it was common opinion that Enoch would accompany Elijah as forerunners of Christ at the end of time."[8]

For those who wonder what Elijah and Enoch have been doing since being taken into the heavenly presence of Almighty God, examine Zechariah 4 and consider the circumstance of preparation required for the "two olive trees" prior to such an awesome assignment.

"*The second woe is past. Behold, the third woe is coming quickly!*"
(Revelation 11:14)

The seventh trumpet/third woe begins the judgments of the second half of the Tribulation, which are far worse than what has come previously.

THE SEVENTH TRUMPET/THIRD WOE: PREPARATION FOR FINAL JUDGMENT

"*Then the seventh angel sounded: And there were loud voices in heaven, saying, 'The kingdoms of this world have become the kingdoms of our Lord and his Christ, and he shall reign forever and ever.'* . . . *Then the temple of*

---

7. For an outline of the varied views, see Rhodes, *8 Great Debates of Bible Prophecy*, 166–67.

8. Oden and Weinrich, *Revelation*, 159; Oecumenius, *Commentary on the Apocalypse* 11.3–6; Tertullian, *On the Soul* 50; Hippolytus, *On the Antichrist* 43; Irenaeus, *Against Heresies* 5.5.1.

God was opened in heaven, and the ark of his covenant was seen in his temple. And there were lightnings, noises, thunderings, an earthquake, and great hail" (Revelation 11:15–19).

With the blowing of the seventh trumpet we exit the previous parenthetical section concerning the little book and the two witnesses, and we are given another glimpse into heaven.

The seventh trumpet/third woe does not initiate anything on earth; however, just as the breaking of the seventh seal in Revelation 8:1 introduced the trumpet judgments with a heavenly silence, the seventh trumpet introduces the seven bowl judgments. These final verses of chapter 11 take place exclusively in heaven, yet the activities revealed project meaning to the earth, which shall be disclosed in detail in Revelation 15 and 16.

The announcement that "the kingdoms of this world have become the kingdoms of our Lord and his Christ" heralds the soon actuation of this fact. The twenty-four elders, initiating worship of Almighty God, offer him praise and gratitude for fulfilling his promises. Compare Revelation 11:17–18 with Psalm 2 and Psalm 50:1–6.

Then there is an awesome display of the Ark of the Covenant as it sits in the temple of God, to which William Barclay shares profound insight:

> Why the special reference to the Ark of the Covenant? This is to remind people of God's special covenant with his own people. Originally that covenant had been with the people Israel; but the new covenant is the covenant in Jesus Christ with all of every nation who love and who believe in Jesus. . . . So this picture is a picture of the coming of the full glory of God, which is a terrifying threat to the enemies of God, but an uplifting promise to the people of God's covenant.[9]

To better comprehend the chronology of the events of the preceding and following passages of Scripture, it helps to realize that immediately after this heavenly introduction to the bowl judgments (via the seventh trumpet), there is *another* lengthy parenthetical section outlining details of events taking place throughout the *entire* Tribulation. These events include a historical summary of Israel, a war and the persecution of God's children (Revelation 12), the Antichrist and False Prophet (Revelation 13), a heavenly vision (Revelation 14), and the introduction to the last half of the Tribulation (Revelation 15).

---

9. Barclay, *The Revelation of John*, vol. 2, 90.

There is an increasing amount of symbolic language as we progress further into Jesus' revelation to John; and this midpoint is where many individuals become further unsure or misled concerning the various interpretations of the book of Revelation. I encourage the reader to recall our earlier instruction (in the Introduction) that all the symbols in Revelation are rooted in the Old Testament and represent literal things or truths—Scripture interprets Scripture.

The odd imagery and signs that John records are not open for everyone to interpret as they wish. Rather, such are founded on clear biblical themes and many traditions and contexts of John's day. Therefore, a thorough understanding of the Bible *and* history make studying Revelation less daunting and much more rewarding. My continuing prayer is that this commentary may be both helpful and enlightening toward such an endeavor.

11

Dramatis Personae and the Cosmic War
Parenthetic Revelation III

REVELATION 12 INTRODUCES US to four key personas:

THE SUN-CLOTHED WOMAN

"Now a great sign appeared in heaven: a woman clothed with the sun, with the moon under her feet, and on her head a garland of twelve stars. Then being with child, she cried out in labor and in pain to give birth" (Revelation 12:1–2).

The woman is referenced as a "great sign," indicating that the woman is not to be taken as a literal woman but rather *represents* some other literal thing. Likewise, her listed attributes will also *represent* something literal. Some believe that she represents Mary the mother of Jesus, or the church; but neither of these suppositions hold scriptural weight as there are no linked passages confirming either one. And this sign appearing to John *in heaven* is not proof that the woman symbolizes the church just because the raptured church is also in heaven.

Indeed, this sign in heaven signifies an *earthly* reality, as determined by the remainder of chapter 12. What the woman does signify is crucial concerning the interpretation of Revelation in that *if* she represented Mary or the church, much of the prophetic context within and surrounding this passage would only offer confusion.

Plainly stated, the woman represents the nation and people of Israel, which gave birth to the Messiah, a fact attested to throughout the Old Testament (Isaiah 26:17–18; 66:7–8; Jeremiah 4:31; 13:21; Micah 4:10; 5:2–3). Beginning with slavery in Egypt and wars of conquest, Israel then endured times of judges and kings, a divided kingdom, an exile, a restoration, and finally, entanglement with the Law. Herein, a centuries-long cycle of bondage and deliverance generated an expectancy for the arrival of Israel's Messiah.

From Abraham to Mary the mother of Jesus, the nation of Israel suffered a long and difficult "pregnancy" as she prepared to bring forth a Messiah to bless the world, as expressed in Revelation 12:2, "Then being with child, she cried out in labor and in pain to give birth." John Walvoord succinctly notes that the woman's "sufferings refer to the nation [of Israel] as a whole, not to Mary the mother of Jesus."[1]

There are some who believe the church brought forth the Messiah into the world, but as Scripture and history reveal, it was Israel from whence the Messiah came and it was Christ who brought forth the church (Matthew 16:18). Many people forget that Jesus was/is Jewish.

Being clothed with the sun, the moon under her feet, and wearing a garland of twelve stars is imagery paralleling Joseph's dream in Genesis 37:9–11 where the sun, moon, and stars represent the patriarch, matriarch, and tribes of Israel. This further affirms that the woman represents national Israel, i.e., the Jewish people.

Another applicable allusion one may glean here is that the sun represents God, who is a Source of light. The moon is a reflector of the sun's light. This evokes the ideal of Israel as God's light-bearer to humanity. However, since Israel failed to reflect his light to the world, she suffered continual judgment; and after Messiah was "cut off" (Daniel 9:26), the *church* took on the mantle of light-bearer as the prophetic program for Israel was placed on hold. That program, the Seventy Weeks, recommences with the signing of the Antichrist's covenant with Israel (Daniel 9:27), which will begin the final Seventieth Week (see chapter six of this commentary). During this Week Israel will once again have the opportunity to be a light-bearer for God in the form of the 144,000 witnesses, representing the Jewish remnant amidst a season of judgment. Sadly, a majority of the Jewish people will still reject Christ as Messiah, some may even worship the Antichrist—for a season.

---

1. Walvoord, *Every Prophecy of the Bible*, 577.

THE DRAGON

"And another sign appeared in heaven: Behold, a great, fiery red dragon having seven heads and ten horns, and seven diadems on his heads. His tail drew a third of the stars of heaven and threw them to the earth. And the dragon stood before the woman who was ready to give birth, to devour her Child as soon as it was born" (Revelation 12:3–4).

Again we have a "sign" appearing to John in heaven, in this instance a great red dragon with seven heads, ten horns, and seven diadems (crowns), representing Satan himself as proven in 12:9. That the dragon is red indicates his bloodlust and warring nature, recalling the red horse of the second seal and the wars that followed (Revelation 6:4). The description of the dragon reaches back to Daniel 7:19–25 and is further elaborated upon in Revelation 13, to which we shall soon turn. What is being described by such terrible imagery is the monstrous nature of not only Satan, but of his earthly kingdoms/empires and its rulers (Revelation 13:1–4; 17). Each are indeed the "beasts" conveyed by Scripture, as they mercilessly devour their enemies and subjects—particularly the Jewish people.

The dragon's tail drawing a third of the stars (angels) from heaven and throwing them to earth recalls the original fall of Lucifer and the angelic rebellion. Daniel 8:9–12, 23–25 is the prophetic root of this reference, where "the little horn" (Antichrist) casts some of the host of heaven to the ground and desecrates the last days temple/tabernacle. Isaiah 14:12–23 and Ezekiel 28:1–19 use this event to illustrate the fall of a Babylonian and Tyrian king for the explicit purpose of revealing that Satan is the ultimate power behind evil Gentile leaders and nations. Further examples of this reality include Satan's attempt to breed out humanity (Genesis 6), his attempt to cut off the Hebrew nation in Egypt (Exodus 1–2), Haman's diabolical decree (Esther 3:8–15), Herod's edict to kill the young Jesus (Matthew 2:16–18), and the religious leaders' plot to kill Jesus (Matthew 26:1–4) leading to his crucifixion.

These are only a few of Satan's countless attempts to thwart God's promise of a Messiah, all of which are cumulatively represented in the vision by the dragon standing before the woman to devour her Child as soon as he was born.

THE CHILD

"And she bore a male Child who was to rule all nations with a rod of iron. And her Child was caught up to God and to his throne. Then the woman fled into the wilderness, where she has a place prepared by God, that they should feed her there one thousand two hundred and sixty days" (Revelation 12:5–6).

The Child is clearly and literally Jesus Christ, confirmed by the statement that he "was caught up to God and to his throne" for this is precisely the circumstance of Christ's resurrection and ascension into heaven (Revelation 3:21). The imagery of Jesus ruling all nations with a "rod of iron" originates in Psalm 2:7–9, is enacted starkly throughout the Tribulation as Israel and the nations are chastised (Revelation 2:27), and is fully realized in Revelation 19:15.

Foretelling events at the midpoint of the Tribulation, Revelation 12:6 describes the woman/Israel fleeing into the wilderness *on earth* after her Child ascends to heaven (a historical reflection of Jesus' ascension). A place and provision have been provided for her by God for 1,260 days (three and one-half years), a clear reference to the latter half of the seven-year Tribulation. The catalyst for Israel's flight into the wilderness is the Antichrist's desecration of the temple/tabernacle (Daniel 9:27). This scenario is expanded upon in Revelation 12:13–17.

Foreshadowings of predetermined places of provision are found in 1 Kings 17:1–7 when Elijah dwelt at Cherith and was fed by ravens; 1 Kings 19:1–8 when Elijah was fed by an angel; and Matthew 2:13–16 when Mary and Joseph and Child fled to Egypt to escape Herod's murderous pride. And of course, Jesus himself promises his followers that he has prepared a place for them in heaven and that he will personally receive them and fellowship with them there (John 14:2–3). Thus they shall escape the "hour of trial" for Israel and the world (Revelation 3:10).

THE ARCHANGEL MICHAEL

"And war broke out in heaven: Michael and his angels fought against the dragon; and the dragon and his angels fought, but they did not prevail, nor was a place found for them in heaven any longer" (Revelation 12:7–8).

Michael the archangel is referenced in Daniel 10:13 as one of the "chief princes," and in Daniel 12:1 as "the great prince" who watches over Israel. Michael is likely the angel who later binds Satan and casts him into the Abyss for 1,000 years (Revelation 20:1–3), since it is indeed Michael who leads the campaign to bar further entrance into the heavens by Lucifer and his fallen brethren.

Revelation 12 also describes two distinct wars:

THE WAR IN HEAVEN

And war broke out in heaven (Revelation 12:7–12). The context of this war is the time of Jacob's trouble, i.e., the time of the end, as proven in Daniel 12:1–4 (ESV), for "*At that time* shall arise Michael [the archangel] . . . And there shall be a *time of trouble*, such as never has been since there was a nation till *that time*. But *at that time* your people shall be delivered" (emphasis mine).

This future war in heaven and the "deliverance" of the woman/Israel (Revelation 12:13–17) is the fulfillment of Daniel 12:1, negating claims suggesting this particular heavenly war to encompass the original Luciferian rebellion shortly after creation.

Though we may understand the *initiation* of the war in heaven to have been the result of Christ's victory over death at his resurrection, followed by the continuing war across the past millennia between holy and unholy angels, the immediate context of Revelation 12 is *specifically* the midpoint of the Seventieth Week, made plain by the fact that upon being cast to earth (12:9) Satan has only a "short time" (12:12) until the end of the Week when he is imprisoned for one thousand years (Revelation 20:1–3). This "short time" is further honed to "a time and times and half a time" (12:14) which is synonymous with three and one-half years, or the last half of the seven-year Day of Wrath.

The war in heaven, which may be understood as the denouement of the age-long conflict between the holy and unholy, results in Satan and his angels losing their "place" in heaven, meaning their privilege concerning access to Almighty God aiming to "accuse the brethren before God day and night" (12:8–10).

Job 1:6—2:10 and Zechariah 3:1–4 offer striking examples of this limited privilege. Also, we need not assume that this present liberty grants Satan entry to the very throne of God or even the third heaven. Rather, his appeals against God's own would (and do) take place on a lower spiritual plane, or lower heaven, where the Lord would meet him (Ephesians 6:12; Job 1–2; Enoch 40:7).

After glimpsing the heavenly war, the apostle John hears a voice in heaven proclaiming several things: the casting to earth of Satan; the coming of the power of Christ to a judgment-ridden world; the victory over Satan by martyrs; and a warning to the inhabitants of the earth and sea concerning an impatient and angry devil (Revelation 12:10–12)! The voice/song John then hears belongs to a particular group of redeemed people, such being those of Revelation 6:11 and 7:13, evidenced by the use of the possessive qualifier "*our* brethren" and "*our* God."

John records that believers overcame Satan by the blood of the Lamb and by the word of their testimony, "and they did not love their lives to the death" (Revelation 12:11). This last phrase closely resembles Jesus' words, "he who loves his life will lose it, and he who hates his life in this world will keep it for eternal life" (John 12:25).

"Therefore rejoice, O heavens, and you who dwell in them!" (Revelation 12:12), for the devil will no longer taint with his presence any of the heavenly planes which he occupied as prince of the power of the air. But, "Woe to the inhabitants of the earth and the sea! For the devil has come down to you, having great wrath, because he knows that he has a short time" (12:12) until he is judged!

THE WAR ON EARTH

Failing his attempt to destroy the Child (in the days of King Herod) and suffering ultimate defeat at Jesus' resurrection, then losing the war in heaven (in the middle of the Seventieth Week) and being cast down and confined to the earth, the dragon determines to destroy the woman (Israel/Jews). But the woman is given two wings of a great eagle that she might fly into the wilderness—a place of protection, nourishment, discipline, and testing (Revelation 12:13–17).

The imagery of eagles' wings evokes God's providence and provision concerning Israel's flight into the wilderness (Revelation 12:6), making it a certainty that she will arrive unharmed. Portentous provision by eagles' wings is also found in Exodus 19:4 and Deuteronomy 32:11–12. Jesus even warns of the dragon's assault in Matthew 24:15–20:

> Therefore when you see the "abomination of desolation," spoken of by Daniel the prophet, standing in the holy place, then let those who are in Judea flee to the mountains . . . But woe to those who are pregnant and to those who are nursing babies

in those days! And pray your flight may not be in winter or on the Sabbath.

The "abomination of desolation" is the act of Antichrist (Satan) desecrating the temple/tabernacle and setting himself up as a god to be worshiped by all. This is the event that prompts those in Jerusalem and all of Israel/Judea to flee to the "place prepared by God" (historically foreshadowed in the *Apocrypha*—1 Maccabees 2:29). Jesus emphasizes that it will be unfortunate for those fleeing if it is the winter season and even less fortunate for those who are with child, those who have children, and those who are bound to religious traditions, as such circumstances would be impediments to said flight and will likely result in being overcome by the enemy.

This remnant of Israel will be nourished for "a time and times and half a time" while being protected from the dragon (Revelation 12:14). The nourishment may be supernatural as it was (via manna) throughout the wilderness sojourn in the days of Moses' leadership.

The dragon will "spew water out of his mouth *like* a flood after the woman" in an attempt to annihilate her (12:15). Note the comparative article "like" which signifies a symbolic comparison between a *flood* and an *assault* on the fleeing Jews; clearly the assault will be swift and powerful like a flood of water. Parallels to this manner of Old Testament imagery can be read in Isaiah 59:19; 43:2; and Psalm 18:4; 32:6; 42:7; 124:4. The idea of a flood spewing from the dragon's mouth suggests that the assault follows *spoken orders and slander* from Antichrist himself who shall have significant military and diabolical resources at his disposal. Antichrist will also have the False Prophet at his side, both of whom are the two beasts detailed in Revelation 13.

The possibility remains, however, for a more specifically literal interpretation due to many modern reservoirs and artificial lakes. For example, if Israel attempts to escape through some valley, the Antichrist may order the release of vast stores of water from an elevated location.[2]

Nevertheless, the flood (of water, military might, or demonic powers) will be swallowed when the earth opens its mouth to protect the woman/Israel. Exactly how this will play out cannot be known, but God's involvement in Israel's survival is certain. A reflection of this event is found in Numbers 16:31–33 when Korah and his cohorts rejected God and rebelled against the leadership of Moses and Aaron:

2. Smith, *A Revelation of Jesus Christ*, 191.

> Now it came to pass . . . that the ground split apart under them, and the earth opened its mouth and swallowed them up, with their households and all the men with Korah, with all their goods. So they and all those with them went down alive into the pit; the earth closed over them and they perished from among the assembly.

Israel's escape enrages the dragon who then makes war with the "rest of the woman's offspring/seed, who keep the commandments of God and have the testimony of Jesus Christ" (Revelation 12:17). Since Satan is powerless to pursue the protected fleeing remnant, he then turns to war against those Jews who remain in Israel and also against those scattered abroad and who have received Christ as Messiah, including the two witnesses in Jerusalem (Revelation 11:7) and the 144,000. This attempted genocide of the Jewish people by Satan will be the most violent and widespread anti-Semitic campaign the world has seen. The Nazi-born genocidal Holocaust was only a tame rehearsal for the coming evil.

The protected remnant in the wilderness will not *only* consist of Jews who have received Christ. The "remnant" of Revelation 12:17 is presented by the Greek word *loipoi* (meaning "destitute remnant") which refers to those not faithful, but blinded (Romans 11:7); whereas the Greek *leimma* and *kataleimma* simply mean "residue or remainder" and are the only two specific word instances in the New Testament referencing the "faithful remnant" of Israel (see Romans 9:27 and 11:5). However, although the protected remnant predominantly consists of unbelieving Jews, they shall indeed believe on Jesus Christ when they suddenly see him descend with power and exceeding glory at his return to earth (then becoming the truly faithful remnant), for

> Though the number of the sons of Israel be as the sand of the sea, only a remnant of them will be saved, for the Lord will carry out his sentence upon the earth fully and without delay. . . . For unless those days were shortened, no flesh would be saved; but for the elect's [faithful remnant's] sake those days will be shortened (Romans 9:27–28 ESV; Matthew 24:22).

THE PLACE IN THE WILDERNESS

To where will Israel flee and remain for three and a half years until Jesus' return? And what is meant by "the wilderness, where she has a place prepared by God" (Revelation 12:6, 14)? This place of refuge is Petra in modern Jordan.

The biblical name of this place is Sela, from the Hebrew *cela'* which means "rocky" or "cliff." Much later, per the Romans, it became known by the Greek name Petra, meaning "rock." Sela was an ancient Edomite city-fortress built in the mountains of northwestern Arabia in the desert wilderness south of the Dead Sea in Israel. In the Old Testament, king Amaziah of Judah conquered the city and renamed it Joktheel (2 Kings 14:7). Obadiah 1:3 gives us another common name for the city that appears throughout the Old Testament: the Rock.

Eventually the site was all but abandoned except for roaming tribal families. Around the fourth century BC a growing clan of traders known as the Nabateans began to establish a vast commercial network across Arabia and beyond. By the first century BC they had settled in, expanded, and smartly outfitted the ancient fortress of Sela, making it their capital city. Throughout the Nabatean's desert kingdom, but especially at Sela, their genius for various desert-adapted agricultural and domestic water systems as well as numerous other engineering and technological skills can be seen. And along with the famous rock-carved facades and cavernous multipurpose quarters, human-built structures continue to be excavated at Sela.

Functioning as a vital caravan trading post, the Nabateans remained independent during the era of Roman dominance, until AD 106 when emperor Trajan decided to consolidate the Near East. He sent Roman auxiliaries into Sela and formally declared it a part of the Roman Empire, effectively ending the Nabatean kingdom. However, with little to no violence resulting, the Nabatean culture and commerce continued unaffected until AD 363 when a calamitous earthquake struck. The loss of their fabled trading hub forced much of their business to transpire through the many other smaller ventures across Arabia, demanding a more mobile existence. As such, Sela was never fully rebuilt or reestablished as a city or trading center, and the Nabateans slowly assimilated into the diverse cultures of the Near East and disappeared from recorded history.[3]

To the present day there has been a continuous presence of Arab Bedouins (some being direct Nabatean descendants) occupying the territory; they love to welcome visiting tourists, archaeologists, and historians

---

3. See Phillip C. Hammond, "Nabateans," in Metzger and Coogan, *The Oxford Companion to the Bible*, 542–43.

from all over the world, and in my own experience they were exceedingly warm and quick to laugh!

Scripture records many prophecies confirming Sela as Israel's place of refuge from Antichrist at the end of the age. Daniel 11:36–45 informs us that Antichrist will regard himself as a god and will overthrow many countries of the Middle East, Near East, and North Africa, including Israel. However, some shall escape from his hand: Edom, Moab, and the prominent people of Ammon (Daniel 11:41). Sela is located in territory once held by the Edomites and Moabites, and to small extent the Ammonites. The capital of today's Hashemite Kingdom of Jordan is Amman, as most Jordanese are descendants from these tribal beginnings. Thus, according to the prophet Daniel, Jordan will (entirely or mostly) escape Antichrist's control and wrath. It is clearly God's sovereignty that orchestrates prophecy despite the intentions and evil of men and devils.

Isaiah 16:1–5 is another prophecy about the flight of Israel into the wilderness, specifically mentioning Sela and the river Arnon in northern Moab where fleeing Israelites will be met by the "daughters [hospitable descendants] of Moab." The Lord God admonishes them to welcome and hide his Jewish "outcasts" from "the face of the spoiler/destroyer" (Antichrist). Verses 4–5 reveal that soon after this the devastating persecution will cease and the oppressors will be purged from the land, then the throne of David will be established and One will sit on it in truth and love, judging and seeking justice and hastening righteousness. A clear reference to the establishment of Christ's rule on earth at the end of the age (Matthew 25:31–46).

Isaiah 26 records Israel's "Song of the Kingdom" that celebrates Messiah's judgment of Israel, the world, and the devil, and also celebrates the consequent salvation of Israel and restoration of the kingdom. Toward the end of the psalm, reference is made to their wilderness refuge and the return of the King:

> Come, my people, enter your chambers, and shut your doors behind you; hide yourselves for a little while until the fury [Jacob's trouble] has passed by. For behold, the Lord is coming out from his place to punish the inhabitants of the earth for their iniquity (Isaiah 26:20–21 ESV).

Hosea 2:14–23 is a prophecy concerning Israel's final restoration per the Jewish remnant. The passage mentions Israel being brought "into the wilderness" to receive comfort, provision, and hope. And most poignantly, the Lord says, "And in that day . . . you will call me 'my Husband' [caretaker], and no longer will you call me 'my Baal.' . . . And I will say to Not My People, 'You are my people'; And he shall say, 'You are my God'" (2:16, 23 ESV).

Psalm 60 is a Davidic song of encouragement in light of God's promises to restore a broken Israel. Psalm 60:9–12 (ESV) specifically foreshadows the flight from Antichrist and a cry for God's protection:

> Who will bring me to the fortified city [Sela]? Who will lead me to Edom? Have you not rejected us, O God? You do not go forth, O God, with our armies. Oh, grant us help against the foe, for vain is the salvation of man! With God we shall do valiantly; it is he who will tread down our foes.

Also see Isaiah 63:1–5, a parallel reference carrying a more vivid description of the Lord God treading down his enemies.

12

The Antichrist and the False Prophet
Parenthetic Revelation III

THE TERM "ANTICHRIST" ONLY appears in the epistles of John (1 John 2:18, 22; 4:3; 2 John 7) and only once refers to a specific individual. The "spirit of antichrist" is what concerned John and other New Testament prophets, for it had already manifested itself within numerous churches by way of false doctrines.

However, in Revelation John foresees the embodiment of the antichrist spirit into one person repeatedly called "the beast," which is symbolically presented in the vision as a horrible monstrosity with great authority and power (Revelation 13:1–10).

The symbolism purposes to show the true nature of an actual satanically influenced person and his terrible violence (via his kingdom) toward all who stand against him, particularly those who testify of Christ. Thus the contemporary name for this individual has become the infamously familiar, and accurate, Antichrist.

Other biblical titles for Antichrist include the wicked one (Psalm 10:2–4); little horn and prince who is to come (Daniel 7:8; 9:26); the spoiler and extortioner (Isaiah 16:1–5); man of sin and son of perdition (2 Thessalonians 2:3); the lawless one (2 Thessalonians 2:9); and the beast (Daniel 7:11; Revelation 13; 14:9–11; 15:2; 16:2, 10; 17; 19:19–20; 20:4, 10).

As one studies the Revelation it eventually becomes clear that the "beast" is both an individual *and* a politico-religious entity, a king *and* the kingdom over which he rules. That the beast was "rising up out of the sea" denotes that he shall rise from the sea of humanity (Revelation 15:17). His ancestry will carry a Greco-Roman (Gentile) origin, a fact John would have discerned and which would have been subtly reinforced since at the time of the vision John was on the island of Patmos in the Aegean Sea, located between Greece and Asia Minor, both formerly of Greek and Roman subjugation. The Aegean is itself part of the Mediterranean Sea which was formerly a "Roman lake," or as the Romans called it, *mare nostrum* ("our sea").

Notably, the Roman flavor of John's day and Rome's historical dominance of the Mediterranean have led most students of prophecy to believe that Antichrist's kingdom will be some form of revived Roman Empire. But contemporary events in our day have generated a more plausible likelihood of both the Antichrist and his kingdom boasting an Islamic flavor, perhaps as a revived Ottoman Empire of sorts. We will examine this possibility in greater detail as we progress.

A GENETICALLY INDUCED "GOD" OF WAR

Evidence supporting Antichrist's *Greek* lineage is provided in Daniel 8:1–12. The prophet Daniel receives a vision of a ram (representing the Mede-Persian empire) in Babylon pushing westward, northward, and southward. None could withstand it and it became great. Then suddenly a male goat with a large horn between his eyes came swiftly from the west (representing a unified Greece under its first king, Alexander the Great ca. BC 331) and broke the power of the ram and trampled it. The goat grew very great, but then the large horn was broken (Alexander died at age 33) and in place of it four notable ones sprang up—four of Alexander's generals established kingdoms for themselves carved from his empire, thus fracturing its power: Ptolemy I in Egypt; Seleucus I in western Asia; Lysimachus in Asia Minor; and Cassander in Macedonia.

Out of these four a "little horn" (Daniel 8:9; not the "little horn" of Daniel 7:8) grew exceedingly great; this was the Greek Antiochus IV *Epiphanes* ("God-Manifest"). He usurped the Seleucid kingdom in BC 175, conquered much territory in the east, including Palestine, and would have conquered Egypt circa BC 168 if Rome had not stopped him. Antiochus exalted himself as a god and upon conquering Palestine he removed the daily sacrifices of Jewish practice, even "casting truth to the ground"

(Daniel 8:12). In this respect, Antiochus was a "type," or foreshadowing, of Antichrist. See Daniel 11:21–45 for more detail.

Evidence supporting Antichrist's *Roman* lineage rests in Daniel 9:26 as he is referenced as a future prince (royalty) of the people (ethnicity) who would destroy Jerusalem and the Jewish temple. This was fulfilled in AD 70 by the Romans under Vespasian, who "sent his son Titus, with a select party of his army, to destroy Jerusalem." A full account of this is rendered by Flavius Josephus in his *Wars of the Jews*, book 4.11.5 through book 5. Like Antiochus, the Roman general Titus was a "type" of Antichrist.

Possible evidence of partial *Jewish* lineage rests in Daniel 11:37, stating that the willful king (Antichrist) shall not regard "the God of his fathers," though the word for God here is the Hebrew *Elohim* which is a general word for God/god and not specifically for *Yahweh*. If he indeed carries any Jewish ancestry, he may use it toward endearing himself to Israel when forming the seven-year covenant. Or he may hide such information, particularly if presiding over an Islamic confederation.

Daniel 11:36–39 offers compelling insight concerning Antichrist's god-complex. Apparent is his atheism, materialism, and inherent desire to conquer, thus elevating himself toward the personification of our contemporary concept of the "god of war":

> Then the king shall do according to his own will: he shall exalt and magnify himself above every god, shall speak blasphemies against the God of gods, and shall prosper till the wrath has been accomplished; for what has been determined shall be done. He shall regard neither the God of his fathers nor the desire of women, nor regard any god; for he shall exalt himself above them all. *But in their place he shall honor a god of fortresses*; and a god which his fathers did not know he shall honor with gold and silver, with precious stones and pleasant things. Thus he shall act against the strongest fortresses with a foreign god, which he shall acknowledge and advance its glory (emphasis mine).

THE RISE AND FALL OF ANTICHRIST

The following seven topics briefly outline the rise and fall of Antichrist but are by no means exhaustive:

Antichrist's Rise to Power

Revelation 6:2 reveals that Antichrist will rise to power through diplomatic prowess, not war. However, he shall remain in power by means militant. Convincing a chaotic world that he can bring lasting peace (perhaps in regard to Ezekiel 38–39), he will eventually (though only for a time) control the world's leaders: "By his cunning he shall make deceit prosper under his hand" (Daniel 8:25 ESV).

In contrast to the thinking of popular culture and much church culture today, the Antichrist will not appear on the scene until *after* the rapture of the church. Thus there is no need for the church to concern itself speculating who the man of sin may be. Second Thessalonians 2:1–12 explains this chronology and provides the understanding that the Holy Spirit via the church is restraining the final rise of evil until the due time when he (and the church) are taken out of the way by rapture; only then will the lawless one (Antichrist) be revealed (2:7–8). The church at Thessalonica had become anxious in reaction to false teaching that the rapture had already occurred, but Paul reminded them he had previously and personally expounded truth to them, stating, "you know *what* is restraining, that *he* may be revealed in his own time" (2:5–6; emphasis mine). This might seem a riddle but the *what* is the church and the *he* is the Holy Spirit within the hearts of those souls who make up the church. This is further evidence that the time of *Jacob's* trouble is not for the church. Also to clarify, though the church and indwelling Spirit are removed from earth (taken out of the way), the Spirit of God will yet remain present during the Tribulation as he was in pre-Christian (Old Testament) history.

The Covenant With Israel

Antichrist will negotiate a unique seven-year covenant with "many" (Israel and other nations), causing the Jews to develop a false sense of security and peace (Daniel 9:27). The first half of this seven years will witness a Jewish consensus toward accepting Antichrist as a long-awaited (political) messiah (if not *the* Messiah), and a return to sacrificial oblation will be encouraged to begin anew or to continue if it has already been reinstated. Also, the political climate may be primed toward construction of the anticipated temple/tabernacle as a result of the Ezekiel 38–39 events; such construction may even be a tenet of the covenant being struck, for

Israel's enemies will have been neutralized and the nations will be reacting convulsively to God's overt and supernatural involvement in world affairs.

The false peace will not last, for in the middle of the seven years Antichrist will break the covenant: "Then he [Antichrist] shall confirm a covenant with many for one week [a prophetic "week" of seven years]; but in the middle of the week he shall bring an end to sacrifice and offering" (Daniel 9:27).

Global Government

A unified global government is prophesied in Daniel 7:7–8 and 7:19–25, and is shown as a strange beast, paralleling Revelation 13:1. The initial success of bringing "world peace" through the covenant with Israel will surely catapult Antichrist toward ever-increasing world prominence, leading him to harmonize and enact already prominent ideals of globalization. World leaders will conclude that they cannot govern themselves, and under a veil of false humility the Antichrist will appoint ten kings who "are of one mind" and who shall then "give their power and authority to the beast" (Revelation 17:12–13), providing Antichrist the most coveted position of humanity's dark side—king of the world.

Global Economy

Revelation 17:13 shows that the kings of the earth "give their power and authority to the beast." This power and authority includes that of military, political, technological, industrial, and *economic* leaning. A unified global government demands a unified global economy. Such an ideal has been pushed for centuries and is even presently being pursued. Restructuring of regional trading blocs such as NAFTA, CAFTA, the European Union, the Eurasian Market, the Southeast Asian Market, ECOWAS (Economic Community of West African States), the Mediterranean Union, and the African Union and Arab Union is encouraged by the international regulatory entities known as the World Bank, the World Trade Organization, the International Monetary Fund, the World Economic Forum, and the United Nations Law of the Sea Treaty.

Consolidation of economic regions of trade will by default necessitate a centralizing of world and regional currencies. This too is on track toward actualization, evidenced by the success of the *euro* which debuted in 1999. The ever-strengthening *yen* and the increasingly unstable American dollar (despite its international allure) has invited response from a global consensus, thus the *amero* is set to be unveiled in the near future with the hope of strengthening a joint economy between America, Canada, and Mexico, thus replacing the present currency of each respective nation. Of course, a global crisis or series of crises may fast track and alter the particulars of international financial integration.

Sooner than later, the globalist agenda will impose further consolidation of world currencies toward the adoption of *one* global currency or credit system, such as the currently active special drawing rights (SDR) system created by the International Monetary Fund (IMF). This would elicit a swift realization (in theory) of the utopian ideal sought for millennia by those who fancy themselves "world rulers." Moreover, global economic crises and a pathogenic pandemic have in all likelihood been an *inspiration* to such world rulers who relish the socialist notion of "never letting a good crisis go to waste."[1]

It is probable that the aforementioned financial behemoths will eventually merge into some sort of single global entity or unified confederation; though whether or not this occurs *before* the Antichrist's rise to power or *as a result of it* is a question left unanswered. However, it is clear within Scripture that he shall tame these monetary behemoths and bend them to his own will (Daniel 11:38; Revelation 17:3–4), ultimately resulting in the totalitarian mark of the beast dictate (Revelation 13:16–17).

Global Religion

The Antichrist's "religion" appears throughout Scripture, most notably in Daniel 11:36–39, referenced above, and in 2 Thessalonians 2:1–12. These passages disclose that

> he opposes and exalts himself against every so-called god or object of worship, so that he takes his seat in the temple of God, proclaiming himself to be God. . . . [for] the coming of the lawless one is by the activity of Satan with all power and false signs and wonders (2 Thessalonians 2:4, 9 ESV).

---

1. Alinsky, *Rules for Radicals*, 89. Alinsky specifically said, "in the arena of action, a threat or a crisis becomes almost a precondition to communication," which is a Machiavellian ideal of defeating good fortune through tactical action to gain ground toward tyrannical rule.

Revelation 17:1–6 shows a woman (false religious system—Mystery Babylon) atop a scarlet beast (Antichrist's kingdom). The Antichrist may approve an ecumenical (universal/unified) world "faith" that serves to bring all world religions together under one banner, just as Nimrod attempted with the Tower of Babel (Genesis 10:8–10; 11:2–9) in Shinar/Babylonia. The aforementioned *Chrislam* may be a precursor (see chapter three, church of Sardis).

Ever since Nimrod's despotism, Babylon has been synonymous with idolatry and political militarism. Revelation 17:18 reveals the underlying truth regarding Mystery Babylon's name, for she is none other than the last manifestation of the great city/entity—Babylon—to reign over the kings of the earth, religiously, commercially, politically, and martially.

Revelation 17:9 further identifies Mystery Babylon with the Roman papal cult by referencing the "seven hills on which the woman sits," an explicit allusion to Rome, and specifically to its cultic foundation per the context of Revelation 17. Even today, the Vatican continues to embody and promote the politico-religious and commercial designs of Babylonianism, which will in all likelihood assist both the False Prophet and Antichrist in their empirical aspirations.

The duel assault of a strategic Babylonian religious spirit and a tactical antichrist spirit are presently softening up the universal church toward its total demonic takeover post-rapture.

Ottomania: the Turkish-Islamic Union

There is also the possibility of an Islamic influence on the Antichrist, though he himself will not be Muslim (unless in name only, for he regards no god but himself). His kingdom therefore may initially consist of a deceptively moderate form of Islam that permits coexistence with non-Muslims, particularly Jews. This accords with widespread interest of a renewed Turkish-led Caliphate. Of course, the world at large (specifically Christians and Israel) would never accept a global kingdom ruled by an ISIS, al Qaeda, Hezbollah, Hamas, Boko Haram, or Muslim Brotherhood. Such violent anti-Semitic and anti-Christian idealism and militarism must be removed or incapacitated (via Ezekiel 38–39) prior to any substantive final peace agreement between Israel and Muslim and non-Muslim nations/entities.

Turkey is a fast-modernizing nation of moderate Sunni Islam. As of this writing, Turkish president Recep Erdogan has aligned himself *against* radical Islam and has launched a domestic campaign promoting the nation's imperial heritage. "Ottomania" describes the Turks' growing fascination with their cultural and traditional past and the mingling of such with modern cultural trends and mores.

On May 9, 2015, in the Black Sea town of Amasya, a statue of an Ottoman prince taking a "selfie" was unveiled: the turban-clad, regally attired figure has one hand resting on the hilt of his sword and the other holding a smartphone aloft. Though this amused more than it offended, it stands as witness to a modernized and western-friendly Turkish culture that is rediscovering the allure of its rich history and desires to "integrate bygone traditions with modern ways."[2]

The Turkish democratic election of June 2015 has made possible "a retuned foreign policy that would return Turkey to its default position as a western-allied, mainly Muslim country that can *transcend the religious, sectarian and ethnic divisions elsewhere in the Middle East.*"[3] A "transcendence" of this scope would be absolutely necessary to win global acceptance or toleration of a legitimately revived and distinctly moderate Muslim caliphate.

Significantly, Iran's leaders possess an apocalyptic bent of Shia Islam but are nevertheless working closely with and willing to temporarily compromise with Sunni-dominant Turkey toward advancing the Islamic cause worldwide, all toward the eventual undermining of America and Israel. This could play out via the long game of false peace through false covenant with an eventual endgame of annihilation.

Satan's Throne

Many Bible commentators believe that Antichrist's seat of power early in the Tribulation (before moving to Jerusalem) will first be located somewhere in Babylonia, for the land/city of Babylon will flourish immensely under his headship.

While this is certainly possible, another option for his initial seat of power is Turkey. I offer this in considering the prospect of an Islamic

---

2. Christie-Miller, "Turkey: Seeking New Cultural Balance," EurasiaNet.org.

3. Ulgen, "Turkey at a Democratic Crossroad," Carnegie-Europe.eu. Emphasis mine.

flavor to Antichrist's kingdom in that Turkey was the epicenter of the Ottoman Empire and Jesus himself mentioned the city of Pergamos (in modern Turkey) as being the location of Satan's throne (Revelation 2:13).

Truly, Babylon's global impact will have nothing to do with Antichrist's preferred base of operations, but everything to do with the commercial and religious devilry it will offer an increasingly corrupt global populace.

Babylonia will be the economic and spiritual center of Antichrist's empire (Revelation 17–18). Any Turkish influence will be by assistance and affiliation. Likewise with the Vatican in Rome. A corrupt Vatican and its politico-religious global network would be (even at present) the perfect pawn for Antichrist's designs. Thus an unholy alliance between a proposed Islamic Caliphate and the Vatican is not so farfetched, especially due to Roman Catholicism's takeover by the Mystery Babylon cult in which the desire for truth is usurped by the mystery of iniquity (Revelation 17:5–6).

Sadly, as we studied in chapter three, Vatican history reveals that well-known idolatrous practices were forced upon churched populations, thereby replacing Christian sacraments, while heathen philosophies replaced instruction from God's Word. This gave rise to the *Roman* Catholic era which heralded a spiritual dark age for the church and Europe wherein the bodies and souls of men and women were trafficked, and truth was exchanged for a lie as the Virgin Mother and Christ Child became the icon of Catholic Babylonianism. Nothing has changed. Even human slavery continues to proliferate globally.

This is not to say that everyone who is affiliated with Catholicism is corrupt or damned, as there are many Catholics (I personally know) who see through the demonic facade and cling to Jesus Christ as their Savior. Yet there are far too many people who are wooed by the Babylonian spectacle of religion (despite benign pretense) and therefore place their identity in *Catholicism* and not in Christ, putting their souls in danger of eternal loss. Certainly the same can be said of souls placing their identity in Protestantism and Orthodoxy.

A Religion of the Sword

Exalting himself above all gods, Antichrist "shall speak pompous words against the Most High, shall persecute the saints of the Most High, and shall intend to change times and law" (Daniel 7:25). This clue is telling, for who might wish to change "times and law" and have a viable replacement ready to go? A Muslim ruler, of course, (or one sympathetic to Islam) decreeing *Sharia* law that is based upon *lunar* reckoning of time, not solar reckoning as the West now prefers. Again, Antichrist will not be a true Muslim even if he proclaims such. It is more likely that he will initially profess no religious affiliation in the spirit of neutrality and political advantage toward self-deification.

Consider also the haunting precision of Jesus' prophecy concerning the coming day when those who persecute and murder Christians (and Jews) will believe they are offering God a service, and when *beheading* is the official method of doing so under Antichrist's dictate (John 16:2; Revelation 20:4; see *Quran*/Sura 47:4).

Indeed, the Antichrist will not believe in this false religion (Chrislam?). He will, however, use it as a tool to assist his ascent to power, for Mystery Babylon's influence carries tremendous wealth and political prowess. That the woman *sits atop* the beast implies a sort of domination/control, though this is only an allowed facade until Antichrist himself gains sufficient strength to throw her off, thereby destroying the false religious system and shifting worship from a generic god to that of himself (Revelation 17:3, 16; 2 Enoch 29:4–5). He shall prosper until God's wrath has been accomplished, "for what has been determined shall be done" (Daniel 11:36).

Antichrist's Death and "Resurrection"

Revelation 13:3, 17:8, and 17:11 reference the Antichrist being killed. Scripture is not specific as to the context of his death, whether in battle or by assassination. His body is then indwelled or reanimated by the beast/dragon (Satan) which creates an illusory resurrection, mimicking that of Christ. This diabolical act deceives the masses and causes many to believe that Antichrist is God: "And all the world marveled and followed the beast. So they worshiped the dragon who gave authority to the beast" (13:3–4).

Satan thus draws on this unholy display and tightens his dictatorial grip on world dominance. As part of this campaign he desecrates the Jewish temple/tabernacle and sets himself up as God in supposed confirmation of the impressionable mob: "Then he opened his mouth in blasphemy against God, to blaspheme his name, his tabernacle, and those who dwell in heaven" (13:6).

He then wages war on the Jews and all who oppose him, and anyone refusing his "mark" to prove their loyalty will be destroyed:

> It was granted to him to make war with the saints and to overcome [martyr] them. And authority was given him over every tribe, tongue, and nation.... He causes all, both small and great, rich and poor, free and slave, to receive a mark on their right hand or on their foreheads (Revelation 13:7, 16).

Antichrist's Destruction

"And then the lawless one [Antichrist] will be revealed, whom the Lord Jesus will kill with the breath of his mouth and bring to nothing by the appearance of his coming" (2 Thessalonians 2:8 ESV).

Revelation 19:19–20 details the Antichrist being cast into the lake of fire, while Revelation 20:1–3 outlines Satan being bound for 1,000 years in the bottomless pit (Abyss).

Following the millennial reign of Christ on earth, Satan will be loosed and will attack the Lord and the holy city, but God will devour him with fire from heaven, sending him to his eternal doom in the lake of fire where he will share said doom with the Antichrist and False Prophet (Revelation 20:7–10).

Revelation 13 contains some passages that are truly difficult to interpret, particularly some of the specific details concerning the "beasts." However, difficulty need not be a discouragement. Recall that John would have been quite familiar with much of what he saw in his visions since God often used *word pictures* to represent literal truths John already understood. Although, much of what John witnessed concerning *future* events likely was not *entirely* comprehended by the prophet, but the principle truths he would have readily discerned.

In essence, John saw what was going to happen but may not have understood *exactly how* it would happen. While intimately familiar with the politics and history leading up to his day, he was not familiar with future politics and future history spanning from his day to the vision's fulfillment.

From this we gain valuable insight in that the greater our knowledge and comprehension is of political and historical trends and progression, then the greater our discernment shall be regarding prophetic progression as we view the world through the lens of Scripture. And we must also remember that knowing prophecy is not as vital as personally knowing the *God* of prophecy; God will always leave some mystery that requires faith and trust in *him*, not in the prophecy itself (Hebrews 1:1–3; Revelation 19:10).[4]

ANTICHRIST—THE BEAST OUT OF THE SEA (REVELATION 13:1-10)

"And I saw a beast rising up out of the sea, having seven heads and ten horns, and on his horns ten crowns, and on his heads a blasphemous name."

With the advent of Satan being cast to earth after the war in heaven he becomes enraged. He knows his time is short and determines to do as much damage as possible before his doom is realized. The damage Satan envisions is caused by delegating his power to the two beasts of Revelation 13—the beast out of the sea (Antichrist and his kingdom) and the beast out of the earth (the False Prophet).

These "beasts" are merely agents and instruments through which Satan will exercise his power on earth. The concept of beasts is initially found in Daniel 7, where four beasts are used as symbols of various pagan empires.[5]

Revelation 13:1 describes the beast from the sea as "having seven heads and ten horns, and on his horns ten crowns, and on his heads a blasphemous name." The sea represents peoples and nations and their governments (Isaiah 17:12; Revelation 17:15) from which this beast arises, symbolizing the lust for world dominion and the persecution of God's people embodied in evil nations and governments throughout history.

The seven heads are not mentioned by Daniel but are again referenced in Revelation 17:9 where it is revealed that the heads are "seven mountains." To clarify, Revelation 17 describes a beast that does not represent only a single empire, but a conglomerate of seven historical

---

4. For a deeply personal treatment of this theme, see Lahaye, *The Merciful God of Prophecy*.

5. Richardson, *Mystery Babylon*, 71.

pagan empires.⁶ Recall the seven-headed beast of Revelation 12. Though there have been many evil empires in history, the seven heads of the beast represent seven specific satanic empires through which the dragon has warred against God's purposes. Moreover, these are empires that have at one time or other ruled over Israel and sought to subjugate or destroy God's people.⁷

It is further revealed in 17:10 that "five have fallen, one is, and the other has not yet come."

The mountains represent a *seat of power* (empire/kingdom) upon which a king sits—specifically Rome in the immediate context of John's vision. Revelation 17:10, as noted above, highlights the idea of *successive* empires.⁸ In keeping with the diabolical designs of the seven-headed beast and with John's vision, we can conclude that five empires had fallen at the time John received the Revelation, one empire was in power (Rome), and one specific empire was yet future, for a total of seven specific empires/kingdoms.

The Final Empire: Roman or Ottoman?

In his book *Mystery Babylon: Unlocking the Bible's Greatest Prophetic Mystery*, Joel Richardson outlines and methodically details the devilish history behind the most powerful empires that sought to conquer the world and annihilate God's people. Beginning with Egypt, which enslaved the Hebrews, and through to the Rome of John's day, which crucified Jesus, destroyed the Jewish temple, and killed countless Jews, the first six empires are:

1. Egyptian Empire
2. Assyrian Empire
3. Babylonian Empire
4. Medo-Persian Empire
5. Grecian Empire
6. Roman Empire⁹

---

6. Richardson, *Mystery Babylon*, 71. Also Duvall, *The Heart of Revelation*, 87.
7. Richardson, *Mystery Babylon*, 72.
8. See Appendix B Expanded Commentary #7.
9. Richardson, *Mystery Babylon*, 72–73.

The Antichrist and the False Prophet

While most commentators agree with this list, it is identifying the *seventh* empire, i.e., the seventh head of the beast, that often brings difficulty. A long-held popular interpretation suggests the seventh empire to be a revived Roman empire led by Antichrist. However, Revelation 17:11 speaks of an *eighth* beast/kingdom that is "of the seven":

> And the beast that was, and is not, is himself also the eighth, and is of the seven, and is going to perdition.

This creates a problem for a revived *Roman* empire, unless Rome were twice revived, making it the sixth, seventh, *and* eighth empires. This is unlikely. Interpretive logic insists that we view each head as a separate empire, which are themselves also referred to as beasts. Richardson says, "The eighth [empire] is the only exception, as it is mysteriously linked to the one before it. The key, then, is to identify the seventh head first. The eighth is the revival of the seventh head. So what empire might this be? Which empire came after Rome?"[10]

Richardson, an expert on biblical prophecy, the Middle East, and Islam, states that the old Islamic empire—commonly known as the Ottoman Empire—is in fact the *seventh head*. He explains that after Muhammad died (AD 632) the Islamic empire swiftly conquered much of the ancient world from India to Spain, including the holy land. "It was far larger than even the Roman Empire at the time of its greatest extent. In its day, the historical Islamic empire, like the previous empires, was the primary satanic steward of the anti-Semitic Jew-hating spirit. . . . If the identity of the seventh head after Rome is the Islamic Caliphate, then this would mean that a revived caliphate, the final yet short-lived empire of Antichrist, is the eighth kingdom."[11]

This completes our list:

7. Ottoman/Islamic Empire
8. Revived [possibly] pseudo-Islamic Empire of Antichrist

Each of the previous six empires ruled Jerusalem and the surrounding Middle East, with each succeeding empire either being destroyed or absorbed by the preceding empire. The Egyptian empire ruled all of Egypt and Israel. The Assyrian empire conquered Egypt and ruled over much of the Middle East, including Israel. Babylon conquered Assyria,

---

10. Richardson, *Mystery Babylon*, 74.
11. Richardson, *Mystery Babylon*, 74.

then expanded, and also ruled over Israel. The Medo-Persians overthrew Babylon (gaining Israel), then were subdued by the Greeks. The Grecian empire (and Israel) were ultimately swallowed by the Romans. The Roman empire fell in two phases: the western half and the city of Rome itself was invaded and harassed by Muslim marauders and widely abandoned during the first few centuries of the violent rise of Islam (early seventh through ninth centuries AD); the eastern Byzantine half did not fall until AD 1453 when it was sacked by the Muslim Turks. Thereafter, the Ottoman empire devoured the Roman empire and ruled over the entire Middle East, including Israel, until 1909. The Islamic caliphate (government), centered in Turkey, was abolished in 1923.[12]

God sovereignly orchestrated the end of the Muslim empire in preparation for Israel's reemergence onto the world stage in 1947–48, hastened by the Holocaust discoveries at the end of World War II. *Israel's national rebirth in the twentieth century would not have been possible without the fall of the Ottomans.*

If we understand the seventh and eighth kingdoms to refer to the historical Islamic empire and its resurgence in the last days, then Revelation 13 and 17 fit seamlessly with Daniel 2 and 7 where the final (Antichrist's) empire is presented as a single empire with *two separate phases*.[13]

In Daniel 2:26–45, Nebuchadnezzar's dream revealed a statue made up of five distinct sections, each representing different historical empires. The first is Babylon (head of gold); the second is Medo-Persia (chest and arms of silver); the third is Greece (belly and thighs of bronze). The last two sections of the statue, the legs of iron and the feet of mixed iron and clay, signify two separate phases of the same kingdom. Similarly, Daniel 7 describes a vision of four beasts, each signifying different historical empires. The fourth beast and the ten horns that "arise from this kingdom" symbolize two separate phases of the same kingdom (7:23–24).[14]

Joel Richardson summarizes, "This would mean that the legs of iron in Daniel 2 and the fourth beast of Daniel 7 represent the historical Islamic empire, while the feet [and toes] of iron and clay [which does not

---

12. Richardson, *The Islamic Antichrist*, 96–98. Also see Bauer's historical volumes: *The History of the Ancient World*; *The History of the Medieval World*; *The History of the Renaissance World*; and Scott's *Mohammed & Charlemagne Revisited*.

13. Richardson, *Mystery Babylon*, 76.

14. Richardson, *Mystery Babylon*, 75.

mix well] in Daniel 2 and the ten horns of the beast in Daniel 7 represent the revival of this empire, which Antichrist will lead."[15]

The ten horns are ten kings (Daniel 7:24; Revelation 17:12) that will rule conjointly, not in succession. That these kings live at the "end time" and are *not* historical is proven because they make war against the Lamb and are overcome by him (Revelation 17:14), which alludes to the future final battle when Jesus returns to earth (Revelation 19:19–20). Also proving that the context is that of the future end time is the fact that the ten kings are said to be of one mind and will give their kingdom to the beast (Revelation 17:13), thus revealing the kings and the beast to be alive *at the same time*. Therefore, in John's day and as of this writing, the Antichrist's kingdom "has not yet come."

The ten crowns upon the ten horns signify the vested (joint) authority or rule of the ten kings over their kingdom. As said, this joint authority is eventually given *in consolidation* to Antichrist by the confederacy of the ten kings. Previously, in Revelation 12:3, the crowns were seen on the heads, not horns, of the beast because the context of 12:1–5 is *historical*, even within John's vision, and the mystery of the ten horns had not yet been disclosed (though it was about to be revealed to John).

The blasphemous name on the heads simply infers the idea of self-deification in that heads of empire often declared themselves as gods, accepting worship and the constructing of temples or images in their names—a practice to also be employed by Antichrist.

The Roman Absence

Why would the Roman Empire *not* be included in Nebuchadnezzar's dream in Daniel 2 or the vision in Daniel 7? Consider that Nebuchadnezzar's dream concerned three distinct kingdoms that would succeed his own (in Babylon). The Roman Empire at its greatest extent only reached Babylon for a few months as a result of Emperor Trajan's Parthian campaign in AD 116. However, in AD 117 Trajan suffered a stroke and died shortly thereafter. Hadrian, a close friend of Trajan, was swiftly hailed as Caesar and halted expansion, being convinced that the empire had reached its viable limits. Legions were recalled from the Lower Euphrates before they settled in and Trajan's fresh Mesopotamian provinces were abandoned.[16]

15. Richardson, *Mystery Babylon*, 75.

16. Constable, *Historical Atlas of Ancient Rome*, 125–26. Also Richardson, *Mystery Babylon*, 76.

Thus, Trajan's frontier expansion along the Tigris and Euphrates rivers was short-lived and hollow, lacking both Rome's bite and digestion. His many campaigns "exacerbated the difficulties of maintaining an empire."[17] With this understanding we cannot claim that Rome (after Medo-Persia and Greece) succeeded or even truly conquered *Babylon*, even though Rome is indeed the sixth head (empire) of the seven-headed beast that seeks to possess or destroy God's people. It is logical, then, that God would not list Rome as a true inheritor of Nebuchadnezzar's Babylon. Although, for first-century churches, Rome certainly embodied the antichrist spirit of Babylon due to the hellish parallels between Roman and Babylonian persecution.

I am aware that this unorthodox interpretation concerning the possible Islamic flavor to Antichrist's kingdom departs from decades (or more) of the traditional mainstay of prophetic scholarship concerning a revived Roman empire. For several years, my own biblical prophecy research was influenced by the idea of a possible "Roman resurgence." I will certainly not discount the years of studying that possibility; however, the September 11, 2001 attack on America by an Islamic entity (tied to Abraham's son Ishmael) introduced another facet to my research that has deepened as a result of the *progressive revelation* of passing years—a factor that reveals mysteries hidden by God only to be discovered by spiritual discernment and shrewd observations based on a depth of knowledge of God's Word in light of world history and unfolding current events (Proverbs 25:2–3). To ever assume that we have mastered the mysteries in Revelation regardless of or based upon prior scholarship is foolish, *for no prophecy of Scripture is of any private interpretation; it is taught and revealed by the Holy Spirit* (2 Peter 1:20–21).

Expectedly, there is much resistance and caution from many respectable and well-intentioned Christian ministry leaders. I join them in warning of the dangers of sensationalist bandwagons and silver-tongued false prophets. Yet just as the unforeseen birth of national Israel onto the world stage in 1947–48 nullified the errant teaching of replacement theology and renewed vigorous research in Bible prophecy, so now the unforeseen and unpredictable foe of radical Islam is forcing believers to reevaluate the history of empires and Islam's impact upon such, particularly concerning how God's sovereignty incorporates it into the end-time context.

---

17. Farrington, *Historical Atlas of Empires*, 41.

By no means do I believe the teaching of a "Roman resurgence" to be intentionally or entirely false, as it remains an astute attempt to comprehend eschatology. Nor am I parroting the increasingly popular but improbable notion of a strictly Islamic Antichrist who leads a radically Islamic empire. Indeed, the Antichrist and his kingdom will be unlike anything the world has seen, with numerous moving parts that cannot be predicted. I believe there will be traits of both Roman *and* Ottoman empires present in the incomparable future kingdom of Antichrist. Thus, as we study God's Word and world history, and as we closely observe global current events and trends, we can then pray for discernment and revelation as we strive to see God's activity so that we may assist and encourage those without hope toward living Christ's kingdom life now, before it is too late.

I believe the Holy Spirit has begun moving upon many individuals primely positioned to keenly discern and disseminate the prophetic winds that have been whipped up by the sudden widespread rise of radical Islam in the twenty-first century. At the vanguard of this company are disciples of Jesus who are proficiently experienced in cross-cultural awareness and who are internationally recognized authorities on the Middle East, Islam, and Bible prophecy. I have benefited immensely from their research which has assisted and affirmed much of what I have prayerfully been studying, discerning, and processing for the past twenty-odd years.

Therefore, I urgently recommend the literature and media programs produced by Joel Richardson, author and commentator for *WorldNetDaily*; Mark Biltz, founder of El Shaddai Ministries; Joel C. Rosenberg, author, commentator, and cofounder of The Joshua Fund; Robert Spencer, director of *JihadWatch*; and Reza F. Safa, pastor and former radical Muslim (Reza Safa Ministries), among others.

A Beast of a Kingdom

Revelation 13:2 reveals the beast as being *like* a leopard, with feet *like* a bear, and a mouth *like* that of a lion. This recalls the prophet Daniel's vision of four great beasts rising from the sea, each different from the other (Daniel 7:3–8). One was like a lion, one like a bear, one like a leopard, and the fourth was described as terrible, exceedingly strong, and having ten horns. As noted above, each beast represented successive empires: the lion, Babylon; the bear, Medo-Persia; the leopard, Greece; and the fourth beast, Antichrist's kingdom. The fourth beast of the Antichrist is identified by it having ten horns and making war against the saints for a "time and times and half a time" until the Ancient of Days (Christ) comes and delivers the kingdom into the saints' possession (Daniel 7:19–27).

Interestingly, when John sees the beast from the sea, it possesses the collective characteristics of each of the imperial beasts that Daniel saw, underscoring the idea that this "terrible beast" is exceedingly more powerful and far worse than any previous world empire. And since Rome was the ruling power of John's day he would have likely thought it a possible candidate for the beast he witnessed. Indeed, in retrospect we can see how the Roman empire has "set the stage" for the future rise of an archetypal entity. The same can be said of the Ottoman Empire. Indeed, when examining both Roman and Ottoman hegemony, an uncanny foreshadowing of Antichrist's future kingdom starkly emerges.

The latter part of Revelation 13:2 simply alludes to the fact that the dragon (Satan) is the basis of the beast's authority and power.

A Beast of a Man—The Dragon's Ascension

Revelation 13:3–4 shows one of the beast's heads (Antichrist) receiving a deadly wound, then being healed, whereupon all the world marvels and subsequently worships him. Occurring at the midpoint of the Seventieth Week, Antichrist will be killed and (his body) shall soon after be indwelled (or reanimated) by Satan himself, lending to the appearance of overcoming death. This circumstance sordidly perverts and imitates Christ's own crucifixion and resurrection and parallels the timeframe of the dragon ascending from the Abyss to make war on the two witnesses (Revelation 11:7). The healing of the deadly wound denotes a restoration to life, made clear from 13:14 which references "the beast who was wounded by the sword and lived." This is similar to the passage concerning Christ, "the First and the Last, who was dead, and came to life" (Revelation 2:8).

Further insight concerning Antichrist's death and healing, and the dragon's ascension, is found in Revelation 17:8:

> The beast that you saw was, and is not, and will ascend out of the bottomless pit and go to perdition [final destruction]. And those who dwell on the earth will marvel, whose names are not written in the Book of Life from the foundation of the world, when they see the beast that was, and is not, and yet is.

The Antichrist and the False Prophet

The phrase "that was, and is not, and yet is" would seem a contradiction according to logic, for how can it be said of something that it "is not, and yet is"? Consider that the context and perspective of "those who will marvel" remains clear as they shall see the beast *that was* alive, *and is not* alive (being killed), *and yet is* alive (being resurrected).

Another devilish perversion is displayed in Revelation 13:4 when the worshipers of the beast proclaim, Who is like the beast?, mocking the Hebrews' praise of God after being delivered from the pursuing Egyptian military: "Who is like you, O Lord, among the gods?" (Exodus 15:11).

In true prophetic form, the beast that is killed and then reanimated may hold a double-meaning: as with the *person* of Antichrist, so with the *seventh empire* (Ottoman) that dies but reemerges as the *eighth* empire (of Antichrist).

Revelation 13:5–7 lists a brief itinerary to be fulfilled by Antichrist. With his mouth he blasphemes God and everything holy. The authority to continue in power for forty-two months (three and one-half years) is *given* to him (showing God's enduring sovereignty), furthering the perverse mimicry of Christ since Christ's earthly ministry lasted the same. It shall also be *granted* to Antichrist to make war with the saints and to martyr them, recalling 12:17 when the dragon makes war with the "seed of the woman" (save those preserved by God in the mountains); and thus he becomes "world ruler."

Revelation 13:8 reveals that Antichrist becomes a politico-religious head to a damned people, i.e., those who *do not* have their names written in the Lamb's Book of Life. This verse offers distinction to 13:3–4 concerning those who follow the beast and worship the dragon. Their end will fare no better than the "worthless shepherd" God gives them (Zechariah 11:16–17).

Revelation 13:9, *"If anyone has an ear, let him hear,"* introduces 13:10 which is a divine promise to avenge the satanic circumstance that envelops the earth. Allusions to Jeremiah 15:2 and 43:11 are apparent.

Highly notable is that verse 13:9 is a truncated version of a passage appearing seven additional times in the book of Revelation at the end of each of the seven letters to the churches. The seven prior instances extend the passage to say, "He who has an ear, let him hear *what the Spirit says to the churches.*" Such an omission in 13:9 carries theistic gravity as it supports the reality that the church is no longer on earth during the Seventieth Week.

THE FALSE PROPHET—THE BEAST OUT OF THE EARTH (REVELATION 13:11-18)

"Then I saw another beast coming up out of the earth, and he had two horns like a lamb and spoke like a dragon. And he exercises all the authority of the first beast in his presence, and causes the earth and those who dwell in it to worship the first beast, whose deadly wound was healed."

This *other* beast is called the False Prophet in later passages (Revelation 16:13; 19:20; 20:10). That this beast comes up "out of the earth" in John's vision (rather than out of the sea) may be a reference to the idea of anti-Christian wisdom deriving from the earth (James 3:15; Philippians 3:19). Although, in referencing the four beasts of Daniel 7 the phrase "out of the earth" is synonymous with "out of the sea," for in Daniel 7:3 the four beasts came up "out of the sea" but in the interpretation found in Daniel 3:17 they are said to be four kingdoms arising "out of the earth."

The False Prophet is seen having two horns like a lamb, denoting an authoritative influence (horns signify authority) tempered by amiability and feigned humility (the lamb indicates a gentle spirit). He also speaks "like a dragon," revealing his cunning to be of satanic stock, and upon exercising "all the authority of the first beast (Antichrist)" the False Prophet shall direct the people of the earth to worship the "resurrected" Antichrist (Revelation 13:11-12). Thus the False Prophet is revealed as more of a religious leader than a political one, drawing much of the world's population into the Mystery Babylon cult (Revelation 17; 2 Thessalonians 2:8-12).

He will accomplish this through "great signs, even causing fire to come down from heaven" and "power to give breath to the image of the beast, that the image of the beast should both speak and cause as many as would not worship the image of the beast to be killed." This extermination results in the multitude of faithful Christian martyrs (Revelation 13:7, 15). The construction of the beastly image is done by the populace at the False Prophet's command, in response to Antichrist "overcoming" death (13:13-15).

One is reminded of the similar circumstance in Daniel 3:1-7 when Nebuchadnezzar made an image of gold nearly ninety feet high and set it up in Babylon, then summoned all his subjects to the dedication of the image and proclaimed that anyone who refused to worship it would be killed.

Apparently, the fabrication and animating of this image will be a technological wonder, if not outright supernatural manipulation. The masses will marvel and follow the beast, ultimately worshiping him as they are wooed by the unholy trinity of the dragon, Antichrist, and False Prophet. And to keep track of all subjects, a macabre scheme is unleashed and purposed toward enforcing allegiance or death:

> He causes all, both small and great, rich and poor, free and slave, to receive a mark on their right hand or on their foreheads, and that no one may buy or sell except one who has the mark or the name of the beast, or the number of his name. Here is wisdom. Let him who has understanding calculate the number of the beast, for it is the number of man: 666 (Revelation 13:16–18).

The Mark of the Beast

The development of a tracking system that forces one to acquiesce to specific demands or die (by starvation or martyrdom) is simply a swift and brutal method toward world domination, and Satan will know he has little time until his doom. Modern technology easily allows for such a system to be implemented broadly and efficiently, thus there is no mystery concerning how this kind of program could work. However, the catalyst toward implementing it would necessitate a maniacal tyrant (Lucifer) exuding a massive god-complex being granted an opportunity (from God) to take over the planet. Of course, this is exactly what Revelation reveals.

The ancient code of calculation referenced in Revelation 13:18 is specifically addressed to Jews who will be the initial target of the future false messiah. At the time of the end, none of the wicked shall understand; but the wise shall understand (Daniel 12:9–10). Here is wisdom: *Gematria* is a Jewish system of letter values where each of the twenty-two letters in the Hebrew alphabet is assigned a numerical value. This means that every person's name in Hebrew holds a specific numerical total. Certainly, countless different name calculations can equal 666. Therefore, using this method of inquiry, it is impossible to figure out *in advance* who the Antichrist will be. However, *when Antichrist appears*, those who have wisdom will be able to confirm his identity by calculating the numerical value of his name to be 666.[18]

Far too much speculation and pop-culture fascination surrounds the "number of the beast." The church need not be concerned with

---

18. Hitchcock, *The Complete Book of Bible Prophecy*, 202–3. Also Fruchtenbaum, *The Footsteps of the Messiah*, 173.

conjecture, for it will have been raptured from the earth and will not suffer the dreaded effects of the mark of the beast. Contemporary fears of receiving the mark inadvertently or by coercion are born of ignorance and hysteria. Paul warned the early church of making this same mistake pre-rapture (2 Thessalonians 2:1–12).

Scripture is our final authority and it states that 666 is the number of man. Mankind was created on the sixth day of creation, and man is not perfect. The number seven signifies perfection, for God rested on the seventh day. The number 666 represents a perverted trinity. Six falls short of seven, as man falls short of the glory of God (Romans 3:23). This is all we need to know.

Fortunately, both the Antichrist and False Prophet meet their final doom when they are cast into the lake of fire for eternity (Revelation 20:10).

The next chapter will conclude Parenthetic Revelation III and cover numerous subjects involving pronouncements, visions, judgment of the wicked, and Christ's victory.

13

Harvest and Vintage
Parenthetic Revelation III

A VISION OF CHRIST WITH HIS 144,000 ON MT. ZION

"THEN I LOOKED, AND behold, a Lamb standing on Mount Zion, and with him 144,000, having his name and his Father's name written on their foreheads" (Revelation 14:1).

In this anticipatory vision John sees Christ *after* his return to earth standing on Mount Zion with the 144,000 witnesses of Revelation 7:4 (Joel 2:32; Revelation 14:1–5). The image here of Jesus standing amidst his witnesses is strikingly similar to Jesus standing amidst the seven lampstands—his church (Revelation 1)—who glorifies Christ alone as the ever-present Light-source of his light-bearers.

John then hears harpers from heaven harping and singing a *new song* that no one but the 144,000 (and the harpists) could learn; the harpers are likely the heavenly congregation of martyred dead referenced in Revelation 7:9–17 and 15:2–3. The 144,000 would learn this new song as part of the celebration of Jesus' return and inauguration of his millennial kingdom. We also see in Revelation 14:1 the nature of the protecting seal from 7:3–4. The 144,000 are sealed—saved forever—with the names of both the Lamb and the Father!

Following the terrible revelation of the dragon, the war in heaven and on earth, and the beasts from the earth and sea, and preceding the more terrible vision of the final bowl judgments soon to unfold, it was surely encouraging for John to glimpse the joyous occasion of triumph and rejoicing at Jesus' return! Perhaps such interludes of joy spared John the season of spiritual sickness Daniel suffered after similar apocalyptic visions (Daniel 8:27; 10:16–18).

Differing schools of thought exist as to whether or not Mt. Zion in this passage means the earthly or heavenly location. Solvency of this issue is reached upon recollection that the 144,000 were sealed (Revelation 7:3–4) to be kept safely alive *through* the Day of Judgment *on earth*, their lives to then continue through the thousand-year reign of Christ *on earth*. The fact that John does not see them in heaven prior or subsequent to Revelation 14:1–5 supports the probability of the 144,000 remaining on the earth without experiencing martyrdom, therefore surviving the Tribulation and witnessing Jesus' spectacular return.

Although, in reference to 14:5 some see a rapture of the 144,000 just prior to Jesus' return. The passage states that the 144,000 "are without fault before the throne of God." For some, this places the entire context of 14:1–5 in heaven, for that is where God's throne, the four living creatures, and elders are. However, divine visionary revelation occasionally offers a mashup of events, place, and time. Therefore, having learned/composed their new song in heaven and incorporated it into the heavenly worship, the harpers (upon their return to earth with Jesus) would then teach the 144,000 the new song in honor of the witnesses' great testimony. Their being faultless before God's throne is likely a reference to being faultless before God in general, just as we "approach his throne" in worship yet remain on earth. Even so, a rapture of the 144,000 at or near the end of the Tribulation followed by their return to earth with Christ is unlikely but not impossible.

Hebrews 12:22–24 presents Mt. Zion as the heavenly Jerusalem, but this does not prove the context of Revelation 14:1 to actually be in heaven in that there is also an earthly Mt. Zion. Ultimately, Revelation 21:2–3 presents the heavenly Mt. Zion/Jerusalem descending *to the earth* after the thousand-year kingdom era.

Revelation 14:4–5 indicates the witnesses' purity in doctrine and morality (2 Corinthians 11:2–3). It is evident that they remain celibate in that they are "not defiled with women," though this is not a negative assault on marriage; it simply reveals that the 144,000 shall serve the Lord in *complete* devotion without any worldly distractions (1 Corinthians 7:32–34).

Some expositors suggest a nonliteral aspect to the 144,000 being virgins, asserting a "spiritually chaste" angle which allows for virtuous marriage as the witnesses fulfill their office—as if the idea of physical celibacy in service to God is unthinkable in light of the world's intensifying carnal culture. However, in that the 144,000 are raised up for a holy mission, it is requisite that they be distinguished in specific ways, as the Scripture passage states. Truly, with Jesus himself as an example, it is not difficult to imagine physically chaste servants of God, particularly if they are raised up when they are zealous *young* men (Jeremiah 1:7; 1 Timothy 4:12) in a time when marriage itself may not be a compelling aspiration due to the more pressing events of a divine call at the end of the age. Note that the apostle Paul proclaims celibate service to Christ to be the highest ideal for *any* age (1 Corinthians 7:1, 7–8).

As the Tribulation begins the remnant of Israel will experience a draw toward recognizing Jesus Christ as Messiah, thus the 144,000 are the "firstfruits to God and to the Lamb" in that they are the *first* Jews of the Tribulation to be restored into a right relationship with God. In this way they are representatives of a soon-to-be redeemed Israel and therefore firstfruits of the kingdom age. This understanding is based on the first of the harvest being dedicated to the Lord (Exodus 23:19; Numbers 28:26; Nehemiah 10:35). God even initially consecrated Israel in this way, for Israel was the firstfruits of all nations to serve him (Jeremiah 2:3). This factor ultimately foreshadowed Christ as the firstfruits of the resurrection harvest of all men (1 Corinthians 15:20–23).

In keeping with thematic flow, even within parenthetical interludes, the literary construct of Revelation reliably juxtaposes judgment with hope, death with victory. The preserving power of Christ is displayed in his servants' perseverance throughout the Day of Wrath. In seeing Christ present with them as they worship and prepare to enter into a millennial rule with him, we are thus prepared to meditate upon the dire details of the last and greatest judgment (the bowl judgments) to befall the earth. We also know that victory soon follows!

THE EVERLASTING GOSPEL PROCLAIMED

Revelation 14:6–7 is the only instance in recorded history that an *angel* is used to proclaim the Gospel. Notice that the angel reasserts God's sovereignty over creation:

> Fear God and give glory to him, for the hour of his judgment has come; and worship him who made heaven and earth, the sea and springs of water.

"And this gospel of the kingdom will be preached in all the world as a witness to all the nations, and then the end will come" (Matthew 24:14). This prophecy in Matthew puts forth "witnessing to all nations" as a sign of the end of the age, thus its *fulfillment* must come at the very end of the age. Assuredly, churches and missions worldwide continuously work toward evangelizing every nation as the end of the age approaches. Yet, contrary to some traditions, the church's efforts do not determine when the end comes—only the Father determines such (Mark 13:32-33).

Therefore, with the raptured church in heaven, only the 144,000 witnesses, multitudes of soon-to-be martyrs, and isolated groups of believers will remain on earth as a faithful testimony to lost souls; and so the Word of God will be presented by an angel of God to *all* the unbelieving world with absolute clarity, accomplishing the prophetic Word of Christ in one single supernatural act just before the end comes. Humanity will have no excuse.

Why is there no call to repentance or to faith in Christ or no mention of peace in the angel's message? God's dealing with humanity at the end of the age is unlike that of the church age, or even the Old Testament era. The witness of history more than suffices and God's direct involvement through his judgment only adds to the burden of truth. Again, humanity will have no excuse.

Some Bible expositors take issue with the idea of an angel proclaiming the Gospel because angels cannot soulfully partake of it. Indeed, salvation is a gift for humanity, but this does not bar angelic messengers from relaying salvation truth or even considering its experiential mysteries (1 Peter 1:12). Scripture frequently mentions unique missions of angels in regard to individuals and nations (Daniel 8:15-27; Luke 15:10; Acts 27:23-24; et al), including delivering Jesus' seven epistles to the seven churches (Revelation 1-3).

Others oddly insist there are separate gospels to be proclaimed (gospel of grace; gospel of the kingdom; gospel of circumcision/uncircumcision; dispensational gospels). To simplify, there is only one Gospel—the Good News of Jesus Christ—which itself can be described or labeled in many ways to be sure. Yet the apostle Paul warned that even if an angel from heaven arrived preaching a gospel different from what he had preached, then such must be rejected as accursed (Galatians 1:8). Moreover, the fact that John described the angel's message as "the everlasting gospel" verifies it to be for all time the genuine Gospel of Jesus Christ.

THE FALL OF BABYLON PREDICTED

In Revelation 14:8 another angel announces, *"Babylon is fallen!"* This prophetic warning of Babylon's impending doom (Revelation 18) offers a final opportunity for heathen to repent before their own destruction. This is also the first reference to Babylon in Revelation.

JUDGMENT ON WORSHIPERS OF THE BEAST

In Revelation 14:9–11 a third angel announces eternal punishment, specifically for those who worship the beast and take his mark.

BLESSED ARE THE DEAD OF THE GREAT TRIBULATION

Revelation 14:12 indicates that "saints" (true believers) are the intended subject concerning 14:13 when John hears a voice from heaven telling him that those who die "from now on" are thus blessed (Philippians 1:21). *From now on* in this context means from the initiation of Antichrist's mark of the beast until Christ's return, a timeframe spanning the final three and one-half years of the Seventieth Week—also known as the Great Tribulation. Martyred saints of this period are "blessed" because living during the Day of Wrath will entail such fear and torment as to be near unbearable, thus to die is a release from torment into heavenly rest.

JUDGMENT AT THE SECOND ADVENT— HARVEST & VINTAGE

Paralleling Joel 3:12–13, the context of Revelation 14:14–20 is that of Jesus Christ in heaven just prior to his glorious appearing and engagement with his enemies at the final battle of Armageddon (Revelation 19:11–21). He is called the *Son of Man* in reference to both his humanity and capacity as divine Judge (John 5:22, 27). J. B. Smith explains:

> The term [Son of Man] is applied to Jesus in the Gospels 84 times, 21 of which refer to his second coming. It is highly significant that it is never used after the Gospels except once in Acts 7:56 in Stephen's vision, and only once in all the epistles (Hebrews 2:6) and that in a quotation from Psalm 8:4. *The term is never used in respect to his personal relation to the church as the body of Christ.*[1]

John sees Jesus sitting on a cloud wearing a golden crown (authority) and bearing a sharpened sickle (judgment), for Christ is the true Reaper of those souls who stand against him: "So he who sat on the cloud thrust in his sickle on the earth, and the earth was reaped" (Revelation 14:16).

The white cloud indicates the divine judgment to be leveled at Messiah's return (Daniel 7:13–14; Matthew 24:30; 26:64; Acts 1:9–11), assuredly a frightening but grand display! John then sees an angel proceed from the temple in heaven to signal the final phase of judgment. Jesus thus begins the reaping and different angels perform their duties accordingly. Recall that these verses are an overview of what follows in greater detail outlined in Revelation chapters 15–19 (bowl judgments and Jesus' return).

With the blessed harvest of Matthew 9:37–38 having already been reaped at the rapture, the harvest of Revelation 14:14–20 is of the wicked. The imagery of angels gathering the harvest of "fully ripe grapes" from the "vine of the earth" and casting them into the "winepress of the wrath of God" recalls Old Testament prophecy (Genesis 49:11; Isaiah 63:2–6; Jeremiah 51:33; Lamentations 1:15; Ezekiel 32:5–6). It may seem strange in 14:15 that an angel instructs Jesus to reap the harvest, but this angel emerges from the heavenly temple, suggesting that his command is being relayed directly from the Father.

At the second advent evil has ripened to a point where God is ready to judge it in absolution (Zechariah 14:3; Revelation 19:15). The "fully ripe grapes" represent the rebellious "vine of the earth" that has brought forth generations of wickedness. Thus divine judgment will fall when Christ crushes those gathered against him, effectively producing a vintage of blood as God's winepress of wrath is trodden.

The "winepress" is noted as being "outside the city" of Jerusalem (Revelation 14:20), indicating that the terrible battle will occur near but not within the Lord's city. The amount of blood coming out of the winepress is stated to reach (or splash) as high as a horse's bridle (Revelation 14:20; Enoch 100:3) while spanning 1,600 stadia/furlongs (160 miles),

---

1. Smith, *A Revelation of Jesus Christ*, 219. Emphasis mine.

suggesting an extensive battleground. This graphic hyperbolic imagery may not be an overtly literal "river of blood," but the literal fulfillment of an indescribable "bloodbath" is distinctly clear.

The picture of a violently but justly judging Jesus does not sit well with many professing Christians, even to the point of some denying such judgment. This level of ignorance or denial begs the question: Do they truly know who Jesus is? If not, how can he be their Savior? A Jesus of the imagination shaped in one's own image will not suffice. I know some believers who have no problem disciplining their own children, other's children, employees, fellow churchgoers, or even friends. But they are convinced they would never personally be disciplined or chastised by Jesus via the Holy Spirit, despite Scripture that guarantees otherwise (Job 5:17; 13:10; Proverbs 1:29–31; 3:12; 30:6; Psalm 39:11; Jeremiah 30:11; Hosea 7:12–13; 1 Thessalonians 2:4; Revelation 3:19). We must serve God on his terms, not ours.

These individuals also choose to soften or ignore the hard truths concerning hell, being in-step with the Spirit, self-examination toward spiritual and personal transformation, weighing others by lack of spiritual fruit, and necessarily disciplined discipleship. I often remind these beloved friends that Jesus himself claimed he did not come to earth to bring peace, but rather a sword of division to determine those who were truly for him or against him (Matthew 10:34–38). Increased Scripture intake and a deeper prayer life are always a remedy to misinformation and a lack of spiritual discipline.

POLITICALLY OR BIBLICALLY CORRECT?

H. A. Ironside states:

> You will remember that our Lord Jesus spoke about the harvest, and he declared that it is the end of the age, the time when the wicked are going to be separated from the just, when he is going to gather the wheat into his garner but burn up the chaff with fire unquenchable. This is what you have here: *discriminating* judgment.[2]

By necessity, law and judgment discriminate. Sadly, political correctness has birthed a generation of relativism that has poisoned both secular and church culture. The only way to counter such vile propaganda is with

---

2. Ironside, *Revelation*, 153. Emphasis mine.

biblical correctness, for God's unbreakable truth exists eternally. As such, humanity can never escape or redefine God's truth. Consider that aspects of discriminating judgment often appear in great literary drama in that it is a direct result of the earth being divinely cursed (Genesis 3) and therefore a part of the human condition. For example, in *Macbeth* we see the eventual harvest of lawless ambition reaped in murder, and in *The Count of Monte Cristo* we see the harvest of avenged betrayal of the innocent.

A SIGN IN HEAVEN ANNOUNCING THE SEVEN BOWL JUDGMENTS

"Then I saw another sign in heaven, great and marvelous: Seven angels having the seven last plagues, for in them the wrath of God is complete" (Revelation 15:1).

In Revelation 15:1–4 John sees another sign in heaven specifically described as being "great and marvelous" because the consequences of the coming judgment will be more terrible than any previous and will effectively showcase the depth of God's wrath, and thus his sovereignty. Unlike the two previous signs John witnessed, which were symbols of literal truth (sun-clothed woman/Israel; multi-headed beast/Antichrist and his kingdom), the sign of the seven angels holding the seven last plagues is itself literal and actual (not a word-picture), though the imagery generated by the scene casts a heavy pall of doom in the mind of those who comprehend the angels' purpose.

Another perfect example of a sign being a literal event is seen in Christ's crucifixion. Jesus said, "When I am lifted up from the earth, I will draw all men to myself," and John explained that he said this *to show*, or signify, the kind of death he was going to die (John 12:32–33). Jesus also referred to his death, burial, and resurrection as "the sign of the prophet Jonah," meaning three days and three nights in the belly of the earth (Matthew 12:38–40). Jesus' manner of death also recalls the literal prophetic event of the bronze serpent lifted up before Israel so that all who had sinned against God might look upon the *sign* and be healed (Numbers 21:5–9). The image of the serpent on a staff thus became emblematic of both sin under judgment *and* healing, penultimately fulfilled in Christ. The emblem persists today in the medical arena.

The seven plagues are said to be the "last" because "in them the wrath of God is complete." This is also indicative of God's systematic judgment detailed in Revelation, for the bowl sequence follows and concludes the sequences begun with seals and trumpets.

THE SEA OF GLASS AND FIRE

The sea of glass mentioned in Revelation 15:2 is most certainly the same sea as in 4:6, though now we see the martyred dead (those having victory over the Antichrist) standing on it worshiping Almighty God. Recall the martyrs under the heavenly altar crying out for vengeance upon their persecutors and being told to rest until their number was completed (Revelation 6:9–11). Here their number is complete and their prayers for vengeance now turn to a song of praise as their petitions are about to be answered in full (8:3–5). That the glass sea is "mingled with fire" denotes both divine glory *and* fury, which is in keeping with the context since judgment is about to be unleashed upon the earth and all things anti-Christ.

PROPHETIC MELODY

The song of Moses and the song of the Lamb in Revelation 15:3–4 indicate thematic elements of *judgment* and *deliverance* and are sung by the martyred dead, whereas the song of the elders in Revelation 5:9 is a song of redemption. The song of Moses[3] offers historical reflection concerning God's faithfulness and justness (Deuteronomy 32) and also his deliverance of Israel from Pharaoh and judgment of Pharaoh's kingdom (Exodus 15:1–21; Psalm 86:9–10). As with Pharaoh and his army, so with Antichrist and his kingdom.

The song of the Lamb avows the martyrs' faith in Christ, for whom they died. The Law and the Gospel have become one, now merged into a splendid psalm of triumph! This song may reflect Psalm 22 which celebrates Jesus' humility, sacrifice, and ultimate victory. Psalm 22:27–28 parallels perfectly Revelation 15:4.

---

3. The Song of Moses and its God-ordained purpose (Deuteronomy 31:30—32:47) has been labeled "a key of all prophecy" by Franz Delitzsch in his *Bible Commentary on the Prophecies of Isaiah*, vol. 1, 74–75 (Edinburgh: T & T Clark, 1879). J. B. Smith described Moses' song as "a comprehensive survey of the entire history of Israel from the beginning to end when she will be a blessing to all the nations of the world" (*A Revelation of Jesus Christ*, 225).

The importance of music in the Bible often gets overlooked outside of the Psalms. The presence of musical themes appears regularly through Scripture, contrasting directly or indirectly light and darkness. Specifically in Revelation we see the contrast between hopeless life-stealing worship of the beast and the gloriously noble and gracious life with Jesus Christ. Note that worship of the beast is devoid of uplifting music. Harpers of God and heavenly choirs in worshipful reverie of the Godhead offer resplendent glimpses of divine harmony.

As a testament to God's truth even when not yet fully revealed in Christ, the powerful inescapable allure of transcendent composition even appears in pre-Christian history. For Homer began his song of the Trojan War by imploring a goddess to sing of the Wrath of Achilles. Truly, a divine source for music elevates earthly finitude to the eternal, even for pagan bards!

THE HEAVENLY TEMPLE

After these things, John looked and saw "the temple of the tabernacle of the testimony in heaven was opened" (Revelation 15:5–8). The imagery and events here, and throughout much of Revelation, repeatedly point to Israel and God's covenant with his chosen people, for the judgment outlined in Revelation is specifically directed at 1) Israel's rejection of her Messiah; 2) the nations that have cursed Israel; and 3) individuals who reject Christ and persist in their unbelief.

The "tabernacle of the testimony" is the Holy of Holies, located within the heavenly temple. The Ark of the Covenant containing the two tablets of testimony is situated here. With the temple opened, God is showing all heaven and earth that he indeed keeps his covenant on every level, and the time of full vindication has arrived. Moreover, John is seeing the *heavenly originals* of things that were constructed into purified earthly copies (Acts 7:44; Hebrews 8:5; 9:23–24). We may even reflect on how the ark that Noah and his family entered into to escape the flood judgment (Genesis 7:7, 16–24) prophetically foreshadowed the act of literally *entering into a covenant with God*, wherein his provision of a saving ark (or sanctuary) for Noah parallels Jesus' sacrificial provision of the same in that we now enter into his presence/sanctuary via the more intimate context of personal relationship—the new covenant (Jeremiah 31:31–34; Ezekiel 37:26; Matthew 26:28; Hebrews 8:6; 9:15).

The seven angels of Revelation 8:2 then proceed from out of the temple, each carrying one of the seven plagues of judgment (contained in a vial or bowl of offering; Revelation 5:8; 8:5) given to them by one of the four living creatures. These will be poured out on the earth in Revelation 16. That the angels proceed from the heavenly temple proves their station and priestly directive, as does their attire which reflects the same worn by Christ (Revelation 1:13)—pure bright linen with golden bands about the chest.

Some have considered that since the seven angels are clothed like the glorified church (Revelation 19:8, 14), they may thus *represent* the church; however, this has no scriptural or logical merit in that angels have never represented the church despite delivering messages to local churches (Revelation 2–3). More probable is that the pure white vestments signify the holy angels as sinless and of pure motive as agents of a Most Holy God.

Again noting the angels proceeding from *out of the temple* to perform their duty, we may conclude that God's judgments of wrath are not vindictive (vengeful) but vindicative (proven just).[4] His holy character *requires* him to punish the obstinate and impenitent, he is not merely inclined to do so per his justice. Yet God's justice is righteously reinforced by his perfect love—his being (personal constitution) and doing (chosen actions) are in absolute undivided accord, absent the carnality of emotional reactivity or indifference (Haggai 2:6–9; Zechariah 14:1–3; Malachi 3:1–6).

THE UNAPPROACHABLE GLORY

"The temple was filled with smoke from the glory of God and from his power, and no one was able to enter the temple till the seven plagues of the seven angels were completed" (Revelation 15:8).

No human is able to enter the temple until the last sequence of judgment is finished (at the end of the Tribulation), for the time of merciful intercession is over. The temple is filled with smoke from God's glory and power, signifying his displeasure which accompanies the vials of his wrath soon to be emptied upon the earth. Such a display is recalled from Exodus 40:34–35 when Moses could not enter into the tabernacle due to

---

4. Smith, *A Revelation of Jesus Christ*, 227.

it being filled by the glory of the Lord, though the context of Exodus 40 did not concern God's anger. Likewise in 1 Kings 8:10–11.

Isaiah 51:17 (ESV) describes this phase of judgment bluntly:

> Wake yourself, wake yourself, stand up, O Jerusalem, you who have drunk from the hand of the Lord the cup of his wrath, who have drunk to the dregs of the bowl, the cup of staggering.

14

The Overturning of the Bowls of God's Wrath

> Then I heard a loud voice from the temple saying to the seven angels, "Go and pour out the bowls of the wrath of God on the earth."
>
> —REVELATION 16:1

THE LOUD VOICE FROM the temple is God himself (Isaiah 66:6).

Upon examination of the bowl judgments one realizes some similarity to the trumpet judgments despite notable differences. The trumpet judgments affected only one-third of the earth, while the bowl judgments generally affect *all* the earth. Further, the bowl judgments occur in increasingly rapid succession, evoking prophetic urgency toward Christ's return.

It remains clear that the bowl judgments contain the completion of God's wrath, proving a supernatural enacting of the plagues. It is God's fury, not nature's fury or the devil's fury. Just as Pharaoh's magicians recognized the worst plagues as the "finger of God," so humanity will recognize God's wrath for what it is (Exodus 8:18–19). Pain and pestilence will be unbelieving humanity's reward for following Antichrist and rejecting Jesus Christ!

Considering the systematic aspect of God's ten-plague judgment of Egypt, there is evidence supporting a *late* Tribulation appearance by the bowl judgments, which effectively *follow* the seal and trumpet judgments rather than accompany them. Interpretive logic determines that a considerable amount of time will pass between the death and reanimation ("resurrection") of Antichrist (at the end of the first three and one-half years) and the emptying of the first bowl (toward the end of the second three and one-half years), which affects those who have the mark of the beast. During this interval the False Prophet's "miracles" will resonate with the masses, serving to solidify his position *prior* to constructing the image of Antichrist and enacting the beast's global mark system, which would entail yet more time (Revelation 13:11–14). Still more time will pass as Antichrist makes war with the saints and pursues those who do not take the mark (11:7; 13:7).

It is during this time outlined above (beginning at the midpoint of the Tribulation) that the trumpet judgments will fall and the three angels will make their proclamations, the last of which specifically warns against worshiping the beast or taking his mark (Revelation 14:6–10). When the first bowl is poured out, it is apparent that such worship and "marking" had become global. These angelic warnings also serve to introduce the seven bowl judgments (Revelation 15–16).

For easier comprehension concerning the last half of the Tribulation we may loosely assume that the trumpet judgments will last for a year and a half and likewise for the bowl judgments, although effects from both the seals and trumpets will remain cumulative as the bowls are poured out upon the earth and Antichrist's kingdom.

Therefore, in considering the comments above, one can see that the chronology of Revelation continues to flow appropriately in contrast to alternate interpretations which place the trumpet and bowl judgments as occurring simultaneously or beginning before the last half of the Seventieth Week.

THE FIRST BOWL: LOATHSOME SORES

"So the first [angel] went and poured out his bowl upon the earth, and a foul and loathsome sore came upon the men who had the mark of the beast and those who worshiped his image" (Revelation 16:2).

It is obvious that the ones affected here are those who "had the mark of the beast and those who worshiped his image," an appropriate judgment since they effectively condemned their own flesh by accepting the beast's mark. Those not having the mark of the beast and who do not worship him will escape this judgment.

Oscar Wilde's *The Picture of Dorian Gray* portrays a man whose inner life and deeds are wholly evil but whose face preserved a temporary appearance of noble morality. However, in the end his face outwardly expressed the repulsive rot of his true self. The foul and loathsome sores bring to the surface the infection of evil for those who bear the mark of the beast, the quality of their souls on public display.

Note Exodus 9:9–11 for a similarly sore experience brought upon the Egyptians.

THE SECOND BOWL: OCEANS TO BLOOD

"Then the second angel poured out his bowl on the sea, and it became blood as of a dead man; and every living creature in the sea died" (Revelation 16:3).

While the second trumpet judgment turned a third of the sea to blood, the second bowl completes the process, rendering the entirety of the world's oceans into blood. Every living creature in the sea dies. It is difficult to imagine the horrific sight, stench, and devastating impact.

Expositors at times will deny that this judgment truly turns the sea into blood, favoring instead the colorful language describing an *appearance* of blood via natural phenomena. Yet John said the sea "became blood," not *like* blood, or *as* blood. Recall our earlier discussion on comparative articles and interpretation. Nothing is impossible with God and the sea becoming literal blood is not beyond him or the poetic severity of his wrath.

Imagine, after a long and treacherous expedition across arid desert and frigid Eurasian mountains, Xenophon's ten thousand Greek warriors shouted with joy when they beheld the Black Sea! But the sea of blood that John describes will elicit no relief.

Note Exodus 7:20–21 when the Nile River in Egypt was turned to actual blood.

THE THIRD BOWL: RIVERS AND FOUNTAINS TO BLOOD

"Then the third angel poured out his bowl on the rivers and springs of water, and they became blood. And I heard the angel of the waters saying, 'You are righteous, O Lord, the One who is and who was and who is to be, because you have judged these things. For they have shed the blood of saints and prophets, and you have given them blood to drink. For it is their just due'" (Revelation 16:4-6).

This judgment expands the previous by striking even the *sources* of drinkable water, degrading humanity's condition exponentially. Revelation 16:5-7 offers divinely poetic justice: Jesus once turned water into wine; now a fatal draft is offered to those who have slain saints and prophets. Blood they have shed, blood they must drink.

In verse 7 the "altar," meaning those whose prayers in Revelation 6:10 are being here answered, responds: "Lord God Almighty, true and righteous are your judgments."

Note Exodus 7:19 when Egyptian rivers, streams, ponds, and pools were turned to blood, including the water in wood buckets and stone pitchers.

THE FOURTH BOWL: SCORCHING HEAT

"Then the fourth angel poured out his bowl on the sun, and power was given to him to scorch men with fire. And men were scorched with great heat, and they blasphemed the name of God who has power over these plagues; and they did not repent and give him glory" (Revelation 16:8-9).

Though the fourth trumpet judgment *darkened* a third of the sun, the fourth bowl does not contradict the former in that it affects the sun's *heat*, not light. Additionally, in understanding that Almighty God holds power over these plagues, there need be no assumption that he gives up any portion of such power to the angel in this passage. The phrase *"and power was given to him to scorch men with fire"* is simply a personification of the sun itself (some say a mistranslation was at fault here), which could be read, "and power was given to *it* to scorch men with fire."

Are *all* men affected by this plague? No. The context of the bowl judgments applies specifically to the beast, his kingdom, and his followers as mentioned concerning the first bowl and shall be noted concerning the fifth bowl. There is also no word qualifier in the above passage suggesting otherwise, or else it would clarify that *all* men were scorched with great heat. More significant is the fact that followers of Christ during this time would not "blaspheme the name of God" or refuse to "repent and give him glory." Therefore, believers will not be harmed.

Life-giving heat will become torturing heat. Men whose burning passions had been their moral undoing will suddenly burn in physical agony. He who has made God his foe has no friend in the universe, not even the sun.[1] The prophet Malachi wrote of this very judgment:

> For behold, the day is coming, burning like an oven, when all the arrogant and all evildoers will be stubble. The day that is coming shall set them ablaze, says the Lord of hosts, so that it will leave them neither root nor branch. But for you who fear my name, the sun [son] of righteousness shall rise with healing in its [his] wings (Malachi 4:1–2 ESV).

Note Exodus 9:8–12. Like Pharaoh, these piteously impenitent souls harden their hearts amidst the most terrible suffering mortal flesh can endure; and like Pharaoh, they shall have their rebellion confirmed as *the smoke of their torment ascends forever and ever* (Revelation 14:11).

THE FIFTH BOWL: DARKNESS

"Then the fifth angel poured out his bowl on the throne of the beast, and his kingdom became full of darkness; and they gnawed their tongues because of the pain. They blasphemed the God of heaven because of their pains and sores, and did not repent of their deeds" (Revelation 16:10–11).

The first four bowls affected aspects of nature (men, oceans, rivers, sun), the fifth bowl strikes the throne of the beast and his kingdom. God here begins to answer the boast "Who is like the beast? Who is able to make war with him?" (Revelation 13:4)

H. A. Ironside states:

> Darkness and anguish do not tend to soften men's hearts or to lead them to confess their sins. Their very suffering but stirs them up to blaspheme God the more. And so, in the outer darkness of a lost eternity, our Lord has told us that there shall be not only weeping and wailing because of suffering endured but also the gnashing of teeth, which implies rage and indignation against God.[2]

---

1. Harmon, *The Interpreter's Bible*, vol. XII, 483–84.
2. Ironside, *Revelation*, 160.

The cumulative effect and urgent succession of judgment is witnessed as the pain and sores of previous affliction remain even as further affliction is applied. The supernatural darkness described here evokes a historical reflection found in Exodus 10:21–23. As darkness saturated Pharaoh's kingdom yet light remained with the Israelites, so it is probable that darkness will affect only the immediate locations of Antichrist's seat of power and regional strongholds. And such darkness may be *felt* (Exodus 10:21).

Predictions of this judgment include:

> Woe to you who desire the day of the Lord! Why would you have the day of the Lord? It is darkness and not light (Amos 5:18 ESV).

> A day of wrath is that day, a day of distress and anguish, a day of ruin and devastation, a day of darkness and gloom, a day of clouds and thick darkness, a day of trumpet blast and battle cry against the fortified cities and against the lofty battlements [tyrannical elite]. I will bring distress on mankind, so that they shall walk like the blind, because they have sinned against the Lord; their blood shall be poured out like dust, and their flesh like dung (Zephaniah 1:15–17 ESV).

Jesus predicted this darkness in Mark 13:24–25:

> But in those days, after that tribulation [distress of prior judgment], the sun will be darkened and the moon will not give its light; the stars of heaven will fall, and the powers in the heavens will be shaken.

Revelation 16 verses 9, 11, and 21 reveal a refrain of willful impenitence amidst terrible and just judgment. This mulish rebellion may seem beyond belief, but those who receive the mark of the beast have indeed sealed their fate (Revelation 14:11). In response to this, commentator William Barclay reflects:

> Nothing that God could do to them either by appeal or by punishment would make them submit to him. We are bound to ask ourselves whether we are so very different. We do not doubt the existence of God; we know that God is interested in us and in the world which he has made; we are well aware of the laws of God; we know the goodness of God, and we know in our heart of hearts that sin has its punishment; and yet time and time again, knowing all this, we go our own way. The tragedy of life

and of the world is not that men do not know God; the tragedy is that, knowing him, they still insist on going their own way.[3]

THE SIXTH BOWL: THE KINGS FROM THE EAST

"Then the sixth angel poured out his bowl on the great river Euphrates, and its water was dried up, so that the way of the kings from the east might be prepared. And I saw three unclean spirits like frogs coming out of the mouth of the dragon, out of the mouth of the beast, and out of the mouth of the false prophet. For they are spirits of demons, performing signs, which go out to the kings of the earth and of the whole world, to gather them to the battle of that great day of God Almighty. . . . And they gathered them together to the place called in Hebrew, Armageddon" (Revelation 16:12–16).

The late John Walvoord, a premier Bible prophecy teacher and author, stated:

> A survey of a hundred commentaries on Revelation reveals fifty different theories, practically all trying to interpret what is meant by the "kings from the east" and also to determine whether the river Euphrates is literal or not.[4]

The volume of interpretations stressing a strictly *symbolic* approach renders those very interpretations unlikely. The absence of comparative articles concerning the river and the eastern kings as well as the logical cause/effect of what John explains in the text is therefore best understood in a strictly literal sense. Also, the river Euphrates is mentioned over twenty times in Scripture and not once does it symbolize anything, its context is always a literal river in Mesopotamia.

The drying of the river Euphrates could be done supernaturally, naturally by severe drought, or physically engineered due to the series of dams within its course; the result is the same—a way prepared for eastern kings and their armies. In fact, the Greek historian Herodotus offers an intriguing account of the Euphrates becoming shallow enough to permit the Persian king Cyrus to capture Babylon circa BC 539.[5]

The Euphrates river was the eastern border of the land promised to Abraham and his descendants (Genesis 15:18; Deuteronomy 1:7–8). And

---

3. Barclay, *The Revelation of John*, vol. 2, 166.
4. Walvoord, *Every Prophecy of the Bible*, 599.
5. Herodotus, *Histories* 1.191.

it was likewise the eastern frontier border of the Roman Empire. Both the Israelis and Romans had powerful enemies residing across the Euphrates. Israel feared the Persians, Assyrians, and Babylonians; Rome feared the Parthian Empire.

Contemporary thought often associates China, Japan, and Korea with the "kings from the east." While this is indeed probable (Japan is the "land of the rising sun"), there is a strong possibility that these *eastern kings* may include eastern *Muslim* nations such as remnants of Iran, Afghanistan, Pakistan, and many of the current "stans" that were formerly Soviet republics.

Perhaps Muslim and Asian nations act conjointly per the economic and military ties that link China, Japan, and North Korea to much of the Muslim world. In fact, as the final push to war plays out late in the Tribulation, the kings of the east ally with kings from both the north and south purposing to destroy the Antichrist and his alliance with powers from the west.

Revelation 16:13–14 is a prime example of Scripture interpreting Scripture, for John sees three unclean spirits *like* frogs issuing from the dragon (Satan), beast (Antichrist), and False Prophet. The three represent an unholy trinity and are listed according to rank. Also, frogs are considered unclean (Leviticus 11:10) and directly recall the second Egyptian scourge (Exodus 8:1–15). That these evil spirits follow the dictates of the unholy trinity is indicated by their issuing from the respective mouths. And it is these demonic spirits that "go out to the *kings of the earth and of the whole world*," not just the kings of the east, with the intent to entice, bribe, or convince them to gather for war in the Middle-Eastern theater, specifically at a location called Armageddon (Daniel 11:40–45).

Psalm 2:2 (ESV) foretells this:

> The kings of the earth set themselves, and the rulers take counsel together, against the Lord and against his Anointed.

Significantly, Gog, king of the north, and his loyal hosts (Ezekiel 38:3, 15) are not included in this prophecy. This is certainly due to their destruction approximately seven years prior at the beginning of the Tribulation, if not earlier.

THE FINAL CAMPAIGN

Armageddon is Greek for the Hebrew term *Har Megiddo*, meaning "mount/hills of Megiddo." Megiddo was an ancient city-stronghold in central Israel approximately fifteen miles inland from the Mediterranean Sea. Due to its strategic location overlooking the pass between the coastal plain and the valley of Esdraelon, the site has seen numerous battles spanning from BC 1468 to AD 1917. It was here that Barak and Deborah defeated Sisera and the Canaanites (Judges 5:19–20). It was also here that Gideon won victory over the Midianites and Amalekites (Judges 6). Even king Saul met his unsavory end in this place (1 Samuel 31:2–7).

The valley is fourteen miles wide and twenty miles long, though still is not large enough to entirely hold the vast gathering of personnel and equipment predicted. Likely the area will serve as a marshaling point since the referenced armies are said to cover a 160–200-mile area north and south of this key location (Revelation 14:20).

Revelation 16:15 seems odd in that it inserts a beatitude into the context of the final battle of the ages. Jesus says, "Behold, I am coming as a thief. Blessed is he who watches, and keeps his garments, lest he walk naked and they see his shame."

This pronounced blessing upon all souls faithful to Jesus Christ during this horrific time is an encouragement to zealously watch for his return. In the historical-cultural context in which Revelation was written it was common for people to sleep naked or minimally clothed. Keeping one's garments simply means remaining awake and alert (by sleeping clothed) so as not to be caught unawares in shameful slumber.

The verse begins with "Behold, I come as a thief." This indicates Christ's second advent since it actually *interrupts* the rising conflict between the gathered armies surrounding Jerusalem (Zechariah 14:1–3; 1 Thessalonians 5:1–11; 2 Thessalonians 1:6–8; 2 Peter 3:10; Revelation 19:11–21). Jesus will surely appear suddenly and unwelcome in the midst of those gathered for the final battle.

THE SEVENTH BOWL: FINAL DOOM

"Then the seventh angel poured out his bowl into the air, and a loud voice came out of the temple of heaven, from the throne, saying, 'It is done!' And there were noises and thunderings and lightnings; and there was a great earthquake, such a mighty and great earthquake as had not occurred since

men were on the earth. Now the great city [Jerusalem] was divided into three parts, and the cities of the nations fell. And great Babylon was remembered before God, to give her the cup of the wine of the fierceness of his wrath. Then every island fled away, and the mountains were not found. And great hail from heaven fell upon men, every hailstone about the weight of a talent. And men blasphemed God because of the plague of hail" (Revelation 16:17-21).

God's voice from the throne saying "It is done!" qualifies the seventh bowl as being the last in the series of judgments, therein indicating the end of Jacob's trouble and global upheaval, thus "finishing the mystery of God" (Revelation 10:7). The previous bowl gathered the armies of the world toward Jerusalem, the epicenter of judgment. The seventh bowl then enacts final judgment upon all gathered, followed by final judgment on all the world when Christ returns.

As God's anger manifests, a great earthquake unlike any before occurs (note Revelation 11:13 where a prior quake caused one-tenth of Jerusalem to fall). Isaiah 2:19-21 and Haggai 2:6-7 may reference this last "great earthquake" that divides the holy city into three parts as well as causing the cities of the nations to fall, the context evidencing a *global* affectation. It may be that this earthquake and subsequent judgment coincide with Christ's return, for

> the Lord will go out and fight against those nations as when he fights on a day of battle. On that day his feet shall stand on the Mount of Olives that lies before Jerusalem . . . and the Mount of Olives shall be split in two from east to west by a very wide valley . . . Then the Lord my God will come, and all the holy ones [saints] with him (Zechariah 14:3-5 ESV).

Some expositors believe "the great city divided into three parts" to be Babylon rather than Jerusalem. However, Jerusalem is clearly intended in that she has already been referenced as "the great city" (Revelation 11:8) and is plainly distinguished from Babylon *and* the cities of the nations (16:19), which would not be necessary if Babylon were meant. Moreover, if "the great city" was indeed Babylon, it would be illogically redundant to list "great Babylon" as another city to be judged, as implied by the conjunctive phrase "*And* great Babylon was remembered before God."

Revelation 16:19 reveals that "Babylon was remembered before God," signifying specific judgment further clarified as "the cup of the wine of the fierceness of his wrath." Details of Babylon's judgment are given in Revelation chapters 17 and 18, which we shall soon examine. From the time of her inception at the Tower of Babel to her role as a commercial/religious center for Antichrist's kingdom, the whore of Babylon has corrupted the inhabitants of the earth and made them drunk with the wine of her fornication, i.e., spiritual adultery (Revelation 17:2). Now, with divine poetic justice, the time has come for Babylon to drink the wine of the fierceness of God's wrath!

The disappearance of islands and mountains, and the plague of 100-pound hailstones described in 16:20–21 act as an understatement of the tremendously terrible final judgment upon humanity, and *still* hearts remain unrepentant (Isaiah 28:17; Proverbs 8:36).

Note the parallel between this plague of hail, that of the seventh plague in Egypt (Exodus 9:22), the hailstorm that destroyed Israel's enemies at Beth Horon (Joshua 10:10–11), the hail and firestorm that shall befall Israel's enemies in the near future (Ezekiel 38:22), and that of the seventh trumpet judgment (Revelation 11:19).

Another compelling reference is found in Job 38:22–23 when the Lord God asks Job if he has *entered the treasury of snow or seen the treasury of hail which he has reserved for the time of trouble, for the day of battle and war.* Mercifully, for those on earth who are Christ's, Psalm 46:6–10 (ESV) provides hope to this hopeless circumstance:

> The nations rage, the kingdoms totter; he [God] utters his voice, the earth melts. The Lord of hosts is with us; the God of Jacob is our fortress. Come, behold the works of the Lord, how he has brought desolations on the earth. He makes wars cease to the end of the earth; he breaks the bow and shatters the spear; he burns the chariots with fire. Be still, and know that I am God. I will be exalted among the nations, I will be exalted in the earth!

Chronologically, Revelation chapter 16 is followed immediately by chapter 19. However, a dreadfully detailed description of the seventh trumpet judgment to befall Babylon is recorded in chapters 17 and 18. This is the last of the parenthetic aspects of the book of Revelation. Before we examine John's record of Babylonian ruin, however, I have provided a brief history of the ancient city and its infernal spirit.

15

Babylon 101

A TALE OF TWO BABYLONS

GENESIS 11:1–9 REVEALS THAT Noah's descendants, rather than scattering across the flood-scarred earth, settled in the plain of Shinar (Babylonia). Here they developed and perfected architectural techniques that were utilized in constructing *ziggurats*, or high-stepped towers, often topped with idols, pools, and/or mirrors and "stargates" for occult purposes. One tower in particular became the focal point of humanity's rebellion against God Almighty: the tower of *Bab El*, a Hebrew word meaning "gate of God."

Due to the rebellious spirit and sinister motives toward world domination, God responded to the proud tower-builders of Babel—who were subject to Nimroud-bar-Cush (a.k.a. Nimrod, Genesis 10:8–2)—by distorting their single unifying language and thus forcing them to scatter abroad, lending to the word "babel" becoming synonymous with the Hebrew verb *balal*, meaning "to confuse, scatter, or mix."

Noah had carried the revelation of God's truth through the great deluge purposing to begin anew, yet his youngest son Ham seemed affected by the early post-flood apostasy (or perhaps the trauma of the flood judgment) and became a rebel, going so far as to reveal and revel in his father's shame amidst Noah's drunken stupor (also likely due to stressors of life; Genesis 9:20–24). Ham's name means "darkened," which is perhaps prophetic in reference to his own seared conscience as well as that of his subsequent generations who settled the continent of Africa following the exploits of his son Cush, meaning "blackened." To clarify, the meanings of Ham and Cush's names are not references to a curse of skin tone but of spiritual darkness. Ham's grandson Nimrod, meaning "mighty," explicitly departed from faith in the Lord God, founded many cities, and sought god-like adoration for himself.

Nearly two millennia after God dispersed the builders and partakers of Babel, the city of Babylon had grown fat in its now infamous ancient glory. In the sixth century BC, king Nebuchadnezzar was strolling about his royal Babylonian palace feeling quite pleased with himself. He remarked, "Is not this great Babylon, which I have built by my mighty power as a royal residence and for the glory of my majesty?"

Immediately, a voice fell from heaven:

> O King Nebuchadnezzar, to you it is spoken: the kingdom has departed from you! (Daniel 4:29–31 ESV)

When we consider the two historical incarnations of "Babylon" we can see the same evil flourishing. And despite many extra-biblical cult histories attempting to elevate Nimrod's Babel, it is Nebuchadnezzar's Babylon that holds more prophetic insight into the last-days Babylon—in part because of its intoxicatingly great wealth and growth into a world empire, but specifically due to its impact on Jews and Jerusalem.[1] The foundational evil of the tower of rebellion, however, will certainly ply its wares in the final conflict of the age.

Nebuchadnezzar's Babylon was used by God to judge the Jews for disobedience. Likewise, the last-days Babylon will be used to chasten Israel's continuing disobedience as a secular state, but it will also afflict Jews *and Christians* around the world. For "the dragon was enraged with the woman [Israel], and he went to make war with the rest of her offspring [dispersed Jews and Christians], who keep the commandments of God and have the testimony of Jesus Christ" (Revelation 12:17).

THE QUEEN OF HEAVEN: FACT OR FICTION?

I have included this short section only for information purposes to be discerningly considered. There are many Nimrodian legends that I have

---

1. Richardson, *Mystery Babylon*, 22–23.

encountered in my studies, but none possess the weight of verifiable truth, although there are some truthful principles and accounts to be gleaned from these narratives.

A major contributor to the lore is Alexander Hislop's *The Two Babylons* published in 1916. The unchanging common thread between the many traditions is the brief Tower of Babel account in the Bible. Author and commentator Joel Richardson advises against placing too much emphasis on "the Nimrod myth" and encourages full trust in God's Word.[2] In full agreement, I earnestly recommend Joel's book *Mystery Babylon: Unlocking the Bible's Greatest Prophetic Mystery*, wherein he discerningly navigates the unfortunately unfamiliar waters between Babylonian myth and God's prophetic truth.

A summation of the most prominent Nimrodian narratives is as follows:

Nimrod's wife was the infamous Semiramis (the First), the foundress of Babylonian *mysteries*, i.e., religions and cults. Thus, Babylon became the fount of idolatry and the mother of world paganism, sending her influence (children) throughout the earth. When Semiramis bore a son she proclaimed the birth a miraculous conception and declared her son, Tammuz, as a divine god-man, an obvious corruption of the Genesis 3:15 promise of the woman's Seed who was to come. From this the *mystery of the mother and child* was introduced, effectively perverting the truth of God and deluding surrounding nations year after year as the earth was repopulated by Noah's descendants.

Semiramis (and her likeness) became known as the "queen of heaven" (Jeremiah 7:18) and the image of her holding a baby boy permeated the world after the scattering of peoples following God's judgment at Babel, leaving only name differences resulting from language distortion. In fact, due to this being the religion of the seafaring Phoenicians, namely Ashtoreth and Tammuz, the apostasy spread swiftly far and wide.

In Egypt the mother and child were known as Isis and Horus; in Greece they were Aphrodite and Eros; in Italy Venus and Cupid, etc. Within one thousand years Babylonianism was a world-dominating religious system, from which Abram/Abraham was separated by the divine call (Genesis 12:1–4). Yet even as Israel began to pursue her identity as a God-chosen nation she was in constant conflict with Babylonian influence, eventually succumbing to it when king Ahab of the northern

---

2. Richardson, *Mystery Babylon*, 30.

kingdom (Israel) joined with a Phoenician princess named Jezebel. The southern kingdom (Judah) had a fondness for *Baal* worship—Baal being the Canaanite name for Tammuz—and ultimately suffered captivity in Babylon itself as judgment for rampant idolatry.

Generations later, after the incarnation of Christ and then his ascension into heaven, the early Christians carried the Gospel into a world saturated by Babylonianism in one form or another. Unfortunately, despite grand gains for the kingdom of God, the *mystery of iniquity* infiltrated the church when Rome adopted Christianity as its state "religion" and the draw of power and prestige usurped the desire for truth. Consequently, heresies such as the mother and child cult became "Christianized."

Truth be told, the earthly mother of Jesus *never* assumed deification or any comparable accolade. The final mention of her in Scripture occurs in Acts 2 where she is seen worshiping and praying with others as they are "all in one accord" under Christ. And though there is truth in the fictions concerning widespread dissemination of bad religion, for want of answers concerning Nimrod's kingdom, certain unquantifiable reports must not overtake the importance of Scripture or the prayerful examination of history and prophecy.

Indeed, the Protestant Reformation brought a slight respite from the actual apostate trends and practices of Roman Catholicism. However, Protestant denominations have repeated the sin of apostasy, falling away from biblical policy and ever toward church politics guided by human reason alone. Suggestions abound encouraging the union of Protestant entities with those of Anglican, Orthodox, Roman Catholic, cultic, and even Islamic faiths; but such would be a world-church confederacy, not the Body of Christ. Moreover, it would be Babel all over again. Outward unity is a façade if truth is compromised. Christendom is unified by those who have been made one in Christ, as members of *his Body*, not a body politic—a kingdom of relationship, not corporate affiliation.

A *CRUDE* NEW BABYLON?[3]

Presently a dusty ruin in modern Hillah, Iraq, approximately fifty miles south of Baghdad, Babylon's historical legacy traverses the peaks and valleys of prominence and decline. Never disappearing completely from the

---

3. Portions of this section are taken from my book *Firestorm: America, Israel, Iraq, and Their Prophetic Future.*

world stage, Babylon's history and ancient structures continue to fascinate historians, archaeologists, and tourists, although her infamous dynasties have branded the "arrogant city" (Jeremiah 50:31) with the metaphorical example of prideful ambition and ultimate evil.

When studying biblical prophecy (Old *and* New Testaments) one realizes that as global events begin quickening toward the final days of this age, Babylon's corporate rebellion will again become a world focus. Therefore, many students of prophecy anticipate Iraq's liberation and reemergence onto the international stage in a grand way. Following the 2003–2004 Gulf War II a "new Iraq" was handed over to the Iraqis and they are now well into their sifting season, plagued by bad politics, sectarianism, and sporadic war. Commentators and authors of history, along with experienced nation-builders, have predicted terminal failure at worst or a decades-long struggle at best for an Iraqi success story.

Yet inside a decade we witnessed impressive strides and accomplishments toward self-governance and international cooperation. Indeed, there are many nations that value a stable Iraq for the overall stabilizing impact it would have on the region, civil and financial. Perhaps as the fresh Iraqi parliament unifies and considers its rich Babylonian roots a "new Babylon" will replace Baghdad as Iraq's capital. Such a possibility is literally fueled by oil.

Beneath Iraq lie the second largest (perhaps first largest) crude oil reserves on the planet, behind only Saudi Arabia.[4] Saddam Hussein never fully harnessed or explored the extent of the sea of oil under the Iraqi desert, due in part to his ego and unsuccessful agenda to conquer territory (Iran; Kurds in northern Iraq; Kuwait), but also because of the volume of sanctions placed on his government as a consequence to his invasion of Kuwait in 1990. Over a decade of these sanctions put a severe financial strain on Iraq (as planned), made worse by Saddam's exploitation of any economic and humanitarian assistance (specifically aided by a corrupt United Nations).

Now with Saddam removed from power, Iraq's hostility toward Israel has ended, and with the cessation of sanctions, the restructuring of Iraq as a civil world player is underway. A total realization of oil exportation is Iraq's most obvious and prospective asset. Numerous nations are currently capitalizing on new credible partnerships with Iraq, for not only are new oil extraction and refinery facilities being constructed, but

---

4. Luft, "How Much Oil Does Iraq Have?" Brookings.edu/The Brookings Institution.

old ones are being rebuilt and improved. The US Department of State's 2015 Iraq Investment Climate Statement outlines the urgent necessity for American and global companies to vigorously assist Iraq's oil industry through multi-tiered investments that ensure all parties a slice of the Iraqi oil pie.[5] As crude and refined oil sales bring in wealth of all currencies, a boom in Iraqi modernization and expansion is resulting.

Geographically, the site of ancient Babylon is near the epicenter of the Middle East and is strategically positioned reasonably close to the borders of Iraq's crude-rich neighbors: Saudi Arabia, Iran, and Kuwait. Think of how *appropriate* it would be for a national/political (Antichrist) figure to have a seat of commercial and economic power literally on two-thirds or more of the world's oil.

The plagues of ISIS and sectarian violence have begun to wane and oil and money have begun to flow. With Iraq swiftly rising within the global community as it exports the "coveted commodity," can we be certain that the now nondescript *Babylon in Iraq* will be the Babylon of the last days?

No, we cannot. At least not yet. Though this is possible, alternatives exist that likewise could fulfill Scripture. We must remember that *Babylon the Great* is prefaced with *Mystery*, as the Bible indicates:

> *Mystery*, Babylon the Great, The Mother of Harlots and of the Abominations of the Earth (Revelation 17:5).

BABYLON . . . LITERALLY?

There will indeed be a literal city of Babylon in the Middle East that dominates much of the world during the reign of Antichrist (Revelation 17:3, 18). Moreover, the heart and allure of the city will be a pagan system of commerce and religion (Revelation 18:15–18). But there are many variables that have yet to disappear or emerge toward solidifying a prediction concerning Babylon's precise physical future location. We will soon examine this. Now, before we turn to Revelation 17 and 18, let us briefly refresh our approach to the mystery and interpretive logic of prophetic Scripture and history.

Biblical prophetic language frequently contains multiple levels of meaning, thus requiring multiple levels of understanding and

---

5. US Department of State, *Iraq Investment Climate Statement 2015*, 4–6.

interpretation. A reference may carry a historical, present, and future fulfillment, or any combination of these. Also look for metaphorical and ideological shadows within the literal fulfillment of prophecy that point to yet further fulfillment and/or reflections of previous prophetic fruition. Prophetic language often simultaneously contains concrete, conceptual, and *specific* (never arbitrary) symbolic meaning.

For instance, in Matthew 24:2 Jesus, in response to his disciples' awe of the buildings of the temple, states that "not one stone shall be left here upon another, that shall not be thrown down." This prophecy was realized forty years later in AD 70 when Roman emperor Vespasian, assisted by his son Titus, finally suppressed the Jewish revolt that began four years earlier in AD 66. The Jewish temple was completely destroyed, literally not one stone left upon another.

Accompanying the literal *concrete* fulfillment of Jesus' words rests the significance of *conceptual* (but no less literal) ideological change. The temple's destruction effectively ended the ritual offering of sacrifice, reinforcing the fact that Christ's sacrificial death was a final and permanent act and the "new temple" was to literally be the body of believers worldwide. Also, the date of the temple's destruction fell on the tenth day of the fifth month (Jewish 9th of Av), the same day that the first temple was burned by Nebuchadnezzar of Babylon in BC 586, thus adding a historical reflection to the AD 70 event.

When the Word of God intends a reference to be allegory or spiritual, it often says so. For example, Revelation 11:8 speaks of "the great city which *spiritually* is called Sodom and Egypt." As mentioned in the Introduction to this commentary, the apostle John here refers to Jerusalem (per its literal iniquity) as being *comparable to* Sodom and Egypt, making it clear that the meaning is *not* stating the cities of Jerusalem, Sodom, and Egypt to be literally synonymous.

Also, the comparative articles "like" or "as" and the subtle comparative phrases "having the appearance of" and "bearing the resemblance of/to" are indicators of metaphorical referencing found in both Old and New Testaments.

There are no such comparative articles or phrases in Revelation 17 and 18 despite the obvious extant symbolism. Rather, John is shown a vision and an angel tells him what each aspect of the vision *explicitly* and literally represents. Both concrete and conceptual meaning are explained.

John would undoubtedly have recalled an ancient prophecy of Zechariah that foretold of what he saw—Babylon's sudden rise and final doom at the end of the age.

BABYLON IN A BASKET

Zechariah, a prophet of the Old Testament (ca. BC 520), was born in Babylon, but returned with his grandfather to Israel/Judah soon after Jewish exiles were free of the Babylonian captivity. The name Zechariah means "Yahweh remembers." This significance of name has many implications, especially concerning the seventh of eight night visions Zechariah received on February 15, BC 519 (Zechariah 1:7). I have chosen to cite the following passage from the New Revised Standard Version for its clarity:

> Then the angel who talked with me came forward and said to me, "Lift your eyes, and see what this is that goes forth." And I said, "What is it?" He said, "This is the *ephah* that goes forth." And he said, "This is the iniquity in all the land."
>
> And behold, the leaden cover was lifted, and there was a woman sitting in the *ephah*! And he said, "This is Wickedness." And he thrust her back into the *ephah*, and thrust down the leaden weight upon its mouth.
>
> Then I lifted my eyes and saw, and behold, two women coming forward! The wind was in their wings; they had wings like the wings of a stork, and they lifted up the *ephah* between earth and heaven. Then I said to the angel who talked with me, "Where are they taking the *ephah*?" He said to me, "To the land of Shinar, to build a house for it; and when this is prepared, they will set the *ephah* down there on its base" (Zechariah 5:5–11, NRSV).

An *ephah*, or "basket" for measuring grain, was the largest measuring container in the Old Testament era, the equivalent to approximately ten gallons. Because of the period's societal dependency on agriculture, this image can be seen to represent *commerce* (locally and regionally).

Once Zechariah was clear that he saw an ephah going forth, the angel revealed a woman inside of it, then went on to identify her as Wickedness, representing the seductive iniquity (sin) in all the land. The image of Wickedness within the ephah indicates *corrupt commerce*.

The leaden cover that was lifted and then thrust back down upon the woman exhibits that the Lord God remains in control of events and their unfolding. God's sovereignty is further emphasized in Zechariah

5:9 as the two winged women (occult symbols of birth and rebirth) are described in their transport of the ephah.

Then Zechariah asks the obvious question, "Where are they taking the ephah?" The angel answers directly, "To the land of Shinar," which is in ancient Babylonia. The angel then explains why. A house (or temple, depending on the Bible version) will be built for the ephah (corrupt commerce), and once this is prepared (or established) the ephah will be set upon its base (or pedestal). The imagery used here of the house/temple being prepared and then set upon its base/pedestal is an archaic allusion to cultic practices and worship.

Through this vision Zechariah witnesses a future event when sin in its fullness again establishes itself with a primary geographic hub from which to offer its corruption to the world through a pandemic of tainted religion and commerce. Note the connection between *religion* and *commerce* made by this subtle vision. Paralleling the same, Revelation 17 and 18 address these two aspects of Babylon in great detail.

In Revelation 17, Babylon the Great, the Mother of Harlots, "with whom the kings of the earth committed fornication, and the inhabitants of the earth were made drunk with the wine of her fornication" (17:2) is none other than the woman of wickedness from Zechariah's vision. The fornication and wine refer to spiritual adultery against Almighty God and the seduction of false religious systems respectively. The power of religion cannot be underestimated. "And the woman whom you saw is that great city [Babylon] *which reigns over the kings of the earth*" (Revelation 17:18).

Revelation 18:3 goes beyond the religious detail and addresses the commercial, making it clear that the entire world has been seduced in both ways:

> For *all the nations* have drunk of the wine of the wrath of her fornication, the *kings of the earth* have committed fornication with her, and the *merchants of the earth* have become rich through the abundance of her luxury (emphasis mine).

Revelation 18:12–13 lists some of the merchandise sold in Babylon, including the "bodies and souls of men," surely a reference to every form of dehumanizing slavery. The tremendous and idolatrous impact that a reborn city of Babylon will have on world commerce and religion is discerned in Revelation 18:9–19 due to references of weeping and wailing kings, merchants, shipmasters, sailors, and all who trade by sea performing extravagantly dramatic rituals of mourning: "Alas, alas, that great city Babylon, that mighty city! For in one hour your judgment has come" (18:10).

SO WHERE *IS* BABYLON?

Conjecture, wild assumption, and bad interpretations of Scripture abound in regard to exactly where in the world the city of Babylon will make her appearance in the last days. It will certainly *not* be New York, Rome, Avignon, Washington DC, or Jerusalem, for the Bible indeed reveals the geography of Babylon's reemergence. And God's Word is the *final* word—the crucial connection between the visions given to Zechariah and John is where Scripture interprets Scripture.

In Zechariah's vision we see a basket containing a wicked woman (representing corrupt commerce and seductive religion) being taken to "the land of Shinar" (Zechariah 5:11). In Revelation 17–18 we see the wicked woman having been established as a great city that has seduced the world via a politico-religious commercial spirit identified as a whore named Babylon the Great. When receiving the vision of Babylon's rise and fall, John informed us that the Holy Spirit carried him away into the "wilderness/desert" where these events will occur (17:3). Part of the mystery rests with exactly where in this wilderness Babylon the Great will be rooted.

The land of Shinar, or Babylonia, is a vastly broad region according to the Bible and to numerous Bible dictionaries, encyclopedias, and biblical/historical atlases. Old Babylonia (ca. BC 1900–1600) at its greatest extent under Hammurabi reached from the Persian Gulf up to Harran and Nineveh in northern Mesopotamia, and east-west from the Euphrates river to the Zagros mountains.[6] Even today the entire area of Mesopotamia is surrounded by desert or mountain wilderness.

Hammurabi's dynasty eventually fell to the Hittites around BC 1595, giving rise to centuries of regional power struggles that would see the birth and death of the Assyrian empire (BC 1420–609). The later short-lived Neo-Babylonian period (BC 612–539) under the Chaldean kings Nabopolassar, Nebuchadnezzar II, and Nabonidas strived to restore

---

6. Hunt, *Historical Atlas of Ancient Mesopotamia*, 68–69; Bauer, *The History of the Ancient World*, 170–76; Keener and Walton, *Cultural Backgrounds Study Bible NIV*, 2343.

Hammurabi's civility and governance and built an empire of majestic splendor and renown. The capital city of Babylon became the largest city in the world. Henceforth, subsequent rulers (Persian, Greek, Seljuk, etc.) endeavored to claim the title "king of Babylon."

Predating Old Babylonia is the kingdom of Shumer (Sumer), of which "Shinar" may be a Hebrew rendering. Sumerian culture coalesced in the first generations (ca. BC 2348–2000)[7] after the great global flood as pioneers moved from the fertile Zagros foothills and settled in the southernmost part of the Mesopotamian plains which would better accommodate urban expansion. Such a migration was possible with the development of irrigation technology to draw and channel water from the Tigris and Euphrates rivers into fields. Remarkable agricultural productivity resulted in an area with virtually no rainfall.[8]

Around BC 2182 Nimrod, Noah's grandson through Ham and Cush, arose as a strongman amidst this prosperity and established the original foundations of the majority of Mesopotamian cities, many of which became the roots of a millennia of waxing and waning empires.

> The beginning of his [Nimrod's] kingdom was Babel, Erech [Uruk], Accad [Akkad/Agade], and Calneh, in the land of Shinar. From that land he went into Assyria [Ashur] and built Nineveh, Rehoboth-Ir, Calah, and Resen between Nineveh and Calah (Genesis 10:9–12 ESV).

Prosperity gave rise to prominence and a unified vision, as the whole earth had one language and one speech (Genesis 11:1). The basic ingredients of civilization as it emerged in Sumer included cities, writing, and the formation of capital and kingship.[9]

Genesis 11:2–4 records that early post-flood settlers journeyed from the east (Zagros), found a plain in the land of Shinar, and dwelt there. In time they began constructing temples and *ziggurats*, which became a source of pride and occult as they began to forsake the Creator God. Truly, any number of the cities throughout Shinar could have fit the

---

7. Using precise dates given in the Bible, the year of the great flood is very near to BC 2348. For meticulous research and exhortation concerning precision dating that reconciles biblical and world history, see Jones, *Chronology of the Old Testament*, 23–28.

8. Time-Life, *Mesopotamia: The Mighty Kings*, 17; Kriwaczek, *Babylon*, 19–20.

9. See William W. Hallo, "Sumer," in Metzger and Coogan, *The Oxford Companion to the Bible*, 719.

biblical description of Babel, for most every city boasted one or more such tower constructs.[10]

Eventually, however, Nimrod's subjects corporately agreed to build a particular city with a high tower so as to make a name for themselves, lest they be scattered over the face of the whole earth (Genesis 11:4). It seems there was a common understanding that such an endeavor was purposefully opposite of God's command for humanity to multiply and fill the earth (Genesis 9:1). Genesis 11:5–9 details God's judgment on this willful rebellion wherein he destroyed the tower and confused the single-language culture of the early Sumerians, forcibly scattering them abroad.

The ancient book of Jasher offers further detail to the biblical account of the tower of Babel, stating that after the tower's destruction Nimrod (also known as Amraphel in the Bible) continued to rule over his kingdom through forceful subjugation.[11] And though he reigned securely for a time, he did not turn to the Lord God. Out of mocking defiance, Nimrod established a new seat of power and called it *Bab El* in scornful commemoration of God confusing the language (Jasher 11:1–8). Here lies a root of willful unrepentant rebellion.

A few years after God's judgment, Nimrod dreamed of his own violent death which came to pass a century later at the hand of Jacob's brother Esau (Jasher 12:45–70; 27:1–16). If the Jasher account is true, Nimrod's death is certainly poetic divine justice.

Despite there being an accurate historical location of Nimrod's Babel (in modern-day Iraq) and its restorations by both Hammurabi and Nebuchadnezzar, God's message through Zechariah and John appears to suggest a specific *region* within which the harlot—Babylon the Great—will rise in the last days. I am not entirely ruling out the possibility of a resurrected religious and commercial Babylon on or very near the ancient ruins in present-day Hillah, Iraq; but it seems less likely now than I imagined only a decade ago.

---

10. Gentz, *The Dictionary of Bible and Religion*, 98. A self-serving spirit of making a name for oneself still manifests in countless ways, but now with truly global appeal via politics as religion. For example, the high rise building of the United Nations in New York provides the lofty platform for member states to implore, promote, and proselytize (many of which are petty dictatorships and corrupt; most of which are anti-Semitic). Former Israeli ambassador to the UN, Dore Gold, disclosed this very corruption in his UN biography, appropriately titled *Tower of Babble: How the United Nations Has Fueled Global Chaos*.

11. See Appendix B Expanded Commentary #8.

Joel Richardson expresses the same sentiment, effectually asking, "If the ancient city of Babylon and end-time city of Babylon are identical... Where is the *mystery*?"[12]

BABYLONIAN ZEITGEIST

Something that actually supports the mystery is the Babylonian *zeitgeist*, or spirit of the times (past, present, and future). One of the oldest villages in Mesopotamia is Eridu, which became a key city in Mesopotamian (and later Babylonian) mythology. An ancient chronicle known as the Sumerian King List was recorded on clay tablets around BC 2100, but surely preserves an older oral tradition.[13]

The record states that "kingship descended from heaven" and eight god-kings ruled for (unrealistic) eons *before* the Great Flood swept over the land. The postdiluvian section of the King List offers more realistic and historically accurate accounts of the region's power struggle, verified by archaeology, with some clear chronological correlation to the much more reliable biblical book of Genesis. The god-kings are in all probability some of the Nephilim/Rephaim we discussed in chapter nine, who would certainly desire to convolute world history away from God's truth. Their post-flood appearance would explain many of the fantastic ancient epics (e.g., *Epic of Gilgamesh*; *Enuma Elish*; *Epic of Erra*) that share similarities with and/or are antagonistic toward the biblical record. In particular, the Babylonian epic *Erra* tells of "seven sages endowed with sublime wisdom . . . who were the councilors of the antediluvian kings . . . and responsible for the invention and the building of cities."[14] These sages were presumably the fallen sons of God, or *Anunnaki*, which would imply that the "city" concept is a product of disseminated divine intelligence.

Eridu was established soon after the flood—likely by Nimrod—and became a hallowed place commemorating the pre-flood god-kings, specifically the original seat of the *first* king Alulim. It is believed by some that Eridu is the actual site of the "tower of rebellion," for it boasts the oldest and largest *ziggurat* ruins found in the region. It was never a

---

12. Richardson, *Mystery Babylon*, 189.

13. Bauer, *The History of the Ancient World*, 3; Kriwaczek, *Babylon*, 17. Mesopotamia is a later Greek name meaning "between the rivers," referring to the Tigris-Euphrates river valley.

14. Leick, *Mesopotamia*, 25.

political city, but rather a long-lived sacred site as can be inferred by the archaeological remains of many multilevel temple structures built on the broken foundations of the original tower *which was never completed and was abruptly abandoned.*[15]

The Sumerian epic poem of *Inanna and Enki* records that in time (after God judged the tower-builders) "one hundred basic elements of civilization" were transferred from Eridu to Uruk (the biblical Erech). One of these basic elements was writing, believed to be a gift from the ruling demigods under Enki, the god of wisdom.[16] Initially, as the first settlements and cities, including Eridu, began to develop on the Mesopotamian plains, oral traditions and civic records began to be inscribed. Then the Lord God confused the languages, causing innumerable trade rifts and, as intended, widespread dispersion. The increasing population and rise of estranged and independent villages and cities throughout the region then led to greater competition between the dynastic families and upstart kings trying to carve out their own separate kingdoms. In a bid for legitimacy, many appealed to the divine mythology and arts of civilization rooted in Eridu.[17]

As mentioned above, when God crushed the unity building project,[18] Nimrod relocated his power center and founded Babel along with many other cities. Uruk once grew so powerful (under Gilgamesh) that the empire's legacy still haunts us today through the name *Iraq.*

In that the *city* of Babylon did not exist until after the tower of Babel was broken, we can better understand a *spirit* of Babylon manifesting at different locations throughout history, though always rooted in the anarchistic spirit that arose in Eridu against the Creator God. Consider, for example, that Hammurabi was crowned in Eridu to honor the Babylonian *zeitgeist* he envisioned as "king of Babylon." By his time, Eridu was merely a shrine, yet the sacred site still captured the hearts of ambitious rulers via historical gravitas as the fabled origin of divine kingship—a Sumerian Eden created by the god-king Marduk. Even the later Neo-Babylonian

---

15. Gilbert, *The Great Inception*, 65.

16. Hunt, *Historical Atlas of Ancient Mesopotamia*, 26, 28. Inanna is later known as Ishtar, the goddess of love and war; Enki is the god of wisdom.

17. Kriwaczek, *Babylon*, 24–27; Leick, *Mesopotamia*, 17–25.

18. Possibly an attempt to construct an unholy mount of assembly for the *gods* toward domination of humanity. On a smaller scale, Mt. Hermon (in modern Syria) long served as an occult center for the post-flood Rephaim *gods* (Joshua 12:4–5; 13:11–12).

king Nebuchadnezzar (of biblical fame) added to his own list of titles, *King of Eridu*.[19]

Research will reveal that "Babylon" does not always refer to the city of Babylon in ancient texts, including the Bible where Babylon often was a veiled reference to Rome (1 Peter 5:13). This reason has erroneously led to speculation that the last-days Babylon would be New York City, Washington DC, Las Vegas, the Vatican in Rome, or Jerusalem. I wholly agree that a Babylonian *zeitgeist* exists in these and many other cities worldwide. However, we have seen that the context of both Zechariah 5 and Revelation 17–18 shows a specific region in the Middle East where the last-days Babylon will emerge. Exactly *where* in that region is the mystery.

Joel Richardson points out scriptural evidence that the last-days Babylon will be a composite of the most rebellious cities that God named and/or destroyed, including Rome, Tyre, Nineveh, Egypt, Damascus, Edom, Sodom, Gomorrah, and even Jerusalem. His book *Mystery Babylon: Unlocking the Bible's Greatest Prophetic Mystery* offers a riveting and compelling case for Islamic Mecca or Saudi Arabia being the heart of the last-days Babylon. Additionally, though, he draws attention to an intriguing report in the UK's *Guardian* concerning the Iraqi port city of Basra on the Persian Gulf.

Basra is called the Bride of the Gulf and the city has grown and modernized radically since Gulf War II in 2003–2004. A massive commercial and tourism center, Basra will soon be the site of the world's tallest building, called "The Bride." At the base of the building's towers will be something called "The Veil," a large canopy over a public area. The Bride will be the centerpiece of this swiftly rising city.[20]

REMEMBER THE FUTURE

Author Derek Gilbert believes that viewing global history with a supernatural worldview allows us to see a long game at work, one that mirrors not only the history of ancient Sumer but of the pre-flood world. In light of globalist modernization, he states that

---

19. Bauer, *The History of the Ancient World*, 8; Kriwaczek, *Babylon*, 30; Gilbert, *The Great Inception*, 53.

20. Richardson, *Mystery Babylon*, 189–90. Cited article by Rose, "The World's Tallest Building Planned—in Ex-Warzone Basra," TheGuardian.com.

the principalities and powers who are the true enemies of humanity are once again pushing us away from self-reliance toward dependence on government; away from an agrarian rural society toward one organized around cities; and ultimately away from independent nation-states toward a world ruled by a king beholden to the lord of the Abyss.[21]

Yet through the revelation of Jesus Christ we possess a blessed hope in knowing the end of our present history will bring the beginning of a new life in eternity with our loving Creator. We shall soon see his justice vanquish forever every injustice. Indeed, even Zechariah's name, which means "Yahweh remembers," carried the promise of fulfilled judgment as he witnessed the events preceding the eventuality of Babylon's final annihilation,

> For her sins have reached to heaven, and *God has remembered* her iniquities (Revelation 18:5).

---

21. Gilbert/Horn, *Saboteurs*, 304.

16

The Doom of Ecclesiastical and Commercial Babylon

Parenthetic Revelation IV

> Alas, alas, that great city Babylon, that mighty city!
> For in one hour your judgment has come.
>
> —REVELATION 18:10

ANY CONTEXTUAL COMPLEXITIES SURROUNDING Babylon the Great are the result of the *mystery* that yet remains. The progression of history, however, brings progressive revelation. As we near the end of the age the prophetic lens we peer through can become less dim, but only if we remain vigilant in our studies and prayers as we humbly serve and worship Jesus Christ, gaining ears that hear what his Spirit is saying to the churches.

Concerning prophecy, the Word of our awesome God informs us most often of *what* will happen but not exactly *how* it will happen. My intent for this commentary is to offer a primer toward developing an unbreakable biblical worldview founded on a strong discipleship complemented by keen observation, contemplation, and revelation. I have seen too many Christians base their worldview on weak discipleship, biblical illiteracy, willful ignorance, and ill-informed assumption.

The Doom of Ecclesiastical and Commercial Babylon

With little to no sound emphasis on Bible prophecy (and its bearing on world history) in both Protestant and Catholic denominations,[1] it is no wonder that many professing Christians lack the necessary biblical worldview. I pray that readers of this book, and more importantly readers of Scripture, will be encouraged and inspired to assist in reigniting a love not only for prophecy but for the *God* of prophecy.[2]

As we survey the doom of Babylon, recall that this judgment is necessary per God's perfect justice. The unrepentant must receive their reward of death and damnation. Jesus even disclosed the heaviness of his heart when he declared a desire for hastening that day in order to move on to the uninterrupted fellowship with his church:

> I came to send fire on the earth, and how I wish it were already kindled! But I have a baptism to be baptized with, and how distressed I am till it is accomplished! (Luke 12:49–50)

JUDGMENT OF ECCLESIASTICAL/RELIGIOUS BABYLON—REVELATION 17

In the last days *religious* Babylon will be in league with *commercial/political* Babylon. Their power base will be physically located somewhere in the land of Shinar, as discussed in the previous chapter. And, as we also previously discussed, if current trends continue it is very probable that a corrupted Vatican in Rome will be allied with both Antichrist and a resurgent Islam toward world dominance.

The conjoined politico-religious entity (made official with the signing of the seven-year covenant; Daniel 9:27) will be led by the Antichrist and False Prophet. For three and one-half years the religious aspect will assert more control over the commercial and political aspects, expressed by Revelation 17:3 where the whore *rides* the beast (Antichrist's

---

1. See Appendix B Expanded Commentary #9.

2. It is crucial to know who God truly is and not simply who we imagine him to be. This is only possible by experiencing him. He must never be a god of our finite imagination, for he is our infinite Creator God and intimately personal Savior, only known in accord with his revelation to us in Holy Scripture and in the Person of Jesus Christ with whom we may enjoy genuine relationship via his Holy Spirit (John 14:1–6, 15–18, 26). Again, I recommend Lahaye, *The Merciful God of Prophecy* for a relational perspective on divine love.

government) that carries her. This serves to bring much of the world populace into the fold of the proffered false faith system.

After three and one-half years the Antichrist no longer requires a broad religious influence and so casts off the whore and destroys her as he demands worship of himself as a god (Revelation 13:12–15; 17:16), ultimately resulting in the Antichrist's desecration of the Jewish tabernacle/temple in Jerusalem. This sets the stage for the last half of the seven-year day of God's wrath.

The Great Whore

In Revelation 17:1–18, John is shown by an angel the great whore/harlot "sitting on many waters," the waters representing "peoples, multitudes, nations, and tongues," i.e., the world, or a large portion of it (17:15). The whore is shown in this context to represent the "great city" of Babylon (17:18) and to have tremendous corrupting influence upon both the earth's general population as well as its leaders and kings, such control exemplified by her sitting upon a scarlet-colored beast (Antichrist and his government) that is clearly anti-Jesus Christ (17:3), a fact further detailed by her being arrayed in the trappings of worldly ideals of religion and nobility (17:4; Jeremiah 51:7).

Consider that the more a religious institution loses its inner morality, the more it strives to compensate for the loss by adorning the outer appearance. The church and individuals are no different (Isaiah 3:16–26).

It is significant that the angel showing John these things is one of the seven angels of God's wrath, for he has one of the seven bowls to be emptied upon the earth. Recall that Revelation 17–18 are a parenthetical retrospective look at events (specifically Babylon's fall) from Revelation 16 when the bowls of wrath are emptied. The seventh bowl heralds Jesus' return which is detailed in Revelation 19:11–21. Again, Revelation 19 immediately follows Revelation 16 with chapters 17–18 being an instructive interlude.

Revelation 17:5 offers an infamous title to the reader which is severely concise and appropriate for the whore: Mystery, Babylon the Great, the Mother of Harlots and of the Abominations of the Earth.

Severe judgment looms when the Lord God identifies cities as harlots (Nahum 3:1–7; Isaiah 23:15–18; Hosea 2:2–13), but here Babylon is named the *mother*, or greatest, of harlots! "Babylon" is a title that identifies all false religions and systems, including those claiming any affiliation with the one true God of the Bible (such as Jehovah's Witnesses, the Church of Jesus Christ of Latter-Day Saints, and Islam). Throughout Scripture we find references to Babylonian worship that has never entirely disappeared, such as weeping for Tammuz/Baal (Ezekiel 8:14) and providing burnt and baked offerings to the queen of heaven (Jeremiah 7:18; 44:17–19, 25).

Following the rapture of the church, Babylonianism will swell and dominate all shells of apostate Christian organizations. In fact, evidence of apostate infiltration of Christendom can presently be seen worldwide via the structure and trappings of most church denominations whether Catholic, Protestant, Orthodox, or Independent.

Revelation 17:6 presents this harlot as drunk with the blood of the saints and martyrs of Jesus Christ, igniting images of historic Romanism and its Inquisitions and portending that similarly worse horrors of slaughter will be unleashed by the Antichrist and his whore during the last days.

Revelation 17:7 describes the beast as having seven heads and ten horns and is the same beast as that seen previously in Revelation 12:3 and 13:1. The seven heads are "seven mountains on which the woman sits" (Revelation 17:9), possibly a sly nod to Rome since in John's day (and ours) Rome was called the city on seven hills. But hills are not mountains, nor are hills "kings" as the seven *mountains* are indicated to represent by 17:10 (as a parallel to empires). Also, many cities have seven hills and Rome itself has more than seven; Constantinople (Byzantium) was likewise known as "the city on seven hills."[3]

Surely, the city and empire of Rome in John's day possessed the nefarious Babylonian *zeitgeist* and was therefore a foreshadowing of Antichrist's future last-days Babylon. But Rome is *not* the last-days Babylon, as previously explained in chapter twelve of this commentary under the subheading: Antichrist—the Beast Out of the Sea. From that section I summarize:

> The mountains represent a *seat of power* (empire/kingdom; Isaiah 2:1–3; Daniel 2:35–45) upon which a king sits—specifically Rome in the immediate context of John's vision. But in broader prophetic context, Revelation 17:10 highlights the idea of *successive* empires (with their kings). In keeping with the diabolical designs of the seven-headed beast and with John's vision, we can conclude that five empires had fallen at the time John received

3. Brownworth, *Lost to the West*, 21.

the Revelation, one empire was in power (Rome), and one empire was yet future (Ottoman), for a total of seven empires/kingdoms. The Ottoman/Islamic empire will later be revived by Antichrist as the eighth empire, though it will be extraordinarily unique.

Revelation 17:8-11 are likewise explained in chapter twelve of this commentary.

The ten horns of the beast (17:3) are ten kings that shall not receive a kingdom until the appointed hour with the beast (17:12), when they shall be of one mind and purpose with Antichrist toward making war with the Lamb of God (17:13-14, 17). Once Antichrist determines that the whore is no longer of use, he casts her off by subjecting her to his ten kings who, out of their hate for her (i.e., religion), "shall make her desolate and naked, and shall eat her flesh, and burn her with fire" (17:16). The idea here portrays the universal truth of human hubris that manifests most readily among those in positions of power, resulting in an aversion to any form of accountability whether moral, constitutional, or religious.

The violent imagery concerning the destruction of religious Babylon reflects the suitably harsh judgment decreed by God himself pertaining to the daughter of a priest profaning herself by becoming a whore (Leviticus 21:9) and the denial of a decent burial, as was the case when *dogs ate the flesh of Jezebel, and her corpse was as refuse on the surface of the field* (2 Kings 9:35-37). Proverbs 5:3-5 also reads as a prophecy of Babylon's end.

Current trends within the global economic and political spectrums reveal a strong push toward an eventual world government headed by a cadre of crafty strongmen (probably unelected), which will choose/accept *one* among them to be their sole dictator, who is referenced in Revelation 17:11 as being the *eighth* king though he is *of* the seven. This odd reference simply evidences the demonic pedigree of Antichrist's impending assassination and "resurrection" (Revelation 13:3-4, 14), allowing for him—per satanic control/possession—to in fact be both the seventh *and* eighth king of the seventh and eighth empires. As with the kingdom, so with the king.

JUDGMENT OF COMMERCIAL/POLITICAL BABYLON—REVELATION 18

The overtly religious influence of Babylon shall govern the first half of the seven-year time of Jacob's trouble, and upon the harlot's end at the hands of the ten kings, the commercial and political influence of Babylon shall become the dominating force for the remaining few years, until its final doom at Christ's return (Revelation 19:11–21).

Note that religious Babylon is judged by the hands of men (per God's design), and commercial/political Babylon is judged directly by the hand of God. Prior mention of Babylon's complete destruction rests in Revelation 14:8 and 16:19, while 18:2 reiterates this surety when John hears the angel proclaim, "Babylon the great is fallen, is fallen!"

The law of retribution, or *lex talionis*, may apply here in reference to Revelation 18:6 (and Isaiah 21:9) where the heavenly voice calls for Babylon to be repaid "double judgment" for her iniquity.[4] Some expositors fittingly offer that the word "fallen" is stated twice in this passage due to the fall of Babylon occurring in two stages—the fall of the whore (religion) *and* the fall of the city (commerce/polity). Of course, the political and commercial Babylon becomes a new "religious" system in which a lost humanity places its faith, if not in the Antichrist himself.

Clarifying the Interpretive Context

There are a number of interpretations insisting that Babylon's prophecies of doom are strictly metaphorical hyperbole outlining the end of the historical Babylonian kingdoms and/or the overall end of evil via spiritual allegory. But as with all other prophecy of Scripture, interpretive logic proves a literal foundation and contextually precise fulfillment, even at the end of the age. We need only take God's Word as his Word indeed.

For example, Isaiah 13 foretells a swift and total annihilation of Babylon in the *last days*, complete with eschatological qualifiers such as "the *day of the Lord* is at hand" (Isaiah 13:6, 9); "I will *punish the world for its evil*" (13:11); "I will shake the heavens, and the earth will move out of her place, in the *wrath of the Lord of hosts* and in the *day of his fierce anger*"

---

4. The Mosaic Law presented *lex talionis* as "life for life, eye for eye, tooth for tooth, hand for hand" (Exodus 21:23–25; Leviticus 24:19–20; Deuteronomy 19:21). But for Babylon at the end of the age, the disregard of greater accountability and the guilt of greater iniquity lead to judgment that is doubly severe.

(13:13); "Babylon . . . *will be as* . . . Sodom and Gomorrah" (13:19). The Sodom and Gomorrah reference offers a historical reflection underscoring how terrible and thorough Babylon's final judgment will be.

Jeremiah 51 expands upon this theme of Babylon's doomed destiny, also including many textual qualifiers placing the detailed judgment within the last days—thus the *when* of the prophecy (as with Isaiah 13). Though imagery of *ancient* warfare is utilized in the prophecies of both Isaiah and Jeremiah—leading some to surmise such passages as having already been fulfilled (clearly missing the *when* context) or carrying metaphorical meaning only—one must consider *what* such imagery symbolizes and therein what literal truth is being conveyed, and to what end? Let us consider, then:

To what end do the prophecies of Isaiah 13 and Jeremiah 51 direct our understanding?

Babylon's complete and final ruin. Revelation 18 is the last and fullest account of this.

What literal truth is necessary to effect such an end?

Literal judgment is necessary to effect a literal complete ruin.

How is an understanding of literal judgment then conveyed?

It is conveyed through imagery of ancient warfare, though this imagery was "modern" in the day of the prophetic utterance. The *idea* being conveyed is that of an overwhelming military invasion against which there can be no hope of survival or escape when it is actually/literally accomplished. This played to the deepest fear of any nation surrounded by powerful enemies, especially a nation that had turned its back on God who would not hesitate to use those enemies to judge disobedience or rebellion.

The devastation to be wrought by the *future* judgment God described would have resonated severely with the prophets as he detailed in horrible measure the most destructive methods of judgment by both natural (warfare; earthquakes) and supernatural means (fire from the sky; angels of death). Moreover, the later disclosure of Revelation 18 adds frightening and final detail to the prophecies of both Isaiah 13 and

The Doom of Ecclesiastical and Commercial Babylon 219

Jeremiah 51, in which we understand the vivid warfare imagery to *symbolize* the literal truth of *actual judgment* that shall come swiftly, totally, and supernaturally.

It also helps to know that many prophecies, upon their utterance, have a near and far (or partial and complete) fulfillment, such as those against Babylon in Isaiah and Jeremiah. The near/partial fulfillment of Babylon's judgment came during Belshazzar's rule (Daniel 5:22–31) and the far/complete fulfillment will commence during the Antichrist's rule. This template is likewise displayed in predictions of Messiah's advent wherein his two *separate* advents were not readily discerned until after the first had been fulfilled.

The Great Whore Is No More

In Revelation 18:1–24 another angel appears to John in the wilderness of Shinar, but this is not the same angel mentioned in 17:1, nor is it one of those with the seven bowls of wrath, for John's words set it apart distinctly:

> After these things [the judgment of the whore] I saw another angel coming down from heaven, having great authority, and the earth was illuminated with his glory (18:1).

It seems this angel is reserved expressly for the final judgment of Babylon, and he descends from heaven with such illumination that dispels the fifth bowl judgment (Revelation 16:10) of supernatural darkness over Antichrist's kingdom. But for Babylon's inhabitants, the great light will only reveal the terror of an angelic bringer of calamity!

The angel then announces the long anticipated final fall of Babylon and designates it a place of foul tragedy (Revelation 18:2–3). The same announcement of Revelation 14:8 was a warning of impending disaster for commercial/political Babylon, but in Revelation 18 the judgment is leveled.

In Revelation 18:4–5 John hears a voice from heaven calling for God's people—all believers—to flee from Babylon and her sins so as not to receive the judgment of plagues she will suffer. It is difficult to imagine any of Jesus' own remaining in Babylon at such a late hour in the Day of Wrath, but apparently some do for reasons not stated (perhaps for evangelistic missions or seeking lost loved ones).

Jeremiah 51:6–9 formerly detailed this warning and the plagues referenced would be those mentioned in Revelation 16:19 as part of the seventh bowl judgment when "Babylon was remembered before God," for "her sins have reached to heaven," recalling the initial circumstance at Babel (Genesis 11:4-9). Also recall Zechariah 5:5-11 discussed in the previous chapter.

Revelation 18:6-8 speaks of divine retribution as applied to Babylon's judgment, namely *lex talionis*—law of retaliation—in that Babylon shall be given double in judgment for all that she herself offered in vice and persecution of God's own. Her proclamations of being a queen, not being a widow, and being impervious to sorrow are classic examples of self-glorification from one who knows the "depths of Satan" intimately (Revelation 2:24).

Moreover, this self-glorification is actually self-delusion, for we may juxtapose Babylon's view of herself with God's view of her: she sees a rich and powerful queen, where God sees a blasphemous worldly whore (Revelation 17:1-5). Her idea of not being a widow plays to her fornicating with the kings of the earth. In reality, she *is* a widow because God has forsaken her, his true bride being the church. And the judgment to come in recompense for her adultery will come swiftly in *one day* as she is "utterly burned with fire, for strong is the Lord God who judges her" (18:8), an indication that said burning will likely be a supernatural or supernaturally triggered event. Also see Isaiah 47:1, 5, 7-11.

Revelation 18:9-19 are a depraved lament chronicling the utter destruction of the city of Babylon and its devastating affect on all affiliated with her commercially, politically, and spiritually. Lust for everything material, sensual, and ungodly has undone every lost soul and the accumulated wealth of every worldly kind has come to nothing (Revelation 18:14).

Certainly John was here reiterating Ezekiel 27:25-36, where seafarers grieve the fall of Tyre. Heaping up corrupt treasure and pleasure in the last days, Babylon's suitors and bastards have fattened their hearts for the day of slaughter (James 5:1-6; Psalm 52:7).

> Neither their silver nor their gold shall be able to deliver them on the day of the wrath of the Lord. In the fire of his jealousy, all the earth shall be consumed; for a full and sudden end he will make of all the inhabitants of the earth (Zephaniah 1:18 ESV).

Weeping for their own dreadful losses and in fear of Babylon's torment, all who saw the smoke of her burning threw dust on their heads and cried out,

> Alas, alas, that great city, in which all who had ships on the sea became rich by her wealth! For in one hour she is made desolate (Revelation 18:18–19).

Placing dust or ashes on one's head is an ancient practice that signifies repentant reflection or an expression of deepest grief (Job 2:12; Lamentations 2:10), symbolically proclaiming humility before God or a base expectation of death (returning to dust). Indeed, Babylon's burning will incite many souls to madness and despair, for God proclaims:

> I will show wonders in the heavens and on the earth, blood and fire and columns of smoke (Joel 2:30 ESV).

In regard to the judgment coming in *one day* or *one hour*, consider that Revelation 18:8 is a broader perspective of Babylon's final doom whereas 18:9–19 are a more precise and personal perspective, lending to greater detail. A similar contextual construct is found in the book of Genesis, wherein 1:26–27 offers a broad account of man's creation while 2:7–25 is more precise and personal.

YAHWEH: THE TRUE AVENGER

"Vengeance is mine, I will repay," says the Lord (Romans 12:19 ESV). "Vengeance is mine, and recompense, for the time when their foot shall slip; for the day of their calamity is at hand, and their doom comes swiftly" (Deuteronomy 32:35 ESV).

In Revelation 18:20–24 the focus shifts from earth to heaven with a triumphant proclamation of martyrs being avenged and Babylon's final doom having been fulfilled. Verse 20 states, "Rejoice over her, O heaven, and you holy apostles and prophets, for God has avenged you on her!"

This is directed to those seen in Revelation 19:1 where we shall witness their response, though the mentioned apostles and prophets receive special recognition for having served and suffered in heavily persecuted ministries from the founding of Jewry to the end of the age. Their burdens are now lifted and their testimony has been proven true.

Babylon is fallen—even the penalty of bearing false witness (against God's own servants) will have been applied (Deuteronomy 19:16–19). In other words, Babylon has slain God's people, and now Babylon shall be slain.[5] Her spiritual sacrilege shall end.

---

5. Smith, *A Revelation of Jesus Christ*, 256.

John sees an angel throw a great stone into the sea (Revelation 18:21), which serves as a symbolic illustration of just how quickly Babylon will be judged and wiped from history, further accenting the prior references to her doom coming in "one hour." John describes the stone being like a millstone, perhaps in reference to Jesus' words from long ago:

> But whoever causes one of these little ones who believe in me to sin, it would be better for him if a millstone were hung around his neck, and he were drowned in the depth of the sea (Matthew 18:6).

These words are eerily prophetic in that now Babylon would have a millstone in place of jewels around her neck, dragging her into the deserved depths of death as she is tossed into the sea.

> How Babylon has become a horror among the nations! The sea has come up on Babylon; she is covered with its tumultuous waves. . . . Thus shall Babylon sink, to rise no more, because of the disaster that I am bringing upon her (Jeremiah 51:41–42, 64 ESV).

Revelation 18:22–23 underscores the complete disappearance of Babylon and verse 24 gives reason for her judgment, particularly recalling her persecution of Jesus' own (Revelation 17:6).

As previously mentioned, Revelation chapters 17 and 18 act as a parenthetical insert between the general event flow from chapter 16 to 19, whereas chapters 17 and 18 thoroughly detail the specific judgment on Babylon alluded to in 16:17–21. With the systematic judgment of seals, trumpets, and bowls now at an end, there is praise in heaven for the saints finally being avenged; and there is great anticipation for the wedding feast and Jesus Christ's imminent return to earth!

17

The Marriage of the Lamb and Return of the King

PRAISE IN HEAVEN FOR BABYLON'S END

"AFTER THESE THINGS *I heard a loud voice of a great multitude in heaven, saying, 'Alleluia! Salvation and glory and honor and power belong to the Lord our God! For true and righteous are his judgments, because he has judged the great harlot who corrupted the earth with her fornication; and he has avenged on her the blood of his servants shed by her.' Again they said, 'Alleluia! Her smoke rises up forever and ever!'"* (Revelation 19:1–2)

In Revelation 19:1–5, the loud voice of a great multitude in heaven, sounding as the sound of many waters and mighty thundering, is the same as in Revelation 7:9–12 and 14:2. This vast host constitutes nearly all of God's servants, and together they shout, "Alleluia!" However, Israel is not yet included in this heavenly chorus as they have not yet been redeemed, which will occur *after* Christ's return to earth. Returning with him will be the raptured church, martyred Tribulation saints, the resurrected righteous dead of all ages, and the holy angels.

Alleluia means "praise God," and is synonymous with *Hallelujah*, a transliteration of the Hebrew *halal* which means "to praise," and *Jah*, a shortened form of Jehovah (God/Yahweh). Psalms 113–18 are called the *Hallel*, or the Praise.

Revelation 19:2 is a direct response to the appeal of Revelation 18:20 and an answer to the prayer of Revelation 6:10 wherein the words "judge" and "avenge" are explicitly paralleled in reference to the great harlot's final doom. The "smoke of her burning rising forever and ever" (19:3) describes the everlasting destruction and eternal torment that Babylon will suffer (2 Thessalonians 1:9–10).

In Revelation 19:4-5 we see the twenty-four elders—previously identified as representing the church (see chapter five of this commentary)—and the four living creatures fall down in worship, followed by a voice from the throne directing the gathered multitudes to give God praise. The voice is certainly that of Jesus, for the Lamb is said to be seated with the Father on his throne (Revelation 3:21; 22:3). A psalm of the cross offers another example of Jesus directing praise to his Father (Psalm 22:22–23).

THE MARRIAGE SUPPER OF THE LAMB

"Alleluia! For the Lord God Omnipotent reigns! Let us be glad and rejoice, and give him glory, for the marriage of the Lamb has come, and his wife has made herself ready" (Revelation 19:6–7).

The praise in Revelation 19:6–9 shifts from gratitude for avenged justice and begins to anticipate the peace and reign of Christ on earth, to commence following his wedding in heaven. The Lamb's wife is clearly the church (Ephesians 5:22–33), which would include redeemed souls from Pentecost to the rapture. This passage is also the first direct reference to the church since Revelation chapters 1–3, reiterating the fact that the church has been *in heaven* whilst God's wrath poured onto the earth. As I stated in chapter four, Christ himself suffered his Father's wrath on the cross in his wife's stead, providing her an escape from the judgment on Israel and the world (2 Peter 2:5–9; Revelation 3:10).

It is Jesus' very act of giving his life for his bride that provides the foundational and prophetic understanding of the institution of marriage itself (Ephesians 5:22–33; 2 Corinthians 11:2). Jesus' bride, the church, will have been made ready at the Judgment Seat of Christ in heaven following the rapture (2 Corinthians 5:10), evidenced by her being dressed

The Marriage of the Lamb and Return of the King

in pure linen that represents both salvation and the righteous acts of the saints, i.e., faith and works (Revelation 19:8; Isaiah 61:10).

John's accompanying angel suddenly reiterates the instruction to write down the events being revealed, stressing that such is from God (Revelation 19:9). Perhaps John had, understandably, stopped recording the vision due to being overcome by the majesty of it all! This is in fact the second instance of *three* (Revelation 14:13; 19:9; 21:5) where John is admonished to "Write!"

The angel then indicates a blessed assembly that is *called to* the marriage supper of the Lamb (19:9), therein *not* being the Lamb's wife/church. Being in heaven, this blessed company includes Old Testament saints (Jew and Gentile, their spirits being in heaven), Tribulation martyrs (as their souls will go to heaven at death), and the angels. And though these three classes form no part of the church, they shall indeed partake of the same heavenly glory and are pictured as wedding guests enjoying the overall gladness and privilege of the occasion.

Markedly, the remnant of Israel is not included in this grouping in that she is still on the earth at this time experiencing judgment, effectively being among the metaphorical virgins with no oil supply that were forbidden to partake of Messiah's wedding (Matthew 25:1-13; also Deuteronomy 31:24-29). This judgment of missing the wedding of the Lamb parallels Moses missing his opportunity to enter the earthly Promised Land due to his lack of anger management as a prophet-judge of Israel before God (Deuteronomy 32:48-52). However, neither Moses nor Israel are rejected by God, but due to willful disobedience they are forbidden certain blessings prior to their ultimate restoration. This is illustrated well by Jesus' parables of the wedding of the king's son and the ten virgins (Matthew 22:1-14; 25:1-13), despite the emphasis on those who miss out entirely on kingdom glory by choice or negligence. Notably, Jesus' invitation to dine with him (Revelation 3:20) is literally fulfilled as the church and wedding guests enjoy blessed feasting and fellowship in heaven with their awesome King! Presumably, Moses will be a guest of the wedding supper along with the Old Testament saints in heaven, though such have yet to receive their resurrection bodies (which will occur at the second advent; Daniel 12:2). Yet Israel's salvation will not be complete until Jesus returns to earth with his bride and wedding guests, and thus Israel's celebration of final deliverance begins with the establishment of the long-awaited kingdom age.

To be sure, there remains a mystery concerning the duration and specifics of the Lamb's wedding celebration and supper that follow the rapture and Judgment Seat, which appear to continue in heaven as divine wrath consumes the earth. It would seem an odd but not impossible juxtaposition. Surely, some truths are not discernible by our finite and fleshly understanding; therefore, let us worship God for what he has both revealed and kept concealed for his future glory!

THE POWER OF JESUS' TESTIMONY

Revelation 19:10 describes John being overwhelmed by the glorious revelation of the Lamb's marriage celebration to the point of falling at the angel's feet in worship. The angel swiftly rebukes John's action, stating that only God is to be worshiped.

This verse also states, *"The testimony of Jesus is the spirit of prophecy."* Indeed this is a powerful truth proving that the primary purpose of prophecy is to reveal the infinite perfection, righteousness, and love of Jesus Christ. Specifically, Jesus' testimony is founded upon his incarnation, passion, crucifixion, and resurrection—his deity *and* humanity.

> And the Word became flesh and dwelt among us, and we beheld his glory, the glory as of the only begotten of the Father, full of grace and truth (John 1:14).

Jesus' testimony also contradicts the testimony of false prophets, for John had previously written:

> Beloved, do not believe every spirit, but test the spirits, whether they are of God; because many false prophets have gone out into the world. By this you know the Spirit of God: Every spirit that confesses that Jesus Christ has come in the flesh is of God, and every spirit that does not confess that Jesus Christ has come in the flesh is not of God (1 John 4:1–3).

A prophetic perspective promotes purpose; therefore, all who truly know Jesus and his testimony have been made free of all bondage and fear by his truth and love (John 8:32; 1 John 4:18). May our hearts burn within us as we encounter the risen Christ and his sure prophetic Word (Luke 24:13–32)!

> For to us a child is born, to us a son is given; and the government shall be upon his shoulder, and his name shall be called

Wonderful Counselor, Mighty God, Everlasting Father, Prince of Peace. Of the increase of his government and of peace there will be no end, on the throne of David and over his kingdom, to establish it and to uphold it with justice and with righteousness from this time forth and forevermore. The zeal of the Lord of hosts will do this (Isaiah 9:6–7 ESV).

THE GLORIOUS APPEARING

"Now I saw heaven opened, and behold, a white horse. And he who sat on him was called Faithful and True, and in righteousness he judges and makes war" (Revelation 19:11).

Revelation 19:11–16 could very well be the apex of biblical *apocalyptic* prophecy—perhaps the apex of biblical prophecy in its entirety. Old Testament prophets Enoch, Ezekiel, Isaiah, Joel, Zechariah, and others, each foresaw the Lord descending to the earth in the last days as a Warrior-Messiah bent upon destroying his enemies and establishing his kingdom. The significance and overwhelming gravity of these few verses cannot be missed by one who takes the time to consider what shall befall the world when this event comes to pass (Zephaniah 3:8; Matthew 24:29–30; 25:31–46).

In his descent to the earth from heaven, Jesus the Christ is vividly described. He is already victorious and astride a magnificent white horse, in direct contrast to the *pretender* of Revelation 6:2. His eyes are like flames that burn away every facade, and the many crowns on his head indicate absolute authority over all creation.

There is a name written that only Christ knows, for there shall always be a mystery concerning his sovereign identity which allows for faith and trust to remain a core aspect of all who believe on his Name (John 1:18). He is clothed with a robe dipped in blood, invoking his perfectly finished work of atonement on the cross and also further identifying him as the Word of God sent by the Father (John 1:1–4, 14).

The armies of heaven, consisting of the church, Old Testament saints, martyred Tribulation saints, and the angelic host, shall follow Jesus to earth, also atop white horses as their victory is assured in the King of Kings and Lord of Lords—a title worthy of the Son of Man and Heir of All Things. The armies shall not engage in battle, however. Victory is Christ's alone as he speaks judgment by the "sword of his mouth" upon those arrayed against him. The two-edged sword indicates the power and authority of the Word of God (Revelation 1:16; Hebrews 4:12; Ephesians 6:17).

The imagery of striking the nations with the sword of his mouth reaches back to Psalm 2:9, Isaiah 11:4, and Isaiah 63:3–6. Although it is difficult to understand *how exactly* Jesus will destroy his enemies, Isaiah 11:4 is a reminder of Genesis 2:7 where we recall that upon the creation of Adam, God *"breathed into his nostrils the breath of life, and man became a living soul."* In light of this, Isaiah records that Christ *"shall strike the earth with the rod of his mouth, and with the breath of his lips he shall slay the wicked."*

Our Creator can give life with his mouth, thus he can also revoke it. Furthermore, the picture of Christ "treading the winepress of the fierceness and wrath of Almighty God" puts forth the idea that his enemies shall be *crushed* (like grapes) and that it shall be a violent and bloody circumstance. Yet the battle at Christ's arrival to earth will not be one of give and take, for Jesus' victory has long been won. His enemies will be routed in an instant with the *breath of his mouth and the brightness of his coming* (2 Thessalonians 2:8)!

THE SWORD OF JESUS CHRIST AND THE WAR OF ARMAGEDDON (REVELATION 19:17–21)

In opposition to the armies of heaven, the Antichrist, the False Prophet, and the armies of the kings of the earth "gathered together to make war against him who sat on the horse and against his army" (Revelation 19:19; 16:14).

This short-lived battle is what is widely referred to as the War of Armageddon, which is the last battle in a series of campaigns that Christ launches against his enemies upon his return. The campaigns include Bozrah/Edom; the valley of Jehoshaphat/Megiddo; and Jerusalem (see Scripture passages below).

Jesus' return in final judgment is also the culmination of the seventh bowl of wrath (Revelation 16:17–21; 17–18), for the Lord declares, "It is done!" He then brings the prophecy to fruition, literally delivering Israel and the world from total destruction, for unless those days were shortened, no flesh would be saved (Matthew 24:22). Following his magnificent descent through the earth's atmosphere and his authoritative arrival over Jordan and Israel, Jesus will finally alight upon the Mount of Olives

The Marriage of the Lamb and Return of the King

to inaugurate what is only the end of the beginning (Zechariah 14:4; Acts 1:9–11).

In dark contrast to the marriage supper of the Lamb there is the supper of the great God (Revelation 19:17–18). John sees an angel inviting all the birds of the air to feast on the flesh of kings, mighty men, horses, and all other rank of persons who have chosen to make war against Jesus Christ. The carnage can scarcely be imagined.

> For the Lord is enraged against all nations, and furious against all their host; he has devoted them to destruction, has given them over for slaughter . . . the stench of their corpses shall rise; the mountains shall flow with their blood. . . . The Lord has a sword; it is sated with blood (Isaiah 34:2–6 ESV).

> Thus says the Lord of hosts, the God of Israel: Drink, be drunk and vomit, fall and rise no more, because of the sword that I am sending among you. . . . You shall not go unpunished, for I am summoning a sword against all the inhabitants of the earth . . . And those pierced by the Lord on that day shall extend from one end of the earth to the other. They shall not be lamented, or gathered, or buried; they shall be dung on the surface of the ground (Jeremiah 25:27–33 ESV).

A similar yet different circumstance of feasting carrion that occurs seven years (or more) earlier can be found in Ezekiel 39:17–20, which details God's destruction of Gog and Magog (Ezekiel 38).

Amidst the Lord God's reckoning the Antichrist and False Prophet are captured and cast *alive* into the lake of fire (Daniel 7:11), bypassing the great white throne judgment that all unbelievers will experience prior to their final sentencing to the fiery lake, which will occur after the 1,000-year reign of Christ on earth. At the end of the millennial kingdom the Antichrist and False Prophet are still in torment in the lake of fire, proving that such torment is not an annihilation of the soul into nonexistence, but rather a perpetual punishment for eternity (Revelation 20:7–10).

In Revelation 19:21 the sword of Jesus' mouth is again referenced, specifically revealing that "*the rest* were killed," meaning *all* of Christ's enemies gathered against him at his return except the Antichrist and False Prophet, who were not killed physically but were sent immediately *in the flesh* to their final doom. Ultimately, after Jesus' victory at Armageddon, all surviving peoples across the earth will be gathered and divided between the wicked and the just; the just inheriting the privilege to live in the millennial kingdom, and the wicked cast into hell (Matthew 13:47–50; 25:31–46).

For additional references to the second advent, see Deuteronomy 30:1–5; Psalm 2; 110:5–6; Isaiah 34:1–6; 63:1–6; Daniel 2:44–45; 7:13–14; Joel 3:1–2, 9–15; Zechariah 12:1–9; 14:1–5; Zephaniah 1:17–18; 3:8; Matthew 24:27–31; 25:31; Romans 11:26–27; 1 Thessalonians 3:13; 5:1–4; 2 Thessalonians 1:6—2:12; 2 Peter 3:10–18; Jude 14–15.

Philippians 2:5–11; Titus 2:11–14; and Hebrews 9:28 explain, correlate, and contrast the first and second advents of Jesus Christ.

18

The Millennial Kingdom and Final Judgment

THE BINDING OF SATAN

"Then I saw an angel coming down from heaven, having the key to the bottomless pit and a great chain in his hand. He laid hold of the dragon, that serpent of old, who is the Devil and Satan, and bound him for a thousand years; and he cast him into the bottomless pit, and shut him up, and set a seal on him" (Revelation 20:1–3).

Immediately after Jesus vanquishes all the armies gathered against him, an angel descends from heaven, having the key to the bottomless pit and a great chain in his hand. This angel may be Michael, an archenemy of Satan (Jude 9) who had cast the devil and his angels to the earth near the middle of the Tribulation (Revelation 12:7). It seems appropriate that Michael would also be tasked with Satan's incarceration. And, as with the angel of Revelation 9:1, this angel also receives the key to the Abyss from Jesus himself (Revelation 1:18). The great chain with which to bind the devil will surely be a literal divine construct that suffices to restrain a supernatural being (2 Peter 2:4; Jude 6; Enoch 88:1). Moreover, a literal binding is necessarily appropriate and just. Eisegetical metaphors are unwarranted.

With the Antichrist and False Prophet being sent directly to the lake of fire, Satan is instead bound and imprisoned in the Abyss (bottomless pit) for 1,000 years *"that he should deceive the nations no more till the thousand years were finished"* (Revelation 20:3). There is no threat of him escaping his bonds, for though he is a powerful being, he yet remains a *created* being subject to the Creator (Ezekiel 28:13, 15).

Also, the purpose of Satan's confinement is not punishment per se, rather it is to prevent him from deceiving the nations.[1] Of course, his deserving punishment shall come at the end of the thousand years.

Why is he not cast immediately into final judgment with the other two beasts? Revelation 20:3 states that *"after these things [the thousand years] he must be released for a little while."* We will examine the reason for this after our look at the thousand years.

THE SEVENTY-FIVE DAYS

An alert reading of Scripture reveals a 75-day interval between the end of the Tribulation and the beginning of the Millennium. Specifically, this interim will begin after Jesus' return to earth and victory over his enemies at the Armageddon conflict. We have previously established that each half of the seven-year Tribulation consists of three and one-half years, or 1,260 days. So now let us consider an intriguing lead from Daniel 12:11–12 (emphasis mine):

> And from the time that the daily sacrifice is taken away, and the abomination of desolation is set up, there shall be *one thousand two hundred and ninety days.* Blessed is he who waits and comes to the *one thousand three hundred and thirty-five days*!

The context of Daniel 12 is a brief vision of the latter half of the time of Jacob's trouble at the end of the age (12:1, 7). Daniel 12:11 confirms this, for the daily sacrifice is taken away and the abomination of desolation is set up at the midpoint of the Tribulation. The timeframe between this desecration and Jesus' return is 1,260 days (the taboo against date-setting the Lord's return only applies to the imminency of the rapture, confirming such to be pre-Tribulation). Therefore, from the time of Jesus' return an additional 30 days complements the 1,260 for a total of 1,290

---

1. Mounce, *The Book of Revelation*, 353.

days. Then the text stresses a blessing for those who wait until the end of the 1,335 days, which tallies another 45 days (30 + 45 = 75).

There is no mystery concerning this 75-day interim prior to the inauguration of the kingdom age. Such time allows for the "sheep and goat" judgment of nations (Matthew 25:31–46), the administrative establishment of kingdom saints and new nations, and any supernatural restoration of a blighted and ruined earth (2 Peter 3:7, 10–13).[2] Indeed, one can barely imagine the blessing of personally experiencing the transition from an earth-shattering age into an age of global peace and truly divine kingship, particularly those who will physically and spiritually endure the Tribulation as new believers and then be privileged to begin a new life in a newly fashioned world!

THE THOUSAND YEARS

"And I saw thrones, and they sat on them, and judgment was committed to them. Then I saw the souls of those who had been beheaded for their witness to Jesus and for the Word of God, who had not worshiped the beast or his image, and had not received his mark on their foreheads or on their hands. And they lived and reigned with Christ for a thousand years" (Revelation 20:4).

Often referenced as the Millennium (from Latin *mille,* meaning "thousand"), a period of one thousand years of predominant peace and progressive prosperity shall ensue following the establishment of Christ as Savior-King over the earth with Jerusalem as his seat of authority.

Let us consider a few common questions:

Is this "thousand years" literally one thousand years?

Yes. If 1,000 is a symbol and not literal, what about the many other specific numbers and durations found in Revelation—¼, ⅓, ½, ⅔, 1; 2; 3; 3½; 4; 5; 7; 10; 12; 24; 1,600; 7,000; 12,000; 144,000; 100,000,000; 200,000,000; 5 months; 42 months; 1,260 days?

When the revelatory message of God to men is specific it ought not be the response of men to un-specify it. Literal numbers can still carry symbolic meaning without disqualifying their literality.

There is no reason to *not* believe in a literal thousand years outside of overt eisegesis, wherein one assumes a personally preferred interpretation

---

2. For further commentary on the 75 days, see Hitchcock, *The End,* 363–66.

over a simple textual exegesis. Moreover, the phrase "thousand years" is mentioned *six times* in the first seven verses of Revelation 20, and there are *no* comparative articles (like/as) signifying a nonliteral meaning. And the passages in Psalm 90:4 and 2 Peter 3:8 that are frequently used to "prove" that the thousand years of Revelation 20 are symbolic do not suffice in that "like" and "as" are used in Psalm 90 and 2 Peter 3 toward promoting the idea of *divine perspective* of time, in which we are to understand that God is not hindered or affected by time for he is outside of it and in fact conceived it for human reckoning (Genesis 1:14–18). This fact imparts God's sovereignty as his prophetic revelation manifests and progresses over the course of time.

Some will postulate that the thousand years represent the present church age, adding that Satan is "bound" by the Gospel and thus diminished in his influence. This is a blatant corruption of Revelation 20:1–3. In direct contrast to this thinking, the New Testament reveals Satan to be a *very active* being, constantly opposing God's purpose in a real and actual manner. The following shows that Satan is presently far from bound:

- he blinds the minds of unbelievers (2 Corinthians 4:3–4)
- he is the god of this world/age (2 Corinthians 4:4)
- he can appear as an angel of light, even though he is fallen (2 Corinthians 11:14)
- he is prince of the power of the air (Ephesians 2:2)
- he commands influences of darkness in the spirit realm (Ephesians 6:11–12)
- he spiritually attacks believers (Ephesians 6:16)
- he walks about like a roaring lion, seeking whom he may devour (2 Peter 5:8)

These references reveal that the binding of Satan must be a *future* event that occurs 1,000 years prior to his final judgment of being cast into the lake of fire (Revelation 20:10). In both Old and New Testaments, God could not have been any clearer in his teaching of a literal kingdom on earth, further clarified in Revelation 20 by his thousand-year specification of the duration of both Satan's binding and the earthly messianic kingdom age. Any interpretation that offers conflicting assumptions and assertions will find itself getting lost in biblical translation at best or, at worst, falling to heresy. Notably, prominent early church fathers

The Millennial Kingdom and Final Judgment

understood the thousand years to be literal, including Justin Martyr, Tertullian, Nepos, and Athanasius. These, among many others, wrote and refuted the rise of the allegorists such as Philo, Origen, Dionysius, and Augustine.[3]

Is a literal "thousand years" necessary?

Yes. The kingdom of God has always existed, though not yet in full representation on earth. At present, Christians are ambassadors for Christ on earth (2 Corinthians 5:20) with citizenship in heaven (Philippians 3:20). The kingdom is not yet seen in full, for it exists *within the hearts of believers* (Luke 17:20–21)—a kingdom of relationship.

Most importantly, the thousand years provides the earthly context in which all of the major biblical covenants are literally brought to completion. In reference to Israel, every Old Testament prophet except Jonah foretold of a great era of restoration, peace, and prosperity wherein the kingdom of God would be ruled by a king of the Davidic/messianic bloodline.

However, only with the actual return of the Messiah will this kingdom finally be actually realized *on earth*, simultaneously fulfilling the Abrahamic Covenant (Genesis 12:1–3), the Palestinian/Land Covenant (Deuteronomy 30:11–20), the Davidic Covenant (2 Samuel 7:4–17), and the New Covenant (Jeremiah 31:31–34). Furthermore, an *actual* messianic kingdom on earth wholly edifies the triumph of Almighty God, reversing and negating the *actual* dominion of satanic rule we presently suffer.

William LaSor succinctly states,

> The messianic kingdom on earth is a vindication of God's creative activity . . . The triumph of God over the satanic dominion of this planet is necessary for the glory of God. If there were no messianic age, if God simply picked up the redeemed remnant and took them off to heaven, then we would have to conclude that God was unable to complete what he began.[4]

Scripture is full of predictions of a literal kingdom on earth to be ruled by the Messiah on a literal throne in Jerusalem (e.g., Isaiah 2:2–4; Ezekiel 37:21–28; Micah 4:1–4; Zechariah 9:10; 14:9), though the length of this kingdom was not disclosed until Revelation 20:1–7 in that God

---

3. Harmon, *The Interpreter's Bible*, vol. XII, 351–53.
4. LaSor, *The Truth About Armageddon*, 160–61.

had hidden such wisdom from those who crucified Christ, for had they known they would not have crucified him (1 Corinthians 2:7–8).

Revelation 20:4 is a reference to the enthroned elders (4:4–8; 5:8–10; 19:4) representing both the church and all other glorified saints and is the realization of a promise introduced in Revelation 5:10 that we would be made "kings and priests to our God; and we shall *reign on the earth*."

And while Israel will be regathered, restored, unified, and living peacefully among the nations of the earth (Ezekiel 37:21–28) as the priesthood among nations it was originally called to fulfill (Micah 4:1–4), it shall also be *judged* by the church, meaning that Israel will be under the church's authority. This future circumstance is confirmed by Christ through his words in Matthew 19:28 and Luke 22:29–30 wherein he expounded the apostles' reward for servanthood:

> So he said to them, "Assuredly I say to you, that in the regeneration, when the Son of Man sits on the throne of his glory, you who have followed me will also sit on twelve thrones, judging the twelve tribes of Israel."

The book of Revelation does not give us a detailed look at the thousand years. For this we must examine the prophets of the Old Testament.

Solomon wrote of the Messiah's earthly reign in Psalm 72. See also Psalm 2:6–8. Daniel prophesied of God's kingdom that would destroy all other kingdoms of the earth and then be established forever, filling the world like a great mountain (Daniel 2:34–45; 7:13–14). Isaiah 2:2–4; 11:1–10 and 66:15–23 detail the transition from a judged and broken world toward regeneration initiated after Christ's return to earth. Isaiah 65:18–25 describes a grand picture of the overall circumstance of the millennial kingdom. Jeremiah 23:3–8 and 31:1–14, 31–34 record further promises of an earthly kingdom to be literally realized in its fullest sense. Ezekiel 43:1–6 presents the return of the glory of the Lord to the temple in the millennial kingdom (see also Ezekiel 34:23–29; 40–48). Joel 2:21–27; Amos 9:13–14; Micah 4:1–7; Zephaniah 3:9–20; Zechariah 8:3–5, 14:8–11, and 14:16–20 also detail the transition from a broken world into the healed situation brought about by an earthly kingdom with Jesus Christ as king.

Upon thorough study of all passages in both Old and New Testaments concerning an earthly millennial kingdom, one must conclude that if it was not eventually literally realized, then God's promises to his people would be illusory at best and deceptive at worst; and neither illusion nor deception are ever a characteristic of God or his promises. Also, the idea that the thousand years is a metaphor for the church age (including present day) does not hold because at his return Christ resurrects those souls martyred for his sake (their martyrdom occurring *prior* to his return) so they can reign with him for a thousand years (Revelation 20:6). This proves the thousand years to be *after* the second advent. Moreover, the thousand-year messianic age is a preparation for the consummation of all things, i.e., eternity future and the life everlasting (Romans 8:18–23; Revelation 21–22).

Who does the millennial kingdom consist of?

Some nations, and thus many people, will survive the global Tribulation (and subsequent separation of "sheep and goats"), extending their physical lives into the millennial kingdom (Isaiah 24:1–6; Matthew 13:47–50; 25:31–46). And children shall continue to be born (to those who survive the Tribulation) throughout the new kingdom (Zechariah 8:5; Isaiah 11:8).

The surviving remnants of many nations will reestablish their destroyed countries rapidly without threat of war, crime, political strife, or impoverishment. These will be expected to honor Israel and perform annual pilgrimages to Jerusalem to worship King Jesus during the Feast of Tabernacles (Zechariah 14:16–18). Interestingly, if any nation neglects the annual worship in Jerusalem they will have specific blessings withheld from them (Zechariah 14:17–19), showing that a choice to obey or disobey with consequences shall yet remain for those new citizens of the millennial kingdom.

There will be different classes of citizens on the earth during Christ's thousand-year reign. Such will be 1) those believing souls who survive the Tribulation and are blessed to enter into the new kingdom, including their future offspring whom will assist in world repopulation; 2) the restored Jewish remnant who survive Jacob's trouble and then see Jesus as their true Messiah; 3) the resurrected righteous dead, Jew and Gentile, from the Old Testament era (Daniel 12:2); 4) the resurrected saints from the church age (effectively the bride of Christ); 5) the resurrected martyrs from out of the time of Jacob's trouble (who will hold a special place of honor serving in God's temple; Revelation 7:13–15); and 6) the holy angels.

Of course, no one class of citizenry will be more favored than another, as God shows no partiality (Romans 2:11; Ephesians 6:5–9; 1 Timothy 5:21; James 2:9; 3:17; 1 Peter 1:17). Yet all will have a role in kingdom harmony.

A RETURN OF SACRIFICES?

Ezekiel 40–46 describes an exquisitely restored temple that will be established in Jerusalem during the millennial kingdom, complete with a reinstated form of the ancient sacrificial animal offerings and order of priests (43:12–27). Of course, Jesus Christ has offered one sacrifice for sins forever (Hebrews 10:12), so the reinstitution of animal sacrifice is no longer a foreshadowing of his atonement, nor is it a return to Mosaic Law. Rather, just as with the Lord's Supper, it will be a powerful *memorial* of the great saving work he has wrought (2 Chronicles 2:4; Hebrews 7:26–27; 9:24–26). See also Isaiah 56:7; 66:20–23; Jeremiah 33:16–18; Zechariah 14:16–21; Malachi 3:3–4.

Even during the Millennium, with Satan bound and demons imprisoned, it will be exceedingly important for the growing *unglorified* human population to know that they are sinners and that their salvation is only possible by the substitutionary blood and death of Christ for their sins. Evil will dwell in the human heart alone. Full devotion to Jesus via a personal faith could be easily mimicked in a peaceful world with no outer enemy foils.

Therefore, the gravity of faith must be evidenced by works (James 2:20), and what better testimony of such a work as Christ's death and resurrection than that which is recorded in Scripture, confirmed by Jesus' own kingly rule, proclaimed by the church and glorified saints, and made starkly real by graphic bloody demonstration of prophetic history. Indeed, *the testimony of Jesus is the spirit of prophecy* (Revelation 19:10).

A GLOBAL RENEWAL

A worldwide renovation process will begin immediately following Christ's victorious return. With his starkest enemies defeated and sent to both hell and the lake of fire, his remaining foes will be rooted out:

> Therefore as the tares are gathered and burned in the fire, so it will be at the end of this age. The Son of Man will send out his angels, and they will gather out of his kingdom all things

that offend, and those who practice lawlessness, and will cast them into the furnace of fire. There will be wailing and gnashing of teeth. Then the righteous will shine forth as the sun in the kingdom of their Father (Matthew 13:40-43; see also 25:31-41).

The earth and its atmosphere will undergo great transformation, progressing from a violently cursed and judged state amidst the Tribulation into an increasingly restored condition in preparation for a final overhaul into perfection at the end of the Millennium (2 Peter 3:3-13; Revelation 21:1):

> I looked when he opened the sixth seal, and behold, there was a great earthquake; and the sun became black as sackcloth of hair, and the moon became like blood. And the stars of heaven fell to earth, as a fig tree drops its late figs when it is shaken by a mighty wind. Then the sky receded as a scroll when it is rolled up, and every mountain and island was moved out of its place. . . . Then the angel took the censer, filled it with fire from the altar, and threw it to the earth. And there were noises, thunderings, lightnings, and an earthquake. And something like a great mountain burning with fire was thrown into the sea, and a third of the sea became blood. . . . And a great star fell from heaven, burning like a torch, and it fell on a third of the rivers and on the springs of water (Revelation 6:12-14; 8:5, 8, 10).

> Behold, the Lord will empty the earth and make it desolate, and he will twist its surface and scatter its inhabitants. . . . The earth shall be utterly empty and utterly plundered; for the Lord has spoken this word. The earth mourns and withers; the world languishes and withers; the highest people of the earth languish. The earth lies defiled under its inhabitants; for they have transgressed the laws, violated the statutes, broken the everlasting covenant. Therefore a curse devours the earth, and its inhabitants suffer for their guilt; . . . [they] are scorched, and few men are left (Isaiah 24:1, 3-6 ESV).

> "Therefore wait for me," declares the Lord, "for the day when I rise up to seize the prey. For my decision is to gather nations, to assemble kingdoms, to pour out upon them my indignation, all my burning anger; for in the fire of my jealousy all the earth shall be consumed" (Zephaniah 3:8 ESV).

> [Yet] the burning sand shall become a pool, and the thirsty ground springs of water; in the haunt of jackals, where they lie down, the grass shall become reeds and rushes (Isaiah 35:7 ESV).

> So shall my word be that goes out from my mouth; it shall not return to me empty, . . . the mountains and the hills before you shall break forth into singing, and all the trees of the field shall clap their hands. Instead of the thorn shall come up the cypress; instead of the brier shall come up the myrtle (Isaiah 55:11–13 ESV).

> Our Father in heaven, hallowed be your name. Your kingdom come. Your will be done on earth as it is in heaven (Matthew 6:9–10).

The world's social and political landscape will also experience drastic transformation as societal fragmentation at every level will cease. Moreover, Jerusalem will not only serve as the place of Jesus' throne, but as capital of the millennial earth:

> It shall come to pass in the latter days that the mountain of the house of the Lord shall be established as the highest of the mountains, and shall be lifted up above the hills; and all the nations shall flow to it, . . . for out of Zion shall go forth the law, and the word of the Lord from Jerusalem. He shall judge between the nations, and shall decide disputes for many peoples; and they shall beat their swords into plowshares, and their spears into pruning hooks; nation shall not lift up sword against nation, neither shall they learn war anymore (Isaiah 2:2–4; Micah 4:1–3 ESV).

> And the Lord will be king over all the earth. . . . Jerusalem shall remain aloft on its site from the Gate of Benjamin to the place of the former gate, to the Corner Gate, and from the Tower of Hananel to the king's winepresses. And it shall be inhabited, for there shall never again be a decree of utter destruction. Jerusalem shall dwell in security (Zechariah 14:9–11 ESV).

> Violence shall no more be heard in your land, devastation or destruction within your borders; you shall call your walls Salvation, and your gates Praise. . . . Your people shall all be righteous; they shall possess the land forever, the branch of my planting, the work of my hands, that I might be glorified. . . . For as the earth brings forth its sprouts, and as a garden causes what is sown in it to sprout up, so the Lord God will cause righteousness and praise to sprout up before all the nations (Isaiah 60:18, 21; 61:11 ESV).

The rule of law and justice—affecting the entire earth—will be forever instated:

The Millennial Kingdom and Final Judgment

> Behold my servant whom I uphold, my chosen, in whom my soul delights; I have put my Spirit upon him; he will bring forth justice to the nations. . . . he will faithfully bring forth justice. He will not grow faint or be discouraged till he has established justice in the earth; and the coastlands wait for his law (Isaiah 42:1–4 ESV).

> Of the increase of his government and of peace there will be no end, on the throne of David and over his kingdom, to establish it and to uphold it with justice and with righteousness from this time forth and forevermore (Isaiah 9:7 ESV).

> Behold, the tabernacle of God is with men, and he will dwell with them, and they shall be his people. God himself will be with them and be their God (Revelation 21:3).

> Thus says the Lord: I have returned to Zion and will dwell in the midst of Jerusalem, and Jerusalem shall be called the faithful city, and the mountain of the Lord of hosts, the holy mountain (Zechariah 8:3 ESV).

The heavenly ideal of perfectly blended knowledge, education, and experience will become an invigorating reality, toward which we are instructed to strive even now:

> Be diligent [study] to present yourself approved to God, a worker who does not need to be ashamed, rightly dividing [discerning] the word of truth. . . . All Scripture is given by inspiration of God, and is profitable for doctrine, for reproof, for correction, for instruction in righteousness, that the man of God may be complete, thoroughly equipped for every good work (2 Timothy 2:15; 3:16–17).

> For at that time I will change the speech of the peoples to a pure speech, that all of them may call on the name of the Lord and serve him with one accord (Zephaniah 3:9 ESV).

> Many nations shall come and say, "Come, let us go up to the mountain of the Lord, to the house of the God of Jacob; that he may teach us his ways and that we may walk in his paths" (Micah 4:2 ESV).

> For now we see in a mirror, dimly, but then face to face. Now I know in part; then I shall know fully, even as I have been fully known (1 Corinthians 13:12 ESV).

Likewise restored to original symmetry will be the relationship between human, animal, and plant kingdoms. With the Curse lifted, toil and strain will come to an end so that all creation can worship the Creator in harmony. The joyous foreshadows of this rhythm that we now experience through successful cultivation, harvesting, gardening, and relating to creatures domestic and wild are rooted in the residual Edenic conscience God has written in our hearts:

> And he will give rain for the seed with which you sow the ground, and bread, the produce of the ground, which will be rich and plenteous. In that day [of renewal] your livestock will graze in large pastures, and the oxen and the donkeys that work the ground will eat seasoned fodder, which has been winnowed with shovel and fork [meaning that even livestock will eat and live well as valued companions rather than as tools or food] (Isaiah 30:23–24 ESV).

> And I will deliver you from all your uncleannesses. And I will summon the grain and make it abundant and lay no famine upon you. I will make the fruit of the tree and the increase of the field abundant, that you may never again suffer the disgrace of famine among the nations (Ezekiel 36:29–30 ESV).

> "Behold, the days are coming," declares the Lord, "when the plowman shall overtake the reaper and the treader of grapes him who sows the seed; the mountains shall drip sweet wine, and all the hills shall flow with it" (Amos 9:13 ESV).

> But they shall sit every man under his vine and under his fig tree, and no one shall make them afraid (Micah 4:4 ESV).

> In that day the branch of the Lord shall be beautiful and glorious, and the fruit of the land shall be the pride and honor of the survivors of Israel [who have escaped the Tribulation]. . . . And in that day the mountains shall drip sweet wine, and the hills shall flow with milk, and all the streambeds of Judah shall flow with water; and a fountain shall come forth from the house of the Lord and water the Valley of Shittim [Acacias] (Isaiah 4:2; Joel 3:18 ESV).

> I will make with them [Israel] a covenant of peace and banish wild beasts from the land, so that they [Israel] may dwell securely in the wilderness and sleep in the woods. And I will make them and the places all around my hill [Jerusalem] a blessing,

and I will send down the showers in their season; they shall be showers of blessing (Ezekiel 34:25–26 ESV).

And I will make for them a covenant on that day with the beasts of the field, the birds of the heavens, and the creeping things of the ground. And I will abolish the bow, the sword, and war from the land, and I will make you lie down safely (Hosea 2:18 ESV).

The wolf shall dwell with the lamb, and the leopard shall lie down with the young goat, and the calf and the lion and the fattened calf together; and a little child shall lead them. The cow and the bear shall graze; their young shall lie down together; and the lion shall eat straw like the ox. The nursing child shall play over the hole of the cobra, and the weaned child shall put his hand on the adder's den. They shall not hurt or destroy in all my holy mountain; for the earth shall be full of the knowledge of the Lord as the waters cover the sea (Isaiah 11:6–9 ESV).

Sing, O heavens, for the Lord has done it! Shout, O depths of the earth! Break forth into singing, O mountains, O forest, and every tree in it! For the Lord has redeemed Jacob, and will be glorified in Israel (Isaiah 44:23 ESV).

A glorious kingdom it will be!

THE FIRST RESURRECTION AND THE SECOND DEATH

"But the rest of the dead did not live again until the thousand years were finished. This is the first resurrection. Blessed and holy is he who has part in the first resurrection. Over such the second death has no power" (Revelation 20:5–6).

The mention of a *first* resurrection and a *second* death implies a *second* resurrection and a *first* death. Revelation 20:6 shows that those who experience the first resurrection are blessed and holy and shall be priests of God and of Christ, and shall reign with him a thousand years.

The event of the first resurrection occurs in different phases and includes Jesus Christ's bodily resurrection, translation, and ascension (Mark 16:19); the rapture of the church (1 Thessalonians 4:13–18; 1 Corinthians 15:51–53); the rapture of the two witnesses at the midpoint of the Tribulation (Revelation 11:3–13); the martyred Tribulation believers receiving glorified bodies just prior to the second advent (Revelation

6:9–11; 7:9–17; 15:2–4; 20:4); and the Old Testament believers likewise receiving glorified bodies just prior to the second advent (Daniel 12:2).

Clearly those blessed by this "first resurrection" are resurrected into glory, not death. And this multi-faceted resurrection is precisely what Paul was referencing in 1 Corinthians 15:20–23 when he said,

> But now Christ is risen from the dead, and has become the firstfruits of those who have fallen asleep [died] . . . *But each one in his own order*: Christ the firstfruits, afterward those who are Christ's at his coming [which references both rapture and second advent] (emphasis mine).

Paul, when testifying before Felix, spoke of two distinct resurrections of the dead, "of the just *and* unjust" (Acts 24:15). Jesus proclaimed the same:

> Do not marvel at this; for the hour is coming in which all who are in the graves will hear his voice and come forth—those who have done good, to the resurrection of life, and those who have done evil, to the resurrection of condemnation (John 5:28–29).

The *second* resurrection, though the phrase itself is not found, is described in Revelation 20:13–14:

> The sea gave up the dead who were in it, and Death and Hades delivered up the dead who were in them. And they were judged, each one according to his works.

This is a resurrection of unbelievers from out of hell to face absolute sentencing to their final judgment, which will be the second death: "Then Death and Hades were cast into the lake of fire. This is the second death." Daniel 12:2 also relates this resurrection of unbelievers, indicating their being raised to "shame and everlasting contempt."

The *first* death, though the phrase itself is not found, is referenced in Revelation 20:5: "But the rest of the dead did not live again until the thousand years were finished."

The "rest of the dead" are *unbelievers* from throughout history to the end of the millennial kingdom who have died the first death and are in hell, where they shall remain for the duration of the thousand-year kingdom of Christ. Being cursed, they do not have part in the first resurrection. But after the thousand years are finished, the accursed souls will be resurrected from out of hell to stand before Christ at the great white throne judgment and receive their just punishment of eternal torment and separation from God. Once each unbeliever has been held to account and sent back to hell, then hell *and death* will be cast into the lake of fire—the second death. To die twice condemned is the penultimate curse, as we saw with Babylon.

Believers do not qualify for the first death, for after one's spirit has been "born again," physical death is simply a transition from one blessed spiritual context to another in relation to God, whereas an unbeliever was never born again, thus their separation from God remains both physical and spiritual. This also lends to why Paul refers to the physical death of believers as "falling asleep," a euphemism evoking a more comforting perspective on the subject (1 Corinthians 15:18–20; 1 Thessalonians 4:13).

SATAN'S RELEASE AND FINAL DOOM

Referring back to Revelation 20:1–3 where Satan is bound in the Abyss for the duration of the thousand-year kingdom of Christ on earth, note that verse 3 reveals "he should deceive the nations no more till the thousand years were finished . . . but after these things he must be released for a little while." I reiterate that Satan is *released*, he does not escape. Revelation 20:7–10 reveals what happens once he is released:

> Now when the thousand years have expired, Satan will be released from his prison and will go out to deceive the nations which are in the four corners of the earth, Gog and Magog, to gather them together to battle, whose number is as the sand of the sea. They went up on the breadth of the earth and surrounded the camp of the saints and the beloved city [Jerusalem]. And fire came down from God out of heaven and devoured them. The devil, who deceived them, was cast into the lake of fire and brimstone where the beast and the false prophet are. And they will be tormented day and night forever and ever.

Why the extended drama of Satan's imprisonment and release before his final doom? It is to prove to yet unglorified humanity that even amidst the Millennium's near "perfect situation" with no evil presence, corrupting influences, or darkness of any kind drawing hearts away from truth and light, there still exists within the human heart a rebellious pride that can become a stumbling block of the most subtle kind. Free human choice remains an abiding construct of salvation.

The prophet Jeremiah was keen to this fact so long ago when he observed that the heart is deceitful above all things, and basely wicked (Jeremiah 17:9). And *when God's judgments are in the earth, the inhabitants of the world will learn righteousness,* even though the wicked will not (Isaiah 26:9–10). The Millennium is no exception.

DEATH IN THE MILLENNIUM?

While there will be worldwide peace, good health, ever-increasing prosperity, and God's truth thoroughly taught and lived with Christ ruling the earth, it may be surprising to learn that disobedience will indeed be a present reality in the millennial kingdom (Zechariah 14:16–19), and not without consequence.

Free will and human responsibility will be tested for those who are yet unglorified—those born and subsequently building lives during this era of Jesus' rule. All other kingdom citizens will have "passed their test" and solidified their standing as saints and servants, just as the angels that refused to join Lucifer's initial insurrection are no longer in danger of succumbing to pride or insurrection.

Notably, Isaiah 65:20 appears to reference a 100-year window of opportunity for those born during the Millennium to come to a personal and *saving* knowledge of Jesus Christ as God and King. In an era of no sinful influence and with Christ and the saints ruling the world with approachability, it will take little to no faith to accept the reality of the time with godly fear and duty—rather than love—driving obedience. Therefore, it will be easy to simply acknowledge the awesome circumstance and enjoy the millennial kingdom blessings without truly surrendering one's soul to Jesus as *personal* Savior.

With longevity of life restored for all, one who has lived for a century will still be considered a child, but will have had ample time to learn who Christ is and to have come to a heart decision for or against him—and even indifference is against him. Today we very rarely have 100 years to make such a choice, and all the while the flesh, world, and devil beset us with deceit, temptations, fears, and doubt. With such evil out of the way, there is no excuse. Thus, *the sinner being one hundred years old shall be accursed [die]* (Isaiah 65:20).

Herein we see that accompanying the graphic death of animals per the sacrificial memorials to Jesus' atonement, *human* death will also provide a necessary gravity amidst a time of pervasive and benevolent peace—for when God's judgments are in the earth, the inhabitants of the world will learn righteousness (Isaiah 26:9).

For many Christians, this idea of disobedience and death in the Millennium is difficult to process due to a lack of both careful prophetic teaching in much of the church and negligent individual study. It is assumed that this is when every tear, sorrow, pain, and death shall be wiped away (Revelation 21:4). However, the actual context of "the former things" passing away is the future eternal state *beyond* the Millennium (Revelation 21–22), which yet remains a mystery we shall discuss in the next chapter.

DEVIL'S DOOM

When Satan is released his evil influence will immediately be felt by those—younger than a century—whose hearts have not truly surrendered to Christ, resulting in a sudden massive campaign to remove Jesus as king and destroy his people. This assault will be swiftly consumed by a devouring fire from heaven (Revelation 20:9; 2 Peter 3:7; Malachi 4:1) that sends all involved human agents to hell and Satan and his devils to the lake of fire, for whom it had been originally prepared (Matthew 25:41).

The reference to Gog and Magog in Revelation 20:8 is a historical reflection recalling an event that unfolds prior to Jacob's trouble detailed in Ezekiel 38–39 wherein Israel's enemies purpose to annihilate her in totality by launching an overwhelming military assault, upon which Almighty God rains down fire from heaven, completely destroying the aggressors. This is very similar to what happens at the end of the thousand years, for fire will fall from God out of heaven and devour his enemies (Revelation 20:9). Then, following the swift end to Satan's attack, the devil himself will be cast into the lake of fire where he shall remain forever.

Without prior knowledge of the Ezekiel 38–39 event, the reference to Gog and Magog in the book of Revelation is surely odd. Some may believe both the Ezekiel and Revelation Gog/Magog scenarios to be one and the same, but the differing contexts in Scripture prove them to be distinctly separate events; in fact, they are a millennium apart!

Ezekiel 38:15 and 39:1–2 show *Israel's* enemies to come from the near and far north; in Revelation 20 *Christ's* enemies come from the four corners of the earth, i.e., *every direction*. Ezekiel 38:11–13 shows that the object of the assault is to conquer and plunder *the land*; in Revelation 20 the object is to destroy the *camp of the saints* and the *beloved city* (Jerusalem), for such contains the earthly throne of Jesus.

The Ezekiel event occurs in the latter years[5] but well *before* Armageddon and Christ's return (thereby *before* the Millennium), proven by the fact that Israel is dwelling securely in the land prior to devastation by the Tribulation judgments and having to flee from the Antichrist (Ezekiel 38:11). The Ezekiel event also transpires *before* God establishes his glory on earth and is personally known among the nations (Ezekiel 38:16, 23); in Revelation 20 the context is at the end of the thousand years wherein *all nations will know the Lord God because his glory has already been established on earth.*

In Ezekiel, Israel's enemies are destroyed, followed by seven months of burials (Ezekiel 39:12–16) and a *seven-year* supply of fuel from war spoils (Ezekiel 39:9); in Revelation 20 the fire from heaven *devours* the enemies of God with no mention of burials or war spoils. Furthermore, Ezekiel offers twenty-one specific details of judgment (Ezekiel 38:19–22; 39:3–11), while Revelation 20 records only one—fire from the sky—which serves simply as the historical parallel between the passages.

After the devil is sent to his doom and the Millennium concludes, the great white throne judgment will commence.

THE GREAT WHITE THRONE JUDGMENT

"As I looked, thrones were placed, and the Ancient of Days took his seat; his clothing was white as snow, and the hair of his head like pure wool; his throne was fiery flames; its wheels were burning fire. A stream of fire issued and came out from before him; a thousand thousands served him, and ten thousand times ten thousand stood before him; the court sat in judgment, and the books were opened" (Daniel 7:9–10 ESV).

This is the final judgment and is for *unbelievers* only. It has nothing to do with the previously expounded Judgment Seat of Christ discussed in chapter four, which follows the rapture and is for souls made righteous through Christ alone (John 5:24).

---

5. In light of Bible prophecy, the end times span from Pentecost to Christ's second advent (Joel 2:28–32), and the *latter years* (or last days) span specifically from Israel's regathering/rebirth (Isaiah 66:7–9; Ezekiel 37:1–14) on the world stage (in 1947–48) to Christ's second advent. The latter years do not include the millennial kingdom, which is an era of prophetic fulfillment all its own.

The Millennial Kingdom and Final Judgment

Matthew 11:21–24 reveals that those with numerous opportunities to receive truth, yet reject it, are subject to *greater* condemnation. Such is the fate of each soul that stands before him who sits on this great white throne. Here, too, the Judge is Jesus Christ, for "the Father judges no one, but has committed all judgment to the son" (John 5:22). John records what he saw in this vision of future judgment for the unsaved and eternally damned:

> Then I saw a great white throne and him who sat on it, from whose face the earth and the heaven fled away. And there was found no place for them. And I saw the dead, small and great, standing before God, and books were opened. And another book was opened, which is the Book of Life. And the dead were judged according to their works, by the things which were written in the books. The sea gave up the dead who were in it, and Death and Hades delivered up the dead who were in them. And they were judged, each one according to his works (Revelation 20:11–13).

This event will be systematically and formally meted out, bringing many verses into complete fulfillment, for "There is nothing covered that will not be revealed, and hidden that will not be known" (Matthew 10:26; Luke 8:17; Ecclesiastes 12:14).

> There will be weeping and gnashing of teeth when you see Abraham and Isaac and Jacob and all the prophets in the kingdom of God, and yourselves thrust out (Luke 13:28).

> Therefore God has highly exalted him and bestowed on him the name that is above every name, so that at the name of Jesus every knee should bow, in heaven and on earth and under the earth, and every tongue confess that Jesus Christ is Lord, to the glory of God the Father (Philippians 2:9–11 ESV; Enoch 47:2–4).

> And no creature is hidden from his sight, but all are naked and exposed to the eyes of him to whom we must give account. . . . It is a fearful thing to fall into the hands of the living God (Hebrews 4:13; 10:31 ESV).

> Vengeance is Mine . . . for the day of their calamity is at hand (Deuteronomy 32:35 ESV).

> And he sat on the throne of his glory, and the sum of judgment was given to the Son of Man. And he caused the sinners and all those who led the world astray to pass away and be destroyed

> from off the face of the earth. They shall be bound with chains, and shut up and imprisoned in their place of assembly, and all their works vanish from the face of the earth. And from that time forward, there shall be nothing corruptible; for that Son of Man has appeared, and has seated himself on the throne of his glory. And all evil shall pass away before his face, and the word of that Son of Man shall go out and be strong before the Lord of spirits (Enoch 69:27–29).

Just as the Judgment Seat of Christ did not take place on earth, but in heaven, so the great white throne judgment will not take place on earth, but elsewhere in the universe, for both earth and heaven/sky fled from the Judge's presence, and there was no place for them (Revelation 20:11).

The books that are opened in Revelation 20:12 are records of the unrighteous works of those being damned (Isaiah 65:6–7; Galatians 3:10–14), accompanied by the Book of Life which is a final record of every individual made righteous by Christ per individual choice. Originally, every soul born is recorded in the Book of Life, but one's failure to receive Christ's salvation results in their name being blotted out (Exodus 32:33; Psalm 69:28; Revelation 3:5). Written records of those who fear the Lord God and meditate on his name may also be opened as points of comparison between righteous and wicked (Malachi 3:16–18), though such records for the righteous are never a basis of salvation by works.

The most heart-wrenching aspect of this circumstance is that every soul sentenced to eternal punishment has made their own choice to reject Jesus' salvation and thus forfeit a relationship with their Creator and Lord who loves them still. Hope will have fled for those facing this final judgment. Their future holds unending torment, unimaginable horror, and a dreadful darkness in forever knowing that the rift between themselves and God will stand fixed for eternity.

Via the resurrection of condemnation (John 5:28–29), each hell-bound soul will be translated from hell to stand before the great white throne, will be condemned forever by their own deeds recorded in the opened books, will kneel before Jesus Christ and worship him as their Creator God (not Savior), and will then be sent back to hell. When all in hell have been individually judged, hell itself will be cast into the lake of fire:

> Then Death and Hades were cast into the lake of fire. This is the second death. And anyone not found written in the Book of Life was cast into the lake of fire (Revelation 20:14–15).

The Millennial Kingdom and Final Judgment

With even death being cast into the lake of fire, Paul's prophecy is realized: "The last enemy to be destroyed is death" (1 Corinthians 15:26 ESV). As harsh as this appears, it is God's perfect justice on evil. And according to J. Scott Duvall, the "only thing worse than evil would be a God who refuses to condemn it."[6]

> Many will say to me in that day, "Lord, Lord, have we not prophesied in your name, cast out demons in your name, and done many wonders in your name?" And then I will declare to them, "I never knew you; depart from me, you who practice lawlessness!" (Matthew 7:22–23)

Such souls shall depart to where Jesus said *the worm does not die and the fire is not quenched* (Isaiah 66:24; Mark 9:44); a place of *outer darkness*[7] and unfathomable sorrow and torment (Matthew 22:13). Like planets possessed of will swinging out of their orbits, the lost will never find their way back to the centralizing sun.[8] Jesus' gravity well shall no longer draw them.

A WORD ON LAST THINGS

Now we finally progress into the long-awaited context of *a new heaven and new earth* in what is considered (in our present time) "eternity future." This awesome revelation is expounded in sparing detail in Revelation 21–22.

Concerning eschatology (the study of last things), Irenaeus declared the future to be intrinsic to everything else in Christian teaching.[9] The key topics of eternal life and death, final judgment, paradise restored, and perfected human destiny are primarily positioned last among the articles of faith; yet according to Thomas C. Oden this in no way implies their triviality, but rather their finality. He expands on Irenaeus' reasoning and states,

> All things in Christian teaching point to a coming consummation. All the vital energies of the doctrines, moral teachings, and liturgies of classic Christianity focus finally on events yet to come that will illumine all present life. Human life attains its final end not in this life but in a future as yet unpossessed. The

---

6. Duvall, *The Heart of Revelation*, 139.
7. See Appendix B Expanded Commentary #10.
8. Ironside, *Revelation*, 199.
9. Irenaeus, *Against Heresies* 5.1.

truest, fullest blessedness does not appear in temporal life, but in eternal life to come (Titus 1:2).[10]

And directly pertaining to our mortality and final destination, Oden offers a challenging consideration: "Human beings are not asked whether they wish to be born. They are asked to live according to God's will between birth and death. Before birth we have no opportunity to choose. After death there is no further opportunity to choose. Having been made [created] without our free choice, we come to a final accounting only as a result of our actual free choices (Hebrews 10:26–31)."[11] Indeed, an understanding of Christianity devoid of the foundational future hope would be self-destructively deficient. And such hope only holds meaning within the eternally transcendent context of Christ's salvation and its immanent construct of moral agency and free choice.[12]

In that we have our beginning in God and have received redemption in God per our fallen nature, it follows that we have our end—our final destiny—in God, or in condemned separation from him. Eschatology, therefore, converges all theological themes from beginning to end and guarantees that all of God's promises will be fulfilled and all injustice will be divinely judged (Psalm 35:24–27; Daniel 12:2; Micah 4:1–4; Galatians 5:5; 1 Peter 4:17; Revelation 19:11–21). Truly, all of creation eagerly anticipates a return to perfection (Romans 8:18–23). With this in mind, "it is foolish to speak of suffering or social justice without reference to the future of God's mercy and justice." The future directly influences the present whether intentionally considered or not (1 Corinthians 15:50–58); but "rightly conceived, the teaching of the end of history is a teaching about the momentous meaning of history."[13]

Studying and contemplating what Scripture says about the future is designed to be a blessed experience (Revelation 1:3). Although, the blessing does not rest in knowing with certainty all that the future holds, but rather in learning to trust wholly in Christ who holds the future (1 Corinthians 13:9–12; 2 Corinthians 4:16–18; 1 John 3:2).

---

10. Oden, *Classic Christianity*, 765.

11. Oden, *Classic Christianity*, 767.

12. For discussion on God's sovereignty, free human choice, and the misleading semantics of predestination, see Birch, *The Morning Star and the Melon*, 4–19.

13. Oden, *Classic Christianity*, 768, 770.

19

The New Heaven, New Earth, New Jerusalem, and Eternity

> *Now I saw a new heaven and a new earth, for the first heaven and the first earth had passed away... Then he who sat on the throne said, 'Behold, I make all things new.'*
>
> —REVELATION 21:1, 5

As THE GREAT WHITE throne judgment is occurring far from the earth, the earth and its atmosphere shall undergo a renovation by fire into a renewed state in preparation for heavenly unity. This renewal will complete the process initiated at the beginning of (and continuing through) the Millennium, which served to foreshadow the fully perfected and glorious eternal state to come after the final judgment.

Just as believers will one day receive new resurrection bodies free from corruption, so the earth will likewise be resurrected to incorruption. The apostle Peter prophesied of this awesome transition and its doomed naysayers:

> Scoffers will come in the last days, walking according to their own lusts, and saying, "Where is the promise of his [Jesus'] coming? For since the fathers fell asleep, all things continue as

> they were from the beginning of creation." For this they willfully forget: that by the Word of God the heavens were of old, and the earth standing out of water and in the water, by which the world that then existed perished, being flooded with water. But the heavens and the earth which are now preserved by the same Word, are reserved for fire until the day of judgment and perdition of ungodly men . . . But the day of the Lord will come as a thief in the night, in which the heavens will pass away with a great noise, and the elements will melt with fervent heat; both the earth and the works that are in it will be burned up. Therefore, since all these things will be dissolved, what manner of persons ought you to be in holy conduct and godliness, looking for and hastening the coming day of God, because of which the heavens will be dissolved, being on fire, and the elements will melt with fervent heat? Nevertheless we, according to his promise, look for new heavens and a new earth in which righteousness dwells (2 Peter 3:3–13).

Peter, having known Scripture and Jesus personally, is certainly informing readers of his epistle as to the context of Jesus' own words: "Heaven and earth will pass away, but my words will by no means pass away" (Matthew 24:35).

ALL SHALL NOT BE FORGOTTEN, BUT ALL SHALL CHANGE

It is commonly taught that before eternity future begins, the earth and the entire universe will be destroyed only to be remembered no more. This thinking is based upon Isaiah's prophecy when God says, "For behold, I create new heavens and a new earth, and the former things shall not be remembered or come into mind" (Isaiah 65:17 ESV).

However, the context of Isaiah 65 is the millennial kingdom wherein much of the prior world conditions—including death—will indeed be remembered along with the entire history of Christ's passion and salvation which removed the sting of death for his own. Such remembrance purposefully points to the glory of our king in that the thousand-year kingdom will literally fulfill every one of the biblical covenants between God and his creation. If there were no remembrance, God's promises would not be actually realized. *Even in eternity future*, if there were no recollection of God's grand story of salvation, then the value of Christ's

The New Heaven, New Earth, New Jerusalem, and Eternity

sacrifice, eternal life, and all of its blessings would be vastly diminished, or at worst pointless.

Isaiah 65:16 (ESV) reinforces this truth in that it sets the specific context for verse 17, stating that anyone who sincerely establishes themselves in the Lord God and in his renewed creation shall be blessed *"because the former troubles are forgotten."*

This may seem to be an instance of biblical contradiction, but the appearance is easily remedied by understanding specific contexts of language and circumstance.

First, as mentioned above, the circumstance in Isaiah 65 is that of the Millennium and its transitional perfection-in-progress toward eternity future. Based on our earlier study concerning the what, when, why, where, and how of the Millennium, we recall that Satan is bound and restricted from interfering in the affairs of men for one thousand years, until loosed at the end of the Millennium. Thus the millennial kingdom shall prosper in the grace, knowledge, and peace of Christ without hindrance. In that sin and evil will not dominate culture anywhere in the world, the overall collective focus of humanity will be one of worship and thanksgiving to Jesus Christ; no longer will education, technology, industry, recreation, or relationships suffer the bent toward abuse, oppression, or worthlessness.

Therefore, the former evils of the world *will be* remembered but *without* debilitating effect, meaning there will be no risk of stirring up emotional bondages and reactions that would cause one to sin (Enoch 91:16–17). Recall of such will be met with the stark truth of and praise for Christ's deliverance from it, for our minds will have been completely renewed (Romans 12:2). This is what is meant by the former troubles being "forgotten." There is a difference between being set free (Romans 6:22) and being *made* free (Romans 8:2). The former involves choice and disciplined obedience to Christ; the latter speaks of established and eternal perfection in Christ by his Spirit as reward for prior righteous choices.

Second, the language in which Isaiah recorded God's words reveals much. The word "new" in reference to the new heavens and new earth that God would form is rendered in Hebrew as *chadash*, meaning renewed, repaired, or rebuilt (on a prior foundation), as opposed to being created brand new from formlessness.[1] Also, the "heavens" that shall be made new does not in this context indicate the entire cosmos/universal

---

1. *The New Strong's Exhaustive Concordance*, Hebrew word #'s 2318, 2319, 8414, 922.

expanse (Hebrew *raqiya*), but rather the earth's visible atmosphere in which the clouds move, as defined by the Hebrew *shamayim shameh*.[2]

Both Jesus and Peter speak of the heavens and the earth "passing away" as rendered from the Greek *parerchomai*, meaning to pass by in time in the sense of passing away from one condition to another, to change; figuratively, to perish.[3] Paul uses the same context when he declares the believer a "new creation," the old self having "passed away" (2 Corinthians 5:17). This idea of passing away does *not* convey annihilation or something ceasing to exist, further supported by Peter's statement that the present heaven and earth are "preserved" or "kept" by God's Word (2 Peter 3:7), indicated by the Greek *thesaurizo* which emphasizes a storing up or amassing (for good or ill).[4]

Both the good and bad things on, around, and in the earth are being stored up for what Peter references as a type of renovation by fire wherein the earth and its atmosphere will "pass away [be changed] with a great noise," and "the elements will melt with fervent heat." The apostle summarizes:

> Both the earth and the works that are in it will be burned up . . . because of which the heavens will be dissolved, being on fire, and the elements will melt with fervent heat (2 Peter 3:10–12).

The "elements" include both the earth and the works that are in it, from the Greek *stoicheion*, meaning order, rudiment, and the first or fundamental principles of any discipline.[5] These elements specifically refer to world systems and religions, evil spirits, climate, geography, and corrupted flesh which are stained by sin and the Curse; they shall be burned up like chaff. The apostle Paul uses the same context in Galatians 4:3, 9 and Colossians 2:8, 20. Such things that humanity has caused, made, or established will not be permitted in the new earth of eternity future; therefore by great heat such shall "melt" and "dissolve," per the Greek word *luo* which means to loose, unbind, set free (from prison).[6]

Fire is a near perfect purifier and simply changes something from one condition to another, eliminating dross and refining or establishing a fertile condition for renewal. Peter shows that the earth will not be

---

2. *The New Strong's Exhaustive Concordance*, Hebrew word #'s 7549, 7554, 8064.
3. *The New Strong's Exhaustive Concordance*, Greek word # 3928.
4. *The New Strong's Exhaustive Concordance*, Greek word #'s 2343, 2344.
5. *The New Strong's Exhaustive Concordance*, Greek word # 4747.
6. *The New Strong's Exhaustive Concordance*, Greek word # 3089.

The New Heaven, New Earth, New Jerusalem, and Eternity

annihilated by fire any more than it was annihilated by water at the flood. We now inhabit the same earth as the pre-flood civilization, though it is indeed a *changed* earth. And so it shall be again changed and baptized/purified—by fire. What will in fact be destroyed is all ungodliness. Fire is also the ever-present biblical symbol of the literal "cleansing, purifying, sanctifying power of God's holiness and justice."[7]

Thus the present heaven and earth shall be *set free* from its present cursed bondage into a new *entirely changed* state where righteousness dwells (Romans 8:21–23; Enoch 45:4–5). Certainly, the great cosmic expanse will also be set free from any contamination by the Curse, namely entropy, the universal process of decay that we presently witness throughout creation. Although the focus of Scripture is primarily on God's involvement with the earth (Isaiah 66:1–2), the cosmos is likewise subject to the creative sovereignty of the Creator.

The Greek word Peter uses for "new" is *kainos*, meaning renewed or refreshed in character, not new in existence or age (*neos*).[8] John uses the same word in Revelation 21:1, and as seen above, Isaiah's use of the Hebrew *chadash* in Isaiah 65:17 is identical to the Greek *kainos*. The same is evident when Paul states, "For the present form of this world is passing away" (1 Corinthians 7:31 ESV).

Hebrews 1:10–12 and 12:26–29 reveal that to bring about this change, ultimately some things on the earth will be removed while others remain. In particular, the millennial kingdom cannot be moved (Isaiah 9:6–7; Daniel 7:18–27; Luke 1:32–33; Revelation 11:15). God's enemies who gather against the heart of the kingdom at Millennium's end will be burned up and sent to the lake of fire to exist forever in torment, but the kingdom with its people and purpose shall remain forever into eternity future.

> Therefore let us be grateful for receiving a kingdom which cannot be shaken, and thus let us offer to God acceptable worship, with reverence and awe, for our God is a consuming fire (Hebrews 12:28–29 ESV).
>
> Yes, the world is established; it shall never be moved (Psalm 96:10; 104:5 ESV).

---

7. Oden, *Classic Christianity*, 821.
8. *The New Strong's Exhaustive Concordance*, Greek word #'s 2537, 3501.

THE LAST ENEMY

"Then comes the end, when he delivers the kingdom to God the Father after destroying every rule and every authority and power. For he must reign until he has put all his enemies under his feet. The last enemy to be destroyed is death" (1 Corinthians 15:24–26 ESV).

With the great white throne judgment complete, and with all of God's enemies, including death, having received just punishment to last for eternity, we may summarize the sweeping history of righteousness: In the present age of grace, those who are Christ's own suffer persecution in that the righteousness accounted to them by Jesus Christ is presently in this world but not of it. Thus righteousness *suffers*. During the millennial kingdom, though there will be death, there will be no persecution. Righteousness shall *reign*. And following the millennial kingdom, in the eternal state, all sin, evil, and death shall be banished. And so, finally, righteousness shall *dwell*.

THE WAY, TRUTH, AND LIFE IN ETERNAL CONTEXT

Eternity future is the reality behind the dream of restoration to perfection. Plato taught that perfect forms and ideas of all things on earth exist in the "invisible world," but that on earth those things are imperfect shadows or copies of the true.[9] The apostle Paul, well-versed in Jewish and Greek philosophy, alluded to this design in Hebrews 9:23–26 (ESV):

> Thus it was necessary for the copies of the heavenly things to be purified with [animal blood], but the heavenly things themselves with better sacrifices than these. For Christ has entered, not into holy places made with hands, which are copies of the true things, but into heaven itself, now to appear in the presence of God on our behalf. . . . once for all at the end of the ages to put away sin by the sacrifice of himself.

So let us now rejoice, for God is indeed the Source of all forms and ideas that are perfect, and he longs to welcome us into his sublimity!

Revelation 21 and 22 offer us a glimpse of a most splendid future in perfect relationship with the Lord our God and with all who shall live in the eternal state. Minimal detail is given within the pages of Scripture

---

9. See Appendix B Expanded Commentary #11.

concerning this future context, though the details written are very specific and do much to stir up hope!

A NEW BEGINNING

Revelation 21:1 is an introduction to the final prophecies of the revelation given to John, prophecies that ultimately close the vision, the biblical canon, and the context of recorded history. The reference to there being "no more sea" indicates that the new earth will be absent vast oceans, accommodating greater land area for habitation. Rivers, streams, lakes, and small seas (with islands) will surely exist, however (Psalm 72:7–8; 97:1; Isaiah 42:9–10; Ezekiel 47:8–12; Zechariah 9:10; 14:8; Jeremiah 31:35–36).

Even the antediluvian prophet Enoch prophesied of eternity future, recording God's words:

> I will transform heaven and make it an eternal blessing and light, and I will transform the earth and make it a blessing . . . All the children of men shall become righteous, and all nations shall offer adoration, and shall praise me, and shall worship me (Enoch 45:4; 10:21).

The new heaven and new earth that John sees is emphasized in 21:5 by Jesus' voice from the throne, saying, "Behold, I make all things new." Everything will again be "very good" (Genesis 1:31). Centuries of Christian meditations have sought to capture the eternal meaning of newness that God makes possible to imagine, though only in part per our finite minds. Along with Dante Alighieri, Gustave Dore, John Bunyan, John Milton, Thomas a Kempis, Augustine, C. S. Lewis, J. R. R. Tolkien, and so many others, we may use our God-given imagination to perceive heavenly splendor, but then *God may use our imagination* to carry us to the very edge of human/divine perception (1 Corinthians 2:9–16).

John the apostle certainly experienced such bliss beyond himself as he received the Revelation. Dante captured the vital burden of self-examination from abysmal depths to celestial heights, and was rewarded with portions of eternal love in the consummation of his grand *Divine Comedy*. Dore masterfully depicted a gritty but celestial surrealism in his art. Milton weaves a striking image of human innocence, frailty, corruption, repentance, and restoration in *Paradise Lost*. A Kempis' *Imitation of Christ* displays divinely discerning dialogue that arrests the soul. Yet even amidst our own most intimate worship of God, nothing we may now ponder compares with what we will ultimately experience.

Revelation 21:2–5 wonderfully presents and fulfills God's overall desire. Verse 3 recalls Leviticus 26:11, proclaiming,

> Behold, the tabernacle of God is with men, and he will dwell with them and they shall be his people. God himself will be with them and be their God.

Remarkably, heaven ultimately comes to earth; the earth does not go to heaven. The heavenly throne will no longer remain beyond the cosmic veil. The new earth and its atmosphere will be prepared by God to receive the New Jerusalem—the final Tabernacle—coming down out of heaven from God. This city will indeed be holy, as will its inhabitants (Revelation 20:6; 22:11); a city for which Abraham waited, whose builder and maker is God (Hebrews 11:10, 16); a city which is the very place Jesus has prepared for his church—his bride—to reside (John 14:2; Revelation 21:9).

Haggai's prophecy is finally realized:

> "The latter glory of this house shall be greater than the former," says the Lord of hosts. "And in this place I will give peace" (Haggai 2:9 ESV).

In fulfillment of Isaiah 25:8–9, God will wipe away every tear and there will be no more death, sorrow, crying, or pain, for the Curse of Genesis 3:17–19 will have been completely lifted—for Christ himself bore and was made the Curse for us so that God could remove it forever (Galatians 3:13; Revelation 22:3).

God reiterates that he is making all things new (Revelation 21:5), and we must logically conclude that all things will forever *remain* new per the removal of the Curse's law of entropy. No thing or person will ever again diminish or decay. Life in heaven will be without time constraints, without distraction, without frustration, without fear, without failure, without weariness, and without idleness or boredom!

AGED TO PERFECTION

Concerning age, Scripture seems to indicate an ideal human maturity being in the early thirties, for Adam and Eve were created as mature adults able to bear and raise children and would likely have remained the same "age" (in appearance) had they not sinned; any children born would

The New Heaven, New Earth, New Jerusalem, and Eternity 261

have presumably grown to a similar maturity as their parents before their age-appearance stabilized.[10] Also supporting early thirties as an ideal maturity is the fact that in order to serve as priests or Levites in the tabernacle/temple, one had to be at least thirty years old (Numbers 4:3). And more poignantly, Jesus began his own public ministry at thirty years of age (Luke 3:23), though he was crucified only three and a half years later. Even his resurrection body, though glorified, remained in similar appearance as that prior to death.

Scripture further reveals that Christ's followers will be "like him" when he returns (1 John 3:3), their natural bodies being transformed and then "conformed to his glorious body" (Philippians 3:21). Plausibly, then, those who die in old age will in heaven be young again but shall retain all their wisdom; and those who die in infancy or youth will in heaven mature to the ideal "age" appearance.[11]

In Revelation 21:6-8 Jesus proclaims, "It is done! I am the Alpha and the Omega, the Beginning and the End. I will give of the fountain of the water of life freely to him who thirsts."

Just as the work of atonement was finished (John 19:30), then the act of global judgment was finished (Revelation 16:17), the work of renewal is now finished. And John certainly remembered Jesus' promises of living water, a reference to both the Holy Spirit and the fountain of the water of life (John 4:14; 7:37-39).

A picture of how abundant our new life shall be is next presented along with the magnificent realization of our grand and long-awaited inheritance. Jesus continues, "He who overcomes shall inherit all things, and I will be his God and he shall be my son" (Revelation 21:7). Thus Isaiah's earnest appeals are answered at long last: To whom has the arm of the Lord been revealed? And who will declare his generation [be Jesus' blessed offspring]? (Isaiah 53:1, 8)

Each of the seven churches (Revelation 2-3) had received a promise for the "overcomers." This final promise for all who overcome is an assurance that Christ's own are indeed joint heirs with him, as he is even heir of all things (Romans 8:16-17; 1 Peter 1:4-5; Psalm 2:8; Hebrews 1:2).

In contrast, Revelation 21:8 offers yet another sharp reminder concerning the fiery fate of those souls who do not overcome sin and evil through Jesus' offered salvation: "But the cowardly, unbelieving,

---

10. Morris, *The Revelation Record*, 441.
11. Morris, *The Revelation Record*, 442.

abominable, murderers, sexually immoral, sorcerers, idolaters, and all liars shall have their part in the lake which burns with fire and brimstone, which is the second death."

THE NEW JERUSALEM

In Revelation 21:2, 9–27 the holy city, New Jerusalem, is the glaring antithesis to Babylon and is seen coming down out of heaven from God, prepared as a bride adorned for her husband.

Although the city is a distinct entity and is not synonymous with the church, this description links the city's *identity* with the church—the bride of Christ (2 Corinthians 11:2; Revelation 19:7–16)—which has overcome the world through Jesus and has received the ultimate reward of Immanuel. The two have become one. The identity parallel is further verified in Revelation 21:9 when the angel speaking with John quantifies the city as "the bride, the Lamb's wife." This city is also the specific place of which Jesus spoke when consoling his disciples in reference to his going away:

> In my Father's house are many mansions; if it were not so, I would have told you. I go to prepare a place for you. And if I go and prepare a place for you, I will come again and receive you to myself; that where I am, you may be also (John 14:2–3).

However, it will not only be the church inhabiting the New Jerusalem. Also present will be non-Jewish and Jewish believers from Adam and Eve to the first advent of Christ, for those under the old covenant received their inheritance (the holy city) after Jesus made atonement for them at the cross—thus enacting the everlasting new covenant (Hebrews 9:12–15; 11:8–16, 40; 12:22–24; 13:14; Romans 3:21–31; 8:29–30; Ephesians 4:7–10; 1 Peter 3:18–22).

Of course, with an entirely renewed earth to inhabit and an awesomely vast universe to explore, to characterize the heavenly tabernacle as an uncomfortably crowded and stuffy place of coerced habitation would prove a lack of imagination. Furthermore, the many glorified believers who rule with Christ will have their thrones in their respective locations across the earth, during both the Millennium and eternity future. Life in heaven will be joyfully active, instructive, and creative. Boredom, indifference, lethargy, and fruitless toil will not exist.

The New Heaven, New Earth, New Jerusalem, and Eternity

John is carried away in the Spirit to a high mountain[12] and is shown in panorama the glory of this heavenly city in dense detail. Symbolism is indeed present in the city's description, but such should also be taken as actual and conveying literal truths. Consider that Washington DC is laid out in specific design utilizing highly symbolic measurements, architectural depth, and even some arcane construction material and forms, yet it indeed remains a very literal and functioning city for its inhabitants.

The holy city is surrounded by a wall 216 feet (144 cubits) high containing twelve gates with the names of the twelve tribes of Israel inscribed on them, for Jesus (a Jew) proclaimed that "salvation is of the Jews" (John 4:22). Perhaps this inscribed aesthetic represents the idea that it was *through* Judaism that Christianity came into the world after the Jews rejected their Messiah (Romans 11:11)—a circumstance that birthed the church which, through Christ, became the light unto the world, thus fulfilling the call to be a "priesthood/light among nations" Israel failed to be (Matthew 21:43). This is why the twelve foundations of the holy city's walls have inscribed upon them the names of the twelve apostles of the Lamb (Ephesians 2:19–20; Luke 22:29–30), for the apostles, through the Spirit, established the church as the foundation of relational connection to God.

Here again we see both Israel and the church recognized as separate but necessary entities in God's great plan of salvation, displaying theological continuity in that the God who revealed himself to the Old Testament patriarchs is the same God who revealed himself fully in Jesus Christ and established the new covenant in his own blood.

That there are three gates on each of the four sides of the city—east, west, north, south—indicates universal access into God's family, for Jesus predicted that "They [believers] will come from the east and the west, from the north and the south, and sit down in the kingdom of God" (Luke 13:29). One universal language will also be established (Zephaniah 3:9).

Each gate being made of *one single pearl* (Revelation 21:21) reminds us that Jesus himself is that "pearl of great price" (Matthew 13:45–46) and that he is also the "door" through which we must pass to be saved (John 10:9). H. A. Ironside poetically states that with each gate being one large pearl we are reminded

---

12. Ezekiel also describes a visionary experience of being carried to a high mountain (Ezekiel 40:2). Such a "mountain" signifies an elevated spiritual perspective from which to see the visions and hear the words of God.

at every entranceway of that one pearl of great price for which our Lord, the heavenly merchantman, sold all that he had with which to buy the church because, although he was rich, yet he became poor that he might make it his own forever.[13]

Some have questioned the need for walls around the city when walls evoke protection from outside threat. This reasoning is founded upon our human experience in a sin-ridden world where threats abound. In eternity future all threats will have vanished and the holy city's walls will stand as majestic symbols of God's own enduring fortitude and embracing presence (Isaiah 60:18). Moreover, in that gates represent a place of judgment in Scripture, every gate in every wall shall be forever open (Revelation 21:25), an *invitation* to every soul in heaven to enjoy the splendor of the holy city where righteous judgment has been established!

Many will dwell within the walls, but all citizens and rulers of the kingdom are welcome and shall come and go according to the Lord's pleasure (Revelation 21:24–26). The majority of non-city dwellers who make up the nations will be those who survived the Tribulation and helped reestablish the nations during the Millennium; they will continue to tend those nations through eternity. Also included are those souls born during the Millennium who truly receive Christ as their Savior-King (thus surviving their one-hundredth birthday!). These souls are grafted into the new covenant at the founding of and throughout Christ's millennial reign after his return to earth; they are not a part of the church, Israel, or Tribulation class of saints and martyrs. Rather, they are a new class of citizenry that Scripture reveals very little about.

Some have described them as general population subjects over which the saints will rule by King Jesus' authority so as to fulfill prophecy. But that seems a bit trite. I suspect a greater relational dynamic and many mysteries to be unveiled that we cannot yet know until the due time.

THE MOUNTAIN OF GOD

The foursquare size of the city equals approximately 1,400 miles in each direction including height![14] In light of God's presently established phys-

---

13. Ironside, *Revelation*, 205.

14. Revelation 21:16 records the holy city being equal in length, breadth, and height as measured in human terms by the angel. Each dimension totaled 12,000 furlongs/stadia, a Greek measure of 600 feet, or roughly 607 English feet. Adding this up

ics, this is far too large to exist on either the present earth or restored earth of the millennial kingdom (the height itself would reach beyond earth's atmosphere into space, complicating planet rotation and gravitational physics). For reference, the elevation of Mt. Everest only reaches 5.5 miles. Yet in light of the completion of the *new* heavens and *new* (much larger) earth of eternity future there need not be any reason why this could not be the actual size of the city (its structure likely a pyramid rather than cube), situated upon—if not in fact being—the *mountain* of God. Human reason devoid of imagination has led many toward bad theology (or simply deprived them of awe-inspiring wonder) in their attempts to insist upon strictly allegorical or humanistic interpretations of this passage.

The precious stones adorning the foundations of the city wall correlate to the stones found in the breastplate of the high priest (Exodus 28:15–21), and they are aglow with the jasper-hued glory of God's being (Revelation 21:11). The streets of the city will be pure translucent gold, evoking God's righteousness so that our paths will be literally *paved in righteousness*.

THE TRUE TEMPLE

In contrast to Ezekiel's vision of the awesome temple of God in the Millennium (Ezekiel 40–43), John declared that he saw no temple in the New Jerusalem, "for the Lord God Almighty and the Lamb are its temple" (Revelation 21:22).

The need for intermediary elements has passed and direct communion becomes reality. This circumstance brilliantly illuminates the relational heart of God, for the true temple is the *family of God* into which every believer is called to be a "pillar," or foundational part. Jesus proclaims,

> He who overcomes, I will make him a pillar in the temple of my God, and he shall go out no more. And I will write on him the name of my God and the name of the city of my God, the New Jerusalem, which comes down out of heaven from my God (Revelation 3:12).

There will also be no need of the sun or moon for the glory of God and the Lamb shall be the city's light (1 John 1:5; Isaiah 60:19–20; Psalm

---

in mileage results in 1,380 miles! For additional insight on the city's size, shape, and capacity, see Hampson, *The Book of Revelation*, 196–98.

36:10). Yet Revelation 21:23, 25 and 22:5 do not teach that the sun, moon, or night will cease to exist in eternity future. These verses simply emphasize the brightness of God's glory as a constant source of light greater than that of the sun or moon; therefore, the holy city will have no need of the sun or moon for light.

In other parts of the earth, however, there will likely remain a need for the light of both sun and moon, practically and as an eternally established witness of God's covenant with David (Psalm 89:34–37; 148:3–6). In fact, Isaiah 30:26 reveals that during the Millennium the sun's radiance will increase sevenfold while the brilliance of the moon will equal the primary light of the sun! Plainly, nighttime will not be as dark as our present experience; yet there is nothing inherently evil in the dark of night, for God created it (Genesis 1:2–5; Isaiah 45:7). The future eternal state, then, shall surpass even the Millennium's wondrous circumstance of luminous bounty.

All told, the intimacy of God's perfect presence, the perpetually open gates, and the absence of the deep dark of night prove that safety and joy will be eternally and internally realized! The New Jerusalem is nothing less than the unveiled and fully realized Holy of Holies.

THE RIVER OF LIFE

"And he showed me a pure river of water of life, clear as crystal, proceeding from the throne of God and of the Lamb" (Revelation 22:1).

Revelation 22:1–2 continues describing the holy city, revealing the awesome spectacle of the river of life proceeding from the throne of God and of the Lamb with the tree of life on each side of the river. The landscaping of this river and its course will differ from the prior circumstance found in the millennial Jerusalem on earth (Zechariah 14:8; Ezekiel 47:1, 12), for the heavenly New Jerusalem offers an all new vista from which the river will descend.

The river flows directly from God's throne—the Fount—at the apex of the holy city and proceeds along the center of a street (or streets if the river pours forth in multiple directions—a probable reality per the great size of the city, as with Eden; Genesis 2:10).

We may assume if the city is pyramidal in structure (i.e., the mountain of God) that the river will descend from level to level, perhaps cascading in various waterfalls and winding its way through intricate and bountiful streams, ponds, pools, and aqueducts, eventually making its way out of any number of the city's gates or waterways and into the surrounding lands, providing its life-giving properties to all the earth.

> There is a river whose streams make glad the city of God, the holy habitation of the Most High (Psalm 46:4 ESV).

> I will open rivers on the bare heights, and fountains in the midst of the valleys. I will make the wilderness a pool of water, and the dry land springs of water (Isaiah 41:18 ESV; Joel 3:18)

THE TREE OF LIFE

"In the midst of its [the city's] street, and on either side of the river, was the tree of life, which bore twelve fruits, each tree yielding its fruit every month. The leaves of the tree were for the healing of the nations" (Revelation 22:2).

The tree of life being on either side of the river of life may reference one specific tree straddling the river as it flows from God's throne, or it may refer to a multitude of *one kind* of tree growing along the river's banks. In either case, the tree is of the same variety as that which God had planted in Eden (Genesis 2:9), perhaps being the very same tree if John's record intends to depict a single source of international abundance (Revelation 2:9). Norse mythology borrows this thematic reality, embodied in Yggdrasil—the tree of the universe.

It seems quite plausible for there to be innumerable *trees* of life lining the river with "each tree yielding its fruit every month" (Revelation 22:2; Ezekiel 47:12). And in that the tree bore twelve fruits monthly, we may understand this as either twelve *crops* of fruit or, more likely, twelve *kinds* of fruit.[15] Consider the parallel that we may individually bear the *varied* fruit of the Spirit (Galatians 5:22–23). The reckoning of months here further confirms the continuation of God's established cosmological order into eternity, entirely in keeping with the wisdom of numbering our days, i.e., cherishing every moment (Psalm 90:12).

The leaves also have great value toward bringing health to the nations. Healing will not be necessary in the eternal state, thus the Greek word *therapeia* can be understood to mean "health, or household service,"[16] indicating a universal usage toward an undisclosed therapeu-

---

15. Morris, *The Revelation Record*, 465.
16. *The New Strong's Exhaustive Concordance*, Greek word # 2322.

tic benefit, conceivably in the form of a heavenly tea. However, Genesis 3:22 does specify that eating fruit from the tree of life will grant life eternal. Additional references include:

> She [Wisdom] is a tree of life to those who lay hold of her; those who hold her fast are called blessed (Proverbs 3:18 ESV).

> To him who overcomes I will give to eat from the tree of life, which is in the midst of the Paradise of God (Revelation 2:7).

> And fragrant trees encircled the throne. And among them was a tree such as I had never smelled, nor was any among them or were others like it; it had a fragrance beyond all fragrance, and its leaves and blooms and wood would not ever wither, and its fruit is beautiful . . . It shall then be given to the righteous and holy. Its fruit shall be for food for the Elect: it shall be transplanted to the holy place, to the temple of the Lord, the Eternal King. Then they shall rejoice and be glad, and enter into the holy place (Enoch 24:4—25:6).

The river of life and tree of life together offer a heavenly picture of life abundant. Fresh flowing water and a bountiful orchard of fruit—the basic necessities of life as divinely designed. Heaven is the new Eden, restoring the original creation into an entirely *better* circumstance of perfect provision and nourishment. And this shall be freely given for redeemed humanity to enjoy the celestial, spiritual, and personally fulfilling plenitude of being in holy fellowship with Jesus Christ, through whom a life of boundless revelation will never end!

PARADISE REGAINED

The description of the city flows into a general description of the overall eternal state of existence with no more Curse, revealing a powerful circumstance: God's people "shall see his face, and his name shall be on their foreheads," signifying our identity in him (Revelation 22:3–5). The fact that God's face shall be seen—via Jesus Christ—holds tremendous gravity, for there will be no temple proxy or veil that restricts our approach to him, a reality that reaches back to Eden prior to the fall of humanity when Adam enjoyed perfect fellowship with his Creator (Matthew 5:8; 1 Corinthians 13:12).

> Beloved, now we are children of God; and it has not yet been revealed what we shall be, but we know that when he is revealed, we shall be like him, for we shall see him as he is (1 John 3:2).

God's people will also serve him in perfection. Surely this service will entail much more than singing and bowing in worship to the Lamb, though such will indeed be a rapturous privilege. Fear of tedium is a misplaced fear, for an eternity of cosmological and unimaginable exploration and relational development awaits every citizen of the kingdom of heaven (1 Corinthians 2:9-13), with all such activity being considered as *rest* in that human endeavor will cease to be stained with toil and strife and will become an enriching heavenly endeavor serving to fulfill our souls and glorify our God and King (Hebrews 4:9-11).

Reiterated is the perpetual luminous glory in the holy city and its surrounding vicinity (Revelation 22:5). Again, the idea of there being no night in the New Jerusalem neither indicates nor implies that night shall not exist elsewhere in the world, as we discussed earlier in this chapter. The repetition here is only meant to reprise the illuminating reality of Jesus' abiding and immediate presence forever and ever!

THE DIVINE EPILOGUE—REVELATION 22:6-21

We are reassured that the words of the prophecy revealed to John by God's angel are indeed "faithful and true," the very name that identifies our Warrior King and Savior (Revelation 19:11). Urgency is emphasized by restating the prophecy of the Revelation as "things which must shortly take place" (1:1; 22:6). Imminency is also discerned, for Jesus' last recorded words are found in these final verses (22:7, 12, 20). *Three times* he says, "I am coming quickly!" This hints at his sudden appearance to the church at the rapture, which is purposed to provoke readiness and motivation toward spreading the word that there soon *will be* a return of the king! Additional indications of Jesus' imminent return are found in Revelation 2:5, 16; 3:3, 11; and 16:15.

In 22:7, the sixth beatitude of Revelation, Jesus recalls the promise recorded in the beginning of Revelation (1:3) that those who keep (or cherish and obey) the words of this prophetic book will be blessed. Truly, Jesus foresaw the end of the age when his very message to those living at such a time would be maligned and distorted by both man and demon, a time in which we now find ourselves as proven (to the diligent disciple) by the prophetic contexts both fulfilled, rapidly converging, and currently blooming throughout the world (Matthew 24:3–34).

No other biblical book has been as misinterpreted, allegorized, feared, and capriciously spiritualized as the book of Revelation. Thus we are to zealously guard the very words of the book in their plainest sense, to be understood and interpreted in light of all previous Scripture, not in light of man's hubristic reason and worldly scorn. In this endeavor we fulfill the apostle Paul's desire that we be found as faithful servants of Christ and *stewards of the mysteries of God* (1 Corinthians 4:1–2), for prophecy never came by the presumptive will of man's interpretation, but by the Holy Spirit (1 Peter 1:20–21; John 14:26).

Immediately following the Lord's words, John again reports that he indeed "saw and heard" the entirety of events in this holy book of prophecy (Revelation 1:1–2, 9–10; 21:2–3; 22:8). He may have felt it necessary to remind his readers and hearers that he had indeed *experienced* such marvelous things first-hand as a reliable witness and was not taking personal liberties in relaying Jesus' message.[17]

Then John "fell down to worship before the feet of the angel" who had showed him these things. John had done this once prior (Revelation 19:10). Certainly the apostle did not intend to worship the angel and was in fact honoring Jesus and his revelatory truth. However, John's reverent response and proximity seems to have made the angel uncomfortable to the point of rebuke for even the appearance of misdirected worship, a clear sign of the angel's humility and sense of divine holiness.

The same angel then admonishes John to "not seal the words of the prophecy of this book, for the time is at hand." This stands in direct contrast to when the prophet Daniel was told to "shut up the words, and seal the book until the time of the end" (Daniel 12:4).

The sealed book of Daniel (revealed in part) is in fact much the same revelation John received, though John was granted fuller disclosure per the progression of prophetic history since the time of Daniel. The time of the end began, as did prophetic urgency, when Pentecost had come to pass, for Jesus had ascended into heaven following his resurrection and the Holy Spirit was sent and made available to all who would become disciples of Jesus (Joel 2:28–29; Acts 2:1–13). Therefore the book of Acts

---

17. The prophet Enoch utilized this same method; for example, "I, Enoch, a righteous man whose eyes were opened by God, saw the vision of the Holy One in heaven, which the angels showed me, and I heard everything from them, and I saw and understood" (Enoch 1:2).

The New Heaven, New Earth, New Jerusalem, and Eternity

remains the context of our day and John's record of the revelation of Jesus Christ serves as a stabilizing resource from the Living Word as the events therein become clear and present realities round about us.

Revelation 22:11 seems a curious placement for the stark statement about those who are unjust and filthy remaining so, and likewise for those who are righteous and holy. Yet Dr. Henry Morris points out the severity of this verse being made apparent by its contextual location between two assertions of urgency and imminency—"the time is at hand" (22:10) and "Behold, I am coming quickly!" (22:12). He explains that

> in view of the certainty of the coming of the Lord and the uncertainty of the time, all men everywhere should evaluate their lives in light of the coming judgments that have just been revealed, as well as all the blessings that have been promised, and then behave accordingly.[18]

The destiny of all shall be one day fixed—forgiveness and salvation shall be complete. There is no purgatory or reincarnation. At the time of the end, "Many shall purify themselves and make themselves white and be refined, but the wicked shall act wickedly. And none of the wicked shall understand, but those who are wise shall understand" (Daniel 12:10 ESV).

MESSIAH'S REWARD

"And behold, I am coming quickly, and my reward is with me, to give to everyone according to his work" (Revelation 22:12).

Here is a powerful reminder that believers will receive their rewards at the Judgment Seat of Christ (2 Corinthians 5:10) according to the quality (not quantity) of their works (1 Corinthians 3:13–15). Of course, such rewarding is not to be confused with one's salvation which is received apart from works. The greatest reward, however, will be to finally enter into a perfectly unhindered relationship with our Creator God. And to know him in such proximity will indeed bring an experiential facet to our conception of his matchless and infinite names.

How magnificent are the names of our Savior when we contemplate their depth: He is called Faithful and True and his name is called the Word of God (Revelation 19:11, 13). "I am the Alpha and the Omega, the Beginning and the End, the First and the Last" (22:13). After hearing Jesus proclaim this, John surely recalled writing in his earlier gospel, "In

---

18. Morris, *The Revelation Record*, 475.

the beginning was the Word and the Word was with God, and the Word was God" (John 1:1).

Comparative titles of Jesus are found in Psalm 90:2; Isaiah 40:28; 41:4; 43:15; 44:6; 48:12; Colossians 1:17; Hebrews 1:2; Revelation 1:8, 11, 17; 2:8; 21:6; and 22:16.

"Blessed are those who do his commandments, that they may have the right to the tree of life, and may enter through the gates into the city" (Revelation 22:14). This is the last of the seven beatitudes of Revelation (1:3; 14:13; 16:15; 19:9; 20:6; 22:7), emphasizing the eternal reward of the righteous in direct contrast to the doom of the wicked: "But outside are dogs and sorcerers and sexually immoral and murderers and idolaters, and whoever loves and practices a lie" (Revelation 22:15). Tragically, the number of damned will far exceed the blessed (Matthew 7:13-14).

Some translated texts render Revelation 22:14 as "Blessed are those who *wash their robes* [in the blood of the Lamb]" in place of "those who do his commandments," possibly to reinforce the scriptural idea that salvation is given by God's grace and not by works or simply keeping God's commandments.

Yet the implication of obedience—sincerely keeping God's commandments—is that those who do so are doing so out of love for him (Matthew 22:37-40). Jesus said, "If you love me, keep my commandments" (John 14:15; 15:10).

And John encouraged us with these words:

> Now by this we know that we know him [God], if we keep his commandments. He who says, "I know him," and does not keep his commandments is a liar, and the truth is not in him. But whoever keeps his word, truly the love of God is perfected in him. By this we know that we are in him. He who says he abides in him ought himself also to walk just as [Jesus] walked (1 John 2:3-6).

THE FINAL TESTIMONY

"I, Jesus, have sent my angel to testify to you of these things in the churches. I am the Root and the Offspring of David, the Bright and Morning Star" (Revelation 22:16).

Here is the first direct mention of the churches since Revelation 3:22. We are reminded that despite the church's absence on the earth during the

The New Heaven, New Earth, New Jerusalem, and Eternity 273

seven-year time of Jacob's trouble, the entire message of the Revelation of Jesus Christ to John is intended for the instruction of the churches in our present age (1:4), and then specifically to any who would come to believe on Jesus' name (3:20) during the dreadful Day of God's Wrath.

Then another powerfully prophetic name is proclaimed by our creator king. The Root and Offspring of David at once identifies Jesus as both ancestor *and* descendant of King David of Israel; Jesus is both David's Lord and David's son (Isaiah 11:1; Matthew 22:41–46).[19] Jesus is both the Origin and Completion of the messianic line.

The Bright and Morning Star is a reference (via the Greek term *orthrinos*) to the planet Venus and its brilliant rising in the early dawn,[20] perhaps inducing the idea of "first light" and that a new day shall soon burst forth at Jesus' return: "I see him, but not now . . . a Star shall come out of Jacob, and a Scepter shall rise out of Israel" (Numbers 24:17 ESV).

Previously, Jesus had promised the "morning star" to overcomers, which is a promise of Jesus himself (Revelation 2:28; 2 Peter 1:19). One may recall that the fallen Lucifer was called "son of the morning" (Isaiah 14:12) and his name has been translated to mean *daystar* or *light-bearer*, again referencing Venus and the fact that he was the most beautiful, the most powerful, and possibly the *first* of the angels that God created.

Although it may seem odd that both Jesus and Lucifer are referred to as "morning star," the scriptural theme of identity and naming is illuminated when we consider that after Lucifer's fall his name became Satan, meaning "Accuser" (Zechariah 3:1; Revelation 12:9–10). The devil therefore lost his innate brilliance and heavenly function and will soon disappear forever. But Jesus—the true Light—reveals that his own brightness will never grow dim and shall forever increase, thus being truly worthy of the name Bright and Morning Star.

"And the Spirit and the bride say, 'Come!' And let him who hears say, 'Come!' And let him who thirsts come. Whoever desires, let him take the water of life freely" (Revelation 22:17). In response to Jesus' proclamation, the Holy Spirit, the holy city (the bride), and those who hear the Spirit's voice all cry out an invitation to any who thirst for truth and eternal life—while there is still time.

Presently within the heart of every true disciple of Christ the Holy Spirit draws and generates a hunger for Jesus' return (Luke 21:34-36; 2

---

19. Morris, *The Revelation Record*, 481.

20. Morris, *The Revelation Record*, 481; *The New Strong's Exhaustive Concordance*, Greek word #'s 3720, 3722.

Peter 3:11–14). For some, however, a deep love for his appearing in the clouds at the rapture captures the heart and quickens the soul toward single-minded obedience set ablaze by a ferocious passion for Jesus' prophecy (2 Timothy 4:8).

Indeed, my own discipleship has been seasoned with prophetic gifting and an insatiable longing for my King's return, expressed by my love for others and my desire for others to likewise love the Lord God above all. Throughout my life the Holy Spirit has faithfully led me into truth, even when I have been entirely unaware or troubled by sin. And he always enjoys bringing to light his handiwork as he and I look back on areas of my unawareness and weakness!

Thus, by the Holy Spirit we are encouraged by Paul to not only approach God in confidence but to also confidently speak on his behalf:

> Therefore, we are ambassadors for Christ, God making his appeal through us. We implore you on behalf of Christ, be reconciled to God. For our sake he made him to be sin who knew no sin, so that in him we might become the righteousness of God (2 Corinthians 5:20–21 ESV).

A FINAL WARNING

Echoing and expanding God's prior counsel in Deuteronomy 4:1–2; 12:32; and Proverbs 30:5–6, a vivid warning is issued in Revelation 22:18–19 for all who encounter the prophecies written in the final book of prophecy:

> If anyone adds to these things, God will add to him the plagues that are written in the book; and if anyone takes away from the words of the book of this prophecy, God shall take away his part from the Book of Life, from the holy city, and from the things which are written in this book.

This grim caution is proven necessary ever more frequently in these latter days in which we live (Enoch 104:9–13). There is no end to the rise of cults and religious systems driven by doctrines of demons and traditions of men (Mark 7:7; Colossians 2:8; 1 Timothy 4:1), but none have done more widespread psychological, emotional, and spiritual damage to individuals than those blasphemous sects that hijack the Bible in a devilish ploy to gain gravitas. A few examples are Islam, Mormonism,

The New Heaven, New Earth, New Jerusalem, and Eternity

Jehovah's Witnesses, perpetuated Judaism, and various strains of Roman Catholicism. A studious reading through the literature and liturgy of each of these will reveal foundational contradictions, omissions, and fantastical augmentations when compared with the New Testament of Holy Scripture.

Note that both Islam and Mormonism boast a vast and highly sacred canon of writings to either replace or append the Holy Bible. Such violations undoubtedly qualify for "adding to" or "taking away" from the Word of God (Revelation 22:18–19). Muhammad, the founder of Islam, even claimed to be the Comforter (or Helper) whom Jesus sent to earth upon his ascension into heaven, effectively claiming to be the Holy Spirit![21] For this evil there is further judgment that Muhammad either ignored or missed but is now well-acquainted with:

> Anyone who speaks a word against the Son of Man, it will be forgiven him; but whoever speaks against the Holy Spirit, it will not be forgiven him, either in this age or in the age to come. . . . but he who blasphemes against the Holy Spirit never has forgiveness, but is subject to eternal condemnation (Matthew 12:32; Mark 3:29).

A FINAL PROMISE

After the exhortation to consider Jesus' revelation as incorruptible and not to be edited, we receive again the oath of imminent return (Revelation 22:20) when Jesus says, "Surely I am coming quickly!"

Then John closes the book of prophecy (22:21) with his own invitation for Jesus to hasten his arrival—*Even so, come, Lord Jesus!*—and a benediction of sublime simplicity: *The grace of our Lord Jesus Christ be with you all. Amen.*

We close with Jesus' words of invitation:

> Most assuredly, I say to you, he who hears my word and believes in him who sent me has everlasting life, and shall not come into judgment, but has passed from death into life (John 5:24).

---

21. See Appendix B Expanded Commentary #12.

Postscript

IN THE PRESENT AGE of profuse affluence, limitless information, and hyper-connectivity, much of the "civilized" world has become distracted and callous toward the idea of that same age coming to an end. Though popular culture the world over seems to celebrate superheroes, anti-heroes, super villains, and apocalyptic scenarios alike, there is indeed a collective and mounting fear that "the end of all things is at hand" (1 Peter 4:7). Such a fear can be deadly if not tempered with discernment.

Anxiety—due to endemic stressors in western culture—now ravages every demographic regardless of social, vocational, or financial status, or age. Even Christians now suffer more than ever from anxiety (and depression), revealing a disturbing lack of discipleship-driven ministry in the western church. Recent research [in 2017] shows anxiety to be 800 percent more prevalent than all forms of cancer![1]

In response to the rampant worry, fear, and cares of this world, the idols of entertainment, comfort, and narcotics have also increased. Christians, too, are guilty of setting up the "golden calves" of our postmodern golden age. Lifestyles of *narcissistic hedonism* eliminate Christ's influence and have resulted in *moralistic therapeutic deism*, a worldview

---

1. Mercola, "Anxiety Overtakes Depression as No. 1 Mental Health Problem," Mercola.com. Anxiety disorders are the most common mental illness in America, affecting one of every thirteen people. See Edmund Bourne, *The Anxiety & Phobia Workbook*, 5th ed. (New Harbinger, 2010), 1–4.

that relishes the existence of an aloof god who demands scant more than being nice, feeling good about oneself, and being *entitled* to divine resolution of our various wants and problems.[2]

And so, with secular culture influencing church culture in greater proportion than the reverse ideal, most churchgoers have become weakened and cowardly caricatures of true disciples of Jesus.

CHRISTIAN COWARDS

Christian cowards replace the spiritual disciplines of Scripture reading, contemplative and conversational prayer, focused worship of Christ, edifying spiritual fellowship, ministry service, et al., with social media scrolling, socializing, polemic politics, streaming media entertainment, and worship of sports teams, pop-culture icons, and self. Anything to avoid the conviction of sin and constructive challenging of the intellect, imagination, and spirit toward Christlikeness. Full of soundbites but no substance, such souls crave spiritual maturity and reward yet despise the time and effort required to achieve it. They idly define their own discipleship by assenting to the Gospel, to faithful attendance to the church house, and promoting their favored church brand rather than by faithful obedience to Jesus Christ and promoting his kingdom first.

Cowardly church leaders only read Scripture and research extra-biblical resources for the sake of wowing their audiences and maintaining their facade of spiritual celebrity. Eventually, their days of actually walking and talking with Jesus are over (if they ever had them) or are severely strained and rare. Any confidence in their personal spiritual gifting has deteriorated due to grieving the Holy Spirit in their own lives and quenching him in others' lives. This then produces a presumption of ministry calling and gifting based on expectation and covetousness that displaces divine revelation, cultivation, and appropriate fruition. Self-preservation, especially if ministry is one's vocation, takes precedence in the schmaltzy church culture of the twenty-first century. Not much has changed since Simon the Sorcerer assumed that God could be bought or fooled (Acts 8:18–23).

I personally know and have known several church leaders who have admitted to *not* reading Scripture regularly if at all! Many more admit

---

2. White, *The Church in an Age of Crisis*, 47, 75. See also Christian Smith's *Soul Searching*, (NY: Oxford University Press, 2005).

to a trite prayer life. Such disconnect from the God one claims to serve has devastating consequences. Sadly, a friend in the ministry who pastors a "culturally relevant," i.e., theologically liberal, church has in fact apostatized and has edified himself as the de facto authority in a cult of personality and posh. Essentially viewing the Bible as somewhat flawed and outdated, he touts the many deviant alternative lifestyles on parade as entirely compatible with biblical Christianity. Moreover, in a social media response to challenges to his heretical hermeneutic he deferred to his doctorate in Old Testament studies, essentially implying at best that he is smarter than everyone else, and at worst that his degree grants him infallibility. I pray my friend owns the error of his way and repents before it is too late (Mark 9:42).

BORED OF THE CROSS

Most believers today live spiritually mediocre and unfulfilled lives because they are not walking in the Spirit or in their calling, often due to the triad of pride, ignorance, and laziness—serving God on their own terms and not his. These souls are brought up on church tradition and fleeting messages about being a good Christian. They remember a few Sunday school lessons and they know who their favorite pastor or author is, but they do not possess an applicable biblical or relational theology nor do they intimately know Jesus or the Holy Spirit. They are bored of the cross and remain spiritually unchanged.

Therefore, as truth is suppressed they suffer regret, frustration, anxiety, depression, and indifference toward God. All of this is then justified by endless excuses that are inexcusably the result of willful ignorance, passivity, spiritual inexperience, and spiritual immaturity. Personal contentment becomes a golden calf on the altar of sloth, fear, and unbelief (1 Corinthians 10:20–21; James 4:17).

The spiritually bored and unsatisfied will often seek to remedy their lack by indulging the industry of quick-fix personal spirituality trends, self-centered spiritually charismatic phenomena, and/or pop-culture presentations of the end of the world. Indeed, there is a genuine Christian alternative to each of these; however, they are not quick fixes, self-centered, or widely popular in the culture at large.

For example, the book of Revelation is possibly the most popular yet most feared, misunderstood, misinterpreted, and *unread* book of prophecy in history. Sure, the spiritually bored may take up and begin to read it, but do they finish? And if they do finish, have they meditated upon its majesty and found their spiritual want remedied?

As I stated earlier in the commentary, a working knowledge of the entire Bible (and specifically Old Testament prophetic literature) *and* a working relationship with the Holy Spirit is necessary to gain the most from the mysteries and arcane language of the book of Revelation. Certainly, there are simple and grand truths and blessings one may readily grasp upon an initial reading. Likewise upon repeat ventures. But Scripture interprets Scripture, and the challenge of interpretation due to biblical illiteracy, spiritual immaturity, intellectual laziness, and an untested imagination too often ends in convenient abandonment of the personal discipline required to persevere. When we become more fascinated with prophecy than with the God of prophecy, we are no better than the Pharisees who worshiped the Law (and themselves) in place of the Law-Giver (Matthew 23:1–33; John 5:39–40).

And so, in one final attempt at fast-track spirituality, biblical commentaries are consulted. But here too one frequently finds daunting synopses of difficult texts and contexts accompanied by grammatical, historical, cultural, and spiritual exegesis of the Bible's literal and metaphorical language. Add to this a fluid and contradictory collection of humanity's traditional views of interpretation that habitually discount the biblical view. This is expressly the case with Bible prophecy in general and Revelation in particular.

G. K. Chesterton agreed with this sentiment when he wrote that "though St. John the Evangelist saw many strange monsters in his vision, he saw no creature so wild as one of his own commentators."[3]

Indeed, I and countless others strive *not* to be wild or monstrous in our endeavors to interpret, exhort, and encourage fellow believers and seekers of God's truth! Yet there remain assorted individuals who are foolish, self-assertive, and—intentionally or not—impious in their aims to have their own voice heard over the Holy Spirit's.

As I also stated earlier, commentaries (and other study helps) are surely a great resource for learning the many nuances of the Bible and acquiring a richer appreciation of the Word of God. But they are tools to be utilized *in tandem* with studying the Bible directly and prayerfully, taking care not to advance only academically. We must not separate the

---

3. Chesterton, *Orthodoxy*, 29.

written Word from the Living Word, for God and theology are not subjects merely to be studied, but are three Persons and a divinely revealed philosophy to be *experienced* simultaneously.

KILLING COWARDICE

To hear what the Spirit is saying to the churches, we must not only believe that he is speaking or know what he is saying through his Word; we must also prayerfully listen for his voice and *imagine* (truly hear) how he is speaking to us individually. Are they divine words of revelation, counsel, or rebuke? Albert Einstein once stated that the imagination is more important than knowledge, which means there can be no meaningful use of intelligence unless there is imaginative perception.[4]

Consider the apostle John imprisoned on the island of Patmos. What might his perception have been? He was there on account of the Word of God and testimony of Jesus. Yet that same Word and testimony made John *who* he was.

> He did not identify himself by his circumstances as a prisoner but by his vocation as a theologian. He did not analyze Roman politics in order to account for his predicament, but exercised his intelligence on the word and testimony of God and Jesus.... The word and witness that shaped his life were then written down by command and under inspiration—in the Spirit.[5]

This would not have been possible had John been playing at being a Christian. John was physically, emotionally, imaginatively, and spiritually available to God (Luke 10:27; Romans 12:1). His identity was thoroughly that of a Christ-follower whose faithfulness and humility precipitated the sublimely luminous and infinitely captivating Revelation. John received and recorded Jesus' Revelation as an ardently devout disciple, theologian, prophet, poet, and pastor fully immersed in the world but wholly owned by his Savior and King.

Soon after his visionary reverie, John was released from Patmos and returned to shepherding the diverse churches he served. Imagine how newly afire his spirit must have been! In all likelihood John was again transformed by such proximity to the author of the Revelation and his infinite story of Love and Life. John's own verbal testimony of what Jesus

---

4. Browne, *Ministry of the Word*, 115.
5. Peterson, *Reversed Thunder*, 2.

had him write also must have persuaded innumerable souls into heaven via his alluring allegiance to the Warrior-King and God of All Creation. Truly, any cowardice in John's nature had long prior been slain by his iron faith in Jesus Christ.

THE DRAGONS OF EDEN

This is how it works. The book of Revelation—and indeed all prophetic Scripture—is an invitation into the very heart of God by way of both our imagination and our spirit so that we may *experience* what is written. Revelation is rooted in all of Scripture and "its intent is to put us on our knees before God in worship and to set the salvation-shaping words of God in motion in our lives."[6] It will bring no comfort or answers to the commonly curious or the skeptic full of questions. Thus, rather than just reading Scripture, we must allow it to read us. So let us not miss out on the life Jesus has for us because we are too busy trying to figure it out for ourselves. Let us recover the lost art of discipleship.

All of us are on a quest for meaning, for true wisdom. We often dream of a world or universe where we have poignant purpose and perfect wholeness, perhaps we even imagine glimpsing the face of God.[7] But then our oft wretched reality beckons and we reluctantly dismiss the pining of our souls only to face the dragons of our imagined Eden—fear and doubt, unbelief, indifference, sadness, unresolved and unhealed emotional trauma, unchecked sin. Yet let us not despair or let go of any Edenic hope, for our heavenly yearnings are evidence of a far greater circumstance that Jesus himself has already prepared for us (John 14:2–3).

In the meantime, have faith that Christ is there among the dragons that beset us—dragons he has conquered (Romans 16:20; Revelation 20:2)! For "Beyond and above the wars and rumors of wars of this world is the greater War that has already been won by the Suffering Servant who bore the iniquity of us all (Mark 13:7; Isaiah 53:6)."[8] We need only appeal to him so that we may indeed be made free by his truth and love (John 8:31–32).

> Other evils there are that may come . . . Yet it is not our part to master all the tides of the world, but to do what is in us for the

---

6. Peterson, *Reversed Thunder*, 24.
7. McGrath, *Glimpsing the Face of God*, 11.
8. Rutledge, *Battle for Middle-earth*, 314.

succor of those years wherein we are set, uprooting the evil in the fields that we know, so that those who live after may have clean earth to till.⁹

Therefore, when we open Scripture and various God-honoring resources, let us also prayerfully open our hearts and minds to the Spirit of God. In so doing, we learn that a mere systematic theology is incomplete in that it is a method toward working out a fully formed and eloquently persuasive *relational* theology—a *revelationship*!

---

9. Prince Imrahil at Aragorn's war council after the battle of the Pelennor Fields. Tolkien, *Return of the King*, Bk V, 155.

Acknowledgments

TWENTY-SIX YEARS AGO, THE Holy Spirit invited (or admonished) me to read his Word with both expectation and scrutiny. Passive devotions and church-house hearsay would not do!

I began to read Genesis, planning to read the Bible from cover to cover. However, after some months, and as is often the case with many souls, I struggled with some of the perceived tedium of Numbers and Deuteronomy. My notes thinned and I pleaded with God to sustain my interest, for I knew that every aspect of his Word was significant—and I was determined to read the entirety straight through! But then came the turn.

The still small voice of the Spirit directed me to read the book of Ezekiel. Though familiar with small portions of the prophet's writing, I had never encountered this historic book of prophecy in all its odd splendor. My first reading led to a second and third, spending months digesting the milk and meat of Ezekiel's record as the Holy Spirit revealed and taught me in a way I had never before experienced (1 Corinthians 2:7–16; 2 Peter 1:20–21). The history, theology, and prophetic visions captured my imagination, yet the reverent and real *relationship* Ezekiel shared with God captured my heart and spirit.

I realized that *proximity* is the key to intimacy with our Creator, and that the art of true discipleship had been largely lost to the western church. Many souls are discipled by mature Christians, but rarely are they discipled directly by Jesus and his Holy Spirit. Thus there is little of

Christ's power or authority in their lives as they accumulate information but lack supernatural *transformation.*

I determined that God would not be an "imaginary friend." He would, in fact, be my God and truest Friend!

The next few years I followed the Spirit's lead from one prophetic biblical Old Testament book to the next, all the while cross-referencing between every other book in both Old and New Testament, particularly Revelation. In this way, Jesus Christ—the Living Word—granted me a grand (and humbling) tour of his written Word in its entirety. I yearned for and learned how to cultivate a discipleship to Christ fashioned after the relationships the prophets had with Almighty God and the first disciples had with Jesus: an invested real-life, real-time, gritty 24/7 endeavor.

Consequently, a deep passion for biblical prophecy and apologetics took root and I soon found myself immersed in numerous books, studies, and teaching opportunities. With a sound biblical foundation and experiential discipleship, the Holy Spirit helped me navigate the turbulent waters of prophetic truth, false teaching, doctrines of demons, and the traditions and con of man. Thus armed, Jesus opened my mind and set his Revelation in my heart (Luke 24:45).

I learned (and still am learning) to approach and understand the Revelation of Jesus Christ from and through the prism of discipleship, an approach that remedies the detachment of strictly academic analysis while enhancing intimately invested inspection. Indeed, Jesus' own encouragement and warning to the seven churches (Revelation 1–3) provides the perfect discipleship template to live by, preparing one's spirit to comprehend both the great wrath and blessed hope that follows.

Truly, and by Christ's design, the grand tour continues and shall never be complete. My flaws—neutral and sinful—keep me humble and striving for Christlikeness. Therefore, I offer heartfelt gratitude to each Person of the triune Godhead: Father, Son, and Holy Spirit. Without them I would never have experienced an earthly adoption or a heavenly one. Gaining both, I am privileged to serve our Everlasting God and Ever-loving Savior.

I am likewise grateful to my parents, Paul and Linda Birch, who adopted me so long ago and raised me in keeping with godly purpose. Growing and maturing in body and spirit amidst the friendly Woodland Community Church family was a true godsend toward keeping me close to the narrow path that leads to life (Matthew 7:13–14).

Acknowledgments

The late Pastor Bob Robinson (USMC, ret.) and the late Pastor Richard Bridge together hold a treasured place in my heart. They exemplified biblical manhood at every level and taught me that personal discipleship is done through the context of friendship and brotherhood/sisterhood—with much humor!

The late Pastor John B. Tripple III also receives my greatest appreciation for his prophetic encouragement when I was just beginning to settle into the divine call on my life—and he left me his entire library!

Corey Franklin Murphy, my best friend with whom I grew up in life and in spirit may be surprised that I include him here. Yet it was he who suffered my numbingly protracted vocal commentaries on prophecy year after year as we both grew in the grace and knowledge of our Lord Jesus Christ! Corey's wife Michelle, too, has been the model of Christian womanhood and a long-term sister-in-Christ. I am fortunate indeed that our life seasons have kept us in proximity so that our camaraderie, tomfoolery, and fireside discourses may continue unabated! Not every soul is so blessed. Thank you both for your love and levity.

Steve and Chelsea Swain have also been a cherished Christian couple with whom I have shared a season of life and ministry. The rigors of discipleship-driven organically relational 24/7 church in the spirit of Acts 2:42–47 must be lived to be truly appreciated. Their friendship and memory remain a blessing.

Shana and Ron Smith are another beloved couple who provided steadfast loyalty and encouragement through a decade of organic church ministry and personal friendship. Amidst the volatile and fickle cultures of both church and society, genuine and lasting affinity is fast becoming scarce—and therefore highly valued. Their authentic love exemplifies the very heart of the church!

I express additional affection (in no specific order) to some of those with whom I have partnered in ministry, to those whose ministries have blessed me, and to those whom I have personally discipled and/or befriended over the years—Dave and Chris Holland, Rev. Isaac Ross, Eric and Casey Miller, the late Dr. Ray Chamberlin, Susie Jarrett, John Murphy, Charlie Green, John and Donna Liammayty, Joel and Heidi Hitchcock, Ray and Sheila Tull, Gary and Karen Johnston, Danny Tice, the 10:10 discipleship class of 2007–2008, Jay Baxter, Greg French, Willie (Popz) and Connie Villegas, Dennis Dailey, Larry Davis, Mark Thomas, Booker Jones, Bill and Wanda Miller, Brandon Miller, Steve Miller, Mark Warren, the late Dave Miller, Kyle Hubbard, Evelyne Colegrove Adams, John and

Blanche Gundry, Tony and Terry Gundry, Jessica Gundry Overstreet, Andrew and Mary Needham, the late Malorie Derby, Mike and Janice McGee, Lindsey English Schilling, Brandon English, Dave Burkhart, Hunter Adkins, Megan Truitt Temple, Derek Ward, Aaron Willey, Aaron Hearn, Travis Brittingham, Chad Shirey, Rob Reinert, Enos Benbow, Larry Whaley, and Bryan Simon. Godspeed you all!

To Melissa Peitsch I extend great thanks for deftly editing this manuscript. Her prowess in finding the slightest typo or suggesting a turn of phrase that makes a world of difference was a help beyond words toward bringing this work to completion.

And I am exceedingly grateful to Wipf and Stock Publishers, particularly Matt Wimer and George Callihan. The world-class expertise and hard work of the entire publishing team has brought my long-prayed-for Revelation project to the next level. You have my deepest gratitude. Godspeed you all!

Appendix A

Ancient Texts

The Book of Enoch, edited by Joseph B. Lumpkin, (Blountsville: Fifth Estate Publishers, 2005). Translation of original manuscripts used are by Richard Laurence (1821) and R. H. Charles (1912) with source verification being the near complete copies preserved by the Ethiopian Coptic Church, several portions of Greek texts, and the fragmented Aramaic texts discovered among the Dead Sea Scrolls in Qumran (*The Dead Sea Scrolls*, Biblical Archaeology Society & Society of Biblical Literature, 2007, 44, 46).

The book of Enoch is a compilation of narrative and prophecy recorded by a few different authors, primarily the biblical patriarchs Enoch and Noah. Most scholars date the earliest known manuscripts of the book of Enoch (or 1 Enoch) to the second century BC. However, what remains elusive but undeniable are the exact earlier oral traditions and/or written sources from which the book originated. Some believe that Noah would have stowed a copy on the ark along with other important works deemed worthy to survive the deluge.

Predating the New Testament and being well-respected as authentic by both Jews and Christians, the book of Enoch certainly influenced New Testament writers. For example: Jude 1:14–15 directly references Enoch 2:1. Genesis 4:8–12 confirms Enoch 22:4–7. Genesis 5:21–24 parallels Enoch 12:1–2. Genesis 6:1–6 confirms Enoch 6–9:9. James 1:6 references Enoch 91:4. Second Peter 2:4 references Enoch 88:1. Matthew 8:28–29 confirms Enoch 16:1. Matthew 25:31–32 parallels Enoch 62:3–5. John 14:2 verifies Enoch 41:2. Revelation 1:13–17 parallels Enoch 71:10–11. Revelation 19:15 parallels Enoch 62:1–2. Revelation 22:1–3 verifies Enoch 25:1–6.

Numerous early church fathers also accepted the book of Enoch as authentic, including Athenagoras, Origen, Irenaeus, Clement of Alexandria, Tertullian, and Justin Martyr. The book was widely accepted and read throughout Christendom for the first three centuries of Christianity. In AD 364, however, a ruling at the Council of Laodicea determined the book of Enoch to be strictly apocryphal and unsavory despite a vastly popular consent to it being highly regarded as historically and spiritually significant—though not a part of the divinely inspired biblical canon. This ruling resulted in regional bans on the book, and with few original copies it soon became scarce. General Christian readership and leadership remains unaware of the theological impact of the book of Enoch in that it reveals great detail concerning fallen angels, giants, spiritual warfare, the dissemination of evil, and the corruption of humanity. Some would say too much macabre detail is recorded in the Enochian record; it is certainly not required reading for the Christian or for salvation of the soul. It simply illuminates and provides theological clarity for many unexplained and truncated truths contained in the Bible.

For those interested, and interest is indeed growing, there is much vetted scholarship on the Enoch text and similar ancient texts (e.g., the *Book of Giants* found among the Dead Sea Scrolls). Dr. Michael S. Heiser's book *Reversing Hermon* (Defender, 2017) is a powerfully informative work on this subject. Notably, another "Book of Enoch" was discovered in 1886 in the Belgrade Public Library archives, referred to as the "Slavonic Enoch" or "2 Enoch." R. H. Charles and other specialists have determined this manuscript to be corrupt due to evidence of many deletions and additions to the original text; they also claim the texts of this Slavonic Enoch to be as recent as the seventh century AD.

The Book of Jasher (J. H. Parry and Company 1840 English edition). The book of Jasher is an ancient history written over 3,500 years ago that details events spanning the books of Genesis to Exodus. Jasher is not a proper name, it is a Hebrew word meaning "upright." The book is approximately the same age as Genesis and therefore older than the book of Joshua, which itself entreats us to read the Jasher account of Joshua's prayer for the sun to stand still (Joshua 10:12–14; Jasher 88:63–64). Another biblical reference to the book is found in 2 Samuel 1:17–18.

Josephus considered the book of Jasher an accurate history of the Hebrews "on account of the fidelity of the annals [records]" (quoted in the Preface of an 1840 English translation edition of The Book of Jasher, Royal Asiatic Society House, London). The ancient *Seder Olam* and the *Babylonian Talmud*, both being Jewish histories, used the book of Jasher as source material, verifying its authenticity.

Beware, however, of a few forgeries. For detailed background on the book of Jasher and an expert English version of the book itself, see Ken Johnson's annotated *Ancient Book of Jasher*, available on amazon.com and biblefacts.org.

The Complete Works of Flavius Josephus, translated by William Whiston, (Nashville: Thomas Nelson Publishers, 1998). English version originally published 1737. Josephus' original Greek and Aramaic text dates sometime late in the first century.

Born into a family of Jewish priests, Josephus spent some of his youth with the Essenes—a fringe religious sect—before becoming a Pharisee at the tender age of nineteen. A colorful life followed for the ambitious young maverick as he was caught up in the Jewish rebellion against Rome (the First Jewish Revolt; known to Jews as the First Roman War) and appointed commander of Galilee. He was eventually arrested and imprisoned in Rome, although he may have stayed his execution when he predicted that the current governor of Judea, Vespasian, would become emperor.

Two years later Josephus' prediction was realized and he was released, deftly expressing his gratitude by adopting the emperor's family name, Flavius. In AD 70 Josephus marched with Vespasian's son Titus as the Roman military dealt a death-blow to the Jewish resistance by destroying the Holy Temple in Jerusalem. Many fellow Jews ever after saw Josephus as a turncoat. His stance against the Jews was certainly only political, for he was indeed sympathetic as he witnessed firsthand biblical prophecy unfold as judgment fell upon Israel, fulfilling Jesus' prediction of the Temple's ruin (Matthew 24:2).

Soon after, Flavius Josephus retired to Rome, became a Roman citizen, and took up wordcraft. His writings include his background and personal adventures, a history of the Jews up to AD 70, a defense of the Jews against anti-Jewry, and various other topics from agriculture and geography to politics and religion. Revealing himself to be a skilled author and historian, Josephus provides invaluable insight into very rich and turbulent eras, particularly the New Testament and inter-testamentary periods.

Appendix B

Expanded Commentary

#1—*The book of Revelation was written circa AD 95.*

The AD 95 date of Revelation's writing was the official consensus of the early church for its first four hundred years and has remained the same for churches that understand the Bible literally. Irenaeus, a disciple of Polycarp (who was a disciple of the apostle John), is considered by all biblical scholars as a trustworthy authority on the first 150 years of Christianity. He wrote *Against Heresies* circa AD 180 and recorded that John received the Revelation on the island of Patmos toward the end of Domitian's reign (see Schaff, *History of the Christian Church*, 750–51). Emperor Domitian, known for banishing souls to Patmos, was killed in AD 96. Irenaeus' history was backed by the early church fathers Clement, Eusebius, Jerome, Tertullian, Victorinus, et al.

The earliest and only objections to the authenticity or dating of Revelation did not surface until late in the second and third centuries by the eastern church via Alexandria, Egypt—the root of Greek-laced allegorical hermeneutic. This loose method of interpretation was advanced by Philo (ca. BC 20—AD 50), Origen (AD 185–253), and eventually Augustine (354–430). I believe Philo was well-intentioned in his purpose to separate Greek thought from Judaism, but his legacy continues to generate more hermeneutical fog than clarity. C. K. Barrett states that "one of Philo's principal aims was to read the doctrines of Hellenistic religious philosophy out of the canonical documents of Judaism. . . . the doctrines

Philo wished to find were not contained in the sources in which he sought them. They existed in Philo's mind, and the means by which he transferred them from their place of origin to the place where he hoped to find them [the Old Testament] was Allegory" (*New Testament Background*, 259). Allegorical exegesis was widely practiced and considered erudite during the Hellenistic era; thus Philo wished to elevate the Jewish biblical canon above all non-Jewish philosophical and narrative writing. His piety is not in doubt, but his exegetical methods were a product of their time with questionable acolytes who even in our day force inappropriate allegorical interpretations onto Holy Scripture.

Spiritualizing or allegorizing Scripture, particularly prophecy, was never the predominant interpretive method within the first-century church. However, a spiritual "dark age" developed in the second and third centuries and then flourished as both Scripture and sound interpretation were closeted away and distorted by the Roman Catholic Church and Gnostics for over 1,000 years.

The allegorical and pseudo-historical interpretive views that persist today are becoming more popular in the western church, primarily for lack of biblical literacy and true scholarship "in the Spirit." Christian academia and culture are trending toward apostasy, as predicted by Paul (2 Timothy 3–4:5). Yet as these false views attempt to rewrite prophecy in general—and Revelation specifically—Scripture remains its own apologetic. For example, in Jesus' letter to the Laodicean church he said they claimed to be wealthy and have need of nothing (Revelation 3:17). But this was impossible if Revelation had been written in AD 64, for the city of Laodicea had been leveled by an earthquake in AD 62, leaving no time for a full city restoration or affluent church presence. Although by AD 95, thirty years later, the city had indeed reclaimed regional prominence to the point of infecting the church with cosmopolitan compromise. Thus, preterist logic does not hold up scripturally or historically.

Tim Lahaye reveals additional fault with the AD 64 date by recalling Jesus' message to the first-century Ephesian church that they "had forsaken their first love" (Revelation 2:4). Lahaye reasons that if Revelation were written in AD 64 or 65, the early church then must have become "cold in their zeal for Christ just thirty years after his ascension, while Peter and Paul were still alive!" Yet history confirms "that was the very period of enormous evangelistic zeal when the gospel was preached 'to every creature under heaven' (Colossians 1:23)" (*Revelation Unveiled*, 27).

For informative and effective comparisons of the differing interpretive approaches concerning the book of Revelation, see Steve Gregg's *Revelation: Four Views—A Parallel Commentary.*

#2—*Constantine's legacy of a Christianized Rome.*

Constantine became emperor of Rome after winning the battle of Milvian Bridge in the name of Christ. He then set to the arduous task of Christianizing the empire. Eventually, Constantine's son Constantius became emperor and faithfully continued his father's legacy. However, Constantius soon edified his cousin Julian, Constantine's nephew, as co-Caesar and assigned Julian the brutal work of pacifying the unruly province of Gaul. Proving to be not only an astute academic but also an ingenious military general, Julian succeeded in subduing Gaul. But Julian was a devout pagan and despised the Christian faith. He zealously promoted and practiced paganism openly and in opposition to Roman law. Yet in gaining decisive victory in Gaul he also, like Julius Caesar, won the loyalty of his legions. Thus in mockery of his uncle Constantine, Julian claimed to receive a sign from Zeus and determined to wage civil war on his cousin and reverse Rome's conversion to Christianity with a reversion back to paganism.

Unknown to Julian, Constantius had been gravely ill and suddenly died in Tarsus. Unknown to Constantius was Julian's apostasy, so the emperor named his cousin as sole ruler just prior to his death. And thus a pagan once again ruled the Roman Empire. Yet in both Constantinople and Rome, Julian did not see the exalted Christian ethic among the imperial aristocracy or the common people; therefore, he sought to subtly subvert Christianity by restoring all outlawed pagan practices and reopening pagan temples across the empire. He was certain that paganism, the old way, would prevail and the new Christian faith would fade. When Christianity did not diminish but steadily spread, the emperor instated restrictive laws against Christians; however, the populace resisted, for even if full of personal vice, the Christians were peaceful and resourceful. Many of Julian's pagan friends were offended by his overt paganism and draconian measures against the harmless Christians. And so in an appeal to the old spirit of Rome, Julian determined to fulfill his uncle Constantine's desire to defeat the growing Persian threat in the east. But he would conquer in the name of paganism, not Christ. Ironically, or perhaps by divine poetic justice, during the campaign he was struck in his side with a spear (like Christ), a fatal wound.

Historian Lars Brownworth summarizes, "Scooping up a handful of his blood, he [Julian] threw it towards the sun and, according to legend, died with the words *'Vicisti Galilaee'* on his lips—'Thou hast conquered, Galilean,' a reference to the triumph of Christianity. [Julian's] words were wiser than the dying emperor meant them to be. The old religion was disorganized and decentralized, a fashionable relic for the cultural elite. It couldn't compete with the personal revelation of Christianity for the hearts and minds of the masses, and its complex jumble of gods and rituals ensured that it was too divided for its partisans to cohesively unite behind it" (*Lost to the West*, 30–37).

#3—*The early church expected and taught a pre-tribulation rapture.*

For example, in AD 372 Ephrem of Nisibis (a.k.a Pseudo-Ephrem) of the Syrian church wrote, "Why therefore do we not reject every care of earthly actions and prepare ourselves for the meeting of the Lord Christ, so that he may draw us from the confusion, which overwhelms all the world? . . . All the saints and elect of God are gathered together before the tribulation, which is to come, and are taken to the Lord, in order that they may not see at any time the confusion which overwhelms the world because of our sins." Cited in Jeffrey, *Apocalypse*, 85–94.

Even earlier in AD 270, Victorinus, Bishop of Petovium, authored a commentary on the book of Revelation wherein he stated, "For the wrath of God always strikes the obstinate people with seven plagues, that is, perfectly, as it is said in Leviticus; and these shall be *in the last time, when the church shall have gone out of the midst*" [St. Victorinus, *Commentary on the Apocalypse of the Blessed John*, vol. III, "The Writings of Tertullianus," trans. R. E. Wallis, (T & T Clark, 1870), 428. Emphasis mine]. For more on Victorinus and his ante-Nicene commentary, see Oden and Weinrich, *Revelation*, xxi–xxii, xxix.

And during the medieval era the rapture was still commonly believed and taught, as revealed by the martyr Hugh Latimer who was burned at the stake for his faith in 1555. Charles Ryrie reveals that Latimer once confidently expressed, "[P]eradventure it may come in my days, old as I am, or in my children's days . . . the saints 'shall be taken up to meet Christ in the air' and so shall come down with him again" (*Premillennial Faith*, 29).

Bible prophecy scholars Thomas Ice and Timothy Demy summarize that "Wherever those who believe in an any-moment return of Christ have realized the implications of such a view, it has always provided a powerful motive for evangelism. [And] Belief in pretribulationism has had and will continue to have a positive impact upon the worldwide missionary effort" (*The Truth About the Rapture*, 44–45).

Tim Lahaye noted concerning missions: "Belief in the imminent return of Christ impels Christians and churches to develop a worldwide missionary vision of reaching the lost for Christ in this generation. We have more reason to believe that Christ will come in our lifetime than any generation since he ascended into heaven and promised to return" (*No Fear of the Storm*, 18).

Distinguishing the rapture from the second advent is key. The New Testament throughout instructs the church to anticipate and look for Jesus' imminent return and to comfort one another with the same (John 14:1–3; 1 Thessalonians 4:18; Titus 2:13). Adversely, Tribulation saints are told to look for signs/events (e.g., appearance of False Prophet, Antichrist, temple desecration, Elijah/Enoch), not Jesus. Moreover, Jesus' return loses imminency at the signing of the seven-year covenant with Antichrist, for he *will predictably return* at the end of the seven years—a sure comfort for those awaiting him!

#4—*Understanding past and future supernatural apocalyptic planetary affect.*

An earth axial shift (not magnetic pole shift) may have occurred (by God's hand) during the flood, contributing to the collapse of a globally temperate climate and the resulting post-flood weather-in-flux we still experience today. The current rate of axial tilt from the equatorial plane (in tandem with the sun's) is 23 degrees with slight cyclical variations. The measured gradual shifting by only a few degrees may have minor overall impact on the planet, but a sudden shift by large degree would be catastrophic to the effect of epic topographical rifting conjoined with catastrophic plate tectonics. Perhaps the judgment of the last days entails such an event, supernaturally initiated by God himself—a scenario that even *good* science cannot explain without mentioning Divine Agency.

A prolific thinker and encourager, Albert Einstein stated, "One can hardly doubt that significant shifts of the crust of the earth have taken place repeatedly and within short time" [May 1953 correspondence to Charles Hapgood concerning developing secular theories of geologic history, specifically earth crust displacement. Within a few decades of this letter the Christian apologetic of Young Earth Creationism would begin to take shape]. For a masterful treatise on this topic that is spiritually, academically, and scientifically balanced, see Dr. Andrew Snelling's *Earth's Catastrophic Past: Geology, Creation, & the Flood*, 2 vol., (Master/ICR, 2009).

#5—*Professor Tolkien acknowledged biblical giant-lore and wove it into his Middle-earth legendarium.*

"The Great among these spirits [angels who sometimes interact with the world] the Elves name the Valar, the Powers of Arda [Earth], and Men have often called them gods" (*The Silmarillion*, 25).

Not widely known is the fact that Professor Tolkien translated into modern English the Old English epic *Beowulf*, completed in 1926. Notably, his translation includes his own detailed commentary on the text. A brilliant edition is available: *Beowulf: A Translation and Commentary* by J.R.R. Tolkien, edited by Christopher Tolkien, (Houghton Mifflin Harcourt, 2014).

In his vastly curious and learned mind, particularly concerning ancient and biblical history, Tolkien clearly recognized that legend and myth are often rooted in truth that can be either mundane or bizarre. He was truly fascinated by Holy Scripture and its palpable impact on ancient language, literature, and understanding of the world. More so when he discovered that even the primeval Scandinavian skalds wrote of the supernatural giants of old, for the sundering of these ill-begotten creatures led them to the unlikeliest of earthly places.

Beowulf is an account, perhaps based in fact, which includes a clan of early Vikings being terrorized by Grendel, whom Tolkien describes as "a fierce spirit that abode in darkness . . . Of him all evil broods were born, ogres and goblins and haunting shapes of hell, and the giants too, that long time warred with God" (*Beowulf*, 15–16, lines 70–91). Tolkien also explains Grendel as "a creature damned irretrievably . . . he is mortal and has to be slain before he goes to Hell" (*Beowulf*, 159).

In his commentary, Tolkien lauds the *Beowulf*-poet's use of literary devices and familiarity of both Scripture and history concerning actual *and* spiritual warfare: "It shows that study of the Old Testament which is characteristic of him. His comparison of the old native legends of strife and heroism, and Scripture, had presented him with two problems, or aroused in him two lines of thought.

"(1) Where do monsters come in? How can they be equated with the Scriptural account of antiquity? And he [the poet] saw also the parallel between the legendary strife of men of old with these implacable misshapen enemies lurking in dark dens, and the strife of Christians with the fallen devils of hell.

"(2) What are we to think of the nobility and heroism of the heathen past? Was it all just evil, damned?

"To his [the poet's] ideas on this second more difficult question . . . I think that he attempted to equate the noble figures of his own northern [Danish] antiquity with the noble figures, sages, judges, and kings of Israel—before Christ. [Though they] were 'damned' owing to the Fall, [and being heathen] . . . The redemption of Christ might work backwards [i.e., prophetically].

"Our poet's answer in the first case he found in the book of Genesis [cha. 6] . . . And the reference to the 'giants' of old clinched the matter for him" (*Beowulf*, 160–62).

#6—*Evidence of giants and their occult status exists worldwide.*

For example: Viracocha, the creator-god of the Incas (Central and South America), was the father of all other gods (demigods) who also created the earth, sun, moon, and every living thing. He is believed to have initially created a race of giants from stone, but they became unruly and Viracocha destroyed them by a great flood, although two giants survived and wandered the post-flood earth. Viracocha then created humans from clay, not stone, and he was very pleased so he spread them across the earth. He gave/taught humanity the gifts of civilization and worship and traveled around the world disguised as an old sage, sharing his civilizing knowledge and arts, though he was not always well received. In some accounts he was assisted by some of the demigods (angels) or surviving giants. When he finished his world mission he disappeared into the west over the ocean, but had promised to return. In some accounts he assigned demigods to supervise and assist humanity in his absence, always aware of his favored creation. This is only one saga of countless others from around the world, all with hints and roots in the universal truth of a Creator God, supernatural angels, giants, and a great flood judgment.

A plethora of print and video media documenting historical, archaeological, cultural, and religious evidences of such giants and their historicity are available. Of course, secular sources often credit the Nephilim and "giant technology" to the ancient alien/UFO ideology where their findings are truly informative but their origin stories are suspect. I suggest that in considering the alien/UFO phenomena as demonic propaganda intending to distort and subvert truth, the Christian can better comprehend biblical insights concerning fallen angels, giants, spiritual warfare, and the Luciferian rebellion that finally comes to an end in the book of Revelation. For primer or review in this arena of study I recommend consulting reputable volumes on ancient Sumerian, Babylonian, and Greek/Roman mythology while remaining aware of the common non-Christian perspective. Particularly, I recommend *Bulfinch's Mythology* by Thomas Bulfinch (Barnes & Noble, 2013) which is a grand tour of Icelandic, Scandinavian, European, Germanic, and Eurasian oral and written tradition and lore. And for a more globally expansive overview of cultural mythologies, I recommend the *Illustrated Encyclopedia of World Mythology* (Hermes, 2022).

Research and evidence chronicling the history of giants in the Americas (and worldwide) and the ongoing global coverup by many institutions (Smithsonian, National Geographic, et al.) has been gaining a following by both secular and faith-based groups and individuals. It cannot be denied that earth's early history witnessed a race of giants bent on dominating humanity, often posing as "gods" and building monuments to themselves that we can still see today around the world. I will caution anyone entering into this vein of study to be wary of wacky New Age fictions masquerading as alternative history or occult lore, much of which is found on YouTube and amidst the deluge of fringe independent resources. A straightforward treatment to get one started is the well-sourced and superb book by Richard J. Dewhurst, *The Ancient Giants Who Ruled America: The Missing Skeletons and the Great Smithsonian Cover-Up* (Bear & Co., 2014).

#7—*Interpreting the seven kings of Revelation 17:10 as seven world empires, not Roman emperors.*

The preterist (historicist) interpretation attempts to identify the "seven kings" of Revelation 17:10 as seven historical Roman emperors, distinctly separate from both the seven heads (world empires) of 17:9 and the beast (final Antichrist empire) of 17:11. This hermeneutic creates unnecessary confusion.

In contrast and better reasoned, G. K. Beale states, "The attempt to identify the seven kings with particular respective world empires may be more successful, since it is more in keeping with the 'seven heads' in Daniel 7:3–7, which represent four specific empires. The first five kings, who 'have fallen,' are identified with Egypt, Assyria, Babylon, Persia, and Greece; Rome is the one who 'is,' followed by a yet unknown kingdom to come" (*The Book of Revelation*, 874).

#8—*Abram rescues his nephew Lot in a post-Babel regional war against Nimrod.*

Just over a decade after the confusion of languages, one of the princes, Chedorlaomer, formerly under Nimrod had established himself as king of Elam, located in southeastern Mesopotamia. Chedorlaomer led a campaign against Babel and the region's most powerful king, Nimrod (Amraphel); he crushed his armies, and subjugated him along with several other kings of the region (Jasher 13:12–16). Barely a decade after Nimrod's defeat, Chedorlaomer called upon four of his vassal kings (including Nimrod) to jointly put down a rebellion in Sodom (Genesis 14; Jasher 16:1–19). During this campaign, Abram's nephew Lot was taken captive as Sodom was plundered. Abram's army of servants aided the kings of Sodom and Gomorrah in repelling Chedorlaomer's invasion, ultimately rescuing Lot and his family.

Due to different names for individuals varying from culture to culture and an arrogant dismissal of the biblical record, most secular histories of ancient civilizations either confuse or ignore key biblical personas and their historical impact, as well as intentionally corrupting dates and timelines. Sir Isaac Newton, a rigorous student of history and prophecy, addresses this biased secular agenda against the Bible in his work *The Revised History of Ancient Kingdoms*. Newton specifically highlights

Nimrod's "unknown empire" of Babel and describes its what, when, where, why, and how (see chapter 3 in his *Revised History*).

#9—*The universal church lacks a unified biblically prophetic missiological worldview.*

This is a general observation of Protestant and Catholic orthodoxy based on my own involvement and personal interviews interdenominationally, including long-term studies and reviews of many specific surveys, doctrinal protocols, and application.

Many denominations hold a high esteem for Bible prophecy but lack genuine prophets and teachers of prophetic exhortation, while many others neglect or discourage prophetic teaching in order to avoid controversies driven by the profuse biblical illiteracy of pop-culture and, sadly, church infighting. Some denominations appear steeped in the prophetic, such as Pentecostal; however, the context is primarily prophetic/miraculous demonstrations of the Spirit at the personal and local church level rather than raw teaching of prophetic passages in Scripture and their bearing on history, discipleship, church governance, the end of the age, and Jesus' return.

Moreover, the universal church is in great need of missionary-theologians possessing a passionate love for Christ combined with the spiritual, intellectual, and physical grit necessary to engage in effective cross-cultural relational evangelism, even in one's own community and various spheres of influence. Jesus and the apostle Paul are our prime exemplars of this level of *living sacrifice* and *reasonable service* offered up for God (Romans 12:1–2). Prophecy is its own apologetic, particularly in the context of discipleship, and is at the core of both Jesus' and Paul's teaching. Missiology and eschatology are the two sides of the coin of evangelism. They are of equal value and should not be separated, yet there is a tendency in the western world to divide them because of theological nuance or perceived controversy. Christians the world over will certainly disagree about the timing, manner, and many variances concerning the end of the age and Jesus' return. However, most Christians agree that the end of the age *is* near and that Jesus *will* return. It is this agreement, then, that must be the focus of missiological eschatology.

Timothy C. Tennent, a proponent of global Christian awareness and outreach, recognizes that "it is increasingly becoming clear that theological scholarship in the West has largely lost its missiological moorings and often operates in isolation from the burgeoning realities of the global church. . . . not only must we adjust to a post-western Christianity, but we must increasingly recognize the new theological challenges of life in a post-Christian West. It is important to recognize the difference between the two phrases, post-western Christianity and post-Christian West. Post-western Christianity refers to the vibrant expansion of Christianity in many parts of the world outside the West. The post-Christian West refers to the equally dramatic recession of Christian faith in the West. This recession does not mean that we resign ourselves to living quietly as an ever-diminishing subculture in an increasingly secular, godless society. On the contrary, it means that the Christian faith must become far more robust in articulating how the Christian gospel is distinct from secular consumerism" (*Theology in the Context of World Christianity*, 250, 268).

Tennent zealously proclaims that the Gospel is inherently a Gospel of action, not a Gospel of reflection or theological isolation. The theology of the New Testament was the foundation of the missiological framework of the first-century church which was born into a hostile world. Likewise today, for the world remains hostile and the theology of the New Testament remains the context of the twenty-first-century church. Eschatology must continue to fuel the evangelistic fire of global and local missions.

#10—*Contemplating hell, the lake of fire, and the outer darkness.*

Though hell/Hades may physically (from our frame of reference) be located at or near the center of the earth (perhaps in another dimension/realm—Deuteronomy 32:22; Isaiah 14:9; 2 Peter 2:4), it eventually gets cast into the lake of fire which must be an even larger location (perhaps in another dimension/realm—Matthew 22:13; 25:29–30; 2 Peter 2:4, 17; Jude 6, 13).

The term "outer darkness" directly correlates to the "everlasting fire," made plain by examining many biblical passages concerning the final place of eternal judgment. *Darkness* denotes the external reality as much as the internal/spiritual separation from God's light forever. And though Scripture does not reveal the exact location or specifications of the lake of fire, there are a few indications of where it will *not* be and what/where it *may* be.

The lake of fire *cannot* be on or in the earth, for the present earth will be dissolved (2 Peter 3:10). Nor could it be on or in the new earth, for righteousness—and God—will dwell there (2 Peter 3:13; Revelation 21:1-3; 22:1-5) and the near presence of such a foul place would not only be odd but would violate Scripture's claims of the damned being separated and cast eternally far away from God's presence (Isaiah 59:2; Matthew 25:29-30; 2 Thessalonians 1:8-9; Revelation 20:15; 21:8).

So what/where *might* the lake of fire be? Consider that Jude describes false teachers as "wandering stars, to whom is reserved the blackness of darkness forever" (Jude 13), and Peter describes false prophets as having reserved for them the same "blackness of darkness forever" (2 Peter 2:17). Henry M. Morris offers a startling possibility, suggesting that in some far corner of the ever-expanding universe the damned will be quarantined on a star, stating, "A star, after all, is precisely that, a lake of fire" (*The Revelation Record*, 431). He also references stars that burn without giving off light in the visible spectrum, thus consisting of both fire and cloudy darkness. To this I would add the possibility of a black hole (a collapsed star), for such is simultaneously a type of *outer darkness* and *separated from the universe proper* due to the gravitational corruption of spacetime (perhaps allowing for extra-dimensional existence of the damned).

#11—*The Spirit paved the way for the Gospel via the Jewish Law and Prophets and Greek philosophy.*

See Plato's Theory of Forms as presented in his *The Republic*. Plato described certain ideas such as Beauty, Truth, and Justice as universal Forms—the highest Form being that of God. He believed all Forms to be connected and rooted in the "invisible world beyond the senses" only to be distorted in the visible world by the division between reality and appearance—the One and the Many.

For example, information we gather about the world is categorized into "knowledge and opinion." Knowledge is sought, but opinion dominates and distorts "true knowledge." One who fancies beautiful things will have opinions about them, which may differ from another who fancies beautiful things. Some find beauty in evil. But the one who fancies Beauty itself can indeed possess true knowledge. For though there are many beautiful things in the world, all truly beautiful things are rooted in the universal Form of Beauty (which would appeal to every soul).

For Plato, seeking meaning beyond the visible world of the senses toward understanding the Forms leads one to ultimately understand the Good, i.e., the meaning of life. This is neatly summed up in his Allegory of the Cave and the Light (see Barrett, *New Testament Background*, 62–65). Notably, the Theory of Forms greatly assisted early Christian philosophers in further developing an understanding of heaven and the soul; however, that is not to say that Christianity is founded on Platonic reason. Far from it.

In the *Timaeus*, Plato describes the supernatural *Logos* (Gk. "the Word") through which the world was created and through which the Forms are levied upon the universe. This "Word" is none other than the Word of God, Jesus Christ (John 1:1–4). Likewise for Aristotle's Changeless Being, the Unmoved Mover. Of course, living in pre-Christian history, Plato and others of like mind would not have *known* Jesus. But the ancient pursuit of the undeniable truths of foundational logic and rational thought are, I believe, evidence of the Spirit of Truth at work in the world preparing the Way that Christ himself would pave with his perfect Gospel and final revelation.

In fact, this is the very same message Paul disclosed to the Athenians in Acts 17:16–34, even referencing pre-Christian history as "times of ignorance that God has overlooked, but now commands all men everywhere to repent" (17:30).

Even the early church father Clement concurs. Marcellino D'Ambrosio states, "Clement goes so far to say that Greek philosophy is actually of divine origin. Though philosophy is not on a par with the Old Testament, God, in his Providence, sent it to the Greeks as a preparation for the Gospel in a similar way that God sent the Law and prophets to the Jews to prepare them for his son.

"Granted, Greek philosophy neither comprehends the truth in its entirety nor conveys the strength to fulfill the Lord's command. Yet it at least prepares the way for Christianity by making a man self-controlled, by molding his character, and by making him ready to receive the truth" (*When the Church Was Young*, 80). For example: Plato, in his *Apology of Socrates*, presents Socrates as a philosophic missionary and martyr who taught men to know themselves, to strive toward improving their souls, to love the God of All Knowing, and to see wisdom as cognizance of one's own ignorance (see Barrett, *New Testament Background*, 60–62).

Concerning the Torah: Jewish literature may be seen as an inverted pyramid. Barry Holtz explains: "The Bible is at the base, but the edifice expands outward enormously—midrashic literature, the Talmuds, the commentaries, the legal codes, the mystical tradition, the philosophical books. All this is Torah. . . . The classic Jewish texts are as much 'classics' as the works of Greek and Roman culture, and although they are far less known, they are as enduring, as challenging, and no less profound. . . . These texts represent a record of [Jewish] struggles with the meaning of law, the nature of interpretation, the conflict of faith and reason, and the elusive power of the divine. In reading them we come face to face with those issues that form the universal core of all great literature, as we see those concerns refracted through the lens of the particular consciousness of the Jewish literary imagination. . . . Jewish literature is strikingly unique: it is creative, original, and vibrant, and yet it presents itself as nothing more than interpretation, a vast set of glosses on the one true Book, the Torah. . . . The traditional writers saw Torah as God's very word and because of that, it itself is eternally 'original'" (*Back to the Sources*, 13–14).

For a brief example of how Plato's convictions and worldview assisted Christian philosophy, via St. Bernard of Clairvaux in the Middle Ages, see Herman, *The Cave and The Light: Plato Versus Aristotle and the Struggle for the Soul of Western Civilization*, 209–10. An outstanding and thorough treatment of this theme is found in Louis Markos' *From Plato to Christ: How Platonic Thought Shaped the Christian Faith* (IVP Academic, 2021). For a concise summary concerning Plato and Aristotle, see chapter 2—Theories of Knowledge—from *A Brief Guide to Ideas* by Raeper/Edwards. And a vital collection of ancient Greek, Roman, and Jewish writings can be found in C. K. Barrett's *The New Testament Background: Writings From Ancient Greece and the Roman Empire That Illuminate Christian Origins*.

#12—*The unpardonable sin of Muhammad.*

The Quran, Sura 61:6, states: "And remember, Jesus, the son of Mary, said: 'O Children of Israel! I am the apostle of God sent to you, confirming the Law which came before me, and giving Glad Tidings of an Apostle to come after me, whose name shall be Ahmad [Muhammad].'

But when he came to them [Jews and Christians] with Clear Signs, they said, 'This is evident sorcery!'"

Note the subtle assertion that Jesus claimed to be confirming the Law which came before him as opposed to Jesus' own revelation in Luke 24:44 that he "fulfilled the Law." This distinction is significant as Islam is based on following laws to earn Allah's favor and mercy with a hope that upon one's death their good deeds outweigh the bad. Yet this is in direct opposition to the biblical teaching that none can earn God's favor or salvation (Romans 5:5–11). The sin of Sura 61:6, however, is Muhammad's attempted usurpation of the Holy Spirit (referenced as the Apostle Ahmad). It is not surprising to learn that the name Ahmad means "praise," with Muhammad meaning "Praised One" [Abdullah Yusuf Ali, *The Quran: Text, Translation, and Commentary* (Elmhurst: Tahrike Tarsile Quran Inc., 2005), 1540].

It is obvious that Muhammad (AD 570–632) read or had knowledge of revelatory New Testament Scripture, specifically John 14:16 which quotes Jesus: "And I will pray the Father, and he will give you another Helper (or Comforter) that he may abide with you forever."

By the eighth century AD, Muslims were citing John 16:7–14 as proof of Muhammad's identity, further perpetuating his unpardonable sin, for Jesus said: "It is to your advantage that I go away: for if I do not go away, the Helper will not come to you . . . when he, the Spirit of truth, has come, he will guide you into all truth . . . he will glorify me, for he will take of what is mine and declare it to you."

Muhammad in no way glorified Jesus as the Christ and Redeemer of humanity, for within the *Quran's* pages Jesus' own words and identity are under assault.

Bibliography

Alcorn, Randy. *Heaven*. Carol Stream: Tyndale, 2004.
Alinsky, Saul. *Rules for Radicals*. NY: Vintage, 1989. Originally published 1971.
Arnold, Eberhard, ed. *The Early Christians: In Their Own Words*. Farmington: Plough, 1997.
Barclay, William. *The Gospel of John*, 2 vols. Philadelphia: Westminster, 1956. Latest edition published 2017.
———. *The Revelation of John*, 2 vols. Philadelphia: Westminster, 1959. Latest edition published 2017.
Barna, George, and Frank Viola. *Pagan Christianity? Exploring the Roots of Our Church Practices*. Carol Stream: Tyndale, 2012.
Barrett, C. K., ed. *The New Testament Background: Writings From Ancient Greece and the Roman Empire That Illuminate Christian Origins*. NY: HarperOne, 1995.
Bauer, Susan W. *The History of the Ancient World: From the Earliest Accounts to the Fall of Rome*. NY: W. W. Norton, 2007.
———. *The History of the Medieval World: From the Conversion of Constantine to the First Crusade*. NY: W. W. Norton, 2010.
———. *The History of the Renaissance World: From the Rediscovery of Aristotle to the Conquest of Constantinople*. NY: W. W. Norton, 2013.
Beale, G. K. *The Book of Revelation: A Commentary on the Greek Text*. Grand Rapids: Eerdmans, 1999.
Beckwith, Isbon. *The Apocalypse of John*. Grand Rapids: Baker, 1979. Originally published 1919.
Birch, Jon Scott. *Firestorm: America, Israel, Iraq and Their Prophetic Future*. Seaford: Signet Ring, 2016.
———. *The Morning Star & The Melon: Pursuing Truth Through Scripture, Science, Philosophy, and Logic*. Seaford: Signet Ring, 2016.
Boa, Kenneth. *Conformed to His Image: Biblical and Practical Approaches to Spiritual Formation*. Grand Rapids: Zondervan, 2001.

Boettner, Loraine. *Roman Catholicism*. Philadelphia: Presbyterian & Reformed, 1962.
Browne, R. E. *Ministry of the Word*. Philadelphia: Fortress, 1976.
Brownworth, Lars. *Lost to the West: The Forgotten Byzantine Empire That Rescued Western Civilization*. NY: Three Rivers, 2009.
Buchanan, Mark. *Your Church is Too Safe: Why Following Christ Turns the World Upside Down*. Grand Rapids: Zondervan, 2012.
———. *Your God is Too Safe: Rediscovering the Wonder of a God You Can't Control*. Sisters: Multnomah, 2001.
Chan, Francis. *Letters to the Church*. Colorado Springs: David C. Cook, 2018.
Chesterton, G. K. *Orthodoxy*. Chicago: Moody, 2009. Originally published 1908.
Christie-Miller, Alexander. "Turkey: Seeking New Cultural Balance." EurasiaNet.org. 5.15.2015. http://www.eurasianet.org/node/73461.
Cohen, Gary. *Understanding Revelation*. Chicago: Moody, 1978.
Conner, Kevin J. *The Church in the New Testament*. Portland: City Bible, 1982.
Conner, Kevin J. and Ken Malmin. *Interpreting the Scriptures*. Portland: City Bible, 1983.
Constable, Nick. *Historical Atlas of Ancient Rome*. NY: Thalamus, 2003.
Cotterell, Arthur and Rachel Storm. *World Mythology*. Cambridgeshire: Hermes, 2022.
Dake, Finis. *Revelation Expounded: Eternal Mysteries Simplified*. Lawrenceville: Dake, 2001. Originally published 1950.
D'Ambrosio, Marcellino. *When the Church Was Young: Voices of the Early Fathers*. Cincinnati: Franciscan Media, 2014.
Duvall, J. Scott. *The Heart of Revelation: Understanding the 10 Essential Themes of the Bible's Final Book*. Grand Rapids: Baker, 2016.
———. *Revelation*. Teach the Text Commentary Series. Grand Rapids: Baker, 2014.
Ellisen, Stanley A. *3 Worlds in Conflict: The High Drama of Bible Prophecy*. Sisters: Multnomah, 1998.
Farrington, Karen. *Historical Atlas of Empires*. NY: Thalamus, 2002.
Fruchtenbaum, Arnold G. *The Footsteps of the Messiah: A Study in the Sequence of Prophetic Events*. Tustin: Ariel Ministries, 1982.
Gansky, Alton. *30 Events That Shaped the Church: Learning From Scandal, Intrigue, War, and Revival*. Grand Rapids: Baker, 2015.
Gentz, William H., ed. *The Dictionary of Bible and Religion*. Nashville: Abingdon, 1986.
Ger, Steven. *The Book of Acts: Witnesses to the World*. Chattanooga: AMG, 2004.
Gilbert, Derek P. *The Great Inception*. Crane: Defender, 2017.
Gilbert, Derek P. and Thomas Horn. *Saboteurs*. Crane: Defender, 2017.
Goggin, Jamin and Kyle Strobel. *The Way of The Dragon or the Way of the Lamb: Searching for Jesus' Path of Power in a Church That Has Abandoned It*. Nashville: Nelson, 2017.
Gold, Dore. *Tower of Babble: How the United Nations Has Fueled Global Chaos*. NY: Crown Forum, 2004.
Gould, Paul M. *Cultural Apologetics: Renewing the Christian Voice, Conscience, and Imagination in a Disenchanted World*. Grand Rapids: Zondervan, 2019.
Grant, Michael. *The Roman Emperors: A Biographical Guide to the Rulers of Imperial Rome 31 BC—AD 476*. NY: Barnes & Noble Inc., 1997.
Gregg, Steve, ed. *Revelation: Four Views*. Nashville: Nelson, 1997.
Hampson, Todd. *The Book of Revelation*. Eugene: Harvest, 2019.
———. *The End Times*. Eugene: Harvest, 2018.

Harmon, Nolan B., ed. *The Interpreter's Bible*, vol. XII. NY: Abingdon, 1957. Copyright renewed 1994.
Hayes, John H. and Carl R. Holladay. *Biblical Exegesis*. 3rd ed. Louisville: Westminster, 2007.
Hendricksen, William. *More Than Conquerors: An Interpretation of the Book of Revelation*. Grand Rapids: Baker, 1998. Originally published 1940.
Herman, Arthur. *The Cave and the Light: Plato Versus Aristotle and the Struggle for the Soul of Western Civilization*. NY: Random, 2014.
Hindson, Edward. *The Book of Revelation: Unlocking the Future*. Chattanooga: AMG, 2002.
Hitchcock, Mark. *The Complete Book of Bible Prophecy*. Wheaton: Tyndale, 1999.
———. *The End: Everything You'll Want to Know About the Apocalypse*. Carol Stream: Tyndale, 2012.
Holtz, Barry W., ed. *Back to the Sources: Reading the Classic Jewish Texts*. NY: Simon & Schuster, 1984.
Horsley, Richard A., ed. *In the Shadow of Empire: Reclaiming the Bible as a History of Faithful Resistance*. Louisville: Westminster, 2008.
Horton, David, ed. *The Portable Seminary*. 2nd ed. Bloomington: Bethany, 2018.
Hunt, Norman B. *Historical Atlas of Ancient Mesopotamia*. NY: Thalamus, 2004.
Ice, Thomas and Timothy Demy. *The Truth About the Rapture*. Eugene: Harvest, 1996.
Ironside, H. A. *Daniel*. Grand Rapids: Kregel, 2005. Originally published 1920.
———. *Revelation*. Grand Rapids: Kregel, 2004. Originally published 1920.
Jeffrey, Grant R. *Apocalypse*. Philippines: Frontier Research, 1992.
Jones, Floyd N., PhD. *The Chronology of the Old Testament*. 15th ed. Green Forest: Master, 2005.
Jones, Peter. *Capturing the Pagan Mind: Paul's Blueprint for Thinking and Living in the New Global Culture*. Nashville: Broadman & Holman, 2003.
Jones, Timothy Paul, PhD. *Christian History Made Easy*. Torrance: Rose, 2009.
Keener, Craig and John Walton, eds. *Cultural Backgrounds Study Bible NIV*. Grand Rapids: Zondervan, 2016.
Kinley, Jeff. *Wake the Bride*. Eugene: Harvest, 2015.
Kriwaczek, Paul. *Babylon: Mesopotamia and the Birth of Civilization*. NY: St. Martin's, 2010.
Lahaye, Tim. *The Merciful God of Prophecy: His Loving Plan for You in the End Times*. Charlotte: Faith Words, 2002.
———. *No Fear of the Storm*. Sisters: Multnomah, 1992.
———. *Rapture Under Attack*. Sisters: Multnomah, 1998.
———. *Revelation Unveiled*. Grand Rapids: Zondervan, 1999.
LaSor, William S. *The Truth About Armageddon*. Grand Rapids: Baker, 1982.
Leston, Stephen. *The Bible in World History: Putting Scripture Into A Global Context*. Uhrichsville: Barbour, 2011.
Leick, Gwendolyn. *Mesopotamia: The Invention of the City*. NY: Penguin, 2001.
Lightner, Robert. *The Epistles of First, Second, & Third John & Jude: Forgiveness, Love, and Courage*. Chattanooga: AMG, 2003.
Limbaugh, David. *The Emmaus Code: Finding Jesus in the Old Testament*. Washington, DC: Regnery, 2015.
———. *Jesus Is Risen: Paul and the Early Church*. Washington, DC: Regnery, 2018.
———. *The True Jesus: Uncovering the Divinity of Christ in the Gospels*. Washington, DC: Regnery, 2017.

Lisle, Jason, PhD. *Understanding Genesis: How to Analyze, Interpret, and Defend Scripture*. Green Forest: Master, 2015.

Livy. *The Early History of Rome: Books I–V of the History of Rome From Its Foundation*. Translated by Aubrey de Selincourt. 18th ed. London: Penguin, 1971.

Luft, Gal. "How Much Oil Does Iraq Have?" Brookings.edu/The Brookings Institution. 5.12.2003. http://www.brookings.edu/research/how-much-oil-does-iraq-have/amp.

Lutzer, Erwin W. *The Doctrines That Divide*. Grand Rapids: Kregel, 1998.

———. *Rescuing the Gospel: The Story and Significance of the Reformation*. Grand Rapids: Baker, 2016.

MacArthur, John F. *The Second Coming*. Wheaton: Crossway, 1999.

Marty, Martin. *The Christian World: A Global History*. NY: Modern Library, 2007.

Mercola, Joseph. "Anxiety Overtakes Depression as No. 1 Mental Health Problem." Mercola.com. 6.29.17. http://articles.mercola.com/sites/articles/archive/2017/06/29/anxiety-overtakes-depression.aspx.

Metzger, Bruce M. and Michael D. Coogan, eds. *The Oxford Companion to the Bible*. Oxford: Oxford University Press, 1993.

McGrath, Alister. *Christianity's Dangerous Idea: The Protestant Revolution—A History From the Sixteenth Century to the Twenty-First*. NY: HarperOne, 2007.

———. *The Genesis of Doctrine*. Grand Rapids: Eerdmans, 1990.

———. *Glimpsing the Face of God: The Search for Meaning in the Universe*. Grand Rapids: Eerdmans, 2002.

———. *Heresy: A History of Defending the Truth*. NY: HarperOne, 2009.

Moller, Lennart. *The Exodus Case: New Discoveries of the Historical Exodus*. 3rd ed. Scandinavia, 2008.

Morris, Henry M. *The Revelation Record*. Wheaton: Tyndale, 1983.

Mounce, Robert. *The Book of Revelation*. Grand Rapids: Eerdmans, 1977.

Moynahan, Brian. *The Faith: A History of Christianity*. NY: Doubleday, 2002.

Newton, Isaac. *The Revised History of Ancient Kingdoms*. Green Forest: Master, 2009. Originally published 1728.

Oden, Thomas C. and William C. Weinrich, eds. *Ancient Christian Commentary on Scripture: Revelation*, vol. XII. Downers Grove: InterVarsity, 2005.

Oden, Thomas C. *Classic Christianity: A Systematic Theology*. NY: HarperOne, 2009.

Otis, George. *Millennium: The 1,000 Year Reign of King Jesus*. Tulsa: Albury, 2000.

Payne, Robert. *The Fathers of the Western Church*. NY: Viking, 1951.

Peterson, Eugene H. *Reversed Thunder: The Revelation of John & the Praying Imagination*. NY: HarperOne, 1988.

Plutarch. *Plutarch's Lives: Romulus*, vol. 1. The John Dryden 1683 translation, revised by A. H. Clough in 1864. NY: Modern Library, 2001.

Raeper, William and Linda Edwards. *A Brief Guide to Ideas*. Grand Rapids: Zondervan, 1997.

Reagan, David, PhD. *Living for Christ in the End Times*. Green Forest: New Leaf, 2000.

Rhodes, Ron. *The 8 Great Debates of Bible Prophecy: Understanding the Ongoing Controversies*. Eugene: Harvest, 2014.

———. *40 Days Through Revelation: Uncovering the Mystery of the End Times*. Eugene: Harvest, 2013.

Richardson, Joel. *The Islamic Antichrist*. Washington, DC: WND, 2015.

———. *Mystery Babylon: Unlocking the Bible's Greatest Prophetic Mystery*. Washington, DC: WND, 2017.

Roberts, Bob Jr. *Transformation: Discipleship That Turns Lives, Churches, and the World Upside Down.* Grand Rapids: Zondervan, 2006.

Rose, Steve. "The World's Tallest Building Planned—in Ex-Warzone Basra." TheGuardian.com. 11.20.15. http://www.theguardian.com/artand-design/2015/nov/20/the-worlds-tallest-building-planned-in-ex-warzone-basra-iraq.

Rosenberg, Joel C. *Enemies and Allies: An Unforgettable Journey Inside the Fast-Moving & Immensely Turbulent Modern Middle East.* Carol Stream: Tyndale, 2021.

———. *Epicenter: Why the Current Rumblings in the Middle East Will Change Your Future.* Carol Stream: Tyndale, 2006.

———. *Inside the Revolution: How the Followers of Jihad, Jefferson, & Jesus are Battling to Dominate the Middle East and Transform the World.* Carol Stream: Tyndale, 2009.

Rutledge, Fleming. *The Battle for Middle-earth: Tolkien's Divine Design in The Lord of the Rings.* Grand Rapids: Eerdmans, 2004.

Ryrie, Charles. *The Basis of the Premillennial Faith.* NY: Loizeaux Brothers, 1954.

Schaff, Philip. *History of the Christian Church.* Grand Rapids: Eerdmans, 1994. First published 1858.

Scott, Emmet. *Mohammed & Charlemagne Revisited: The History of a Controversy.* Nashville: New English Review, 2012.

Scott, Michael. *Ancient Worlds: A Global History of Antiquity.* NY: Basic, 2016.

Sekulow, Jay. *Jerusalem: A Biblical and Historical Case for the Jewish Capital.* NY: Center Street, 2018.

———. *Unholy Alliance: The Agenda Iran, Russia, and Jihadists Share for Conquering the World.* NY: Howard, 2016.

Shelley, Bruce L. *Church History in Plain Language.* 3rd ed. Nashville: Nelson, 2008.

———. *Church History in Plain Language.* 5th ed. Grand Rapids: Zondervan Academic, 2021.

Smith, J. B. *A Revelation of Jesus Christ: A Commentary.* Scottdale: Herald, 1961.

Spencer, Michael. *Mere Churchianity: Finding Your Way Back to Jesus-Shaped Spirituality.* Colorado Springs: WaterBrook, 2010.

Stark, Rodney. *The Triumph of Christianity: How the Jesus Movement Became the World's Largest Religion.* NY: HarperOne, 2011.

Strauss, Ed. *Heaven: The Inside Story From the Bible.* Uhrichsville: Barbour, 2016.

Strong, James. *The New Strong's Exhaustive Concordance of the Bible.* Nashville: Nelson, 1990.

Sweet, Leonard and Frank Viola. *Jesus: A Theography.* Nashville: Nelson, 2012.

Tennent, Timothy C. *Theology in the Context of World Christianity.* Grand Rapids: Zondervan, 2007.

Time-Life. *Mesopotamia: The Mighty Kings.* Lost Civilizations Series. Alexandria: Time-Life, 1995.

Tolkien, J. R. R. *The Lord of the Rings: The Return of the King.* NY: Houghton Mifflin Harcourt, 2001.

———. *The Silmarillion: The Myths & Legends of Middle-earth.* NY: Harper Collins, 1998. Originally published in Great Britain, 1977.

Towns, Elmer. *The Gospel of John: Believe and Live.* Chattanooga: AMG, 2002.

Ulgen, Sinan. "Turkey at a Democratic Crossroad." Carnegie-Europe.eu. 6.17.2015. http://carnegieeurope.eu/2015/06/17/turkey-at-democratic-crossroad/iapp.

US Department of State. *Iraq Investment Climate Statement 2015.* http://www.state.gov/documents/organization/241811/pdf.

Vine, W. E. *Vine's Topical Commentary: Prophecy*. Nashville: Nelson, 2010.

Walvoord, John F. *Every Prophecy of the Bible*. Colorado Springs: Chariot Victor, 1999.

Weima, Jeffrey A. D. *The Sermons to the Seven Churches of Revelation: A Commentary and Guide*. Grand Rapids: Baker Academic, 2021.

White, James E. *Christ Among the Dragons: Finding Our Way Through Cultural Challenges*. Downers Grove: InterVarsity, 2010.

———. *The Church in an Age of Crisis: 25 New Realities Facing Christianity*. Grand Rapids: Baker, 2012.

———. *Rethinking the Church*. Grand Rapids: Baker, 2003.

Wills, Garry. *Why Priests? A Failed Tradition*. NY: Penguin, 2013.

Witherington, Ben III. *Is There a Doctor in the House?* Grand Rapids: Zondervan, 2011.

Zuck, Roy B., ed. *A Biblical Theology of the New Testament*. Chicago: Moody, 1994.

———., ed. *A Biblical Theology of the Old Testament*. Chicago: Moody, 1991.

Zuck, Roy B. and Charles R. Swindoll, eds. *Understanding Christian Theology*. Nashville: Nelson, 2003.

www.ingramcontent.com/pod-product-compliance
Lightning Source LLC
Chambersburg PA
CBHW070231230426
43664CB00014B/2267